# MIDNIGHT
## IN MOSCOW

# MIDNIGHT IN MOSCOW

*A Memoir from the Front Lines of
Russia's War Against the West*

## JOHN J. SULLIVAN

*Former U.S. Ambassador to Russia*

Little, Brown and Company
New York  Boston  London

Copyright © 2024 by John J. Sullivan

Little, Brown and Company
Hachette Book Group
1290 Avenue of the Americas, New York, NY 10104

littlebrown.com

First Edition: August 2024

Little, Brown and Company is a division of Hachette Book Group, Inc. The Little, Brown name and logo are trademarks of Hachette Book Group, Inc.

The publisher is not responsible for websites (or their content) that are not owned by the publisher.

Little, Brown and Company books may be purchased in bulk for business, educational, or promotional use. For information, please contact your local bookseller or the Hachette Book Group Special Markets Department at special.markets@hbgusa.com.

Print book interior design by Taylor Navis

ISBN 9780316571098

Library of Congress Control Number: 2024936536

Printing 1, 2024

LSC-C

Printed in the United States of America

# CONTENTS

# CONTENTS

*For my wife, Grace*

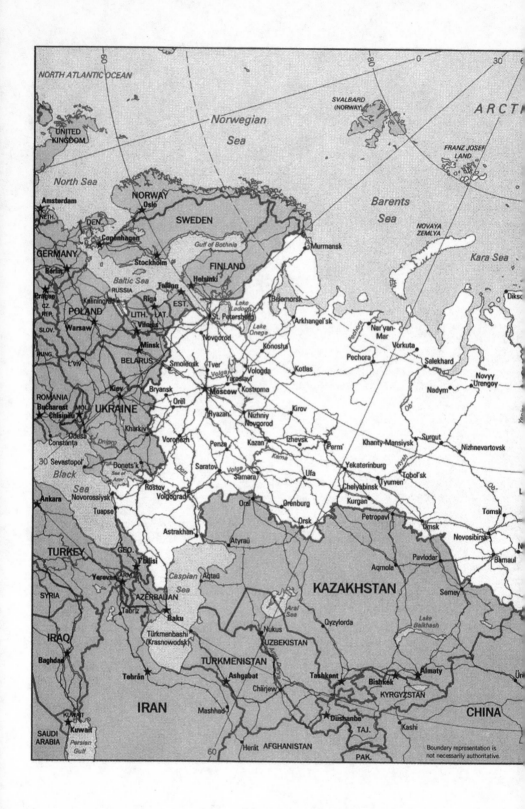

150    180    80    U.S.

*Chukchi*
*Sea*

OCEAN

*Wrangel*
*Island*

Providerniya

*East Siberian*
*Sea*

Pevek

Anadyr'

*Bering*
*Sea*

180

NEW
SIBERIAN
ISLANDS

Cherskiy

SEVERNAYA
ZEMLYA

*Laptev*
*Sea*

U.S.

*Kolyma*

Tiksi

*Arctic Circle*    *Lena*

*Vilyuy*

Yakutsk

Magadan

Petropavlovsk-
Kamchatskiy

*NORTH*

Vilyuysk

*Okhotsk*

*PACIFIC*

Lensk

*Aldan*

Aldan

*Sea*
*of*
*Okhotsk*

*OCEAN*

*KURIL*
*ISLANDS*

Neryungri

Okha    *Sakhalin*
*Island*

Occupied by
Soviet Union in 1945,
administered by Russia,
claimed by Japan.

150

Ust'-
Ilimsk

*Angara*

Ust'-Kut    Nizhneangarsk

Berëzovyy

Urgal

Sovetskaya
Gavan

Yuzhno-
Sakhalinsk

*Lena*

Tynda
Never

*Amur*

Komsomol'sk

Kansk

Bratsk

*Lake*
*Baikal*

Birobidzhan

Khabarovsk

40

Krasnoyarsk

Chita

Blagoveshchensk

*isey*    Kyzyl

Irkutsk

Ulan-
Ude

Borzya

**CHINA**

Harbin

Vladivostok

Khasan

*Sea*
*of*
*Japan*

Aomori

**JAPAN**

Tokyo

**MONGOLIA**

Shenyang

*NORTH*
*KOREA*

P'yongyang    Seoul
*SOUTH*
*KOREA*    Pusan

# Russia

——— International boundary    ┼┼┼┼ Railroad

★   National capital    ——— Road

Dalian

*Yellow*
*Sea*

Fukuoka

0    250    500    750 Kilometers

0    250    500    750 Miles

Qingdao

*East China Sea*

Lambert Conformal Conic Projection, SP 47/62 N

120

Base 801995 (R00183) 9-94

# FOREWORD

LONG BEFORE HE ARRIVED AT Spaso House in Moscow as the new US ambassador to Russia, in early 2020, John Sullivan was a true exemplar of excellence, as a public servant and as a citizen. In his principled service to five US presidents during an increasingly challenging series of positions, John was also continuing a family tradition. His father and several uncles were veterans of World War II and had a deeply embedded sense of service.

Ambassador William Sullivan, John's uncle, was a revered member of the Foreign Service. He not only served as US ambassador to Laos, the Philippines, and Iran, but was a Navy man in World War II whose ship, the USS *Hambleton,* participated in the Normandy invasion. John comes by his patriotism and his mighty heart for service quite honestly. It is unsurprising, but nevertheless noteworthy, that John was one of very few Trump appointees asked to remain in his post by the incoming Biden administration, a decision that reflected enormous trust in John's leadership and loyalty.

In *Midnight in Moscow,* John Sullivan takes us inside his most demanding assignment—US ambassador to Russia. While there is never an uncomplicated time in the US-Russia relationship, readers will learn John's perspectives from a particularly eventful period whose challenges included the rise of Covid-19, the chaos of the 2020 election transition in the US, the death of Mikhail Gorbachev, the Britney Griner detention, the SolarWinds hack, the constant efforts by the Russian government to undermine his mission, and, most important, Russia's inexorable march to war in Ukraine and the resulting support for Ukraine from the United States and our allies.

Starting life as a pugnacious Irishman in Boston turned out to be excellent preparation for John's amazing career, and his cheerful determination to capably manage tough challenges comes through on every page. The roster of public servants who have held that ambassadorial post in Moscow includes names like George Kennan and Averell Harriman, and John has earned a place in the same sentence as those celebrated gentlemen. John's first trip outside of North America was to Russia in 1989, and he never lost his appreciation for Russian history and culture and his affection for the Russian people, notwithstanding whatever policy tensions occurred during his tenure.

On a personal note, his tenure in Moscow also included the passing of his beloved wife, Grace, and he writes movingly about the many sacrifices public service requires and the burdens placed on family members of our diplomats around the world.

*Midnight in Moscow* is not only a compelling account of John Sullivan's years as our ambassador to Russia and a brilliant assessment of what lurks inside the mind of Vladimir Putin, but also a master class in how to be an effective, thoughtful, and humble public servant. People like John Sullivan—people of integrity, independence, and intelligence—are in regrettably short supply in public life these days. We are lucky to have had John Sullivan's service over so many years, including the service rendered by writing this important book, which I can't recommend highly enough.

James N. Mattis
General (Retired), US Marine Corps
Richland, Washington
March 6, 2024

# MIDNIGHT
## IN MOSCOW

# INTRODUCTION

# AUGUST 31, 1939

SEVENTY-SEVEN YEARS. IT HAD BEEN that long since the apocalyptic war in Europe of the mid-twentieth century. My father and uncles fought in World War II, and I grew up listening to their stories about the war. As I sat alone in my residence in Moscow late on February 23, 2022, it seemed surreal to me that I was present at the start of the next major war on the continent—and even more so that I was on the wrong side of the front line.

By that night, more than two years after I arrived in the Russian Federation as the US ambassador, I knew that a "reinvasion" of Ukraine by Russia was imminent. This time it would not be an incursion with stealthy "little green men," as had occurred in Crimea in 2014 and spread to the Donbas. What was coming in February 2022 was going to be much worse: an invasion of Ukraine by all the elements of the Russian armed forces and security services. Russia's earlier offensives would look tame by comparison.

To prepare for war, my colleagues and I at the embassy had established a twenty-four-hour watch and had agreed upon a coded message to be conveyed by a watch stander to me on an open—and thus monitored by our host government—phone line if the invasion began, as expected, in the middle of the night while I was at my residence. The American ambassador in Moscow had lived for many decades in a beautiful old mansion known as Spaso House, which was a short drive from the embassy, but which did not have secure communications equipment (apart from the monitoring devices planted over the years by the deeply inquisitive KGB and its successors).

The "code" was a not-too-complicated signal that I needed to come to the embassy immediately because the war against Ukraine had started.

To snickers from my colleagues, I had chosen a memorable line from the 1980s action movie *Predator*, four classic words uttered by Arnold Schwarzenegger's character: "Get to the choppa!" I thought if the Russians went to the trouble of listening to everything I said on the phone, then let them puzzle over that message.

When Rear Admiral Philip W. Yu, the embassy's highly capable defense attaché, called me a few hours after midnight on Thursday, February 24, with that message, I was only dozing. It was difficult to sleep knowing what was about to happen. Several days earlier, on a February 19 phone call with Secretary of State Antony J. Blinken, the secretary asked about the mood at the embassy. I said it felt like August 31, 1939, the night before Germany invaded Poland. I believed that Russian president Vladimir V. Putin, without legal, military, or moral justification, was going to launch an aggressive war on Ukraine. It was a bold statement, but I knew the secretary shared my assessment.

After the call from Admiral Yu, my bodyguards assembled in the predawn darkness and we drove to the embassy, through empty streets, in one of the armored vehicles they used to transport me. It was cold (below freezing) but not frigid (below zero, as it often was) that awful morning. In fact, I thought it might turn into a nice day by Moscow winter standards. But I knew that I would not be spending any time outdoors.

Upon arrival at the quiet compound in the middle of the night, I was immersed in a stream of cables, reports, meetings, telephone calls, and videoconferences on the brutal and wide-scale Russian invasion and the heroic Ukrainian resistance. Over the next twenty-four hours, with the heightened pace of secure communications with officials at the State Department and the White House, as well as my need to have secure conversations with my embassy colleagues and access to highly classified documents at unpredictable hours around the clock, I concluded that I could not continue to live at Spaso House. Living there meant assembling the bodyguards and making the drive to the embassy every time I needed to receive or convey classified information. On February 25, I moved into a townhouse on the embassy compound, next to the office building, the chancery, where I had my office.

My decision to move was a matter of logistics, but it also had a deeper, symbolic significance. Spaso House had been the US ambassador's residence in Moscow since shortly after the United States, under President Franklin D. Roosevelt, established diplomatic relations with the Soviet Union in late 1933. Illustrious residents over the years who served as ambassador included legendary diplomats in the US Foreign Service, such as George F. Kennan and Llewellyn E. Thompson Jr. Famous political and military leaders, such as W. Averell Harriman, who later held a variety of senior diplomatic and political offices, including governor of New York, and General Walter Bedell Smith, chief of staff to General Dwight D. Eisenhower during World War II, had also lived there as ambassador. The residence had hosted many gala dinners and important conferences with distinguished guests ranging from American presidents (Nixon and Reagan) and Soviet leaders (Khrushchev and Brezhnev) to famous artists, including Leonard Bernstein and Ray Charles. Spaso House was a cultural and historic icon, particularly for Russians in Moscow.

Alas, on February 25, 2022, I became the first American ambassador in over eighty years not to live in that famous residence. This, too, offered an ominous parallel for any student of history: Ambassador Laurence A. Steinhardt had left Spaso House for a few weeks in October 1941, shortly before America's entry into the war, and, with other foreign ambassadors, relocated to Kuybyshev as the Germans threatened to overrun Moscow. Through the dramatic eras that followed—America fighting as Russia's ally in World War II (when the residence suffered bomb damage during a Luftwaffe raid), the Cold War, the Cuban Missile Crisis, the Soviet invasion of Afghanistan, the dissolution of the Soviet Union, the post-breakup chaos, and the rise of Vladimir Putin—the American ambassador had always lived in Spaso House. But no longer. The reasons for the move were pedestrian—my need for secure communications and to be able to get some sleep—but the symbolism was not lost on Russians and Americans who noticed the move.

A few speculated, erroneously, that safety concerns were behind my relocation to the embassy compound. During my time as ambassador, even after the war had started, I never felt physically insecure, or at least no less secure than any other high-profile American official who serves or travels abroad. I believed the Russian government did not want any physical harm to come to me while I was in Russia, since it would not reflect well on the host of our US mission. On the other hand, the Russian government devoted a huge number of personnel and resources to try to annoy, provoke, criticize, frustrate, embarrass, and compromise me. That special attention was a known feature of the post to which I had been appointed.

No, what my move out of Spaso House symbolized, in a trivial way considering the brutal war in Ukraine but ominously given the broader context, was the declining trajectory of US-Russia relations. Our relationship with Russia had been among the most important dynamics in international affairs over the past century and would likely remain at least as important in the next. Nevertheless, as the war began in Ukraine, that essential relationship appeared to be careening toward the ground.

---

For years before this moment, I had warned that relations between the United States and Russia were at a post–Cold War low, and I often paired this warning with another earthly image: we needed to stop digging the hole that we were in. That was a common talking point for both American and Russian officials to use in describing our relationship. Before I became ambassador in December 2019, I had served for almost three years as the US deputy secretary of state, and I invoked the hole metaphor many times in both positions.

Until February 2022, the fundamental policy of the United States was, on the one hand, to confront and push back hard on the Russians in the many areas where we were opposed—cyberattacks, election interference, and the wrongful detention of innocent Americans, to name a few from a growing list—but, on the other hand, to seek progress in those few narrowing areas where the interests of our countries could be more aligned: for instance, arms control, counterterrorism, and space exploration. We also continued to engage with the Kremlin on important regional issues involving national governments that were hostile to the United States, but which had better relations with Russia, such as Syria, Iran, North Korea, and Venezuela. There was bipartisan consensus on this approach in Congress and among the three secretaries of state for whom I worked as deputy secretary or ambassador: Tony Blinken, Michael R. Pompeo, and Rex W. Tillerson.

But there had been virtually no progress in addressing any of these challenges, and the overall bilateral relationship continued to sink lower, its descent hastened by the reckless and outrageous actions of the Russian security services. Among the most notorious was the attempted assassination of Sergei Skripal, a former Russian intelligence officer, in the United Kingdom in March 2018 with a dangerous chemical weapon—a so-called Novichok nerve agent—that killed an innocent woman, gravely sickened many others, including a police officer, and shut down large parts of the city of Salisbury.

By the time I arrived at Embassy Moscow, the pace of deeply disturbing events was nonstop, particularly the sweeping crackdown on any political opposition to Putin, on civil society generally, and on what was left of the few independent media organizations in Russia. The crackdown was intimately related to another disturbing development: the putative constitutional and legal reforms introduced by the Kremlin in early 2020 that would allow Putin to avoid the existing term limits in the Russian constitution and serve as president until 2036, if he so chose (and lived that long).

The 2020 election in the United States played out against this dark backdrop. The violent and anarchic scenes from the US Capitol on January 6, 2021, were catnip to Russian propagandists. I responded publicly that our republic under the US Constitution—commonly described as "the world's longest-surviving written charter of government"—was resilient and would continue to serve the American people in January 2021 and beyond. Thankfully, our Constitution functioned as it had since 1789, and the transfer of power in Washington occurred on January 20, 2021.

President Joe Biden asked me to remain in my post as ambassador, and I was honored to continue to represent the United States in Russia during such unsettled and dangerous times. My life as ambassador and my approach to our Russia policy did not change significantly after I was retained in January 2021. There were, however, significant differences in the policymaking process in the new administration. For example, I had much more contact with the White House and President Biden himself than I had in the prior administration. My point of contact in Washington in the Trump administration had been Secretary Pompeo, and I had never spoken to President Trump—not once—during the entire time I was his ambassador in Moscow.

Some things remained unchanged after the change in administrations. My principal goal as ambassador was to work to stabilize US-Russia relations while defending US national security and our democratic values. This goal was reaffirmed in June 2021, when I accompanied the president to his meeting with Putin in Geneva. Biden made clear that we would continue to confront and oppose the Russians in the many areas where they threatened or undermined US interests, but also that we would seek dialogue on those few issues on which the interests of our two countries allowed.

The White House called it a search for "guardrails" with Russia. Sadly, limited engagement with the Russians had barely begun following the summit when there was a seismic shift in the relationship. In the months that followed, US intelligence agencies reported on Putin's plans for Ukraine. The Russians were on the verge of crushing any guardrails under the treads of their tanks.

———————

The painful and bloody history of Russia's intervention in and seizure of territory from Ukraine, a war of aggression begun in 2014, had hung over every aspect of US-Russia relations up to February 2022. It was a topic in virtually every high-level engagement between senior officials of both governments, but the conflict, while still deadly, was essentially frozen. The Germans and the French had taken the lead in negotiations from the beginning, and in the so-called Normandy Format with the Russians and the Ukrainians, to seek a resolution. But by 2021, the Normandy Format talks had stalled and the Russians would not engage meaningfully in direct negotiations with the government in Kyiv (I use the Ukrainian-derived transliteration Kyiv for all references to the capital of Ukraine in this book).

Ukraine had cast a pall over the relationship between the United States and Russia but had not yet completely broken it. Relations with Russia were terrible, but my US colleagues and I kept trying to find some common areas on which to work with the world's only other nuclear superpower.

What senior American policymakers learned in late October 2021 about Russia's preparations for an invasion of Ukraine, however, stopped or transformed everything we were doing. Detailed intelligence showed the scale of a huge Russian military buildup around Ukraine, and over the next four months the United States had tense negotiations with the Russians to try to avoid a disastrous war. Once again, we achieved little success—but this time, the consequences of failure were catastrophic.

When it began, Putin's invasion of Ukraine completely upended the relationship between the United States and Russia. The war blasted through the bottom of the hole that our two countries had been digging and we plunged to new depths. I gave an interview to Reuters in March 2022 in which I said, in response to a question invoking the hole-digging metaphor, that relations had reached the depth of the Mariana Trench in the Pacific Ocean—the lowest point on earth. My statement elicited a few emails from friends in Washington curious to know what the Mariana Trench was, but no one disagreed.

The war changed things large and small, from Russia's place in the world to where I lived in Moscow. Not to mention the slaughter of thousands of innocents and the unspeakable suffering of millions of Ukrainians because of a policy choice by the Russian president. There was no threat to Russia's national security that would justify any military action by Putin, let alone a massive invasion or the indiscriminate civilian casualties that followed.

Putin called the invasion a "special military operation." Russian state media, the only domestic source of news for most Russians, propagated his narrative that the invasion of Ukraine was necessary to "denazify" and "demilitarize" the Ukrainian government, which, but for the "special military operation," was engaged in a "genocide" against Russians in Ukraine. The brazenness of Putin and his state propagandists was breathtaking. They were alleging that the democratically elected government of Ukraine—headed by a president who is a Russian-speaking Jew, who lost relatives in the Holocaust, and whose grandfather fought in the Red Army against Germany in World War II—was in fact a rogue conspiracy of Nazis implementing a modern genocide against Russians.

Ironically, considering my prior use of a movie quote from him, it was

Arnold Schwarzenegger who in the first month of the war produced a video addressed to the Russian people that was among the most compelling takedowns of their government's justification for invading Ukraine. Schwarzenegger was a credible voice because he and his movies were popular in Russia; his 1988 movie *Red Heat* was the first American feature film shot in Red Square.

In his March 2022 video, Schwarzenegger spoke movingly of his love for the Russian people, the lies their government was telling them, and the brutality of the war being fought in their name in Ukraine. He scoffed at the notion that Ukraine was run by Nazis, and he invoked his father's service as a soldier in the German Wehrmacht at Leningrad, "all pumped up on the lies of his government," who later in life was wracked with guilt and broken physically and mentally from the experience. He warned Russian soldiers not to succumb to the lies of their government and suffer the same fate as his father.

I watched the Schwarzenegger video after our public affairs chief, Jennifer Palmer, remarked about how powerful it was, at the morning country team meeting, the regular gathering of section and agency heads at the embassy. I thought at first that Jenny was exaggerating or pulling my leg because I had picked a Schwarzenegger quote as our code to signal the start of the war. After I saw the video, it was clear she was not. This was brilliant public diplomacy—albeit conducted by a US citizen, not the US government. Yet, as impressive and persuasive as the Schwarzenegger video was, I knew it would have no impact. It was a tiny drop in the roiling sea of disinformation in Russia at the dawn of the "special military operation."

---

After my relocation to the embassy compound, I worked in a sad, gloomy world, sitting in an office with the blinds drawn—as they always were, around the clock, to try to limit the ability of the Russians to monitor the activities in my suite. I was convinced that Russia had crossed a threshold from which there would be no return. Former Russian president Dmitry Medvedev, channeling the rage of Russian nationalists, wrote that Russia and the West should "padlock the embassies and continue contacts looking at each other through binoculars and gunsights." Fortunately, we had not yet reached that stage, but we were coming much closer to it than I would have thought possible when I was appointed ambassador.

Adding to the diplomatic challenges were the restrictions and isolation of the Covid-19 pandemic, and their impact on Russia and the Kremlin. Another handicap was the dramatically reduced staffing at the US mission in Russia—the result of an impasse over visas and a series of diplomatic expulsions and consulate closures by both sides in the prior five years. The US mission shrank from an embassy in Moscow and three consulates to a thinly staffed Embassy Moscow with no consulates, making it even harder for the United States to conduct diplomacy with Russia.

Serving as the US ambassador in Moscow had always been difficult, as evidenced by the photographs of bomb damage at Spaso House during World War II. My friend and predecessor as ambassador to Russia, William J. Burns, who was CIA director during much of my time in Moscow, had said that he got his gray hair when he served in Moscow. The post had never been a cushy job of cocktail parties and polite banter with diplomatic colleagues and foreign ministry officials. To the contrary, traditionally it had been so difficult that long before there was a war in Ukraine, I had two presidents (Trump and Biden) each separately question my judgment, if not my sanity, in light of my desire to serve them in Russia.

But the new challenges that my embassy faced during the war and the deadly pandemic, combined with greatly reduced staffing and a ruthlessly hostile host government, were extraordinary. Our relations with Russia had entered a period as low, and as dark, as any during my lifetime. If the Russians could call their failed invasion of Ukraine a "special military operation," then the US mission to Russia in these difficult circumstances of failed diplomacy could fairly be called a special diplomatic operation.

The story of that mission is a piece of the historical record of Russia's aggressive war against Ukraine that also sheds light on the potential future of US-Russia relations. At the time of this writing in March 2024, that relationship is at risk of hitting a new low—one that will make the Mariana Trench look like Mount Everest. Can we stop digging, and can we climb out of the pit? That is among the most urgent questions of our time. I hope that this book, my final dispatch from my service as ambassador, will help inform the answer.

PART I

# THE ROAD TO MOSCOW

# CHAPTER 1

# A NEW CHALLENGE

THE ONLY TIME I SPOKE to President Trump about my nomination to be the US ambassador to Russia, he seemed amused. It was the afternoon of August 20, 2019, and we were departing the Cabinet Room at the White House following a meeting with President Klaus W. Iohannis of Romania. President Trump walked up to me and said he had been talking about me to the media.

Earlier in the day, during a media scrum in the Oval Office, a reporter had asked the president whether he was going to nominate me to be the new US ambassador in Moscow. As *Politico* reported, Trump responded cagily: "Sullivan 'could very well be' his pick to be the new envoy to Russia . . . , saying that the current No. 2 to Secretary Mike Pompeo was 'very respected' and that Pompeo likes him 'very much.'" Actually, the president had decided days before to nominate me, but the news had leaked prematurely. That had become common in the Trump administration but was alien to my experience in past administrations, where high-profile nominations were guarded closely until announced later in the process.

As we stood in the doorway to the Cabinet Room, President Trump told me of the press inquiry and said that if I really wanted the job, he would nominate me to be ambassador. But when I told him that I did, a quizzical look came over his face.

By this point in the administration, I had had many interactions and conversations with the president, and he knew me. In an almost avuncular way, he asked whether I was certain, and before I could respond, he volunteered to say that I did not have to leave my position as deputy secretary.

I reassured President Trump that I really did want to go to Russia, but as our conversation continued, it became apparent that he did not believe me—or at least that he thought I was not making the decision voluntarily.

The president, I realized, thought that my boss at the State Department, Secretary Pompeo, was forcing my departure. This seemed to him to be the only reason a sane person would leave my senior position on Mahogany Row of the seventh floor at the State Department for cold and hostile Moscow.

Finally, after my repeated reassurances that this was what I wanted, the president shook his head in feigned disbelief and said, in that case, my nomination would go forward.

I returned to the State Department and told Secretary Pompeo of my conversation with the president. We both laughed and agreed that the president's questioning of my sanity was legitimate, but that he was mistaken about anyone forcing my departure. In fact, I had raised the idea myself in a meeting with the secretary earlier in the summer, proposing that I replace Ambassador Jon M. Huntsman Jr. at Embassy Moscow.

When I told the secretary of my interest in the post, he was not initially enthusiastic about letting me go. He asked me why I wanted to leave, and I laid out my rationale.

By the summer of 2019, I had been the deputy secretary of state for well over two years. In ordinary times, it was a difficult and stressful job. In the Trump administration, it was a pressure cooker. Going to Moscow seemed like a reprieve, which was really saying something.

---

My background and preparation for what many considered the most challenging job in US diplomacy—ambassador to Russia—was as a lawyer with substantial experience working in Washington. I was born and raised in the Boston area (South Boston and Medfield) in an Irish Catholic family with grandparents who had emigrated from Ireland. I grew up a typically militant Bostonian with a wicked devotion to Dunkin' Donuts, all four of our professional sports teams, and my patron saint, the greatest ice hockey player ever, the incomparable Bobby Orr. After a terrific education at Xaverian Brothers High School in Westwood, Massachusetts, I attended Brown University and Columbia University School of Law. I was then a judicial law clerk for Judge John Minor Wisdom on the US Court of Appeals for the Fifth Circuit in New Orleans, and for Associate Justice David H. Souter on the Supreme Court of the United States.

I moved into my first job in the Executive Branch working in the Office of Legal Counsel (OLC) at the US Department of Justice in the George H. W. Bush administration. It was a young assistant attorney general, William P. Barr, the future two-time attorney general, who hired me. I had considered working as a prosecutor (and even inter-viewed with the then US attorney for the Southern District of New York, Rudolph W. Giuliani, whom I would subsequently run across in very different circumstances much later in my career) but chose OLC instead because that small office was deeply involved in national secu-rity issues advising Attorney General Richard L. Thornburgh and the counsel to the president, C. Boyden Grey. I was attracted to foreign affairs and national security, with no real urge to be a trial lawyer.

I admired President Bush and was honored to work for him. When he lost his reelection campaign, on November 3, 1992, to Governor Bill Clinton of Arkansas, I was crestfallen. The following day I was present on the South Lawn of the White House with many others to greet him and the First Lady as they returned from Houston. The atmosphere was funereal, with many people in tears, but the president tried to cheer us up. He urged everyone to work hard to have the best presidential transition possible: "Let's finish this job with style. Let's get the job done, cooperate fully with the new administration. The government goes on, as well it should, and we will support the new president and give him every chance to lead this country into greater heights." He was, as always, a patriot who put his country ahead of grief over a crushing personal defeat.

In February 1993, I entered private practice in the Washington office of a Chicago-based law firm, Mayer, Brown & Platt. My decision to stay in Washington, rather than return to Boston, was heavily influenced by my wife, Grace M. Rodriguez, whom I had met when we were in law school. Grace was a native New Yorker from Queens (she grew up near Shea Stadium) and was equally devoted to her hometown and her beloved Amazin' Mets. That was an issue we successfully overcame as a couple after the Mets tragically beat the Red Sox in the 1986 World Series. I always joked that when we survived this trauma (as I had experienced it), I knew we were meant to be together, and that nothing would separate us after we married in August 1988.

Staying in Washington was a compromise and an act of marital diplomacy. Grace was adamant about not moving to Boston. For some reason, even though she had lived in Cambridge for four years as an undergraduate at Harvard, she thought Bostonians were smug, tribal, mean, and talked funny. I never understood why. (Years later, after the Patriots became the greatest franchise in NFL history and we Patriots fans were proudly chanting, "They hate us, 'cuz they ain't us," I wondered whether Grace had been onto something, because she was usually—frustratingly—right. But then again, so were Tom Brady and Bill Belichick.)

At Mayer Brown in Washington, I practiced in the Supreme Court and appellate group during the eight years of the Clinton administration, writing briefs and occasionally arguing cases. When Governor George W. Bush became president, in January 2001, I considered going back into government service, and Grace and I talked about it. With three young children, it was not the right time for me to leave Mayer Brown, where I had been elected a partner in 1997. I turned down an offer to serve as a deputy assistant attorney general at the Justice Department.

September 11 changed my perspective. On that awful Tuesday morning, the weather was stunningly beautiful, and Grace was in her law office at King & Spalding, where she was a partner, at the corner of Seventeenth Street and Pennsylvania Avenue, directly across from the White House complex. Everyone at the firm was ordered to leave and to get out of the area after American Airlines flight 77 crashed into the Pentagon. On the street outside Grace's building, uniformed Secret Service officers told those exiting to run away, because another hijacked plane was thought to be headed toward the White House, and to avoid the Metro.

At that moment, I was sitting in my car in traffic near my office at Mayer Brown, several blocks north and west of where Grace was. I also had no cell phone service, so I was only able to get in touch with Grace—and pick her up—hours later, after she jogged and walked miles up

Connecticut Avenue toward our home in Maryland. Later that night and for days and nights thereafter, we heard jet aircraft flying overhead, even though all civilian air traffic had been grounded. It was the sound of combat air patrols over the nation's capital and our peaceful neighborhood in Bethesda. Grace and I could not believe how our world had changed so quickly.

The September 11 attacks also changed our view on whether I would return to public service if the right opportunity came along. In 2003, the White House Counsel's office approached me about serving as the deputy general counsel of the Department of Defense under Secretary Donald H. Rumsfeld. I had never served in uniform, and nor had I ever been inside the Pentagon before I went for my first interview with Jim Haynes, the general counsel. It was an intimidating experience. When I was offered the position, Grace and I agreed that this was a job I should take even though it meant leaving my partnership at Mayer Brown.

My service at the Defense Department turned into the most intense educational experience of my life. Just navigating the enormous bureaucracy was difficult and time-consuming, to say nothing of learning the language, culture, and processes of each of the military departments and the Joint Staff. I also had to master whole new areas of the law while giving legal advice to a department that was fighting wars in Afghanistan (Operation Enduring Freedom) and Iraq (Operation Iraqi Freedom), as well as navigating interagency battles in Washington. My work was so personally transformative that I felt as though I were born again professionally. I also gained confidence in my ability to manage stressful situations.

After President Bush won reelection in November 2004, the White House Office of Presidential Personnel reached out to me to discuss possible new jobs in the president's second term, but I loved working at the Pentagon and was not looking to leave. The sense of purpose and mission among my colleagues was inspiring, and almost daily there was a new challenge to keep me on my toes. My job was never boring, and although the hours were long and the pace was unyielding, I was running on adrenaline and would do anything to avoid letting down my colleagues. Most of all, I had nothing to complain about, because I was not in harm's way, unlike for example, the marines of the First Marine Division under the command of then major general James N. Mattis, who had begun Operation Phantom Fury in early November 2004 to liberate Fallujah, Iraq, from Islamic insurgents led by Al-Qaeda in Iraq. Mattis would later play a significant role in my professional life.

Then in 2005, the White House made me an offer I could not refuse: a presidential appointment (requiring Senate confirmation) as the general counsel of the Department of Commerce. I would be my own boss as a lawyer, and the office carried more responsibility as the number three position in the hierarchy of the department. I accepted the nomination, was confirmed by the Senate, and was appointed in July 2005. Two years later, I was nominated to be the deputy secretary of commerce and, after another Senate confirmation, was the number two official at the department.

Serving as the chief operating officer of the Commerce Department was the first nonlegal job in my career and gave me significant management experience. I also did a lot of international travel to promote US businesses abroad. And because of my prior experience at the Defense Department, I became deeply involved with promoting the economy of Iraq, where the US military was still heavily engaged, and encouraging US investment there.

When the Bush administration ended, on January 20, 2009, I left office and returned to private law practice. The Obama administration in 2010 appointed me to the US-Iraq Business Dialogue, a government advisory committee on US commercial relations with Iraq, to which I was later elected chair—but that was a part-time position without compensation. I had no expectation that I would ever serve in government again.

---

On November 8, 2016, I was as surprised as many were when Donald Trump was elected president. I had not been involved in the campaign and did not know anyone who worked for the president-elect. I was not an active Trump supporter, but I did still believe in Ronald Reagan's famous Eleventh Commandment, "Thou shalt not speak ill of any fellow Republican." Even though Trump himself did not follow that directive, I had voted for him with no thought that I ever would be invited to work in his administration.

It did not take long for the seed of the idea to become planted in my mind, however. I was introduced to the incoming Trump administration in January by Jim Mattis, the now-retired Marine four-star general whom the president-elect had announced on December 1, 2016, would be his secretary of defense. A representative of General Mattis called me shortly thereafter to inquire whether I would be interested in working for him as the general counsel of the Department of Defense.

General Mattis was legendary in the US Marine Corps, as I knew from my prior service at the Pentagon. I was enthusiastic about the idea of working under him, because of my enormous respect both for him and for the institution he would be leading: a place where I had enjoyed such an extremely rewarding experience in the George W. Bush administration under Secretary Rumsfeld. The thought of turning Mattis down never entered my mind—unless Grace objected.

My wife and I made every important life decision together, and I valued her opinion. In addition to being the love of my life for thirty years, Grace was a sophisticated lawyer and now a senior partner at King & Spalding, an international law firm that afforded its attorneys a deep understanding of the inner workings of governments at home and abroad. She had not voted for Trump and would not have been supportive if I were going to work for him at the White House. But working for Secretary Mattis at the sprawling Defense Department was a different story. She also thought the new secretary would need the help, noting incredulously that the president-elect insisted on calling him Mad Dog. That was neither his call sign while he was in uniform (which was Chaos) nor a sobriquet that anyone but the president would think to use in his presence. In any case, to my relief, Grace was in complete agreement: I should accept Mattis's offer.

I considered General Mattis's job offer an honor in and of itself, although I knew that it was only the start of a clearance process run by the White House that if successful, would lead to my nomination by the president. This ordeal had already proved frustrating to General Mattis, because several of his personnel selections were not approved by the White House. In my case, however, as a lawyer put forward to serve as a general counsel, I went through a special review overseen by the White

House Counsel's office. The process moved quickly, not just because it was on a different track but also because I had served in the two Bush administrations with several of the lawyers involved in the review. They knew me personally and thought I would be a good choice for the position. I also was well known in the legal community and had worked for two prominent senior Republican officials, former attorney general Bill Barr and Judge J. Michael Luttig, at the Justice Department, and they would vouch for me.

As I awaited the approval of my nomination, the Trump transition team asked me to help certain cabinet secretary nominees prepare for their confirmation hearings, including Rex Tillerson, nominated to be the secretary of state, and Wilbur L. Ross Jr., nominated to be the secretary of commerce. I was invited to participate in a mock confirmation hearing—a so-called murder board, a common feature of every consequential nomination by a president reviewed by the Senate—for Secretary-designate Tillerson in the early morning on January 7, 2017. The opportunity to engage with the recently retired chairman and CEO of ExxonMobil Corporation and the soon-to-be secretary of state made it worth the effort to get to the transition headquarters in Washington, DC, before 8 a.m. on a Saturday.

As the least distinguished member of a panel consisting of former senators and a few other very senior former officials, however, I was tasked with asking the secretary-designate questions intended to be provocative, personally embarrassing, or just plain annoying. The former senators and other eminent members of the panel would ask deep, thought-provoking questions on US foreign policy and national security. The organizers of the panel urged me to focus on nasty questions that would "throw the nominee off his game" and "get under his skin." It was typical to ask wealthy cabinet nominees such as Tillerson, for instance, about the current price of a gallon of gasoline or a loaf of bread in the hope of exposing them as out of touch with average Americans. I knew the routine but thought some of the suggested questions were a waste of time. I was confident that Tillerson—who until days earlier was CEO of one of the largest oil companies in the world—knew the price of a gallon of gas.

I did my best to try to annoy and rattle the nominee—quite a challenge given his stature and imposing demeanor. I asked him about the Order of Lenin he had received from President Putin years before. Among other things, I wanted to know what he had done for Russia to deserve the award, and whether his friend Putin was wearing a shirt when he presented it. Secretary-designate Tillerson stared at me for a moment with a serious countenance and then said in a slow, deep voice that President Putin had presented him the Russian Order of Friendship in 2013 for ExxonMobil's "contribution to strengthening cooperation in the energy sector," and that Putin had not presented him the Soviet-era Order of Lenin. He also noted dismissively that Putin was fully clothed when presenting the award.

I thought at the time that if I were lucky enough to be nominated and confirmed as the general counsel of the Defense Department, I should seek to avoid crossing paths with the future secretary of state, who could not have a high opinion of me after our exchanges that morning. Seeming to confirm my suspicion, a fellow panelist, former senator Kay Bailey Hutchison of Texas, and our future US ambassador to NATO, put her arm around me at the end of the session and joked to her old friend Secretary-designate Tillerson that I had played a "great snarky Democrat." The secretary-designate did not appear to be amused. I hoped he would not complain to General Mattis, but I figured he had more important things on his mind.

Not long after President Trump's inauguration, the White House approved my nomination, and I started filling out the voluminous paperwork for my background investigation. I was one of the first personnel choices by now Secretary Mattis to be approved by the White House, along with Heather A. Wilson, the former member of Congress who was nominated to be the secretary of the air force. On March 7, 2017, the White House announced my nomination publicly and sent it to the Senate Armed Services Committee for review.

Days after the announcement, Grace and I went to Boston with our three adult children, Jack, Katie, and Teddy, for a long-planned visit with family and friends. We were having a large dinner party at my favorite restaurant, The Inn at Bay Pointe, in Quincy, Massachusetts, on Saturday night, March 11, when I received a surprising text message to call Secretary Tillerson's office at the State Department.

I stepped outside and spoke to Secretary Tillerson's chief of staff, Margaret J. A. Peterlin, who said the secretary would like to meet with me, and asked whether I could be in his office at the department on Monday. Of course, I said—but I was curious as to why. Margaret said that Secretary Tillerson wanted to speak with me about serving as the deputy secretary of state.

Was the secretary aware, I asked Margaret, that the president had already nominated me for a position at the Pentagon? She said he was and that he had spoken to Secretary Mattis earlier in the day to get his approval before asking her to reach out to me. In that case, I said, I would see Secretary Tillerson on Monday.

My head was spinning as I returned to the dinner table. I told Grace briefly about the conversation and she gave me one of her "you have got to be [kidding] me" looks. We both shook our heads at this completely unexpected turn of events. She knew, as did I, that serving as the deputy secretary of state would be an enormous change from serving as the chief lawyer at the Defense Department: a job that would be not only more demanding, but also with a much higher profile, and which was sure to impose enormous burdens on both of us and our family. If nothing else, my plans to steer clear of Secretary Tillerson had been completely upended.

————

I arrived at Foggy Bottom—as the State Department complex in Washington is informally known—on Monday afternoon and waited in the reception area directly outside Secretary Tillerson's large office. There was nervous energy and a flurry of activity among the staff in the suite because the secretary was leaving on his first trip to Asia that evening and there was light snow falling that might complicate his departure. I sat there alone amid the commotion, wondering what I was going to say when I saw Secretary Tillerson for the first time since the murder board two months ago, where I had asked him snarky questions about Vladimir Putin. I assumed that there would not be a problem, since he had asked to meet with me, but there was still a lingering question in my mind.

Any doubts that I was harboring vanished as soon as I was invited into the secretary's office. He greeted me with a grin and started teasing me about the "grilling" I had given him. That was not the way I remembered the morning, I replied, trying to match his good humor, and anyway it sounded like a terrible way to impress a potential boss.

With the air cleared, Secretary Tillerson and I each took a seat and settled into a more formal interview. We discussed my background and my previous service in government, including my management experience as the deputy secretary of commerce. I told him of my substantial work in those prior roles with the State Department, and of my family's connection to the Foreign Service. My late uncle Ambassador William H. Sullivan had been a senior officer and three-time ambassador who, at the end of a distinguished thirty-two-year career, had served as the last US ambassador to Iran. Bill's children (my four cousins) had lived the Foreign Service life all over the world. Secretary Tillerson and I also discussed his desire to modernize the State Department by applying the rigorous management skills he had honed over forty years at ExxonMobil.

After an hour, the secretary's staff interrupted to say that it was time for him to leave for Joint Base Andrews and his flight to Tokyo. I had enjoyed our conversation, but I walked out of the department into the late-afternoon snow not knowing whether he would ask me to take the job. Two days later, Margaret Peterlin, who was traveling with the secretary, emailed me to expect a call from him.

Grace and I had discussed the matter extensively since our dinner had been interrupted on the prior Saturday night. We agreed that I would accept the nomination if it were offered, and our rationale was premised on trust in Tillerson, like my prior decision to accept the Defense Department nomination, which was based on trust in Mattis. Both men had assumed positions vitally important to the nation's security and I was supremely confident that they would always put the nation's interests ahead of any other, political or personal. The position of deputy secretary of state would be more burdensome and risky because of its high profile, but it would be worth the sacrifice if I could help Secretary Tillerson with the responsibilities he had taken on.

The following day, March 16, I received a call from the State Department's Operations Center connecting me with Secretary Tillerson as he was flying from Tokyo to Seoul. The secretary said he wanted me to serve as his deputy secretary and I said yes when he asked whether I would accept the job. The next step was to get White House approval, which the secretary assumed would require a meeting with the president. Secretary Tillerson said he would arrange the meeting and accompany me to the Oval Office after he returned from Asia. I immediately called Grace and told her the news, but we knew it was not final until the president had signed off.

Based on Secretary Tillerson's advice that a meeting with the president would be necessary, I was surprised when I received an email the very next day from the White House Office of Presidential Personnel with paperwork to fill out for my nomination to serve as the deputy secretary of state. I knew the person who had sent the message—she was an experienced professional who had worked in prior Republican administrations and on my recent nomination to be the general counsel of the Defense Department—and I asked her whether the president had approved the nomination. She said he had; and I asked again whether she was sure, in the light of my conversation the day before with Secretary Tillerson. She said she was certain the president had just approved my nomination and that no meeting would be necessary. It was March 17, an auspicious day for a Boston Irishman.

This turn of events was not what I had expected, but I chalked it up as another example of the "unconventional" style of the nascent Trump administration. I emailed Margaret Peterlin, Secretary Tillerson's chief of staff, to ask her to relay the news to him—and then I began filling out a new set of forms for my State Department nomination. Not only would it need to be reviewed and approved by the Senate Foreign Relations Committee, but it would also require an expanded background investigation because of the scope and significance of the position.

Exactly one week later, on March 24, 2017, news of my proposed nomination leaked to the *New York Times*. I was surprised again, because in the two Bush administrations in which I had served, the White House always kept a tight hold on a presidential nomination until it was final—in particular, until the background investigation was completed. I had been nominated by President George W. Bush and confirmed by the Senate twice, and in neither case did news of my nomination leak. I was finally, however, beginning to internalize a fact that was already apparent from the abundant reporting about President Trump: his administration was going to be nothing like its Republican predecessors.

The remainder of the nomination and confirmation process proceeded without drama. My nomination was officially announced on April 11, and the Foreign Relations Committee held a confirmation hearing on May 9. The full Senate considered my nomination on Wednesday, May 24, and confirmed me in a bipartisan 94–6 vote, which was a gratifying result in the increasingly hostile political climate in Washington. I attributed the large vote in my favor to the reputation I had earned in Washington over twenty-five years and, more importantly, to the fact that highly accomplished figures with substantive backgrounds as diverse as Rex Tillerson, Jim Mattis, and David Souter had vouched for me. Secretary Tillerson left me a congratulatory message saying that I had hit a home run.

I immediately resigned from Mayer Brown (again) and drove to the State Department, where I took the oath of office and assumed the duties of my new position at 4:30 p.m. that Wednesday afternoon. Any thought I had to savor the moment was quashed when I was immediately handed an enormous stack of binders and told that I needed to prepare for a deputies committee meeting run by the National Security Council (NSC) staff at the White House the following day on the US government's ongoing nuclear posture review. It was a welcome-to-the-big-leagues moment if ever there was one.

———————

My first afternoon as deputy secretary set the tone for the next two years and eight months, which were a grueling, seven-days-a-week marathon. The traditional heavy stress and long hours of the job were compounded by the chaotic and undisciplined style of the president and the many unfilled positions at the State Department. The Trump administration had decided not to fill the second deputy secretary position at the department, a role that had been created by Congress at the end of the Clinton administration. The State Department is the only cabinet department with two deputies: a principal deputy secretary (my job) and a deputy secretary for management and resources. The Trump administration intentionally left the second deputy position vacant; I would perform the functions of both.

I agreed with that approach, which President Bush and Secretaries Colin Powell and Condoleezza Rice had also adopted, but I did not agree with a process that left many of the other senior positions at the department unfilled for months or years. For example, for more than half my time as deputy secretary, the department did not have a Senate-confirmed legal adviser. Because of my background as a lawyer and the fact that I was nominated to be the general counsel of the Defense Department, everyone naturally looked to me to be the responsible senior official for legal matters at the State Department. Similarly, the department did not have a Senate-confirmed under secretary of state for management during most of my tenure as deputy secretary.

There were a variety of reasons for the dozens of vacancies, but the cumulative effect was to layer added responsibilities on the few senior leaders of the department who were confirmed by the Senate, such as Ambassador Thomas A. Shannon Jr., a career ambassador, the highest personal rank in the Foreign Service, who was the highly capable and richly experienced under secretary of state for political affairs during my first year as deputy secretary. In addition, the secretary and I had to ask more junior officers and other appointees to serve on an acting basis in performing the functions of the numerous unfilled senior positions. The women and men stepping into this void rendered extraordinary service to their country in difficult and often unheralded roles.

I learned something about the challenges of serving in an acting capacity in a senior position when President Trump fired Secretary Tillerson unceremoniously via a tweet in March 2018. In retrospect, the episode captured the tumult of the Trump administration and the resulting stress on all those involved in US foreign policy and national security affairs. At the time, it was simply an all-consuming emergency for me—the biggest that I had to deal with at the State Department as deputy secretary.

An inkling of the chaos ahead came a week prior to the infamous tweet while Secretary Tillerson was on an extended trip to Africa. I had to call him late on Thursday, March 8, waking him in the middle of the night in Addis Ababa, Ethiopia, to tell him of the president's extraordinary meeting earlier that day with Chung Eui-yong, the South Korean national security adviser. I had been present in the Oval Office—with, among others, Vice President Mike Pence; Secretary Mattis; General Joseph F. Dunford, the chairman of the Joint Chiefs of Staff; and Lieutenant General H. R. McMaster, the national security advisor—when the South Korean official conveyed an offer from North Korean leader Kim Jong Un to meet with Trump. I told a groggy Secretary Tillerson that the president had accepted the offer from the leader—whom Trump had called Little Rocket Man—on the spot, without asking for any input from his advisers. Instead, Trump leapt to considering venues for the meeting, including, amazingly, Las Vegas (which was an obvious nonstarter).

The secretary was at first dumbfounded, but he immediately pivoted to how we would manage this new and profoundly challenging situation. In the interim, his important trip to Africa would continue—that is, until he received calls over the weekend from White House Chief of Staff John F. Kelly, the retired Marine general, advising him to return home. Tillerson arrived at Joint Base Andrews before dawn on Tuesday, March 13, and went to his residence to rest before coming to the office later in the day.

I was at the department that morning, preparing for a busy day, when Tillerson's deputy chief of staff told me that the president had just fired the secretary. To say I was stunned is, of course, a gross understatement. I turned on the television in my office to see that at 8:44 a.m. that morning—just moments before—the president had tweeted:

Mike Pompeo, Director of the CIA, will become our new secretary of state. He will do a fantastic job! Thank you to Rex Tillerson for his service! Gina Haspel will become the new Director of the CIA, and the first woman so chosen. Congratulations to all!

That is how Secretary Tillerson and I, along with the rest of our country and the world, learned of this significant development.

My immediate reaction was that whoever was going to serve as the acting secretary of state until Director Pompeo's confirmation was going to have a tough job. I guessed that the president would not designate me, because I was associated so closely with Tillerson. I convened a meeting of the department's senior staff in the secretary's conference room to try to reassure everyone and to impress upon my colleagues the need to remain calm and to present a controlled and disciplined image and message to a variety of audiences: the department and our posts around the world, the rest of the US government, our country, our allies and partners, and most especially our adversaries and those who wished us ill. I said our goal as a department would be to have the smoothest transition possible from the sixty-ninth secretary of state, Rex Tillerson, to the seventieth, Mike Pompeo.

Later in the morning, I received a call from General Kelly, who was on *Air Force One* with the president. Kelly gave me the very opposite news that I had suspected I would hear: he told me that I would be the acting secretary of state until the new secretary was confirmed. The president had confidence in me, John said, and so did he and the White House staff, including General McMaster, and of course Secretary Mattis.

I was not completely surprised, because the deputy secretary was usually the default option to step into the role of secretary of state in circumstances like this—insofar as there had *ever* been circumstances like this. I also was relieved, because Kelly's call answered another question that had occurred to me in the intervening hours: namely, whether I was about to be fired.

I thanked John for his kind words of reassurance. I then started reaching out as acting secretary to the senior leaders at the department who had not been able to attend the earlier staff meeting I had chaired, as well as our ambassador to the UN, Nikki Haley, and other colleagues across the national security departments and agencies. I had the same message of calm reassurance to each person about the stability of the State Department despite this otherwise very unsettling development.

At this point, Secretary Tillerson arrived at the department, and I went to meet with him in his office. He was, as always, composed and thoughtful, despite the turmoil swirling around him and our department. I told him how shocked and saddened I was by what had happened, and that I owed him enormous gratitude for selecting me to be the deputy secretary of state—the best job I would ever have. He was gracious in response, saying that he would submit a resignation letter to the president with an effective date at the end of the month, on March 31, but that he would delegate all his authorities and responsibilities to me that very afternoon. He said that he would be available for consultations with me at any time, but that from this moment on I was the acting secretary of state. I accompanied him to the press room, where he spoke from the podium and told the media what he had told me.

Secretary Tillerson was a model of strength, decorum, and wisdom. He had vast experience working and living around the world for Exxon-Mobil, but never lost touch with his Texas roots and the values he had learned as an Eagle Scout. Trained as an engineer, he had climbed the corporate ladder at ExxonMobil to the top and had negotiated for decades with heads of state, foreign ministers, oil ministers, and other global leaders. In many ways, Rex Tillerson had all the talent and experience one could ask for in a secretary of state, which was why former secretary Rice and former secretary of defense Robert M. Gates had strongly endorsed his nomination. But in other significant ways, he was completely miscast for his role—any role—in an administration as undisciplined and unconventional as this one.

President Trump had chosen as his new secretary of state CIA director Mike Pompeo. The secretary-designate had a military background and was extremely smart (first in his class at the US Military Academy), having gone to Harvard Law School (serving on the *Law Review*) after his army service, and then into business. He was also a political figure, elected to Congress with the Republican wave in 2010, and a skilled participant in the hurly-burly of national politics.

My first meeting with the secretary-designate was a breakfast on March 16, 2018, in his office at the CIA. We had worked together for almost a year and knew each other but were not close personally. Our breakfast meeting was an opportunity to discuss his preparation for what would surely be a contentious confirmation process and how the State Department and I could support him. We also discussed my approach to what I hoped and expected would be a brief tenure as the acting secretary. In a dangerous world, the United States needs to have a Senate-confirmed secretary of state guiding its foreign affairs.

I ultimately spent six weeks as the acting secretary of state, much longer than I had anticipated. The time passed very quickly, however, with several major events, including the state visit to the United States of President Emmanuel Macron of France (whom Grace and I hosted for lunch at the State Department) and the visit of Prime Minister Shinzo Abe of Japan to Mar-a-Lago for meetings with President Trump. During this period, I welcomed the advice and assistance of Secretary Mattis, who would call me regularly to check on how I was doing and to coordinate our policy positions. This was important when, for instance, it came to planning the joint strike on April 14 by the militaries of the United States, France, and the United Kingdom on multiple chemical-weapons-related sites of the Assad regime in Syria after a chemical weapons attack on civilians in Douma.

Yet even with the backing of Secretary Mattis, serving as the acting secretary of state was a huge challenge, and one that I overcame only with the support of the great team I had assembled in the office of the deputy secretary. They were led by my chief of staff, Gregory D. LoGerfo, a highly respected and experienced senior Foreign Service officer. Like me, Greg was from the Boston area, although from the other side of the Charles River and a rival school, Boston College High School (alma mater of General Dunford). Grace would give me an eye roll for being "tribal" when I would point out those important (at least to me as a Bostonian) distinctions.

Over the years we worked together, Greg and I developed a very close personal and professional relationship. We shared a keen interest in the *Godfather* trilogy, and our signature office motto, "And there will be the peace," was a quote from Don Barzini in the first film. Quite appropriate for a diplomatic office, we thought. I had complete trust in Greg, and he never let me down. Ironically, I had been warned by a political appointee in the department that officials at the White House would prefer that I not select any career officer as my chief of staff and that I pick instead a political appointee. I ignored that advice and urged anyone who inquired about the position to trust my judgment, which turned out to be impeccable in the case of Greg.

During my tenure as deputy secretary, Greg and I recruited several very talented special assistants from among the ranks of the Foreign Service and the civil service at the State Department, each of whom was responsible for one of the department's six regional bureaus as well as a functional bureau (e.g., counterterrorism or arms control). I also had a political appointee as a senior adviser, Marik A. String, who came with a stellar reputation from private law practice at the prestigious Wilmer-Hale firm, after working for the Senate Foreign Relations Committee. Marik also served in the US Navy Reserve while he worked at the State Department.

My experience as the acting secretary was an extended reminder that the pace of global events does not slow to accommodate the US government, whether for a lengthy confirmation process or for any other reason. In the history of our country, the important office of secretary of state had rarely been held by an acting secretary for more than a few days. My tenure as acting secretary, from the day Secretary Tillerson was fired on March 13, was among the longest in history.

To my relief, Director Pompeo was finally confirmed as secretary at midday on April 26. Early that afternoon, I went to the US Supreme Court for a small swearing-in ceremony at which Associate Justice Samuel A. Alito administered the oath of office to him. Without skipping a beat, or even stopping at the department, the new secretary then rushed directly to Joint Base Andrews for an overnight flight to attend a meeting of the NATO foreign ministers in Brussels the next day.

That was typical of my experience with the new secretary. He was full of energy, working round-the-clock, and a voracious reader. From the very start, he and I worked well together. We never discussed whether I would stay as his deputy or whether he wanted me to stay. We just went about the business of the department. Most important, Secretary Pompeo tried to improve the State Department's difficult relationship with President Trump. For instance, shortly after returning from Brussels, the secretary invited the president to speak at the department in the Ben Franklin Room on May 2 to introduce the president to the diplomats who worked for him. And he began to run interference for the department, and for me personally, with the White House.

In my case, the secretary's influence was most important in August 2018, when President Trump almost fired me. The cause, if that is the right word, was the raft of sanctions that the United States had imposed on Russia in response to the use of a Novichok nerve agent—a chemical weapon—by Russian military intelligence, the GRU, in Salisbury, England, earlier in the year. US law required the sanctions, and they were the right thing to do as a matter of policy, whether they were legally required or not. I reviewed the draft sanctions order, and before signing, I informed Secretary Pompeo and the White House of what was forthcoming.

Unfortunately, the National Security Council staff did not tell the president in advance of the sanctions. Trump learned of them from the front pages of the morning newspapers. He was blindsided and incensed, thinking that someone in the "deep state" was acting without his approval to subvert his relationship with Putin and Russia. That relationship had been the subject of immense speculation due to credible reports of Russia's attempted interference on Trump's behalf in the 2016 presidential election, and had come under renewed scrutiny after Trump's comments at a summit with Putin in Helsinki the month before, when our president had appeared to take Putin's word denying election interference, over the assessment of the US Intelligence Community.

The president called Secretary Pompeo very early in the morning on August 8, just as I was walking into his office for our daily morning check-in, a little before 7 a.m. The president said in colorful language that he wanted the person who had signed the sanctions order to be fired. The secretary told the president he would find out what had happened. Pompeo hung up and looked at me for an explanation. I told him that the sanctions were right as a matter of policy and required by law. I also said that I had given the White House notice of the sanctions and had heard no objection. The secretary nodded and said he would take care of the situation.

I went back to my office down the hall while the secretary spoke to National Security Advisor John Bolton, and—to Ambassador Bolton's credit—he intervened with the president to explain what had happened. As a result, the president did not demand my firing, but the whole situation made for a hectic day. Through it all, however, I was relatively serene. If I were going to be fired by the president, this was as good a reason—imposing sanctions on Russia for the attack in Salisbury—as I could imagine.

Partly because of this brief, disturbing episode, I developed a solid relationship with Secretary Pompeo as I continued my service as the deputy secretary of state in the Trump administration over the following year. Over time, thanks to hard work by the secretary and his team, a number of senior positions at the department were eventually filled, which relieved some of the burden on those of us who had been there from the start of the administration. Some of the burden—but not all.

———————

No matter how long many of us survived in the Trump administration, our jobs never got easier. The chaos and unpredictability of the White House remained a vexing problem. Sooner or later, it became too much for some to tolerate any longer.

Secretary Mattis, who had brought me into the administration, decided that he could not continue to work for President Trump and resigned in December 2018. In his resignation letter, the secretary emphasized that the president needed (and deserved) a secretary of defense whose views were more in line with the president's views than Mattis's were. His resignation was a great loss for the country, as well as for me personally. I wondered whether I could continue to serve the president responsibly if the person I originally trusted to bring me into the administration was leaving in these circumstances.

I spoke to Secretary Mattis about my reservations, and he urged me to stay. Among other things, he told me that Secretary Pompeo and my colleagues at the State Department needed me to remain in my position, if only because somebody had to do the job and because the global challenges that the United States faced were not going away. His comments had the intended effect: I resolved to stay, although I remained deeply troubled that the two people responsible for my being the deputy secretary of state—Rex Tillerson and Jim Mattis—were no longer serving in the administration. I could not shake the feeling that my days in office might be numbered, too.

That foreboding grew stronger during a slow-burning intrigue involving representatives of the president (including Rudy Giuliani) and a senior US diplomat. Months before Mattis's resignation, I had learned from Secretary Pompeo that the president was concerned about our embassy in Kyiv and the US ambassador there, Marie L. Yovanovitch. I knew the ambassador, and her deputy chief of mission, George P. Kent, having visited the embassy in February 2018. I also was very familiar with the situation in Ukraine, having met twice with the Ukrainian president, Petro Poroshenko.

Ukraine was a festering problem for Europe and the United States. The country confronted two staggering challenges. The first was existential: Russian aggression. Putin's government had seized Crimea and occupied the eastern Donbas region in 2014 in response to the Ukrainian Revolution of Dignity in February of that year. Putin refused to accept the Revolution of Dignity as reflecting the will of the people of Ukraine in removing President Viktor Yanukovych, who had fled to Russia. The second challenge was widespread and ingrained corruption, which made governing Ukraine difficult and the country's desired integration into the European Union (EU) and NATO a fraught subject at best.

Secretary Mattis and I had met with President Poroshenko in Munich on February 17, 2018, to discuss both issues. The Trump administration had agreed, at my urging and in contrast with the Obama administration, to provide lethal aid to Ukraine to resist the continuing Russian aggression. The security assistance included Javelin anti-tank missiles. Mattis discussed this with Poroshenko but spent more time emphasizing the need for legal and other reforms in Ukraine to address rampant corruption. The secretary said that I would follow up with the Ukrainian president on anti-corruption reforms soon.

That was the purpose of my trip to Kyiv the next week. While there, I was thoroughly briefed by Ambassador Yovanovitch and her team on anti-corruption reform efforts the United States supported and on the security situation in Ukraine. When I met again with President Poroshenko, late in the afternoon of February 21, I urged him to adopt vigorous anti-corruption measures, which would not only improve the economy but also strengthen the country to push back against the violent Russian encroachment on Ukrainian territory. Before the meeting with Poroshenko, Ambassador Yovanovitch and I toured Maidan Nezalezhnosti (Independence Square) in Kyiv, which had been the focal point of the Revolution of Dignity.

Later in 2018, when Secretary Pompeo told me about President Trump's concerns with Ambassador Yovanovitch, I recounted for the secretary my visit to Embassy Kyiv and my favorable experience with the ambassador and her team. My strong impression was that they were doing a good job under very difficult circumstances, and faithfully implementing US policy with respect to Ukraine. The secretary said he did not know the factual basis for the president's concern, but he would make further inquiries.

In the months that followed, I would occasionally hear from the secretary that the president was asking again about our ambassador in Kyiv and why she was still there, to which the secretary would respond that Ambassador Yovanovitch was doing her job and that there was no basis to remove her. Eventually, the president directed the secretary to speak to his personal lawyer, former New York City mayor Rudy Giuliani (the former US attorney who had interviewed me for a job decades before). But Giuliani had no clear justification for the president to recall Ambassador Yovanovitch, other than the vague and unsubstantiated accusation that she was "anti-Trump," as described by some dubious Ukrainian sources that Giuliani knew. There was serious concern among US national security officials that Giuliani was being influenced by Ukrainians who were affiliated or working with the Russian security services. Secretary Pompeo declined to take any action in those circumstances without a firm factual basis for his decision.

By the spring of 2019, however, President Trump was becoming more insistent. Secretary Pompeo warned me that the president was going to go around him and fire Ambassador Yovanovitch by tweet, just as he had fired Secretary Tillerson the year before. The secretary asked me to speak to the ambassador, explain the situation to her, and ask her to end her service in Kyiv early rather than subject herself to such a painful public ordeal. She was approaching the three-year mark for her service as ambassador later in the summer, which is about the average tenure for the post in Kyiv. Leaving a few months ahead of time seemed like a comparatively small price to pay for avoiding another social-media spectacle, with its corresponding implications for morale at the State Department and for America's national security more broadly.

Through the director general of the Foreign Service, Ambassador Carol Z. Perez, I asked Ambassador Yovanovitch to return to Washington to meet with me in early May 2019. I proceeded to have a series of difficult conversations with her over two days in my office. I told her everything I knew and answered every question she had to the best of my ability: she had done nothing wrong, but the president had lost confidence in her and did not want her to remain as the US ambassador in Kyiv. I did not agree with that assessment, but it was not my judgment that mattered. Only the president determined when an ambassador's tenure was over. I told her that my uncle, Ambassador William H. Sullivan, had been recalled by President Carter as the US ambassador to Iran in 1979 over the objection of then–secretary of state Cyrus Vance. As she knew, the confidence of the president is the coin of the realm for an ambassador. If the president has lost confidence, then the ambassador must come home whether the secretary of state or his deputy agrees or not.

I explained to the ambassador bluntly that if she did not leave her post, the president was likely to fire her by tweet at any moment. This was an extremely difficult message to convey to a person who had done nothing wrong to merit her recall. Ambassador Yovanovitch was understandably upset by, and disagreed with, the message. But she handled the situation with poise and professionalism. We discussed the logistics of her return to Kyiv and how she would disengage from the embassy over the next few weeks in the context of the upcoming inauguration of the new president-elect of Ukraine, Volodymyr Zelensky.

So it was that Ambassador Yovanovitch concluded her service in Kyiv early and returned home. This was a bad outcome for US diplomacy and our relations with Ukraine, and it sent the wrong signal to Russia about US resolve in supporting Ukraine. But it was, in my opinion, a marginally better outcome than having another senior State Department official endure dismissal via social media. After she returned from Kyiv, Ambassador Yovanovitch remained in the Senior Foreign Service and took a position teaching at Georgetown University before her eventual retirement in January 2020.

After dealing with Ambassador Yovanovitch's departure from Ukraine, yet another in a series of deeply troubling developments, I started to think seriously about leaving my position as deputy secretary. I was ready for a change. The Tillerson firing, the Mattis resignation, and now the recall of Ambassador Yovanovitch: these were all extreme examples of the stress and disorder that I had to deal with every day, beyond the usual daunting challenges of formulating and implementing US foreign policy in a dangerous and ever-changing world.

When I began my service at the start of the Trump administration, I often wondered—considering the chaos at the White House and the high turnover in personnel—whether I would be able to remain in office until the end of 2017. As the summer of 2019 began, I was grateful that I had been able to serve in a critical position in the US government for well over two years. But Secretaries Tillerson and Mattis were gone, and I began to ponder my eventual departure. I wanted to do so on my own terms and with the least disruption possible for the department. I also had my eye on a new challenge—a country that was malevolently undermining the interests of the United States and its allies and partners around the world, from Salisbury to Kyiv and beyond. I refer, of course, to Russia.

# CHAPTER 2

# THE GAUNTLET

I MET WITH SECRETARY POMPEO IN his office on June 17, 2019, to propose that I resign as the deputy secretary of state. The secretary was surprised by the idea and said he did not want to lose me. Why did I want to leave an important job supporting him—a job that, according to him, I had mastered?

My rationale was simple: I was burning out.

The magazine *Foreign Policy* noted at the time that I had served as "deputy secretary during one of the most tumultuous periods in modern State Department history." After more than two years, I was ready to get off the hot seat.

But I was deeply conflicted about the idea of leaving my post, much less retiring from government entirely. I felt guilty, for one thing, because my resignation would not make things easier for my colleagues remaining on duty in the department—or for my successor, if she or he were lucky enough to be confirmed by the Senate in the deteriorating political environment in Washington. I also did not want to leave public service and abandon the broader mission of defending America's interests around the world. So, on the one hand, I was worn out and needed a change. Yet, on the other hand, I wanted to stay the course.

I had just begun to grapple with this dilemma and to consider other positions in which I could continue to serve, when, shortly before my meeting with Secretary Pompeo, an appealing opportunity presented itself.

At the beginning of June, Ambassador Jon Huntsman returned on leave from Moscow to tell the president and the secretary that he was going to resign his post on October 1, 2019, to run for governor (again) in Utah. He and I met in my office at the department on June 4 before he walked down the hall to tell Secretary Pompeo the news. Jon and I discussed the importance of the job he was leaving and who might be good candidates to succeed him.

I did not mention it in my first meeting with the ambassador, but the threshold question in my mind was whether his departure presented a solution to my professional dilemma. The ambassadorial post in Moscow was a role in which I could remain engaged in the key foreign policy issues on which I had worked as deputy secretary. Russia, as a permanent member of the UN Security Council and a nuclear and energy superpower, was involved in some way in virtually every issue of significance to American interests and security. On a personal level, too, Russia was a nation of particular interest to me. I had from my youth been fascinated with the country.

In subsequent meetings and phone conversations with Ambassador Huntsman over the next ten days, we discussed the possibility that I would succeed him. Jon was very enthusiastic about the idea, explaining not only the obvious importance of the position, but also the satisfaction he had derived from it. He thought that I would be a good fit for the post and could have influence with the Russians because they would respect me as a former deputy secretary of state. He said he would advocate for my selection with the president if I wanted the job. In the time between these conversations and my meeting with Secretary Pompeo, I had decided that I did.

———

My interest in serving as the US ambassador to Russia only increased as I considered the advantages of making the move. There were many, some of them professional or service-oriented, and others more idiosyncratic.

The preeminent reason, of course, was that I would remain meaningfully involved in public service implementing US foreign policy with no guilt that I was abandoning my colleagues at the State Department. But I also would be my own boss in running the US mission in Russia and less subject to the undisciplined machinations of the White House. I would control my day-to-day schedule, for example, which meant that—perhaps most appealingly—there would be no more last-minute substitutions by me for the secretary in important meetings when he was summoned to the Oval Office on no notice, a not infrequent occurrence in the Trump administration.

On one occasion, Secretary Pompeo had been summoned by the president to the White House, with no option to decline or delay, shortly before he was to meet at the department with Mexican foreign secretary Marcelo Ebrard. I was handed the secretary's briefing book for the meeting by his staff and told that I would be hosting the foreign secretary to discuss topics on which I had not recently been involved—including the situation on the southern border of the United States—and with only minimal time to prepare. Although I pulled it off, and the meeting ended with smiles and handshakes, last-minute substitutions such as this were no way to conduct US foreign policy.

Another consideration that influenced my decision was the abundant (and mostly erroneous) public speculation and media reporting that President Trump had a corrupt relationship with President Putin and Russia—for example, that Trump was compromised by the Russian security services or had conspired with Russian election interference in the 2016 election. In my tenure as deputy secretary, I never saw evidence of a corrupt bargain between Trump and Russia. To be sure, the president would not genuinely admit that the Russians attempted to interfere in the 2016 election (which they did), but only because he thought that to do so would be to concede that the Russians were somehow responsible for his victory. He would not or could not draw a distinction between his own interests and those of the country he was leading. Although it was not definitive evidence that Trump himself had colluded with Russia, this was nevertheless a problem for those of us in the administration who were dealing with Russia, as it undermined our work against future Russian election interference. By taking the job in Moscow, I would have a chance to help mitigate some of this damage, I thought, while also getting a clearer picture of the relationship between America's president and one of our foremost geopolitical adversaries.

With respect to Putin, President Trump had his own (mostly misguided) ideas about how he could develop a relationship with the Russian leader to achieve a diplomatic win—for example, on trade, investment, or energy—that would benefit Trump politically, and therefore, in his mind, the United States: what was good for Trump, he seemed to think, was also good for the United States, although not necessarily vice versa. When it came to Russia, this attitude of the president's had led him to seek a personal friendship with Putin, which he thought would benefit the United States and him politically.

In a sense, Trump was approaching Putin in exactly the same way that he approached other world leaders. I saw in his dealings with President Xi Jinping of China, Prime Minister Narendra Modi of India, and President Recep Tayyip Erdoğan of Turkey, for instance, a similar, highly personalized form of diplomacy that did not consider the larger strategic interests and values of the United States—only the simple, misguided assumption that whatever benefited President Trump politically also benefited the United States. That approach to foreign leaders was rightfully subject to withering criticism, but as applied to Putin it did not constitute evidence of unique collusion (or a corrupt relationship) with Russia.

This did not mean, however, that it was wise. To the contrary, when it came to Russia in particular, this mode of foreign relations was downright self-defeating.

In pursuit of his personal diplomacy with Putin, for example, President Trump would not accept the unanimous recommendation of his foreign policy team that he should not congratulate Putin on his overwhelming reelection victory in March 2018. Even in a so-called "managed democracy" like the Russian Federation, Putin's victory was at best tainted by substantial corruption and political manipulation. Most Western leaders thus declined to congratulate Putin, but Trump insisted he had to do so to develop a personal rapport with the Russian president. The American president had little concern for the boost that his message gave to Putin, a committed adversary of the United States, nor for the negative impact of that message on US promotion of democracy and anti-corruption policies worldwide.

To make matters worse, at the same time that President Trump was seeking personal diplomacy with Putin, senior officials like me in his administration—and with the president's own express approval—were hardening and expanding the policies toward Russia that we had inherited from the Obama administration. The Trump administration, for example, increased sanctions on Russia, expelled Russian diplomats and closed Russian consulates, provided Javelin anti-tank missiles to Ukraine, and not only documented Russia's intentional violation of the Intermediate-Range Nuclear Forces (INF) Treaty but also withdrew the United States from the treaty as a result. It would have been a revelation to Vladimir Putin that the United States was going soft on Russia during the Trump presidency, even if this was the public perception—one reinforced in large part by the president's own rhetoric.

Relocating to Moscow as ambassador while the 2020 election approached would put me firmly in the middle of this whirlwind of conflicting policies and statements. This would add to the complexity of the job, but in a way that I found meaningful and appealing.

But this was by no means the most difficult or enticing part of the proposition. Rather, the most professionally challenging and attractive feature—at least to me—of the position of US ambassador to Russia was the way that it would require me to engage with the Russians, and to do so on their own territory, under the intense scrutiny of the Federal Security Service (FSB), the principal heir to the notorious KGB, which was responsible, among other things, for domestic security. This was one of the key features and bugs of the US ambassadorship to Russia—and indeed had been since the early days of the Soviet Union.

---

For almost ninety years, since the United States recognized the Soviet Union, our diplomatic post in Moscow had always been among the hardest assignments for any American diplomat. This difficulty was intertwined with a unique opportunity, however: the chance to study one of our most formidable adversaries up close. This is what made me so interested in the post.

Six years before the legendary US diplomat George Kennan became ambassador to the Soviet Union, while he was the deputy chief of the US mission in Moscow under Ambassador Averell Harriman, he wrote a classified cable in 1946 to Secretary of State James F. Byrnes on a diplomatic strategy for dealing with the Soviet Union. In that since-declassified cable, known to history as the Long Telegram, Kennan concluded that confronting the "political force" of the Soviet Union, which was "borne along by deep and powerful currents of Russian nationalism," would be "undoubtedly [the] greatest task our diplomacy has ever faced and probably [the] greatest it will ever have to face." Kennan spoke with authority as a Russian linguist and a keen observer of Russian history, who had been among the first US diplomats to join Ambassador William C. Bullitt in establishing the US mission to the Soviet Union in 1933, just over a decade after its founding in late 1922.

Kennan followed the Long Telegram with an article in 1947, published anonymously in *Foreign Affairs* and titled "The Sources of Soviet Conduct." Writing under the pseudonym X, Kennan warned that the United States was "going to continue for a long time to find the Russians difficult to deal with," and urged a "policy of firm containment, designed to confront the Russians with unalterable counter-force at every point where they show signs of encroaching upon the interests of a peaceful and stable world."

I reread the Long Telegram and the X article as I thought about my future, and I found the challenge that they described irresistible. The Russians, like their Soviet predecessors, were relentless in pursing their interests and in using any means available to do so—facts, law, and morals were never obstacles for them—especially when seeking some sort of advantage against the United States. The Russian government under President Putin viewed the United States as its implacable adversary, just as the Soviets in Kennan's day approached the United States with "innate antagonism," as he put it. And the effects of this outlook on Russian behavior were the same as I perused Kennan's writings as they were eighty years ago: "the secretiveness, the lack of frankness, the duplicity, the wary suspiciousness, and the basic unfriendliness of purpose." As Kennan correctly predicted, those "phenomena are there to stay."

It was vitally important, consequently, for any American diplomat to approach the Russian government with careful preparation, attention to detail, and an iron commitment to the interests and values of the United States. It was always a test of wills, as the Russians would seize on any sign of weakness and remember any ill-advised concession, no matter how seemingly insignificant, or how long ago it was offered. My experience was that they would never reciprocate a goodwill gesture, viewing it simply as a vulnerability—something to be exploited, rather than honored.

The idea of dealing with such a well-known and entrenched adversary appealed to me because the stakes were so high on such a wide range of topics, whether it was the continued operations of the American Embassy in Moscow, the wrongful detention of American citizens in the Russian criminal justice system, or the status of our respective nuclear arsenals. I thought that I could continue to contribute to protecting US interests and national security by taking responsibility for our relationship with this uncompromising foe.

The difficulty of the assignment would only be enhanced by the fact that I would be working in the most hostile counterintelligence environment for American diplomats anywhere in the world: Moscow. The Russian security services, once overseen by the KGB but now led principally by the FSB, have a long-standing and well-deserved reputation for espionage in our embassy; for harassing, provoking, and assaulting US embassy personnel; and for disrupting the traditional tasks of US diplomats authorized by the Geneva Conventions, like consular visits to detained American citizens in Russian prisons and labor camps.

I relished the idea of standing up for and protecting our mission, our personnel, and our citizens in this hostile environment, against the worst that the FSB could inflict on us. It might have been my Boston Irish heritage, but I thought, like an old-fashioned beat cop, that I could make a difference, however slight, in protecting the interests of the United States and the lives of Americans in Russia.

Finally, I had deeply personal reasons for wanting to serve in Russia. Simply put, I have always been intrigued by Russian history and culture. My interest was first piqued when the Soviet national hockey team played Team Canada in the famous Summit Series in September 1972. I was passionate about hockey, like most Bostonians at the time, after the Bruins had won the Stanley Cup twice, in 1970 and 1972, led by our sainted Bobby Orr. Several of my Bruins heroes were playing on Team Canada, but not Orr, because he was recovering from knee surgery. Harry Sinden of the Bruins was the coach and general manager of the Canadian team.

The tournament was supposed to be a slaughter by the veteran NHL players on Team Canada, but they barely won the series, and only after Bobby Clarke of the Flyers had intentionally slashed one of the absolute best Soviet players of all time, Valeri Kharlamov, severely injuring his ankle in game 6.

My twelve-year-old mind was completely puzzled: who were these Soviet players who could match my Bruins and the best players in the NHL, and why had everyone in North America underestimated them? Why did we not know about them? What was this Communist system that could produce such talented players and a great team? I remember that before the series began, Boston hockey commentators denigrated the quality of the Soviet equipment and warned that Soviet players could get hurt playing against professionals from the NHL. It turned out that the only thing wounded during the series, beyond Kharlamov's ankle, was Canadian pride, even though Paul Henderson scored for Canada in the last game to win the series.

Eight years later, I was in college and the roles were reversed. The Soviets underestimated the United States at the Lake Placid Olympics, and, like millions of Americans on February 22, 1980, I watched a miracle on tape delay with Al Michaels making the call of the iconic victory by Team USA. At this point, I was hooked on all things Russian and Soviet. I could name the complete rosters of the Soviet national hockey teams from 1972 and 1980. That trivia won curious admiration years later from the former Russian ambassador to the United States, Sergey Kislyak, when I participated in a panel discussion with him at the Munich Security Conference in February 2018.

My interest extended far beyond ice hockey, however. I took Russian history classes in college, although I did not speak Russian and ended up majoring in American history. I became as knowledgeable as an amateur could be on Russian history and culture. I did not change my plans to go to law school, but I was a budding amateur Russophile.

I never talked about this background or my interest while my nomination to be ambassador was pending, because I thought it would sound too contrived and hokey. The United States does not need an amateur Russophile in our embassy in Moscow. Instead, I presented myself as someone with policy and leadership experience in government service over decades.

But my personal interest in Russia was quite real. My first trip outside North America was to the Soviet Union, for over a month in July and August 1989. Grace and I traveled to Moscow, Leningrad, Kyiv, and Yalta. At the time, I did not take significant notice of the fact that two of those cities (Moscow and Leningrad) were in the Russian Soviet Federative Socialist Republic and two (Kyiv and Yalta) were in the Ukrainian Soviet Socialist Republic—they were all in the Soviet Union, which is the only fact on which I focused. That difference, however, would have major significance for me years later as a US government official.

In sum, I had various interlocking reasons for wanting to serve as US ambassador to Russia. All the attractions of the job would be irrelevant, however, if my wife, Grace, did not agree. We had many conversations about the potential move before I raised it with the secretary. The overriding problem was that Grace would not be able to live in Moscow full-time, because of her high-profile law practice at King & Spalding and her clients in the United States. The issue came close to ending my consideration of the position.

But as we discussed the matter further, Grace and I thought we could adapt to a less than ideal situation. We agreed that she would spend as much time as she could in Moscow, and I would travel home as often as I could. Our three children were out of college and lived on their own. Moreover, our lives had already been severely disrupted by my service as deputy secretary. I traveled a great deal, and when I was not traveling, I was working long hours, seven days a week, at the department. How much worse would it be, traveling back and forth between Washington and Moscow?

Those, at least, were all of the pragmatic factors that we weighed in our decision-making process. But at the end of the day, Grace simply wanted to continue to support me in my public service, as she had throughout my career. I was enormously grateful at the time for her sacrifice, and that love and gratitude only increased over the next three years.

---

In my meeting with Secretary Pompeo on June 17, I did not just reveal that I was considering resigning. I also explained that my motivation for doing so was to enable me to throw my hat in the ring for Ambassador Huntsman's job. As we sat together, I laid out for the secretary all the reasons I had for wanting to leave Washington to serve in Moscow. The secretary said he understood, respected my reasoning, and that, although he did not want me to leave, my years of service, including as the acting secretary of state, had earned me the right to the appointment. He said he would clear it with the president.

I returned to my duties as deputy secretary, confident that Secretary Pompeo—a man of his word—would do as he promised. And sure enough, in early August, I learned that the president had signed off on my nomination.

Interestingly, I never spoke to President Trump about the job until he approached me quizzically in the Cabinet Room in August 2019, after the meeting with the Romanian president, when he thought (erroneously) that Pompeo was forcing me out. By then my nomination was already progressing through the bureaucracy for clearance before it was formally sent by the White House to the Senate.

There was just one part of the process to be completed before my nomination formally was announced: the background investigation. I assumed that would not take long, since I was already the deputy secretary of state and held the highest security clearances in the executive branch, as the alter ego of the secretary of state—an office that I had held on an acting basis not that long before. If the government trusted me to be the acting secretary of state, what more could it need to know before allowing me to take a demotion to serve as ambassador?

I was wrong: it took six weeks for the investigation to conclude. As is standard for background investigations, I sat for an interview with the investigator toward the end of the process, in September. I thought he might give me an indication of what was causing the delay. The only hint I got was from one of the few questions he asked me. He wanted to know why in 2008 I had not registered as a lobbyist when I was representing a client at Mayer Brown. I told him that in 2008 I was the deputy secretary of commerce and had no client other than the United States of America.

The investigator accepted my answer as good and sufficient with no follow-up, and the brief interview concluded. It was clear to me that the investigation was not a high priority, given the lack of scrutiny and understanding of my public record.

All the work in support of my nomination, including the delayed background investigation, was successfully concluded shortly after that interview, and the nomination itself was announced officially in early October. The confirmation process required review by the Senate Foreign Relations Committee, which I welcomed, as I had good relations with the senators on the committee and did not expect any major problems.

I continued my work as deputy secretary and joined Secretary Pompeo in New York City on the evening of September 22, 2019, for the annual High-Level Week at the United Nations General Assembly, when many world leaders descend on Manhattan's Turtle Bay neighborhood, including the president of the United States. The pace of meetings during this annual ritual was always grueling, and especially for me as the deputy secretary of state. During the prior High-Level Week, in September 2018, the *Washington Times* published an article describing me as a "busy deputy" who "may be the most vital player on the Trump administration's team this week," participating in many diplomatic engagements and back-to-back meetings. It would be the same intense tempo again at High-Level Week in 2019.

In New York, I had little time to focus on anything other than preparing for my next meeting. A few days before I left Washington, however, the *Washington Post* broke a story about a whistleblower who had filed a complaint in August concerning a telephone call between President Trump and an unidentified foreign leader. That story, which unfolded while I was in New York, turned out to have enormous implications for the country, for me personally—and for our already fraught relationship with Putin's government in Russia.

---

As I hustled from meeting to meeting at the UN during the week of September 23, 2019, the story about the presidential phone call exploded with media reporting that the call was with Ukrainian president Zelensky on July 25, 2019. I had previously been unaware of either the phone call or the subsequently filed whistleblower complaint. I occasionally participated in or monitored presidential phone calls with foreign leaders, but I was traveling on July 25 and was not included in, and did not receive a readout of, the call with President Zelensky.

It was only as I sat on an Amtrak train back to Washington on the afternoon of Friday, September 27, that I had time to assess the congressional and media interest in the July 25 phone call. Speaker Nancy P. Pelosi had already announced on September 24 that multiple committees of the House of Representatives would launch impeachment inquiries. The focus of the inquiries was the allegation that President Trump had "call[ed] upon a foreign power to intervene" in the 2020 election by pressuring President Zelensky to investigate former vice president Biden and his son Hunter's dealings in Ukraine. The pressure was allegedly exerted when President Trump threatened to withhold security assistance to Ukraine that the country needed in resisting Russia's aggression.

An offer of security assistance for Ukraine to resist Russian aggression in exchange for a criminal investigation of the Bidens was extremely problematic—and not something I would have supported. I enthusiastically endorsed criminal justice reform in Ukraine and the reduction of corruption in the country, but not a political focus on only one particular (albeit potentially egregious) case. The whole sordid mess was a disgrace, including Hunter Biden's "business dealings" in Ukraine and his father's tolerance thereof as vice president.

I knew immediately that this was a scandal that would have a substantial impact on all of us at the Department of State. But it soon became apparent that the impact on me would be focused on the review of my nomination to be ambassador to Russia, which was sent to the Senate on October 11. Unlike many of my administration colleagues, I was not asked for an interview or a deposition in connection with any of the House impeachment inquiries. In fact, I had no contact with any of the House impeachment investigators at all. I assumed, and was later told by congressional staffers, that was because I had not been aware of the July

25 presidential phone call until the media broke the story in September, and I was not involved in the hold by the administration on security assistance to Ukraine.

While the House impeachment investigators did not want to speak with me, the members of the Senate Foreign Relations Committee were extremely interested in my role in, and knowledge of all the circumstances surrounding, the July 25 Zelensky phone call and related issues. The *New York Times* observed that by "jumping into an impeachment fight that so far has been waged in the House behind closed doors, Senate Democrats used Mr. Sullivan's nomination to be President Trump's next ambassador to Russia to bring the drama into the open."

Indeed, as the House investigations were picking up speed, I began a long series of meetings with senators and their staff to discuss my nomination. In virtually every meeting, the July 25 phone call was a major topic of discussion. I told anyone who asked exactly what I knew and did not know: I was completely unaware of the July 25 phone call and the whistleblower complaint until the first media reports. I was aware of a hold on assistance for Ukraine, but in the summer of 2019 I was focused principally on unblocking a contemporaneous hold on funding for Central American countries to compel them to reduce migration north to the United States. The senators and staff were most interested in the fact that none of the House impeachment inquiries had asked to speak with me.

The only Ukraine-related issue about which I had direct knowledge was the recall of Ambassador Yovanovitch earlier in the year. That, too, had become a subject of the inquiries by the House impeachment investigators, presumably because of the unusual interest of President Trump and his personal representatives in Ukraine and its politics and corruption. I explained to the senators and their staff exactly what I knew and what I had done in connection with the recall of the ambassador from her post in Kyiv. I said I would repeat under oath in a public hearing everything I had told them and would not decline to answer any of their questions.

My confirmation hearing was scheduled for October 30, 2019. Preparation for the hearing—reading background materials and receiving in-depth briefings on Russia policy—was in many ways also preparation to assume the post of ambassador to Russia. But the overlay of the impeachment inquiry made the work tense and tiring. At this point, my chief of staff as deputy secretary was Katharine B. Nanavatty, who replaced Greg LoGerfo in April 2019 after he left to serve as the deputy chief of mission in our embassy in Tunis.

Kate, like Grace, was a New Yorker, and she had a stellar record and reputation in the Foreign Service. Kate and I had worked together for almost two years before she became my chief of staff. She ran the team supporting my nomination at the department, soliciting the memoranda I needed, arranging the appropriate briefings, and organizing a murder board as the hearing approached. I was immensely fortunate to have her succeed Greg as the leader of the office of the deputy secretary. Grace once told me how impressed she was with Kate, with her intellect, poise, and personality, and how successful she would be in the private sector for a much higher salary. We agreed that our country was lucky to have her as an American diplomat.

I needed the help of Kate's entire team because my nomination was going to be scrutinized under a microscope. Washington media predicted that I would face "an increasingly skeptical and partisan Senate confirmation hearing" (as *Foreign Policy* put it on October 17). The ranking Democrat on the Foreign Relations Committee, Senator Robert Menendez of New Jersey, said in an interview with CNN about my nomination: "[Sullivan's] got a lot of questions to answer.... This is going to be one tough nomination hearing, as far as I'm concerned."

The difficulty ahead would transcend the Senate hearing itself, I knew. In one sense I had two audiences. I would always tell the truth and answer the senators' questions to the best of my ability, which I hoped and suspected would result in my confirmation—maybe even with a bipartisan vote. There was another audience at the White House, however, and if the president was not satisfied with my performance, he might not sign the commission appointing me as ambassador, even (or maybe especially) if I were confirmed unanimously by the Senate.

I resolved not to overthink the matter and simply to answer the questions put to me by the members of the committee. In the final analysis,

I would rely on my extensive public record and, as *Foreign Policy* noted, on "the fact that [Sullivan's] reputation is high in Washington.... He is widely respected by career diplomats as a capable and amicable manager." None of that would guarantee my confirmation, however, in the politically charged atmosphere in which I would appear before the august Senate Foreign Relations Committee.

I met with Secretary Pompeo shortly before the hearing to tell him that I would not refuse to answer questions about Ukraine and the July 25 phone call. Although the White House had advised administration officials not to cooperate with or give testimony to the House impeachment inquiries, I told the secretary that I did not believe I could decline to answer questions at my confirmation hearing merely because the questions were also relevant to the House impeachment inquiries. I believed the senators were entitled to ask relevant questions to assess my suitability to be ambassador to Russia, and that included questions about what I had done and said as deputy secretary of state. Secretary Pompeo did not try to dissuade me; he simply advised me to exercise my best judgment.

Despite the extraordinary scrutiny of me and my nomination, and the frenzy of the burgeoning impeachment inquiries, I was gratified to discover that I continued to have bipartisan support. That support was reflected at the start of the hearing on October 30, when Senator Ben Cardin, a senior Democrat from Maryland, and Republican senator Dan Sullivan (no relation) of Alaska jointly introduced me to the Foreign Relations Committee. The chairman of the committee, Senator James Risch of Idaho, then submitted for the record a letter the committee had received supporting my nomination, from dozens of former senior officials—Democrats and Republicans, political appointees and career officers, including Secretary Mattis (now out of office and reviled by President Trump).

With the departure of the two senators who had introduced me, I sat alone before the committee. The most notable question posed to me came early in the hearing. Senator Menendez asked whether it was ever appropriate for a US president to demand an investigation by a foreign government into a domestic political opponent. I said, "I don't think that would be in accord with our values." The senator followed up with several questions involving Ukraine and the recall of Ambassador Yovanovitch:

**MENENDEZ:** What did you know about a shadow Ukraine policy being carried out by Rudy Giuliani?

**SULLIVAN:** My knowledge in the spring and summer of this year about any involvement of Mr. Giuliani was in connection with a campaign against our ambassador to Ukraine. . . .

**MENENDEZ:** You were aware that there were individuals and forces outside of the State Department seeking to smear Ambassador Yovanovitch? Is that correct?

**SULLIVAN:** I was.

**MENENDEZ:** And seeking to remove her. Is that right?

**SULLIVAN:** I was.

**MENENDEZ:** And did you know Mr. Giuliani was one of those people?

**SULLIVAN:** I believe he was. Yes.

I was also specifically asked why Ambassador Yovanovitch had been recalled. As the *New York Times* subsequently reported, "testifying under oath and on camera, . . . Mr. Sullivan . . . became the highest ranking official to publicly affirm that Ms. Yovanovitch had served 'admirably and capably.' He also went on the record with his belief that Mr. Giuliani helped to coordinate an effort to denigrate her." The *Times* further noted that I had told the committee that Ambassador Yovanovitch "had done nothing wrong, but that the president had lost confidence in her. [Mr. Sullivan] added that it is a president's prerogative to recall diplomats he believed he could no longer trust."

Following those questions and answers, the remainder of the hearing focused more on issues of US policy toward Russia—and there were many important topics, such as the Nord Stream II pipeline, arms control, and wrongfully detained Americans—and less on questions about Ukraine and the recall of Ambassador Yovanovitch. I assured the committee that I would "be relentless in opposing Russian efforts to interfere in US elections, to violate the sovereignty of Ukraine and Georgia, and to engage in the malign behavior that has reduced our relationship to such a low level of trust."

After each senator had an opportunity to ask me questions, the hearing concluded. Grace, along with my family and many colleagues and friends, had sat behind me the entire time. After the hearing, she and I chatted briefly with those senators who had stayed until the end. Grace and I then exited the hearing room, on the fourth floor of the Dirksen Senate Office Building. Once in the hallway, we were immediately approached by representatives of Russian state media—*Sputnik* and *Russia Today*—who wanted to interview us. We politely declined but smiled knowingly at each other, a silent acknowledgment of the new phase that our lives would be entering if I were lucky enough to be confirmed as ambassador.

The US media coverage following the hearing was factual and straightforward. There was no glaring criticism, with one exception. Former mayor Giuliani objected to my testimony that he was involved in a "campaign" to oust Ambassador Yovanovitch. He tweeted: "The Amb. nominee doesn't know what he's talking about and shouldn't be incorrectly speculating." But I heard nothing from the White House, and Secretary Pompeo assured me that I should not have any difficulty with the most important audience (Trump) in the West Wing.

With the hearing behind me, I could do nothing but wait for the Senate to vote on my nomination, which would be delayed by the intervening Thanksgiving holiday and congressional recess. I was confident that I would be confirmed, but I was still holding out hope for a bipartisan vote like the one I had received to be deputy secretary of state. That would be important, not as a personal honor, but as an indication to the Russian government that I had the full support of the US government. It was increasingly rare in Washington for nominees to high-profile positions to receive bipartisan support, which was a sign of our polarized politics and a change from prior decades. When my uncle Bill Sullivan was confirmed as US ambassador to Iran, in 1977, the Senate vote on his nomination was 99–1. Uncle Bill later asked the senator who had voted against him what his objection was, and the senator replied sheepishly that it was a clerical error and he had intended to vote yes. Times have certainly changed.

I was relieved, therefore, when on December 12, 2019, I was confirmed with a strong, bipartisan 70–22 vote. But the competitor in me noted that I had received sixteen more "no" votes from Democrats than in the prior vote on my nomination to be deputy secretary. I was reassured by Grace and Kate that a 70–22 Senate vote to confirm me as President Trump's ambassador to Russia, during a blistering impeachment inquiry that implicated Russia, was a success beyond what any of my friends and State Department colleagues had thought was possible in those circumstances. I was personally gratified that the members of the Foreign Relations Committee—those senators with whom I had worked most closely over the prior three years—had voted overwhelmingly in support of my nomination.

The final hurdle in the appointment process was the president's acceptance of my resignation and his signature on my commission as ambassador. This step was delayed because the administration did not want me to vacate the position of deputy secretary of state until my successor, Stephen E. Biegun, had been confirmed by the Senate. Steve, an accomplished and highly respected foreign policy professional who was then serving as our special representative for North Korea, had been nominated to succeed me as deputy secretary on the day after my confirmation hearing at the end of October. He had his own confirmation hearing in November and there did not appear to be any doubt that he would be confirmed. The problem was that, as the calendar wound down to the end of 2019, it was uncertain whether the Senate would vote on Steve's nomination before the senators took their Christmas recess. If his confirmation were delayed until sometime in January, that would further delay my appointment and departure for Russia.

By the late afternoon of Friday, December 20, I was not optimistic that Steve's nomination would be voted on before the Senate recess. I left the department that evening assuming that I would be working as the deputy secretary through the holidays and into the New Year—during which time the United States would not have a confirmed ambassador in Moscow. That was a problem in any country, but especially so in Russia because of the importance of the issues that could arise at any moment and the Russians' unwillingness to deal with anyone other than a Senate-confirmed and presidentially appointed ambassador. They are sticklers for protocol and sensitive to any perceived diplomatic slights, such as leaving an ambassadorial post unfilled for any length of time.

Later that night, however, I received an email from Kate informing me that in one of its final votes before the Christmas recess, the Senate had confirmed Steve, and that following the vote, the president had accepted my resignation and appointed me as the tenth US ambassador to the Russian Federation. I would ring in the New Year as an ambassador, after all—and be in Moscow, and on a whole new hot seat, before long as well.

———

Secretary Pompeo administered the oath of office to me—a necessary formality to do anything as ambassador—in a quick, informal ceremony in his office on the morning of Monday, December 23, with Kate holding the Bible. None of my family members were present, as the plan was to hold a ceremonial swearing-in event in two weeks, after the holidays.

After he swore me into office, the secretary and I had a conversation about my departure for Moscow, my priorities as ambassador, and whether I needed anything from him. I asked the secretary for a final meeting with President Trump. I wanted, at a minimum, another picture of me meeting as ambassador with the president for my credibility with the Russians. There were plenty of pictures of me with him as deputy secretary, but a photo taken together now would demonstrate unequivocally that I continued to have a relationship with President Trump and his White House after my confirmation hearing and the criticism from Giuliani. Secretary Pompeo said he would arrange the meeting and attend with me.

In the meantime, I was assigned a large office on the first floor of the department for my use as I made the unusual transition from deputy secretary to ambassador. It had been many decades since anyone had done that, going from almost the very top of the hierarchy to a lower-ranking position. The last person to move directly from deputy secretary of state to ambassador was John N. Irwin II, who in 1973 resigned to become ambassador to France. The number two position at the State Department was always viewed as such a desirable post that even members of the president's cabinet had resigned to take the job. In 1966, during the Johnson administration, Nicholas Katzenbach resigned as the US attorney general to become under secretary of state (as the number two position in the department was then called).

I remained in Washington for a couple of weeks because of the lengthy holiday in Russia in early January for the New Year and Orthodox Christmas, when the government and much of the country shuts down. I had no more responsibilities as deputy secretary and spent my time preparing for my new post. My plan was to depart for Moscow on January 15, 2020, after the Russian government had reopened. The meeting with the president and the secretary was scheduled for 1 p.m. on Friday, January 10, which was also the day the department had scheduled a more formal swearing-in ceremony for me as ambassador. It would be at 3 p.m. in the department's large and richly appointed Ben Franklin Room.

I arrived at the White House on January 10 well in advance of my scheduled Oval Office meeting with the president. Secretary Pompeo arrived separately. Unbeknownst to me, former governor Chris Christie of New Jersey had also arrived at the White House, unannounced. President Trump asked him into the small presidential dining room off the Oval Office and Secretary Pompeo was invited to join them. The president proceeded to blow up his afternoon schedule to chat with former governor Christie. I waited almost two hours, with no idea what was causing the delay, and was growing increasingly nervous as the time for my swearing-in ceremony approached. Aides appeared from time to time to reassure me that the president would see me shortly, but there were several hundred people gathering at the State Department for an event that I could not miss.

As I sat stewing in the reception area of the West Wing, the clock approaching 3 p.m., Secretary Pompeo swept out of the Oval Office suite and offered me a ride back to the department—which I gratefully accepted, since otherwise he (as host) and I (as guest of honor) would have been late for my swearing-in ceremony. During the short car ride, the secretary told me he had several times reminded the president, to no avail, that he should meet at least briefly with his ambassador departing for Russia.

I marveled at the president's lack of discipline, but I was not completely surprised. It was just another reminder that Donald Trump had no interest in the ordinary duties of his office, like conferring with the ambassador he was sending to a challenging and critical post. If not a shock, however, it was still a disappointment, and did not augur well for the new mission on which I was about to embark.

Arriving at Foggy Bottom, Secretary Pompeo and I went straight to the Ben Franklin Room on the eighth floor of the department, for the ceremony. There was a large crowd of my family, friends, and colleagues. Several cabinet members were in attendance, as well as senior White House officials, including Jared and Ivanka Trump. Justice Alito administered the oath of office while Grace held our family Bible. I was grateful that the justice was available and willing to preside over the ceremony on short notice after Chief Justice John G. Roberts, who had sworn me in as deputy secretary, was unable to attend because of preparations for the imminent Trump impeachment trial in the Senate. The chaos of the White House was spreading across the federal government.

I never did end up speaking to President Trump before I left for Moscow. In fact, I never spoke to him again.

———————

My remarks at the ceremonial swearing-in ceremony on January 10 were a reflection on the very first line of dialogue in *The Godfather,* spoken by the undertaker Amerigo Bonasera, "I believe in America." I talked about the significance of patriotism and the commitment to public service in my extended family of immigrants that greatly influenced my life and career, including my decision to go to Moscow. My grandparents were from Ireland and Grace's parents were from Cuba. Among the many American patriots with whom I grew up and whom I mentioned in my remarks were my late father, John H. Sullivan, who was a World War II US Navy combat veteran, and Grace's great-uncle Jose Pujals, who had survived as an unbroken political prisoner in Fidel Castro's Cuba for decades until he was released to his adopted country, the United States, a week before Grace and I were married in 1988. All of them inspired me because they believed in America.

I also revealed at the ceremony my personal—as opposed to professional—interest in living in Moscow. I mentioned my attraction to Russian culture and history to emphasize that I was departing with an open mind and a desire to find areas in which I could work with the Russians. I was adamantly opposed to many of the policies and actions of the authoritarian Putin government, but I was not a Russophobe looking only for conflict with Russia and the Russian people. To convey that message, I invited the Russian ambassador to the United States, Anatoly I. Antonov, to attend the ceremony, which he did. In fact, he was in the front row when I delivered my remarks.

With my departure imminent, my memories of Russia and ice hockey flooded back as I packed over the weekend following the ceremony. Among other things, I packed my old hockey bag, which included some equipment that was almost as old as the 1972 Summit Series itself. I looked forward to skating with local players in the numerous men's leagues in Moscow. Most of all, I looked forward to traveling to Russia as the US ambassador thirty years after my first trip to the Soviet Union. I knew that no matter what happened, it was going to be an eventful experience—but just how consequential, I could never have guessed.

# CHAPTER 3

# EARLY SKIRMISHES

IN THE SIX MONTHS BEFORE my arrival in Moscow in January 2020, I had dedicated a great deal of time to readying myself to represent the United States in Russia. Much of this preparation occurred in the context of meetings—and although only some of these were explicitly fact-finding missions, all of them gave me an enhanced understanding of what I would be up against if and when I was sent to Russia. The picture that emerged was not pretty.

Perhaps most helpfully, I had the chance to receive briefings by experts from across the US government and from the academy and the private sector. The culmination of this effort came in mid-November 2019, when I traveled to Stanford University, which has an impressive range of experts with enormous experience dealing with the Russian and Soviet governments. There, I was able to meet with former secretaries of state George P. Schultz and Condoleezza Rice, as well as former secretary Mattis, former national security advisor H. R. McMaster, and former US ambassador to Russia Michael A. McFaul. I was grateful to each of them for their willingness to share their insights, even if they were decidedly pessimistic about the prospect of any improvement in US-Russia relations.

For his part, Secretary Schultz urged a long-term view, citing his experience in President Reagan's second term and the US engagement with the Soviet government under the leadership of the general secretary of the Communist Party, Mikhail S. Gorbachev, who ultimately presided over the breakup of the Soviet Union. But, as Secretary Schultz himself noted, Putin was no Gorbachev. Indeed, as I learned three years later,

Putin had absolutely no respect for Gorbachev or his leadership in the last years of the Soviet Union.

Although no one I spoke to in the United States was optimistic about our relationship with Russia, they all agreed that we needed to continue to talk to the Russians. I was eager to do just that. Thus, while I was consulting with US experts, I also had several meetings abroad as deputy secretary of state with senior Russian officials from the Ministry of Foreign Affairs (MFA). Those meetings were an important prelude to my arrival as ambassador and signaled how the Russian government would receive me.

The signals were mixed at best. I worked hard to find the slightest reason for optimism. But in retrospect, it was a fool's errand.

---

On July 17, 2019, I met with Russian deputy foreign minister Sergei A. Ryabkov at the US mission in Geneva, Switzerland, where I had traveled as the leader of a US interagency delegation to a long-delayed convocation of the US-Russia Strategic Security Dialogue, which is focused principally on arms control and related issues like missile defense. The US delegation was composed of senior officials from the State and Defense Departments, including representatives of the Joint Staff. Deputy Foreign Minister Ryabkov led a similar Russian delegation of senior officials and experts.

I arranged for a one-on-one meeting with the deputy foreign minister before the security dialogue began. He and I had spoken periodically on the telephone during the prior two years but had not met in person. I knew Ryabkov by reputation as a highly respected and experienced career diplomat. A deputy foreign minister of Russia since August 2008, he was responsible for, among other things, bilateral relations with the United States and other North and South American countries, as well as nonproliferation and arms control issues.

Ryabkov and I exchanged pleasantries, and we agreed it was important for us to get to know each other better. I did not tell him that I was interested in serving as the next US ambassador to Russia or that my proposed nomination was pending at the White House. I knew, however, that if—as I hoped and expected—I became the US ambassador in Moscow, he would be my principal point of contact with the Russian government. (Foreign ministers tend to leave to their seconds-in-command any meetings with ambassadors and other officials who are similarly lower in the governmental hierarchy.)

From all appearances, I could not have asked for a much better interlocutor on the Russian side. Ryabkov was exactly my age, and he cut an impressive figure. He wore glasses and had a full head of gray hair, looking every inch the part of a savvy Russian diplomat, which he was. Sergei was very smart, he had a good sense of humor, and his English was impeccable. But more than appreciation, I felt a real affinity for him. I felt about him the same way that former UK prime minister Margaret Thatcher once professed to feel upon meeting Gorbachev in December 1984: "I like Mr. Gorbachev. We can do business together." I liked Ryabkov and thought I could work with him.

In an early test of that hypothesis, I had one important matter to raise with Ryabkov before we went into the large conference room down the hall to begin the security dialogue: the case of Paul N. Whelan, a former US Marine from Detroit, Michigan, who was arrested by the FSB in Moscow on December 28, 2018, while attending a friend's wedding. Whelan was charged by the Russians with espionage. Later, Trevor Reed would be arrested in August 2019, one month after my meeting with Ryabkov, and would become the next high-profile, wrongfully detained American. But in July 2019, Whelan's case was the most prominent example of this problem, which unfortunately continued to grow in the years ahead.

I told Ryabkov that—as the FSB surely knew—Whelan was not a spy for the United States or any of our allies, and I added that his arrest was going to be a significant impediment to any improvement in US-Russia relations. Ryabkov responded that neither he nor anyone else in the Russian government would talk about the Whelan case or any possible terms for his release until the Russian criminal justice system had run its course, which could take some time. I asked why the Russian government wanted to delay talking about the matter, when the FSB could bring its case against Whelan to trial and get a conviction whenever it wanted to do so, as early as tomorrow. Even without yet having served as ambassador to Russia, I knew there was no independent judiciary in the country.

But Ryabkov responded that I needed to respect the Russian system, so I did not press the matter. Clearly, he was not authorized to talk about the case, and anyway we needed to rejoin our delegations to begin talking about strategic security and nuclear weapons.

This particular strategic security dialogue was especially important because the New START treaty, which set limits on US and Russian strategic nuclear weapons and delivery systems, was due to expire in less than two years. The scope of our discussion was open-ended, including topics like anti-satellite weapons and cybersecurity. The dialogue was merely the first step in what I expected would be lengthy negotiations leading not only to the renewal of the New START treaty but also to a discussion of new cutting-edge technologies, such as artificial intelligence, in the future.

One additional geopolitical issue that I raised with the Russian delegation was the inclusion of the People's Republic of China (PRC) in our future arms control discussions. That was an important subject for the United States, and for Russia too, considering the People's Liberation Army's (PLA) program to substantially expand the PRC's nuclear arsenal. President Trump was personally interested in the issue and raised it periodically. His interest in nuclear arms control grew out of the staggering cost of maintaining and modernizing our nation's nuclear weapons and triad of bombers, ballistic missiles, and submarines, as recommended by the NSC-led nuclear posture review in which I had participated at the start of my service as deputy secretary. The president quite rightly wanted the PRC and its growing nuclear arsenal to be included not only in our own strategic calculations, but also in direct discussions with us and the Russians to limit the risk of nuclear war and, with it, the huge cost of nuclear deterrence—money that could be spent in any number of more useful ways.

Some news coverage of arms control issues at the time misinterpreted the proposal by the Trump administration as an effort to include the PRC in the New START treaty itself, which was never suggested or considered. The New START treaty is a bilateral agreement between the United States and Russia, tailored to our respective nuclear arsenals. Rather, the proposal that I raised in Geneva was to include the PRC in negotiations about the future, including what would follow or supplement the New START treaty, which would expire by its terms in 2026 even if there were a full five-year extension of the treaty agreed to by early 2021. Five or seven years in the context of arms control negotiations is a short period of time, so I believed that we needed to get the ball rolling on the PRC's inclusion in any new treaty.

Although I made what I thought was a strong case for why it was in the interests of the United States and Russia to include the PRC in future arms control discussions, the negative response from the Russian side was not unexpected, given Russia's improving relations with the PRC, which was not interested in arms control. Deputy Foreign Minister Ryabkov said Russia was not opposed to including the PRC in future negotiations, but that the PRC itself was not interested in participating. Furthermore, he said that Russia would not discuss the issue with the PRC or attempt in any way to persuade the PRC to participate in future negotiations. I replied that the PRC's nuclear weapons program was a concern for both of our countries that we would have to address, and it was better to do so sooner rather than later. But the Russian delegation was not interested in any further discussion of the topic.

Another issue I raised at the security dialogue was Russia's enormous stockpile of nonstrategic nuclear weapons. Russian tactical nuclear arms were not covered by the New START treaty, which limited only the number of deployed strategic nuclear warheads by each country. Furthermore, Russia already had blatantly violated the Intermediate-Range Nuclear Forces Treaty—which prohibited "intermediate range" (310 miles to 3,420 miles) ground-launched missiles—by deploying the Novator 9M729 cruise missile, which exceeded the prescribed range criteria. As a result of the Russian breach, the United States suspended its participation in the INF Treaty on February 1, 2019, and was planning to withdraw formally on August 2, 2019.

My questions about Russia's nonstrategic nuclear weapons were related to the development of the Russian military's doctrine of "hybrid" or "new generation" warfare, particularly in preparation for a potential conflict in Eastern Europe or the former republics of the Soviet Union, which Russia considered part of its exclusive sphere of influence. Facing a mismatch in conventional military forces in any conflict with NATO now or in the near future—as opposed to the Cold War era, when the Red Army and the Warsaw Pact typically held the upper hand in conventional forces in Eurasia—the Russians were seeking to combine political, economic, cyber, and informational tools to offset that disadvantage.

A key element of Russia's new vision of warfare involved the use of nuclear weapons or, at the very least, the threat of nuclear war. Indeed, there was a growing concern among NATO leadership that the Russian military had lowered the threshold for the use of nuclear weapons. In what is known as the escalate-to-deescalate doctrine or scenario, the Russians could potentially make a limited nuclear strike at the start of a conventional conflict to force their adversary to back down under the threat of a wider, catastrophic nuclear war. The success of this strategy depended on, as the arms control expert Ulrich Kühn at the Carnegie Endowment for International Peace observed "(1) an ambiguous nuclear doctrine; (2) nontransparency and noncompliance with arms control agreements; and (3) continued nuclear threats and acts of signaling."

I sought to remove some of the ambiguity and engage with the Russians on their tactical nuclear arms. I asked how the stockpile of these weapons fit into their military doctrine and strategy. But the Russians were stone-faced. They would not even provide a rough estimate of the number of nonstrategic weapons in their arsenal—unfortunate, but consistent with their long practice of resisting efforts by the United States to increase transparency in the Russian nonstrategic nuclear weapons program.

I was very frustrated by our inability to make even the slightest progress in discussions with the Russians on this important topic, but I did not let it show in the meeting. I had learned that patience was very important in these circumstances, and I resolved to try to always maintain my composure. Kennan had advised that the "sine qua non of successful dealing with Russia" is for any foreign diplomat to "remain at all times cool and collected." The Russians view "loss of temper and of self-control" as a sign of weakness, which "they are quick to exploit." Personally, I also found that an occasional touch of humor, at the right moment, could both defuse a tense situation and display a sense of calm confidence. But the instances where humor was appropriate were rare, because the Russians would not respect anything resembling frivolity in a discussion about something as deadly serious as arms control.

At one point in the dialogue, during a very lengthy (almost two hours) and tense discussion that was going nowhere, I looked across the long table at more than a dozen red faces on the Russian side (all older men). They were clearly in dire need of a restroom or cigarette break. I slapped my hand on the table and said in a stern voice, "This has to stop." Then I paused. Everyone on both sides of the table turned with wide eyes toward me, expecting an angry outburst about the lack of progress in our discussion. Instead, I smiled and said it appeared that we needed to take a break before there were more red faces or worse around the table. Ryabkov laughed, as did many of his relieved colleagues. I made sure not to avail myself of the facilities during the break, to signal that I was strong and focused and taking a break only to accommodate my Russian friends.

When we reconvened, I cannot say we made any progress in the discussion, but the conversation was somewhat less stilted and tense. It was a trivial and fleeting gesture, but one by which I wanted to convey to Ryabkov and his colleagues that I was a confident but reasonable person, unfailingly committed to my country's interests and my principles, to be sure, but a person with whom they could do business.

Through small steps like this, I had tried to build a working relationship with the Russians as deputy secretary of state. Now, I intended to approach my future mission in Russia in the same way.

The strategic security dialogue concluded at the end of a long day with no agreement other than that the future agenda was lengthy and complicated, and that we should meet again. I stopped in Brussels on my way home to Washington to brief our NATO allies on the substance of the talks in Geneva, particularly on nonstrategic nuclear weapons. Alliance members were concerned about Russia's breach of the INF Treaty—which was not surprising, given that many allies were within the intermediate range of the Russian missiles covered by the treaty—and the resultant imminent withdrawal of the United States from the treaty.

At the time, there was little more that I could do. But now, as I was preparing to take my new post in Moscow, I hoped that the chance to engage more extensively with the Russian government might allow me to succeed where the talks in Geneva had failed. Nor was this the only unfinished business that I hoped to address once I landed in Russia.

———————

Two months after the security dialogue in Geneva, I led the US inter-agency delegation to participate in the second round of the US-Russia Counterterrorism Dialogue, in Vienna, Austria, on September 9, 2019. The US delegation included representatives of the FBI and the Intelligence Community. The Russian delegation was led by Deputy Foreign Minister Oleg V. Syromolotov. Unlike Ryabkov, who was a career diplomat, Syro-molotov was a senior career intelligence officer who had been a general in the FSB and the head of its counterintelligence service for eleven years. In March 2015, he was removed as the head of FSB counterintelligence and transferred to the Foreign Ministry, where he was made responsible for, among other things, counterterrorism issues.

The counterterrorism dialogue with Syromolotov and his delegation grew out of the infamous meeting between Presidents Trump and Putin in Helsinki, Finland, in July 2018. At that meeting, which I did not attend, the two presidents discussed many issues. Some were extremely contro-versial, like election interference by the Russians, about which Trump astonishingly accepted Putin's denial, despite the contrary conclusion of US intelligence agencies. Others were less so, like Putin's request for a counterterrorism dialogue, to which Trump agreed. Although the Rus-sians were very interested in meeting on counterterrorism, I was less enthusiastic but saw little downside; if we could stop just one terrorist plot in either country and save innocent lives, it was worth the effort.

The two sides met for the first dialogue in December 2018, which is when I originally met Deputy Foreign Minister Syromolotov. A heavy smoker in his mid-sixties, he was a large man of few words, with deep roots in the KGB and FSB. He did not strike me as a promising busi-ness partner the way that Ryabkov would half a year later. Indeed, we accomplished virtually nothing at this meeting beyond introductions— although we did agree that we would meet again in 2019.

The result of the first counterterrorism dialogue was no surprise to anyone in the US delegation. The Russians wanted to make a public show of meeting with US officials on the topic but did not seem seriously committed to actual cooperation. Our experience in prior counterterrorism exchanges with the Russians was that the conversation was always one-sided. The United States, through the Intelligence Community and the FBI, would provide actionable information on terrorist cases to the Russian security services but receive no such information in return.

In December 2017, for instance, information from the United States helped the FSB prevent an attack on Saint Petersburg's Kazan Cathedral by plotters affiliated with the Islamic State of Iraq and the Levant (ISIL). Putin was sufficiently grateful to thank President Trump in a phone call after Christmas. But there was little reciprocity. Often the Russians would purport to identify, or designate as terrorists, individuals who were political dissidents or members of a religious group disfavored by the Kremlin, like the Jehovah's Witnesses. This was not only of no use in helping the US government stop real terrorists, but also completely antithetical to our commitment to human rights and religious freedom.

The most notorious failure in communicating on counterterrorism with the Russians involved the Tsarnaev brothers, who committed the Boston Marathon bombing on April 15, 2013—an act of terrorism that, for obvious reasons, was especially personal to me. The Russians had provided a tip about the brothers in 2011, which allowed the FBI to begin an inquiry. But the Russians declined follow-up requests for more information that would have justified a more substantial investigation under US law. Only after the bombing did the Russians provide the FBI with intelligence, in particular an intercepted telephone conversation, that might have prompted further investigation if provided earlier. Years later, while I was serving in the State Department, resentment for this particular instance of uncooperative Russian behavior continued to run deep among US law enforcement professionals, and Bostonians like me.

The second round of the counterterrorism dialogue, in September 2019, was as unproductive as the first. In a one-on-one meeting with Syromolotov during a break, I told him that the United States needed to see a more constructive approach from the Russian government to justify our continued participation in this dialogue. Syromolotov was noncommittal.

I later reiterated the basic point in remarks to both delegations—but added that whether we continued meeting in the format of the dialogue or not, the United States would continue to provide actionable intelligence to save lives in Russia from terrorist attacks. I no more wanted to see innocent blood on the streets of Saint Peterburg than I did on the streets of Boston.

On my recommendation, the United States later suspended future meetings of the counterterrorism dialogue. But true to our values, the United States continued to provide information to the Russian security services on terrorist threats in Russia. Indeed, in December 2019, intelligence from the United States disrupted another terrorist plot in Saint Petersburg. Not much later—shortly after I was appointed US ambassador to Russia—Putin called President Trump again to thank him for the support of the United States in stopping a terrorist attack and saving innocent Russian lives. Not for the last time, I remarked to myself that the Russian president had a funny way of showing his gratitude.

---

My last two meetings with a senior Russian official before I arrived in Moscow as ambassador were with the Foreign Minister himself, Sergey V. Lavrov. On November 23, 2019, three days after my nomination was voted favorably out of the Senate Foreign Relations Committee, I met with Lavrov in Nagoya, Japan, on the sidelines of the G20 foreign ministers meeting. Secretary Pompeo was not enthusiastic about attending such meetings if they required long-distance travel, because the focus of the G20—an assembly of the world's twenty largest economies—was principally on economic matters and the group itself was not as impactful as the G7. Pompeo preferred to focus on political and security issues. He had sent me in his place to the G20 foreign ministers meeting in Buenos Aires, Argentina, in May 2018, but the 2019 trip to Nagoya was more auspicious for me, given my aspiration to go to Moscow.

I was eager to attend the gathering in Nagoya because it would be the first opportunity for me to engage with senior Russian officials after my nomination to be ambassador had become public. I was not sure whether Lavrov would attend or whether he would have time to meet with me. A conference of twenty foreign ministers is inevitably hectic, and my own schedule was busy: after two and a half years as deputy secretary, including service as acting secretary, I had come to know well many of the foreign ministers attending the meeting, which meant that I had received many requests for bilateral meetings.

As it turned out, Lavrov was in Nagoya for the G20 foreign ministerial and was pleased to meet me. Although I had met Putin before, when I was traveling in November 2018 with Vice President Pence in Asia, I had not met Lavrov. I had participated in telephone calls that Secretaries Tillerson and Pompeo had with him, but had not spoken to the foreign minister directly. This made me look forward to meeting him all the more.

Lavrov was a legend in international diplomacy. He served from 1994 to 2004 as the Russian ambassador to the United Nations, after which he was appointed foreign minister by Putin. He was among the longest-serving foreign ministers in the history of the Russian Federation or the Soviet Union (Andrei A. Gromyko served over twenty-eight years as Soviet foreign minister). Expressing himself in perfect English, Lavrov was very knowledgeable about the United States from his years living in New York. He was everything one would expect a senior diplomat with his experience to be: brilliant, urbane, charming when he wanted to be, and witty. Yet, as a Voice of America profile noted in 2014, "at the same time, Lavrov is known to be withering in his criticism, dismissive, condescending, stubborn, and even icy cold."

Lavrov was also very loyal to Putin and cynically towed the Kremlin line on every issue. Among those who followed Russia closely, there was much debate about whether he was in Putin's "inner circle" or not. The consensus seemed to be that he was not, but that he was, at a minimum, a skilled and important advocate for Putin—someone with global stature who could use that preeminence to help advance Putin's aims. And Putin did not want to lose him, which is why Lavrov had stayed in his position for as long as he had.

The foreign minister and I met in the late morning in a small conference room at the Nagoya facility hosting the G20 gathering. A tall, impeccably dressed man, Lavrov wore wire-rimmed glasses and was a heavy smoker with a deep voice. Preternaturally self-confident, he tended to dominate most diplomatic or social settings. Just how much so, I would soon see for myself.

I began the meeting by thanking Lavrov for the Foreign Ministry's quick approval of my proposed appointment to be ambassador. In international relations, the receiving government must give its consent—or agrément, the French word used in diplomatic parlance—to the appointment of a diplomat. In the United States, the White House will not put an ambassador's nomination forward for Senate consideration until the receiving state has given its agrément. The review by the receiving state can take time, sometimes months, and is occasionally refused. In my case, the Russian MFA had provided agrément in eight days, which I was told was a record.

Lavrov's response to my expression of gratitude was interesting. He said that of course they had provided agrément quickly, because I was the deputy secretary of state and someone of that rank deserved such treatment. I was reminded of Kennan's observation that Russians place great stress on "prestige" and "punctilious attention to protocol." In my case, it was important to the Russians that the United States had nominated a senior official—with the second highest rank in the State Department—to represent it in the Russian Federation. Jon Huntsman had made that point to me months before. It did not matter what my personal qualities were. The most important thing, from Moscow's perspective, was the prestige of the appointment and the way that this reflected on Russia and the importance assigned to it by the United States.

After our initial exchange of pleasantries, Lavrov took out several folded pieces of paper on which he had extensive handwritten notes. He said that although he looked forward to working with me, he wanted to point out several misperceptions that I had of Russia and its government's policies. He then proceeded to critique my recent testimony before the Senate Foreign Relations Committee at my confirmation hearing. He reviewed every criticism I had made of Russia—and there were many, ranging from energy blackmail and the Nord Stream II pipeline to election interference—and told me why I was mistaken in each instance. He did so in a very businesslike way, without invective, as if it were a courtesy by him to correct my embarrassing errors before I arrived in Moscow and repeated them.

This performance took up most of the thirty minutes allotted for our meeting; soon we would have to rejoin the other G20 foreign ministers. I did not have time to respond to each of Lavrov's criticisms, so I chose to focus on Russian election interference as a serious problem in our bilateral relationship. Lavrov responded tersely that the Russian government had nothing to do with any purported interference in the 2016 or 2018 elections in the United States. Obviously, I did not believe him, and he did not expect me to believe him. It was simply a conversation stopper, because he was not going to engage in a back-and-forth on the topic and we did not have the time for that anyway because the G20 foreign ministerial was resuming.

With our bilateral meeting concluded, Lavrov and I returned to the G20 meeting and stood near the entrance to the large ballroom where the event was being held. The PRC foreign minister, Wang Yi, approached us. Lavrov introduced me to Wang, whom I had not met before and who seemed surprised; he recognized my name but had not recognized me. He looked me up and down, grunted my last name, and then walked away. Lavrov smiled as I wondered which of my recent critical public statements about the PRC had caused that undiplomatic reaction.

The Russian foreign minister and I did not have another opportunity to speak in Nagoya, but I would not have to wait long to see him again: Lavrov visited Washington on December 10, 2019, to see Secretary Pompeo, and I joined them for a meeting in one of the ornate diplomatic reception rooms on the eighth floor of the State Department. Among the items on the agenda was Ukraine. Lavrov had just come from a conference in Paris the day before of the leaders of the so-called Normandy Format countries: Russia (Putin), Ukraine (Zelensky), Germany (Chancellor Angela Merkel), and France (Macron). The Normandy Format group, created in June 2014 to try to find a peaceful resolution to the violent conflict initiated by Russia in eastern Ukraine in 2014, had been in stalemate without a meeting since 2016. The fact that the leaders of the four countries were meeting at all to discuss the war in eastern Ukraine was viewed as progress. Lavrov relayed that at the nine-hour meeting in Paris, Ukraine and Russia had agreed on a cease-fire and a prisoner exchange, but there was no breakthrough on a path to peace.

The issue of Russia's aggression toward Ukraine continued to loom menacingly and darken the relationship between the United States and Russia, month after month, year after year, with no diplomatic solution in sight. The United States was not independently driving efforts to solve the problem, deferring mostly to the negotiations led by the German and French governments, which were not producing results. The impeachment scandal over Trump's July 25 call with Zelensky (and the odor of Hunter Biden's "business dealings" in Ukraine while his father was vice president) exacerbated the problem of a lack of American influence and resolve. I was episodically involved in Ukraine policy, as during my February 2018 trip to Kyiv, but there were always other pressing matters or outright crises with which I had to deal that laid claim to my time.

Listening to Lavrov's report on the December 9 meeting in Paris confirmed what I already knew: the Ukraine conflict would be at the top of a long list of intractable problems I would confront in my new job in Moscow. I resolved to dig more deeply into the matter and try to position the United States to play a more active and constructive role. That would be more than a tall order, what with the ongoing impeachment proceedings against Trump—which after all were focused on Ukraine. The major problem was not in Washington, however. It was the Russian government's unrelenting aggression against Ukraine that undermined its sovereignty and made the search for a peaceful solution so difficult.

Lavrov and Pompeo concluded their meeting over lunch and then held a joint press conference before a sizable audience in the Ben Franklin Room. Deputy Foreign Minister Ryabkov had accompanied Lavrov on the trip, and we exchanged pleasantries. I told him how much I was looking forward to working with him in Moscow. When the press conference started, I took a seat in the front row among the journalists who would be asking questions. The *New York Times* reported that when asked about my potential appointment as ambassador, Lavrov "praised Mr. Sullivan. 'We know him as a very highly professional diplomat. . . . We'll be happy to cooperate with him.'"

With that benediction from the Russian foreign minister, I departed for my new post on the afternoon of January 15, 2020. Grace and our elder son, Jack, who was between semesters at Columbia Business School, joined me in Moscow for my first week as ambassador. Grace was already on a business trip in Europe and Jack was coming from New York, so the three of us traveled there separately. Our daughter, Katie, who had injured her knee and recently had surgery, could not travel. Our younger son, Teddy, stayed behind to look after Katie during her recovery. The plan was for our whole family to gather in April, when we would celebrate the Easter holiday together during the spring in Moscow.

I wrangled several large suitcases and my hockey and stick bags into a car headed to Dulles Airport. That was when it really hit me: I was not the deputy secretary of state anymore. I no longer had a black State Department SUV, driven by a man who had become my good friend over the last three years, to take me where I needed to go. I boarded a plane by myself for the first time since May 2017, having always traveled with someone else when I was the deputy secretary. It was a lonely way to relocate to an uncertain future at Embassy Moscow. As it turned out, I would have to get used to being alone.

# PART II

# NIGHT FALLS

# CHAPTER 4

# POLITE RECEPTION BY HOSTILE GOVERNMENT

WHEN I ARRIVED AT Moscow's Sheremetyevo International Airport, I was met by representatives of the Russian Foreign Ministry and by some of my new colleagues from Embassy Moscow. It had been a very long trip, involving a connection in Amsterdam (there were no direct flights to Moscow from Washington), and I had spent it alone with my thoughts, reviewing my plans and priorities as ambassador. The talented embassy spokesperson, Rebecca Ross, who would subsequently guide me through my many interactions with the Russian media, led the embassy team to greet me at the airport.

As Rebecca took pictures to document and publicize my arrival, she tried to reassure me that I did not look as tired and haggard as I felt. We drove to the ambassador's residence, Spaso House, through a cold Moscow night, but the city was awash in light and glistening with decorations from the recent Christmas and New Year celebrations. The city was much different from the grim Soviet capital that Grace and I first visited thirty years before, which even in the middle of a summer day seemed dark and depressing. It gave me a spark of hope that the city had changed so much, although tinged with disappointment that Grace was not with me. She and our son Jack would arrive the next day.

As I set foot on Russian soil, I had a solid grounding in all the important policy issues from my meetings with senior Russian officials as deputy secretary. I also had a good sense of how the Russians would treat me: respectfully but with no sign that they wanted to negotiate seriously or seek compromise on any issue, large or small. As I would say frequently during my time as ambassador, nothing is ever easy with the Russians—a point not as eloquent as Kennan's observations, but just as valid. The degree of difficulty, however, did not relieve me of the obligation to continue to try to find those rare issues on which we could make some progress and, at a minimum, always defend zealously the interests of the United States and its citizens.

Within days of my arrival, I began a series of meetings at the Ministry of Foreign Affairs and the Kremlin. My first order of business was to present my credentials as ambassador, signed by President Trump, to Deputy Foreign Minister Ryabkov, which I did on January 20, 2020. I received in return an identity card (a *kartochka* in Russian) issued by the ministry that identified me as the US ambassador entitled to diplomatic immunity, which was not an insignificant matter, considering our troubled relationship. I was authorized to conduct business as ambassador on behalf of the United States with the Russian government, and I could live in Russia with complete confidence that I would not be subject to arrest or any other Russian legal process—because the Russians themselves relied on diplomatic immunity all over the world, including in the United States. They could expel me, if they wanted to, but they could not arrest me. Nonetheless, I was careful to keep my *kartochka* with me wherever I went in Russia.

With my new imprimatur, I scheduled meetings to introduce myself to the other deputy foreign ministers at the MFA—or to catch up with them, in the case of Ryabkov and Syromolotov. In another meeting with Ryabkov on January 27, I joked that whatever gaps there were between the United States and Russia in arms control, politics, economics, or any other field, there was one indisputable advantage the Russians had over the United States: ten deputy foreign ministers as compared to one (at least when I served as) deputy secretary of state. During our meeting, Ryabkov and I discussed issues in the Arctic, a huge geographic area of mutual interest to both countries. The Russians were seeking to promote the so-called Northern Sea Route, a shipping route through the Arctic that in a warming climate would be shorter than traditional routes between Asia and Europe. The United States was concerned about recent Russian military activities and development in the Arctic.

One of the other deputy foreign ministers with whom I met was Mikhail L. Bogdanov, who covered the Middle East. In our first meeting, on January 28, we discussed Syria, where Russia's support of the brutal Assad regime was a continuing problem, and Libya, where the conflict between rival governments and their militias was exacerbated by Russia and the intervention of the Russian government's (at that point unacknowledged) military contractor known as the Wagner Group, led by Yevgeny Prigozhin.

The following day, I saw Deputy Foreign Minister Syromolotov, with whom I had met twice before in the counterterrorism dialogue. By the time I arrived in Moscow, the dialogue had stopped meeting and our discussions on counterterrorism had not progressed. Quite the opposite: the Russians had been falsely and outrageously accusing the United States of fomenting terrorism by allegedly creating the infamous jihadist group known as ISIL, or the Islamic State. I told the deputy minister that was an insult to the many Americans, including friends and former colleagues of mine, who had lost their lives or been grievously injured fighting the Islamic State. I also pointed out that we had helped to thwart the ISIL-affiliated attack on Saint Petersburg's Kazan Cathedral in 2017. For the duration of my service in Moscow, the United States did not resume the counterterrorism dialogue with Russia.

As I made my way through the roster of deputy foreign ministers, I also had meetings with senior Kremlin leaders. (Although commonly referred to as "Kremlin" officials, in fact they do not work inside the Kremlin; rather, they work on Staraya Square, near Red Square, in office buildings that house the Presidential Executive Office.) I began with Yuri V. Ushakov, the assistant to the president of the Russian Federation for foreign policy.

A senior career diplomat, Ushakov served as the Russian ambassador to the United States from 1999 to 2008. When Putin returned to office as president in May 2012, he appointed Ushakov as his chief foreign policy adviser. Ushakov's role for Putin was like a White House staffer's, performing some of the functions carried out by the national security advisor to the US president. Ushakov was experienced, savvy, and trusted by Putin. Although not an influential policymaker, he had Putin's ear and could be counted on to get a message through to the Russian president when needed.

The most significant thing I noted about Ushakov in our introductory meeting on January 23 was that he preferred to meet alone, with no one else in the room. Virtually every other Russian government official that I met with in my time as ambassador had at least one staff member present for a meeting with me. Ushakov, on the other hand, preferred a quiet, intimate atmosphere, as though he were taking me into his confidence, which suited his personality. In his early seventies, Yuri was genial and soft-spoken, but I knew he was completely committed and unfailingly loyal to the man he called the Boss—Vladimir Putin.

In our first meeting, Ushakov and I discussed whether President Trump would accept Putin's invitation to attend the upcoming Russian Victory Day parade on May 9, 2020, on Red Square in Moscow, to commemorate the Allied victory over Nazi Germany in World War II. This was going to be an extremely important event for Putin in shaping his ongoing narrative about the greatness of the Russian civilization, and he especially wanted the international prestige of having the US president attend. Trump had made positive statements about considering the invitation but had not decided. I conveyed to Ushakov that President Trump was grateful for the invitation and was still considering it. I did not tell him that I was firmly opposed to the US president participating in this disinformation spectacle that would weaponize history in support of Putin's quest for empire, nor that I would do everything I could to convince Trump not to attend.

Ushakov and I also discussed a variety of other matters, including trade and investment and wrongfully detained American citizens. Those diverse topics unfortunately were related. Putin had asked Trump at their Helsinki meeting in 2018 for a US-Russia business leaders dialogue. Since then, however, the Russian government had arrested the most successful and prominent US business leader and investor in Russia, Michael Calvey, on a phony charge of fraud. I told Ushakov that a business dialogue was not possible because US business leaders would not attend, and the US government would not facilitate, any such meeting so long as criminal charges were pending against Calvey. Ushakov promised to investigate the matter, but I did not expect any relief, because I believed the Russian security services were involved in the case, and they had much more clout than Ambassador Ushakov.

Although we discussed some difficult subjects, Ushakov and I had a polite and cordial conversation. We promised to stay in close touch with each other. Like my reaction on meeting Ryabkov, I thought I could do business with Ushakov. He would be an important link to Putin.

———————

In my series of initial meetings at the MFA and the Kremlin, the most prominent issue on which it was virtually impossible for me to get traction with Russian officials was the conflict in Ukraine. In the six years prior to my appointment as ambassador, the Russians had become entrenched both geographically, in Crimea and the eastern Donbas, and diplomatically, in their views on negotiations about a resolution. It all came down to the orientation of Ukraine, East or West.

The original conflict traced its roots to a dispute over whether Ukraine would align with, and in due course join, the European Union. In 2013, there was wide support in the Ukrainian parliament (known as the Verkhovna Rada) for an "association agreement" with the EU that would establish a political and economic relationship, including a trade pact, between Ukraine and the EU. The agreement would be a step forward in the lengthy (yearslong) process for Ukraine to become a member of the union. Even to be eligible to sign the association agreement, Ukraine would have to implement certain legal, judicial, and electoral reforms required by the EU, including the release from prison of the country's former prime minister Yulia Tymoshenko, a political rival of the current Ukrainian president, Viktor Yanukovych.

The Russian government under President Putin (recently reelected after his four-year "sabbatical" as prime minister) was resolutely opposed to the association agreement. A Ukrainian embrace of the EU would severely undermine Putin's plan to create a Russia-led Eurasian Economic Union focused on the former republics of the Soviet Union, which Kazakhstan and Belarus had already agreed to join. Not including Ukraine—the second largest country by geographic area in Europe—in this union was unthinkable to the Kremlin. Even more objectionable was Ukraine in the EU. A Putin economic adviser, Sergei Glazyev, scoffed at the notion, calling Ukraine joining the EU a "sick self-delusion." Glazyev warned that Russia would respond with much "tougher" trade measures if the Ukrainians made "this suicidal step of signing the EU Association Agreement."

The agreement itself had been the subject of years of negotiation between Kyiv and Brussels and would firmly root Ukraine in the West. Most Ukrainians endorsed the concept of an association with the EU. Polls at the time showed that a majority supported the agreement, but the backing was not overwhelming or universal across Ukraine. Large swaths of the population in southern and eastern Ukraine, as well as on the Crimean peninsula, were Russian speakers who identified much more closely with Russia. The association agreement was not widely popular in those regions. As a result, Ukrainian president Yanukovych was in a very difficult political position.

The contradictions were stark: the association agreement was generally popular but not in the regions of Ukraine where Yanukovych had the strongest electoral support (Crimea and the Donbas). A future in the EU was better in the long run for Ukraine, but the implacable opposition of the Russians threatened immediate and potentially devastating economic and political harm to Ukraine if it pursued that westerly path. Equally costly to Yanukovych as a condition of the association agreement was the release of his most bitter political enemy—whom he had beaten in the 2010 presidential election and then had prosecuted and imprisoned— former prime minister Tymoshenko. If released, she would likely be an opponent in his upcoming reelection campaign.

Amid this swirl of conflicting interests in the fall of 2013, Yanukovych was on the verge of signing the association agreement, in advance of an EU summit meeting at the end of November, when he blinked. On November 21, under enormous pressure from Russia, his government, led by Prime Minister Mykola Azarov, abruptly issued a decree "suspend[ing] the process of preparations for the conclusion of the Association Agreement." It was a shock to many Ukrainians and the EU. The government decree cited the need to "ensure the national security of Ukraine" in the face of economic threats by Moscow and announced that Ukraine would "renew active dialogue" with Russia.

The capitulation to Russian coercion triggered large protests in Ukraine, eventually leading to the Revolution of Dignity. Protest leaders called for the resignation of Yanukovych and Prime Minister Azarov, and the protesters occupied Independence Square (Maidan Nezalezhnosti) in Kyiv. The uprising became known as the Euromaidan protests. During clashes with the Ukrainian security services (the most notorious of which was the special riot police, the Berkut) in January and February 2014, over one hundred protesters were killed, and many others were wounded. The escalating violence by the security services included sniper fire from rooftops. On February 20, thousands of protesters in Kyiv advanced toward the Rada (parliament) under fire from police snipers. There was strong evidence, and many accusations, that Russian FSB and GRU officers were among the Ukrainian security services resisting the advance and that Russia provided extensive logistical support for the crackdown on the Euromaidan protesters.

The next day, Yanukovych and opposition leaders in the Rada agreed to establish an interim government under Arseniy Yatsenyuk (Prime Minister Azarov had already resigned on January 28). When the security services stood down in Kyiv later that day, the protesters had won. In the evening, Yanukovych left the capital for Kharkiv in far eastern Ukraine. The Rada then voted unanimously (328–0) on February 22 to remove Yanukovych as president, because he had fled and was unable to fulfill the duties of his office, and set May 25 as the date for a presidential election to determine his successor. From Kharkiv, Yanukovych denounced the Rada vote as illegal: "I am not leaving the country for anywhere. I do not intend to resign. I am the legitimately elected president." The response from thousands of protesters against him in Kharkiv was the chant "Ukraine is not Russia!"

With his position untenable, Yanukovych escaped to Russia with Putin's assistance on February 24. The interim government of Prime Minister Yatsenyuk was recognized internationally (but not by Russia) and later signed the association agreement with the EU. Petro Poroshenko was elected the new president of Ukraine on May 25, as the government continued to remove officials associated with the Yanukovych regime. A related process of "decommunization" (or "de-Sovietization") also was underway. In February 2014, for example, Lenin Square in Dnipropetrovsk was renamed Heroes of Maidan Square. President Poroshenko formalized the process one year later when he signed legislation requiring the removal of Soviet Communist monuments, but not World War II memorials, and the renaming of streets and places named after Soviet Communists.

Putin would not take those affronts lying down. The Russian government condemned the Revolution of Dignity as a coup. The Russians argued that the Rada had acted illegally by removing Yanukovych without an impeachment vote by three-quarters of the total members (450) of that body, as required by the Ukrainian constitution in effect at the time. The unanimous vote of 328 members on February 22 was ten votes short of that threshold. The contrary constitutional argument was that the Rada had not impeached Yanukovych because he (like other senior members of his government) had abandoned his office by fleeing Kyiv. The vote of the Rada merely recognized that fact and was not an impeachment for treason or another crime as the constitution provided.

The fall of the Yanukovych government in Ukraine was too significant to the Kremlin to limit Russia's response to quibbling over constitutional issues. The Russian answer to the Revolution of Dignity started well before February 22. While the Euromaidan protests were underway, counterprotests supporting Russia were launched in southern and eastern Ukraine. The counterreaction was strongest in the Autonomous Republic of Crimea, as it was called in the Ukrainian constitution. The Crimean government vocally supported Yanukovych and condemned the Euromaidan protesters as "threatening political stability in the country."

At the end of February, Russian soldiers with no insignia—the infamous "little green men"—moved to occupy airports and other strategic locations in Crimea, including the parliament (the Verkhovna Rada of the Autonomous Republic of Crimea) in Simferopol. On March 1, the Crimean government requested, and the Russian parliament approved, the deployment by Putin of Russian troops in Ukraine. With the Russian military embedded throughout the peninsula, the Crimean parliament scheduled a referendum on March 16 for Crimeans to decide whether to join the Russian Federation. The Ukrainian government in Kyiv strenuously objected, but the referendum went ahead with turnout reported at 83 percent and the vote in favor of joining Russia proclaimed to be over 95 percent. It was widely suspected that those who supported remaining in Ukraine boycotted the election or were afraid to vote, thus leading to intense skepticism about the election returns.

Foreign governments did not recognize the results of the election, which was hastily organized on less than two weeks' notice under the threatening gaze of the Russian military. The United States and the EU denounced the referendum as illegal and illegitimate and declined to accept the outcome. One hundred countries in the UN General Assembly subsequently passed a resolution taking the same position. Nevertheless, on March 17, the day after the referendum, the Crimean parliament requested admission to the Russian Federation, which was granted on March 21.

Putin had acted with lightning speed to invade (stealthily) and annex (illegally) Crimea because there was little the Ukrainian government could do to resist. The situation was different in the Donbas, where in March 2014, just as Putin was moving to seize Crimea, pro-Russian protests began in the Donetsk and Luhansk Oblasts, or provinces. In April, armed Russian-backed separatists seized government buildings and declared the independence of the Donetsk People's Republic (DPR) and the Luhansk People's Republic (LPR). The Ukrainian military and security services responded and launched a counteroffensive, while Russia secretly provided troops and weapons to the separatists. Ukraine succeeded in retaking much of the separatist-held territory, and the Russians countered by moving thousands of its troops, tanks, and artillery into the Donbas to help the separatists recapture some of the territory that they had declared was independent of Ukraine. During the conflict, the Russian military supplied an air defense system to the separatists that was used on July 17, 2014, to shoot down a commercial aircraft flying over Ukraine near the border with Russia en route from Amsterdam to Kuala Lumpur: Malaysian Airlines flight 17, killing all 298 passengers and crew on board.

International outrage at the tragedy was met with stonewalling and denials by the Russian government. Meanwhile, efforts to broker a cease-fire were unsuccessful until September 5, when negotiations in Minsk, Belarus, spearheaded by the French and German governments, led to the signing of the Minsk Protocol by the Trilateral Contact Group on Ukraine: Ukraine, Russia, and the Organization for Security and Co-operation in Europe (OSCE). The leaders of the DPR and LPR also signed the document, which was the first of the two Minsk agreements, but it failed to stop the violence. Cease-fire violations were routine, and intense combat resumed in January 2015.

The parties returned to the negotiating table and signed a second agreement, Minsk II, on February 12, 2015. This agreement provided for, among other things, a cease-fire, the withdrawal of heavy weapons from the line of contact, the release of prisoners of war, and certain legal reforms in Ukraine that would afford limited self-government in the separatist areas of the Donbas. While most major combat operations ended after Minsk II, the violence never fully ended, and the agreement was never fully implemented. Artillery exchanges and skirmishes continued, but the line of contact did not materially change. This stalemate led many to call the situation a "frozen conflict." To those on the front lines in the Donbas, it remained a war zone, with casualties reported regularly by both sides.

This was the status of the conflict in Ukraine when I was appointed ambassador, in December 2019. The challenge I faced in Moscow was to get Kremlin and MFA officials to acknowledge that Russia should negotiate directly with the government in Kyiv. Instead, the Russian response was to deflect responsibility by insisting that Russia was not a party to the conflict and that Ukraine had to negotiate directly and exclusively with the two separatist republics, the DPR and the LPR.

The biggest concern—the brightest redline—that Putin had with Ukraine was its continuing desire to join NATO. Although the Euromaidan protests and the Revolution of Dignity were triggered by the proposed EU association agreement in 2013 and the hostile reaction by the Kremlin, it was Ukraine's proposed NATO accession that was most objectionable to the Russians, because NATO is a military alliance, albeit a defensive alliance. Talks between NATO and Ukraine on membership had waxed and waned since the early 2000s but accelerated after the events of 2014. During the administration of President Poroshenko in 2017, the Verkhovna Rada enacted a statute enshrining NATO membership as a foreign policy priority for Ukraine. After Zelensky was elected in 2020, he reaffirmed Ukraine's strategy to join NATO. And, although the application process for NATO membership was uncertain and could take years or decades, the Russians were adamantly opposed.

I would have an opportunity to test the Russian government's views on Ukraine and willingness to negotiate constructively about the conflict when I met with Nikolai Patrushev, the secretary of the Russian Security Council, who was a powerful figure in the Kremlin. His role in the Russian Presidential Executive Office was more closely analogous to the role of the US national security advisor than Ambassador Ushakov's role as foreign policy adviser to the president. Like Putin, Patrushev was a former KGB officer from Leningrad. In fact, the two men first met while working for the KGB in Leningrad in the mid-1970s. Patrushev transitioned from the KGB to the FSB in the 1990s and eventually succeeded Putin as director of the FSB when Putin became prime minister in 1999, before going on to assume his current position on the Security Council in May 2008.

Apart from Putin himself, Patrushev was the quintessential example of the *siloviki*—translated as "people of force" or "strongmen"—in Russia. The *siloviki* are men typically trained in the security or intelligence services, for example, the KGB/FSB, the SVR (foreign intelligence), the GRU (military intelligence), or the FSO (Federal Protective Service, which bears some resemblance to the US Secret Service but is more powerful and closely connected with Putin). These men maintain their intimidating influence after they leave their official positions in government to create wealthy lives for themselves. But it was what they got up to within the Russian government that most concerned me and my colleagues in the State Department.

Putin's inner circle was populated with *siloviki,* and Patrushev was among the most influential in that small group. He had influence not only because of his background of long service in the KGB/FSB and his close personal relationship with Putin from their youth in Leningrad, but also because of his position as secretary of the Russian Security Council. All decisions involving security in Russia, broadly defined to include the conflict in Ukraine, ran through him to the president. He therefore was, or could be, involved in every important issue in Russia at any given moment.

My first meeting with Patrushev on February 4 was brief. He did not speak English and I hardly understood any Russian, so my need for translation slowed the pace of the discussion. He initially conveyed a desire for improved relations with the United States but said that would happen only if the United States changed all aspects of its harmful and dangerous policies toward the Russian Federation. Those policies, he added, would never succeed in undermining Russia, in any event. On the situation in Ukraine, he would not give an inch. The conflict was internal to Ukraine, he insisted, and stemmed from an illegitimate coup in February 2014. If the United States wanted to resolve the conflict in Ukraine, then we should speak to our clients in Kyiv who had started it.

I was not surprised by his views, based on what I knew of his prior statements and writings. He appeared to be paranoid and conspiracy-minded, an ultranationalist, and an implacable adversary of the United States. He was the type of Russian leader who, as Kennan described, could not "tolerate rival political forces in the sphere of power which they coveted. Their sense of insecurity was too great." They were, Kennan said, "too fierce and too jealous" to negotiate in good faith with another party. Patrushev, it was clear, was someone for me to watch out for and not someone interested in stopping the violence in Ukraine.

———————

The Patrushev meeting was in many ways a template for my future engagements with senior Russian government officials, particularly during my first several months in Moscow. As a threshold matter, I had no complaint about access; virtually every senior Russian official with whom I sought a meeting granted my request. I met with, among others, the finance minister, the governor of the Central Bank of Russia, the energy minister, the minister of trade and industry, and the health minister. Foreign Minister Lavrov hosted a lunch to welcome me to Russia on January 31.

Every door was open, with one exception: Defense Minister Sergei K. Shoigu declined a meeting with me. I suspected it was because Secretary Mattis had refused to meet with the Russian ambassador in Washington. (Mattis had said that it was a waste of his time, and I could not disagree.) But with that exception, I had the access I wanted and needed. I reported on these developments to Washington and said so publicly in statements to the media. Equally important, I was treated with respect. There were no intentional efforts to provoke or embarrass me, with staged protests or media leaks, for example.

The insuperable problem, though, was the substance of the discussions at the many meetings I attended. The conversation that stands out in my memory as the most illustrative occurred when I met with Energy Minister Alexander V. Novak on the afternoon of February 6. The minister welcomed me into his conference room, and as we sat down, he launched into a heartfelt lament about the state of US-Russia relations. He said it was intolerable for two great countries to be unable to work together. As he went on, it seemed as though he were reading my talking points about the downward spiral in our relations and how we had to stop digging the hole we were in. I nodded my head as he continued speaking and I thought to myself that he might be another Russian official with whom I could do business.

Finally, as Novak reached his peroration and I prepared to raise with him some areas on which I thought we could work together, he looked at me directly and said, "This dreadful state of affairs is entirely the fault of the United States, and I wonder what you plan to do about it, ambassador." Try as I might, it was difficult to bring the conversation back into a constructive mode after an opening like that. The meeting continued, again with pleasantries on both sides, but with no effort on the Russian side to have a real give-and-take.

In each of my meetings, a through line quickly emerged. My welcome by the Russians was polite and completely by the book as a matter of protocol. But the net result of my meetings was zero progress on the most important policy issues on my agenda, a dispiriting result and one brought even lower by the Russians' accusations of hostility, hypocrisy, arrogance, and malfeasance on the part of the United States. I wondered whether this pattern would hold in the most important event in my early tenure: a one-on-one meeting with Putin during the ceremonial presentation of my credentials in the Grand Kremlin Palace.

That milestone was still weeks away when I disembarked in Moscow. In the interim, besides meeting my new counterparts on the lower strata of the Russian government, I would try to settle into my new surroundings—both the singular diplomatic environment of twenty-first-century Russia and the unique embassy that I now found myself leading.

# CHAPTER 5

# MISSION RUSSIA

THE DIFFICULT SUBJECTS THAT I discussed with senior Russian officials before and after I arrived in Moscow were vital to US foreign policy and national security, but none was more significant to me than the protection of Americans—everyone, private citizens and US government personnel—as well as American diplomatic posts (the embassy and our consulates) and corporations present in the Russian Federation. I spent more time on the welfare of Americans (broadly defined) in Russia than on any other issue during my service as ambassador.

My immediate priority on arrival was to focus on the embassy, which was in the heart of Moscow, across the street from the Russian White House (officially, the House of the Government of the Russian Federation) on the Krasnopresnenskaya Embankment along the Moscow River. The Russian White House, which was made internationally famous by the image of Russian president Boris Yeltsin speaking to a large crowd while standing on a tank during the failed coup in the final days of the Soviet Union in August 1991, was where the prime minister of Russia and the deputy prime ministers had their offices. The fact that the US embassy sat so close was both a testament to the importance of the US-Russia relationship and, occasionally, a complication of it, as I will explain.

Embassy Moscow, like all other US embassies and consulates around the globe, was a diplomatic property, protected under international law and the Vienna Convention, which meant it was inviolable, and no Russian government official could enter without the permission of the United States. Surrounded by a high wall, the compound was a twelve-acre American community with a dining facility, gym and pool, basketball court, pub, commissary, hair salon, travel agency, and health unit. Most of the several hundred Americans who worked at the embassy also lived in the many townhouses and apartments on the compound. Some lived in the city, with a cluster living near the Anglo-American School (pre-K through high school), where virtually all the children of embassy personnel went to school. The embassy had school buses to take the children who lived on the compound to and from the school.

The heart of the embassy, in the middle of the compound, was the chancery, the building where most offices, including mine, were located. Next to the chancery was a new building that housed our consular services section, which assisted American citizens in Russia and provided visas to Russians seeking to visit the United States. Embassy Moscow supported not only State Department personnel but also representatives from a variety of US government departments and agencies, ranging from NASA and the FBI to the Departments of Commerce and Defense. The embassy was the hub that connected Russians and Americans: students, academics, family members, tourists, business leaders, and all levels of government officials. It was a cornerstone of the US-Russia relationship— and yet its existence had grown increasingly precious as that relationship had deteriorated in recent years.

I had made that very point as deputy secretary in March 2018, in a briefing for President Trump with other officials on the proposed expulsion of Russian diplomats from the United States in response to the Russian GRU's use of a dangerous nerve agent in the attempted assassination of Sergei Skripal in Salisbury, England. In an Oval Office meeting, I cautioned that the Russian government's certain retaliatory expulsion of US diplomats from Russia would further weaken our already depleted mission in Russia. I was not arguing that we should not expel any Russian diplomats, only that we needed to be careful and proportional in our actions because the Russians would respond reciprocally.

President Trump cross-examined me, contending that I was merely protecting State Department property and interests. I disagreed and said it was our nation's embassy and his embassy, housing the ambassador he had appointed, as well as many other departments and agencies of the US government that reported to him. Although legally not US territory, it was the diplomatic equivalent and an invaluable and inviolable presence for the United States in a hostile country. The president, perhaps reflecting his background in the real estate business, accepted the point and thanked me for the clarification, which was not typical in my dealings with him.

At the conclusion of the meeting with the president, everyone agreed on a compromise in which the United States would close the Russian consulate in Seattle and expel sixty Russian diplomats—forty-eight from the Russian mission to the United States and twelve from their mission to the United Nations. After that decision was announced, and as I had predicted, the Russians closed the US consulate in Saint Petersburg and expelled sixty US diplomats. This followed a pattern of tit-for-tat closures and expulsions that began after the Russian interference in the 2016 US presidential election and extended through my time as ambassador. The net result was a greatly diminished US mission in Russia when I arrived, consisting of the embassy in Moscow and consulates in Yekaterinburg in the Urals and Vladivostok in the Russian Far East, on the Sea of Japan. Whereas the US diplomatic presence in Russia had once numbered over a thousand people (including third country nationals and Russian citizens), by the time I arrived in Russia there were fewer than five hundred—and that number would drop lower in the years ahead.

Of course, the diplomatic expulsions would not have had such a long-term impact on the staffing of our mission if we had been able to get visas from the Russian MFA for US personnel to replace the expelled officers and staff. I was often asked why we did not simply send new diplomats to replace those expelled, and the short answer was that the Russians would not allow us to do so. And the reason they would not give us the requested visas had everything to do with how they use their diplomatic missions around the world.

The key to understanding the issue was the distinction between declared and undeclared intelligence officers in a foreign mission in a host country. As was true for most countries, including Russia, some personnel in a mission were intelligence officers who were declared as such to the host government and who were granted diplomatic visas on that basis. For example, the SVR *rezident*, who oversaw the *rezidentura*, or Russian intelligence station, was a declared intelligence officer. An undeclared intelligence officer, however, was one who was admitted to a country surreptitiously under the cover of a diplomatic office, for example as a trade officer; they, too, received a diplomatic visa, but under false pretenses. (A third and completely different category of spies, not relevant to diplomatic exchanges but popular in movies and television dramas like *The Americans*, were so-called illegals—foreign intelligence officers who entered a country without ever seeking diplomatic cover or immunity at a foreign mission.)

Among the insoluble problems for US-Russia diplomacy was the fact that the Russian government insisted on flooding its foreign missions with undeclared intelligence officers, mostly from the SVR but also from the other security services. An ambassador from a European country in Moscow once told me that in his country they euphemistically refer to Russian embassy personnel as "multifunctional diplomats." The problem was particularly acute in the United States, because we hosted so many Russians at their missions to both the United States and the UN. There were hundreds of Russian diplomats accredited to the United States or to the UN and many were present under diplomatic cover as undeclared intelligence officers engaged in espionage. It was an indication of the problem that all sixty of the Russians who were expelled in response to the Salisbury attack in 2018 were assessed by the United States to be Russian intelligence personnel.

This was a massive security challenge for the FBI, but also a diplomatic challenge for the State Department. In accordance with diplomatic practice, the Russian MFA periodically provided the State Department with a list of personnel identified by name, title, and position that the Russians proposed to send to the United States, and they sought diplomatic visas for them. The State Department similarly provided a list of proposed US diplomats to the MFA. Upon careful review of the Russian list, however, some would be identified by US officials as Russian intelligence officers who were posing as diplomats (e.g., a political officer) or staff (e.g., a cook or gardener). The State Department generally would not issue a diplomatic visa to an undeclared Russian intelligence officer. And for every visa that the United States declined to issue, the Russians would decline to issue a visa to an American.

Over time, this dynamic had led to a diplomatic standoff. For example, the Russians might need visas for thirty incoming staff, and the United States might need an equivalent number. If we declined to issue diplomatic visas to the ten Russian intelligence officers presented by the MFA on their list, then they would typically deny ten of our thirty visa requests. Sometimes the whole package of thirty visas per side would be scuttled. Each country's mission was adversely affected, but the Russians maintained an advantage because they had started with a larger number of diplomats in the United States and allowed them to stay longer than we would allow a US diplomat to stay in Russia (for, among other reasons, the stress and hardship). Moreover, while the United States declined to issue visas to Russian spies, the Russians in retaliation denied visas to the personnel they deemed most important to the functioning of the US mission: for instance, IT specialists who keep the diplomatic facilities' computers and phones working, or engineers who keep the elevators and HVAC systems running.

Although we were more adversely impacted, the Russians were also frustrated. I told Deputy Foreign Minister Ryabkov that this problem would not abate until the Russians stopped trying to send so many undeclared intelligence officers—I used the undiplomatic word "spies" at one point in the discussion to emphasize the point—to the United States. But I knew this was not going to happen under President Putin, because, as one of my colleagues once observed, these were exactly the sorts of Russian "diplomats" one should expect from a nation led by a former career KGB officer.

To keep our respective missions running in the face of this impasse, the two sides had to engage in detailed and time-consuming negotiations over small-scale visa trades (for example, swapping two US diplomatic visas for two Russian diplomatic visas), which made staffing and planning difficult and added to the stress on the US embassy that I was taking over. Incoming officers did not know when or whether they would get visas to assume their new posts; some had to wait over a year before they could move to their new destination, whereas others never got to go at all. Officers with onward assignments from Moscow were delayed in their departures until their successors could get visas. It was an intolerable situation and no way to conduct diplomacy.

Most significantly, engineers and technical experts with required expertise and security clearances to maintain our facilities, including the embassy's secure areas and equipment, were not getting visas. For example, the fire suppression system in the chancery was long overdue for repairs (the water pump in the basement was covered with rust and needed to be replaced), but we could not get visas for the right people to do the work, nor could we hire local workers for the job, because that would provide an opening for the Russian intelligence services to penetrate our diplomatic facilities. The Russians were forcing us to choose between our safety and the security of our mission.

In an embassy already under intense scrutiny by the FSB and a hostile Russian government, the visa impasse was one more problem for our mission. It was also why I was so focused on reviewing the staffing and functioning of the embassy and meeting as soon as possible with all my new colleagues upon my arrival to get their views on how we could maintain our facilities while improving our operations and effectiveness. Before I departed Washington, I received extensive briefings from Ambassador Huntsman and his team on the embassy and the two consulates, but there was no substitute for personally assessing the situation on the ground.

———

My education on the US mission in Russia began on my first night. At Spaso House, I was welcomed to my new residence by the section and agency heads of the embassy, led by Bartle B. Gorman, the deputy chief of mission who had been the chargé d'affaires until I arrived. Bart was on his third assignment in Moscow during a long and stellar career in the Foreign Service. Trained as an officer in the State Department's Diplomatic Security Service—a law enforcement agency that among other things, protects US personnel and diplomatic properties around the world—he had served as the senior regional security officer at Embassy Moscow from 2014 to 2016. But he was far more than a security specialist. Bart was a fluent Russian speaker with a PhD in Russian literature and language from the University of Southern California, and he had lived in Russia as a graduate student before he joined the Foreign Service. He knew more about the Russians and their government than anyone I had worked with at the State Department. He was also a seasoned manager and leader. I could not have asked for a better deputy and colleague, and I told Jon Huntsman how grateful I was to him for originally picking Bart as his deputy.

The rest of the State Department team at the embassy were also experienced and highly capable. Its members included Tim Richardson, the political section chief; John Kuschner, the management section chief; and Karl Stoltz, the public diplomacy chief. Stephen Sexton was the regional security officer overseeing not only the diplomatic security agents and engineers assigned to the embassy but also the Marine Security Guard (MSG) Detachment, which was the largest detachment at any US embassy in the world. A former marine himself, Steve had exactly the right training and experience for his difficult job. He was also a hockey player from Detroit who, along with one of our defense attachés, US Army colonel Jon Dunn, played at night in two local men's leagues in Moscow. Steve had me out on the ice for a skate not long after I arrived.

I was excited about the prospect of working with such an impressive group of colleagues. I knew from my prior experience as deputy secretary of state and earlier as deputy secretary of commerce that the US government sends extraordinary Americans to work at its missions abroad. In the case of Russia, special care is given to selecting the women and men who serve there under the intense scrutiny and pressure of the host government. The stressors were various and compounding: every nonsecure phone call monitored, audio surveillance inside the embassy (except, we hoped, in secure areas), video and audio surveillance off the compound, "close access" physical surveillance every moment outside the embassy (e.g., a "random stranger" suddenly sticking a cell phone in a US diplomat's face and taking a picture), approaches on the street soliciting cooperation with the FSB, poisoned pets, and, for those living off the compound, home invasions by the FSB when no one was home.

These were just some of the methods the FSB used, not only to harry and intimidate the staff of Embassy Moscow, but also to slowly smother our mission in the country. Individually, these acts were annoying or upsetting. Cumulatively, over time, they were absolutely stifling. Secretary Mattis had told me that the Marine Corps selects only the best of the NCOs in its MSG program for the detachment in Moscow, young marines—our "diplomats in blue"—who were guaranteed to be the targets of repeated provocations and harassment by the Russian security services when they were off duty and left the compound. They had to be mature enough to avoid new Russian "friends" who were unusually inquisitive, bartenders who were overly generous in serving alcohol, and tough guys who were looking to instigate a scrap. The ways in which young marines could be set up or exploited was limited only by the imagination of the FSB officers monitoring them twenty-four hours a day, seven days a week.

I thought the most inspiring aspect of the entire team at the US mission in Russia was their resilience in the face of these challenges far from home, which would have broken the will or the spirit of others. Although shorthanded, our staff continued ably to represent the United States to the Russian people, to keep Washington fully apprised of political, social, economic, security, and military developments in Russia, and to maintain the safety and security of the aging facilities at the embassy. The toughness of these men and women extended to their families who lived with them in Moscow. They had to endure the same challenges, and children were not immune. For instance, when I was ambassador, a school bus with the children of diplomatic families on board was stopped by police for a purported traffic offense and the vehicle and young passengers were searched in a "safety inspection."

I was proud to join a group of Americans with such commitment to our mission, and one of my most immediate concerns was what I could do to help them. They had training and experience in their fields of expertise that I did not have, and they were doing their jobs superbly well. What could I add? I was there to provide leadership, of course—but what would that leadership entail?

First, I made it clear to the country team at the embassy that I would take the lead on difficult engagements with the Russian MFA and the Kremlin. I would deliver any unpleasant message personally and not delegate any task, no matter how small, that would include absorbing a vitriolic Russian response. Most important, I would defend the mission against Russian harassment or aggression, and would make sure that the MFA did not treat our mission differently from the way we treated their mission to the United States, whether regarding matters of diplomatic visas, staffing levels, travel restrictions, or any of the numerous other aspects of our operations on which the Russians sought to exert malign influence.

I told my colleagues that we would insist on reciprocity, which the Russians always said they wanted but were loath to see implemented. Insisting on reciprocity was important not only as a matter of common-sense policy (I cited the Golden Rule: "Do unto others..."), but also for morale, so that everyone at the US mission knew that the ambassador was standing up for each of them as well as for the United States. For example, the Russian MFA had rules different from the State Department on the length of time a diplomatic visa was valid and the continuation of diplomatic immunity after a visa had expired. In the United States, a Russian diplomat with an expired visa retained immunity, while an American diplomat in the same situation in Russia did not and was subject to arrest. This had practical adverse effects on the operations of Embassy Moscow. In at least one case, we had to restrict an officer to the compound until his visa was renewed, and the renewal was unreasonably delayed by the MFA for many days. I would not tolerate that type of asymmetry.

As ambassador, I also would apply our rules faithfully and impose discipline on our personnel where it was merited. We had a rule at the US mission that anyone who drove under the influence would be sent home immediately, whether the Russian government was aware of the behavior or not. The Russians in the United States, on the other hand, had a more flexible approach. In one case, a Russian diplomat accredited to the UN was arrested for drunk driving in Washington State, not too far from Naval Base Kitsap, where the US military has large and sensitive facilities. I never found out why we had allowed a Russian "diplomat" assigned to the UN in New York City to travel across the country to Washington after the Russians had already breached (by obstructing the travel of US diplomats in Russia) the so-called Open Lands Agreement of 1992, which had liberalized the travel rules for US and Russian diplomats.

Even more frustrating was the Russian MFA's refusal to send their drunk driver home. They said he would be denied driving privileges in the United States. At my urging, the State Department said no, he would either be sent home by the Russians or be declared persona non grata by the United States, which meant he had to leave or else would be prosecuted. The Russians forced us to declare their diplomat persona non grata, and then expelled one of our diplomats in retaliation. Such was the give-and-take with the Russian MFA, but I knew that we needed to practice what we preached for the Russians to take us seriously. Anything less would be a sign of weakness and would be viciously exploited by them—making the US mission less safe and successful.

I made it clear that US diplomats in Russia would not quietly take our lumps—even if it meant an ugly confrontation with the Russians over actions against our mission or personnel. To emphasize the point and lift some spirits at post, I gave this policy an unclassified name and called it Operation Twisted Sister, which many Americans, at least of my generation, would associate with the band's 1984 hit single "We're Not Going to Take It." My colleagues and I chuckled about how long it would take the FSB (which closely monitored everything that we said and did in the nonsecure areas of the embassy) to figure out what our references to OTS and Twisted Sister meant. The consensus was not long. (I also knew that Secretary Pompeo was a fan of heavy metal music, and this name would not hurt if I ever had to defend my approach to him.) The members of the political section at the embassy, led by Tim Richardson and his deputy, Sonata Coulter, so liked the name and what it stood for—American resolve—that in December they gave me for Christmas a Twisted Sister T-shirt autographed by each member of the section. I displayed it proudly in my office for the next two years.

Second, in addition to intervening with the Russians, I would be the mission's chief advocate and intermediary with Washington, so that US government officials—in the executive branch as well as in Congress—and the American public would understand exactly what was happening in Russia and at our embassy and consulates. Because of my most recent service at a prominent level in the administration, I had easier access to many senior officials than another ambassador might have had. This would be important when I needed support in implementing a tougher policy on reciprocity with the Russians.

Finally, I wanted to inspire a quiet confidence in our mission. I had seen how important the "tone at the top" is for an organization. In my first weekend as deputy secretary of state, I was working in my office, with the television on in the background, when Secretary Mattis appeared on the CBS News program *Face the Nation*. He was asked by John Dickerson, "What keeps you awake at night?" The secretary of defense answered, quietly and without hesitation, "Nothing. I keep other people awake at night." I was taken aback and had to rewind to hear him say that again. I could only imagine what a boost in morale that quip—and what it revealed about the secretary—had on our men and women in uniform. It certainly gave me, and many of my colleagues at the State Department who heard the remark, a lift.

That was the type of quiet confidence I sought to convey and inspire at Embassy Moscow and our consulates: confidence in our mission and in our values as Americans that are expressed in, among other documents, the Bill of Rights. We would treat each other, and the Russians, fairly and with respect; and we would defend ourselves and our nation's interests zealously. Quiet confidence, however, is not arrogance and must be tempered and leavened with humility. No government or society is or has ever been perfect. To be taken seriously—to be effective—we must not pretend to be any different.

I sought to lead a US mission in Russia that would have pride in the US Constitution and our system of government, in the American people and our history, but that would have the courage and strength to admit our flaws—something the Kremlin could never muster. And the enduring need for humility was affirmed in my first spring in Moscow, after the murder of George Floyd in Minneapolis, and the subsequent protests and riots in the United States. It was important—in the face of the Russian government's constant disinformation campaigns, efforts to exacerbate racial divisions in the United States, and contempt for our society—for the US mission in Russia to keep faith with our principles and values, but also to be truthful and acknowledge that the United States is not perfect. Our founders said so expressly in drafting the US Constitution "to form a more perfect Union"—emphasis on *more* and less on *perfect*. It was a subtle message, and sometimes not an easy one to convey to a jaded Russian public, or any foreign audience, but that is one of the reasons why the

United States has embassies and consulates around the world: to engage in such public diplomacy.

We had a memorial service for George Floyd at the flagpole in the courtyard outside the embassy chancery. Everyone at the embassy stood around our flag in silence for eight minutes—the time that a police officer knelt on Floyd's neck, killing him. The Russian security services monitored everything we did. I hoped they understood the significance of what they were monitoring.

My leadership as ambassador extended beyond the walls of the embassy compound to our two consulates, small but important US diplomatic outposts in the vast Eurasian colossus that is the Russian Federation. The consulate in Yekaterinburg, two time zones and almost a thousand miles from Moscow, was led by our very capable consul general, Amy Storrow, and was an important link to this politically and culturally significant city in the Sverdlovsk Oblast, home to the Yeltsin Presidential Center. The Yekaterinburg consulate also provided access to the many businesses and manufacturing facilities in the Urals region, a traditional hub of heavy industry with access to abundant metal ores, coal, and precious stones.

Five time zones and thousands of miles farther east of Yekaterinburg was the US consulate in Vladivostok, led by our dynamic consul general, Lou Crishock, who was an enthusiastic representative of the United States in eastern Siberia. Among his other talents, Lou could do a rousing Elvis Presley impression, but under his good-natured persona was a deeply serious Foreign Service professional and a strong leader with an extremely important remit. The embassy in Moscow was about as close to the State Department in Washington as it was to the consulate in Vladivostok— such is the geographic breadth of Russia—but our presence in the Russian Far East was vital as it helped us to monitor the development of the political, military, and commercial relationship between Russia and China, whose border lay only about twenty miles west of Vladivostok, as the crow flies. It was also an important post from which to assess Russia's interaction with North Korea (also only a short distance from

Vladivostok) and the reception in Russia of North Korean "guest workers" who made hard currency for the regime in Pyongyang.

The embassy and two consulates constituted the US mission to Russia; and as diminished in staffing and resources as the embassy was, the consulates were even more vulnerable. Each had a skeleton team of a dozen or fewer US diplomats supported by local staff, mostly Russian citizens and a few third country nationals who worked for us. Neither consulate had a secure space for reviewing and storing classified material, or a secure means of communicating with the embassy in Moscow or with Washington. Whenever we needed to convey sensitive or classified information to the consulates or vice versa, someone had to travel from those remote locations to Moscow.

I met with Amy and Lou in Moscow on February 3, soon after my arrival, to discuss the operations of their consulates and the challenges they faced. Among the most significant challenges was the scale of the territory they and their teams were expected to cover. Each consulate was asked to report on developments across a huge swath of Russia, the largest country by landmass in the world. It was not possible for them and their small teams to get to know all the local political and civic leaders in their territories the way they ordinarily would in a typical consulate covering a far smaller area. Even more challenging, it was extremely difficult for them to provide consular services to an American who needed help in a distant location in the Urals or Siberia.

Among the lessons I learned as ambassador was that there were a surprisingly large number of Americans who got into trouble or needed help in Russia, whether they were arrested, were the victims of crime, lost their children, or had no money to get home. When I arrived, in January 2020, there were tens of thousands of American citizens living in or visiting Russia, many of whom were in the Saint Petersburg–Moscow corridor. Some were dual Russian-American citizens, but the hyphenation was irrelevant to me. Each American citizen was entitled to our maximum support—they were my most important constituency as ambassador. The problem was that the US mission's consular section was so shorthanded that we had to perform triage. And because those most in need of our help were in the custody of the Russian criminal justice system, these were the people who often got our fastest attention.

The chief of the consular section who oversaw the provision of American citizen services across Russia was Cathy Holt. As a veteran consular officer, she was an invaluable resource to me. I spent hours meeting with Cathy, touring the consular section and meeting the consular officers and the local staff, Russians and third country nationals, who not only provided services to American citizens, including new passports, but also issued a huge number of visas to Russian citizens. The consular section at Embassy Moscow, as is true at most large embassies in big cities, was an extremely busy operation.

Cathy briefed me on the cases of three American citizens who were arrested without cause and incarcerated in pretrial detention in Moscow: Paul Whelan, Trevor Reed, and Michael Calvey. Whelan had been detained for over a year at this point, on the spurious but extremely serious charge of espionage, and I had already raised his case with Deputy Foreign Minister Ryabkov. The injustice of his detention was compounded by how badly he was being treated in the old and notorious Lefortovo Prison, which was nominally under the jurisdiction of the Russian Ministry of Justice but which was used by the FSB for interrogations, as it had been by the KGB.

I insisted on visiting Whelan at Lefortovo as soon as possible, and holding a press conference outside the prison to draw international attention to his plight. He was being denied medical treatment, access to his lawyers, and the ability to communicate with his family. I met with Paul on January 30 in a small, shabby room at Lefortovo. The prison, built in 1881, was cold, dark, dilapidated, and depressing, just as one would imagine a notorious KGB/FSB interrogation center to be. It was as forlorn and godforsaken a place as any I had ever seen. Cathy Holt accompanied me to the meeting with Paul, and Rebecca Ross assembled the press on the street outside the prison.

Paul and I sat on either side of a wooden table and there was nothing else separating us, but we were not allowed to shake hands or reach across the table. An FSB colonel sat with us, along with an interpreter. Everything I said in English had to be translated for the colonel before

Paul could respond. Similarly, everything he said to me had to be translated for the colonel before I could respond. Paul was bundled up in sweaters from the cold and looked very pale. Nonetheless, he was smiling and glad to see me. I joked with him that I had worn a green tie that day to show solidarity with a fellow Irish American. Paul laughed and I thought, after all he had been through, he was not in bad shape.

I conveyed messages from his family and we discussed his case at length, as well as the conditions of his confinement. I assured him that I would do everything I could to get him the medical attention and legal counsel he needed, as well as his mail and phone calls with his family in the United States. He seemed relieved to learn that I had been following his case closely and would be a zealous advocate for him until he was allowed to return to the United States. I could only imagine what courage it took to survive as an innocent man in such an alien and forbidding place. After two hours, we had to end the meeting and I left to address a large group of international media that Rebecca had gathered outside the prison gates.

I was slightly surprised that the FSB allowed me to talk to the press so close to the prison. I was even more surprised that the focus of the media seemed not to be Paul's innocence or the horrible conditions of his confinement but the question of who the United States would trade for him. I said the United States does not arrest people—from Russia or anywhere else—to trade them. Paul was innocent and in his pretrial confinement at Lefortovo he was being denied his rights guaranteed under Russian law and international law. The press questions, however, reflected what the Russian government was telling these members of the media. I was dealing with a justice system that was not centered on guilt or innocence, but on how the system could be used by the FSB and the Kremlin to gain an advantage against the United States or another adversary.

That Russian approach was reflected in their criminal case against Trevor Reed, another wrongfully detained American, who was arrested for assaulting two police officers in Moscow in August 2019. Like Paul Whelan, Trevor was a former marine and was plainly innocent of the charges against him, as was subsequently demonstrated at his trial, where even the presiding judge laughed out loud at the contradictory and palpably implausible testimony and other evidence presented by the prosecution.

Unlike Whelan's case, however, Trevor's case was not handled directly by the FSB, because he was not charged with a crime as serious as espionage. He was held in the regular pretrial detention system (in the SIZO-5 facility in Moscow), along with ordinary Russian criminals, and not in the custody of the FSB at Lefortovo Prison. Thus, he was not subject to the same interrogations and psychological pressure as Whelan was. Because of these differences, I tried a different strategy with Trevor's case. I decided not to make prominent statements to the press, in the hope (and it was only a faint hope) that if the profile of the case were not high, then this obviously innocent man might be acquitted, or, if convicted, then sentenced to time served. My public advocacy for Paul had failed so far, and thus I thought it was worth trying a low-profile strategy for Trevor. As it turned out, this long-shot strategy was destined to fail because the Russian justice system is not constituted to adjudicate guilt or innocence but rather to produce outcomes that the Russian state wants. What is more, the FSB always has an interest in a case that involves an American, particularly a former member of the US military.

The third case of a wrongfully detained American that was on my agenda when I arrived as ambassador was the prosecution of Mike Calvey, the founder of the largest private equity firm in the country, Baring Vostok Capital Partners. Calvey was arrested in February 2019 and charged with fraud in connection with a commercial dispute about a bank of which he had been a director. The matter was the subject of pending arbitrations in London, but the Russian private parties to the dispute had decided to use their connections to the Russian security services to initiate a criminal case that would disrupt the arbitrations. After his arrest, Calvey spent several months in pretrial detention in the Moscow SIZO system before he was released to home detention and required to wear a monitoring device on his ankle.

I first met Calvey in his home near Red Square on February 14, 2020. We discussed his situation and how I could support him. His case was different from the Whelan and Reed cases, as indicated by the fact that he was in home detention and not incarcerated. Additionally, there were

significant downsides to the Russian government in continuing the prosecution. A bogus criminal charge of fraud against the founder of Baring
Vostok—who also happened to be among the most prominent and effective spokespeople for doing business in Russia—was bad for the economy
and for the investment climate in the country. We decided that I would
try to maintain a low profile by not making public statements, while Mike
and his team of lawyers worked on the case. The charge against Calvey
was eventually lowered to embezzlement, an equally spurious accusation but one that would carry a lower penalty, and the terms of his home
detention were loosened. But the criminal case against him continued.

In connection with the Calvey case, I met with the board of directors of the American Chamber of Commerce in Russia (AmCham). The
AmCham, working through the US Commercial Service at Embassy Moscow, would become a vital link for me to US businesses in Russia. When
I arrived, there were over twelve hundred US companies doing business
in the country, and they were another important constituency for me as
ambassador. While the challenges that they faced were markedly different from those confronting individuals such as Whelan and Reed, these
problems were all connected, and the solutions would need to be as well.

The US Commercial Service is part of the Department of Commerce
and an organization with which I was very familiar from my days as the
deputy secretary of commerce. The Commercial Service is charged with,
among other things, being an advocate for US companies in foreign markets, and was led in Russia by Jim Golsen, a highly regarded senior Foreign
Commercial Service officer. On January 27, Jim introduced me to Alexis
Rodzianko, a former banker in New York and later in Moscow, who was
the president and CEO of the AmCham. Alexis, Jim, and I spent a significant amount of time working together to establish a two-way channel of
communication between me and the US business community in Russia.

In my initial meeting with Alexis and the AmCham board, we discussed the negative impact of the Calvey prosecution on American businesses in Russia, and the impossibility of having a US-Russia business
leaders dialogue—the gathering of Russian and American CEOs that
Putin wanted—while a phony criminal charge was pending against the
most prominent American business leader in Russia. We also discussed

more generally the problems that US businesses were having in Russia with corruption, antiquated and arcane regulations and regulatory regimes, and the lack of a judicial system that would protect the interests of an American company.

There would be many similar discussions in the years ahead, most of them including Alexis—who turned out to be not only a valuable business connection but also a remarkable source of information on Russia generally. His knowledge extended deep into Russian history. His great-grandfather Mikhail had served as chairman of the Russian Empire's State Duma from 1911 to 1917, under Tsar Nicholas II. Talking with Alexis always reminded me that the largest constituency on which I needed to focus, after my fellow Americans, was the Russian people themselves. I had to work hard to present a more accurate and positive image of the United States to the Russians than what was conveyed in the overwhelmingly negative reporting by the Russian media controlled by the Kremlin. I owed this to the Russians, just as I owed it to the American people.

———————

The closest Russian audience to me was comprised of the hundreds of locally employed staff (mostly Russians, but some third country nationals as well) who worked at the embassy and the two consulates. These men and women were the permanent backbone of the mission. Many of them had worked for the United States for decades. I enjoyed meeting with them individually and in groups to thank them for their work. Our reliance on local staff was standard for all US missions around the world, and logical when one considers the benefits, from their knowledge as natives of the host country to the fact that it is much less expensive to hire a local employee for certain roles than to send someone from the United States to do the same job.

The problem in Russia was that the host government viewed our local staff as a vulnerability for us that they could exploit. They did so in at least two ways. First, to gain leverage in negotiations, the Russian MFA would threaten to make it illegal for the United States to employ Russian citizens or any third country nationals in Russia. There was a precedent for this, and the MFA knew that we remembered it well and the pain it had caused. In the mid-1980s, the Soviet government barred Soviet citizens from working at the US mission, which caused enormous disruption to our operations and left highly trained Foreign Service officers doing double duty in the motor pool and cleaning floors (the euphemism for this was "all-purpose duty"). To avoid this weakness in their own missions, the MFA never employed local staff at their diplomatic posts anywhere in the world. The Russian embassy in Washington, and consulates in Houston and New York, as well as their mission to the UN, were all staffed exclusively by Russians. When I complained about their threat to cut off access to our local staff, my interlocutors at the MFA pointed out that it was our own foolish decision to leave ourselves vulnerable in ways the Russian government never would.

I doubted that at the end of the day the Russians would follow through on their threat to remove our local staff—because of the second way in which they exploited them. For as much as the FSB targeted Americans at our mission, they were even more relentless in pursuing our local staff and putting pressure on them to provide information that the FSB wanted. They had inducements and threats to gain cooperation. I was briefed on one case in which the FSB approached a longtime Russian employee of the embassy and reminded him of his teenage son's serious medical condition. I interrupted the briefer and asked, "So they were offering medical treatment?" My colleague said no, the FSB officer told the father that if he did not provide the information the FSB wanted, the son would lose the expensive medical treatment for which the father had already paid. What parent, no matter how dedicated to his employer and friendly with his American coworkers, could ignore that unconscionable threat? On the other hand, we could not employ someone subject to such coercion and had to separate the employee.

I did not believe that the Russian government would cut off our ability to employ local staff, because they were too valuable to the FSB. Indeed, by employing Russians and third country nationals (the non-Russians we employed could be threatened with loss of their immigration status if they did not cooperate), we were the ones putting our local staff at risk, not to mention the security of the mission and the United States. I resolved that as part of Operation Twisted Sister (standing up to the Russian MFA and insisting on reciprocity), we would have to significantly reduce our reliance on local staff in our embassy and consulates. But we would have to do so in an orderly way that would not completely upend the functioning of the mission, given our overreliance on local staff and the long time, not to mention the great expense, that it would take to get Americans trained, cleared, and in Russia to replace them. It was clearly a hole in our armor that had to be patched.

———

I did not allow our dreadful relations with the MFA and the FSB to distract me from engaging with the Russian people and immersing myself in Russian culture. I toured the Kremlin museums with Grace and our son Jack on the weekend after we arrived. A few weeks later, I had lunch at the Pushkin State Museum of Fine Arts. I went for exploratory walks along Old Arbat Street, which is near Spaso House, and went for runs with my bodyguards (I never went anywhere outside the embassy or Spaso House without them) in the city in the early morning to combine exercise with sightseeing.

Pursuing a personal interest and following up on what I had promised would be my own version of hockey diplomacy, I attended a hockey game on February 1 between two Moscow-based teams in the Kontinental Hockey League (KHL), which was formed in 2008 out of the former Russian Superleague. Passion for ice hockey was something that unites almost all Russians, the way it unites Canadians. My hosts for the game were Russian hockey legends Alexander Yakushev, known as Big Yak, and Viacheslav (Slava) Fetisov. Yakushev was the leading scorer on the Soviet national team in the 1972 Summit Series with Canada that had so impressed me in my youth. Fetisov, an Honoured Member of the Hockey Hall of Fame in Toronto, was one of the greatest players ever in the game: the youngest captain in the history of the Soviet national team in the 1980s, and a two-time Stanley Cup champion with the Detroit Red Wings in the 1990s (but still no Bobby Orr).

I spent time with Big Yak and Slava before the event and agreed to drop the puck at the ceremonial opening face-off. The game was between the visiting Dynamo club and Spartak, a club that Big Yak had once coached and with which he still had a relationship. The third KHL team in Moscow is CSKA Moscow, known as Red Army and founded by the Russian Armed Forces in 1946. Slava had played for Red Army as an officer in the Soviet military from 1976 to 1989. Flanked by Big Yak and Slava, I walked out on a red carpet to center ice at Spartak's home arena, the Megasport Sport Palace, which was full to its capacity of fourteen thousand fans.

As I reached center ice and the captains of the two teams skated over, the game announcer identified Yakushev, Fetisov, and me, the new US ambassador. The crowd immediately started booing. I had never had fourteen thousand people boo me before. I did my best to keep my composure as I dropped the puck and shook hands with the two players towering over me. Big Yak, Slava, and I turned to walk off the ice, and I said to Slava, "Well, that wasn't great, getting booed by a huge crowd in my first major public appearance as ambassador." Slava replied, "They are not booing you; they are booing me. Watch." He waved to the crowd and there was an immediate chorus of boos. We stepped off the ice, into the penalty box, and I told him I was confused. Why were Russian fans booing one of the greatest players in the history of Russian hockey? He said, "These are fans of Dynamo and Spartak, and when I played for CSKA we kicked their asses every year in the '70s and '80s." I concluded that Russian hockey fans, like their counterparts the world over, have long memories and are unforgiving.

We watched the game from Big Yak's box at the arena. Unlike Slava, Big Yak did not speak English well and seemed taciturn that evening. I had tried to talk to him about the '72 Series and impress him with my knowledge of his team, but he was not engaging. I mentioned the infamous slash by Bobby Clarke of the Philadelphia Flyers on Kharlamov during the series, but that did not improve his mood. I told him that as a lifelong Boston Bruins fan, who was now a longtime Washington Capitals season-ticket holder and fan of Alexander Ovechkin, I was not fond of Clarke or the Flyers. Big Yak grimaced when I mentioned the former captain of the Flyers. I thought that might give me an opening.

After the game, Big Yak, Slava, and I spoke to the press. As I stood between them, I started to give my spiel on hockey diplomacy and how the game can bring us together: Russians, Americans, Canadians, Swedes, Finns, Czechs, Poles, Germans, hockey players, and fans everywhere. I said hockey unites us and we can all agree on one thing. I repeated that mantra several times in different ways and I could see from the looks on the faces of my colleagues from the embassy press office that they were wondering where I was going with this stem-winder. I finally looked at Big Yak and said the one thing that all hockey fans around the world could agree on: "The Flyers suck." Big Yak was taken aback, then smiled and said loudly, "Yes, the Flyers suck." Slava laughed and said he had not seen anyone get a rise out of Big Yak like that in a while. I had some explaining to do with the press and others gathered around us, but I had made an impression on Big Yak, who gave me one of his autographed sticks. I hoped it was a tiny step toward more positive engagement not only with Russian hockey fans but with the Russian people.

I spoke to the Russian media frequently as ambassador, and I was not afraid to speak my mind. After I finished a lengthy interview with an influential Russian daily newspaper with national distribution, *Kommersant,* which was focused on politics and business, Rebecca Ross described my interview style as "spicy," which I took as a compliment. My goal was to speak honestly to the Russian people—in a way they did not hear their own leaders speak—to get their attention and give them a different perspective on US-Russia relations and the news of the day.

My first large meeting with the press was a lunch with the editors of TASS, the famous Russian state-owned news service, and correspondents from a variety of Russian media, on January 30. There were at least fifty people gathered in a large conference room at the TASS headquarters in Moscow. The conversation was polite and nonconfrontational, as the Russian reporters sized me up as the new US ambassador. The meal was sumptuous, and I was enjoying the discussion. I thought maybe they were taking it easy on me in my opening encounter with the Russian media.

That was, until a series of questions from two young Russian journalists changed the tone. They questioned me aggressively on the US Foreign Agents Registration Act (FARA), which predates World War II and requires registration with the Department of Justice by persons representing foreign principals in the United States, particularly foreign governments and political parties (lobbyists for foreign commercial interests are allowed to register with Congress under the more permissive Lobbying Disclosure Act). The Russian journalists tried to make the case that FARA was much more onerous than recent (and further proposed) changes to the Russian law on foreign agents and their influence. I disagreed completely and pointed out the substantial differences between the simple registration statute in the United States and the more draconian restrictions enacted and proposed in Russia.

The lunch continued, but the questions on foreign agents and FARA from representatives of the Russian state media piqued my interest. They were a signal of what was important to Putin and the Kremlin in January 2020. The Russian government was in the middle of a sweeping crackdown on civil society, using, among other things, the label of "foreign agent" as a pretext for arresting and incarcerating independent journalists and political leaders. The Kremlin, through its state media, was engaging in disinformation by trying to make the false case that what Russia was doing was no different from what the United States has done under FARA. I was witnessing that disinformation campaign in my presence at the TASS lunch, and I had to push back hard. In doing so, I relearned an old lesson: there are no free lunches.

The Russian crackdown on civil society, including the dissolution of organizations and arrest of individuals designated as foreign agents, gathered momentum during the following months and continued throughout my tenure as ambassador. The crackdown dovetailed with constitutional reforms that Putin had introduced as I arrived in January—new rules—that would entrench his power and allow him to continue to serve as president, despite existing constitutional terms limits, until 2036.

It was not long after the TASS lunch that I got to make my own personal assessment of the Kremlin leader who was causing such tumult in Russia and the world.

# CHAPTER 6

# THE CHEKIST

I HAD MET VLADIMIR PUTIN BRIEFLY on several occasions as deputy secretary of state and had sat behind him for hours at the East Asia Summit in Singapore in November 2018, but had not had a full conversation with him. My first meeting with Putin as ambassador, scheduled for February 5, 2020, was thus also the first time that I was able to speak with him at length.

Our February 5 meeting was part of a formal credentialing ceremony for ambassadors recently arrived in Moscow, which was hosted by Putin once or twice a year in the Grand Kremlin Palace. Foreign Minister Lavrov and Ambassador Ushakov were present, as more than twenty ambassadors presented their credentials to Putin personally. I was told that I would have a meeting with Putin after the ceremony, for which he was customarily late. Like autocrats throughout history, his practice was to keep people waiting and then make a dramatic entrance without a hint of contrition, no matter how large or august the audience was. It was a blunt way to show his interlocutors that he was the boss.

I was intensely curious about the man, having read as much as I could about him from open sources and classified reporting over the years. Putin was good with languages, I knew; he was fluent in German from his five years of service in the 1980s with the KGB in Dresden, and he would converse as president in that language with Chancellor Merkel. He also could speak English, having begun English lessons in 1990 shortly before he retired from the KGB. It was rumored that he intensified his study when he began attending G8 leaders' meetings in 2000 (until Russia was suspended in 2014) and did not like to have the other leaders talking among themselves in English without him. Nonetheless, he relied on a translator in most public meetings with English speakers—though he did switch between Russian and English in a high-profile interview with Oliver Stone in 2017—and he used a translator with me. Indeed, when we met after the ceremony in the grandeur of Saint Alexander Hall in the palace on February 5, it was just the two of us and a translator.

During our meeting, I was impressed with Putin's physical appearance. For a sixty-seven-year-old Russian male—not known as the healthiest cohort—he was fit and trim, with clear blue eyes and a healthy complexion. He spoke in a soft voice and exuded an air of supreme confidence and nonchalance. He walked with a bit of a strut, swinging his left arm but holding his right arm by his side in an odd manner that was widely reported to be the result of his years of training to keep his right hand near the weapon he wore on his hip as a KGB officer. Whether or not he had received such training, or whether it could possibly have had an impact on his gait decades later, it certainly bolstered the swaggering KGB image that he cultivated for the Russian people and projected to the world.

With his affectations—late arrivals, KGB swagger, slow movements and posturing, and sotto voce style—Putin reminded me of the gangster Paul Cicero, played by Paul Sorvino in Martin Scorsese's classic film *Goodfellas,* about whom the narrator, Henry Hill, observes, "Paulie might have moved slow, but it was only because Paulie didn't have to move for anybody." Putin let everyone who came within his orbit know that he did not have to move for anybody.

During our meeting, Putin had two messages to convey. First, he repeated a proposal that he had recently announced, to organize a meeting of the leaders of the five countries (the United States, the PRC, the UK, France, and Russia) that are permanent members (the so-called P5) of the UN Security Council to commemorate the seventy-fifth anniversary of the founding of the UN in 1945. I told him that President Trump was aware of the proposal and considering it. Putin then offered as a rationale for a P5 leaders meeting a potential topic for discussion that I had raised previously in the strategic security dialogue with the Russians about including the PRC in our future arms control negotiations. Clearly aware of this idea, Putin said if the P5 leaders met in the format he suggested, nuclear arms control could be a relevant topic for discussion, because all five countries had nuclear weapons. Piggybacking on his point but trying to direct the discussion toward what I viewed as a much more substantive issue, I observed that the most important country to be included in any future arms control negotiations was the PRC, because of its large and growing nuclear arsenal and plans for increased growth. The UK and France had nuclear weapons, but their programs were smaller and relatively static compared to the PRC's program.

But Putin was not really interested in multilateral arms control negotiations, which my subsequent discussions with officials at the Russian MFA confirmed, and he was even less interested in talking about the subject with the American ambassador. What he was most interested in was a P5 leaders meeting. He concluded our discussion of the topic by shrugging his shoulders and saying he thought a P5 leaders meeting was a good idea, but if we disagreed, that was fine with him.

Putin was affecting a "Why would I care what you think?" attitude—but I knew that he really wanted a P5 leaders meeting. He had come up with the idea himself. The meeting would give him increased stature on the world stage, something he craved and believed he had earned and deserved. Yet his response to me was classic Putin, as I would come to understand: the more he wanted something, the less he was willing to show it, as that would be a potential weakness or vulnerability to be exploited by an adversary. In his mind, the projection of strength and control was paramount.

Once he had distanced himself sufficiently from his pet project, Putin moved on to his second topic, his invitation to President Trump to attend the large Victory Day parade on Red Square, on May 9, 2020, to commemorate the seventy-fifth anniversary of the Allied victory in the Great Patriotic War—what we call World War II. It was very important to Putin for world leaders, and especially the American president, to join him in Moscow in front of Lenin's Tomb to honor the Soviet Union's victory over Nazi Germany and watch a long and impressive Russian military parade. I responded the same way I had in my earlier meeting with Ambassador Ushakov: President Trump was grateful for the invitation and would consider it as he reviewed his spring schedule in what was shaping up to be a busy reelection year. Putin's reaction was another shrug with an "I don't care whether Trump attends or not" look on his face. Again, the more he wanted something, the less he allowed himself to show it.

Putin nodded and smiled to indicate that our meeting was over. He had made the points he wanted to make and was done with me, although he had allowed me to say more to him than I thought he would. I would see him in the future, but most likely in the company of a more senior US official (the president or the secretary of state). It was rare for Putin (as for many heads of state) to meet with any ambassador and therefore very unlikely I would be in his presence again one-on-one.

What struck me most about my conversation with Putin was how important the historical memory of World War II was to him—politically and emotionally—even as the world was entering the third decade of the twenty-first century. The two subjects he presented to me in that first meeting, and that he knew I would promptly relay to the White House and the State Department, were both inextricably connected to the same period at the end of World War II in mid-1945, when the UN was created and the Allies triumphed over Nazi Germany. The insidious problem with his invocation of World War II, however, was that Putin twisted popular memory—fake history, as opposed to fake news—to suit his political needs and justify his imperial ambitions.

Indeed, the history of World War II was a fraught subject for me as ambassador, and it came up repeatedly during the seventy-fifth anniversary year. The Russian government and political commentators were watchful for, and quick to pounce on, any inadvertent statement by an American official that did not, in their opinion, give proper credit to the Red Army and the sacrifices of the Soviet peoples in the defeat of Nazi Germany. The Russians were fierce guardians of this proud historical legacy. I was always careful in this regard, both as a matter of diplomacy and as a matter of historical accuracy, to recognize the heroic and bloody sacrifices of the Soviet Union and the Red Army in the war, citing the 27 million Soviet dead (according to recent Russian historical sources, which I accepted for the purposes of any remarks that I gave in Russia). And to be sure, whichever statistics one uses, Russia's losses dwarfed the losses of the other Allies who fought against Nazi Germany. What bothered me was the warped narrative that Putin and the Kremlin nationalists pushed—a narrative in which it was Russia that won the Great Patriotic War against Nazi Germany, and Russia alone that should be celebrated.

There were several significant problems with this version of history. First, it equated the Russian Federation with the Soviet Union, when in fact they were not the same country. The Soviet Union was composed of fifteen republics, including Russia, Ukraine, Belarus, and Georgia, each of which has been for decades an independent country. The wartime Soviet leader was a Georgian, Joseph Stalin. The largest Soviet republic was indeed Russia, which suffered huge losses during the Great Patriotic War, but Russians were not the only ones who sacrificed and were killed. The per capita casualty rate was higher for Ukrainians than for Russians. And according to Ukrainian sources, almost one in five Soviet citizens named a hero of the Soviet Union during the war was a Ukrainian. The glorious Soviet victory was not solely a Russian victory.

Second, the narrative put forth by Putin and the Kremlin nationalists had no place for the real and essential contributions that the other Allied powers made to defeating Germany. For example, the Russian government in 2020 did not properly acknowledge that in 1940 and the first half of 1941, while the Soviet Union was at peace with Nazi Germany under the August 1939 Molotov-Ribbentrop Pact, known officially as the Treaty of Non-Aggression between Germany and the Union of Soviet Socialist Republics, the United Kingdom stood alone against the Nazis and fought and won the Battle of Britain.

Nor could the Russian government in 2020 properly acknowledge the contributions of the United States to the Allied victory in Europe, and its indispensable (in fact decisive, as even Soviet leaders Stalin and Nikita Khrushchev concluded) material support to the Soviet Union and the Red Army. During the darkest days of the war, the United States contributed over $180 billion (in today's dollars) in equipment and resources under the Lend-Lease Act, starting in November 1941. The United States provided a vast supply of jeeps, trucks, tanks, aircraft, and fuel, and a large percentage of the explosives used by the Red Army during the war.

Even more egregiously, the war in the Pacific against the Empire of

Japan was virtually ignored in the Russian nationalists' 2020 narrative of the Great Patriotic War, except for criticism of the United States for using atomic bombs to destroy Hiroshima and Nagasaki. Indeed, the Soviet Union was neutral in the war against Japan until days before the Japanese announced their surrender in August 1945, when the Soviet Union declared war on and seized territory from Japan. Neither the Soviet Union nor Russia executed a formal peace treaty with Japan, and none exists to this day because of a continuing dispute over the Kuril Islands, a territory seized by the Soviets at the very end of the war. Thus, as a legal matter, Russia and Japan are still technically at war.

History, and particularly the history of World War II, is a potent tool for Putin and the Kremlin, because that history still resonates powerfully with the Russian people in ways that are difficult for an average Western observer to understand. The staggering scope of the destruction, and the loss of so many millions during World War II still linger, and in many ways are still fresh in popular memory. The United States celebrates its "greatest generation"—including close members of my family—but not on the scale or with the emotional intensity that Russia mourns, honors, and proudly celebrates the victory of *its* greatest generation. The parade of the Immortal Regiment in Victory Day celebrations in Moscow and cities across Russia is a poignant example: thousands and thousands of ordinary Russians march, almost all of them carrying pictures of dead relatives or friends, to "immortalize" the men, women, and children who sacrificed so much to defend their homeland and defeat Nazi Germany.

Putin himself marched in Immortal Regiment parades and had a personal claim to this legacy. Although he was born seven years after the war, his family had endured great suffering and loss during the brutal siege of Leningrad by Nazi Germany. His father was severely wounded while serving in the army, and his older brother Viktor died of diphtheria and starvation during the siege in 1942. Putin had a deep connection to this history, in short, and he spoke with real passion about the Great Patriotic War.

But Putin also used a distorted history of the war and its aftermath in support of his geopolitical ambition for Russia. The *Christian Science Monitor* reported in 2016 that one of the founders of the Immortal Regiment movement "complained that [the] idea for spontaneous, voluntary, and noncommercial acts of memory has been hijacked by the Russian state and turned into a regimented spectacle that validates official views."

Putin manipulated popular memory of the war in Russia and turned it into a geopolitical weapon, because of an even deeper connection that he felt to Russia's history—or at least one particular aspect of it. This dimension of the Russian experience was much darker and more nefarious, a far cry from the sacrifices of the country's "greatest generation." Tellingly, however, it exerted an even greater emotional claim on him: defining him not only as a Russian, but also as a person.

---

The single most important thing to know about Vladimir Putin, I came to realize, was that he was, and proudly called himself, a Chekist. This was widely acknowledged among Russia experts in the West: as a former Western diplomat in Moscow observed, "If Putin were to agree to describe himself in one word, his likely choice would be 'Chekist.'" But the implications of this self-description for Russia, its government, and its place in the world were not well understood.

Chekists were a subset of the *siloviki*, the "strongmen" in Russia. Rather than being members of a fraternal organization, like Freemasonry, or some secret society, Chekists were specifically the product of the security services: the FSB, the KGB, and their predecessors throughout Russian and Soviet history back to the Russian Revolution in 1917. A former KGB general quoted by *The Economist* said that "a Chekist is a breed....A good KGB heritage—a father or grandfather, say, who worked for the service—is highly valued" among the members of the "breed."

The original Chekists worked for the All-Russian Extraordinary Commission, commonly known as the Cheka (a shorthand based on the commission's Russian language acronym). The Cheka was created on December 20, 1917, by the Council of People's Commissars of the Russian Soviet Federative Socialist Republic, chaired by Vladimir Lenin, and was led by Felix Dzerzhinsky, a former Polish aristocrat who became a Bolshevik revolutionary. Established to combat counterrevolutionaries and prevent sabotage, the organization was turned by Lenin and Dzerzhinsky into a dreaded secret police service that arrested, imprisoned, tortured, and executed all opponents of the revolution, real or imagined, without any constraints imposed by law or an independent judiciary.

The Cheka, as a secret police organization, was not a novel development in Russia. In the late Russian Empire, the tsars had the Department for Protecting the Public Security and Order, known by its English acronym as the Okhrana, which was founded in 1881 to combat political terrorism and revolution. Like the Cheka, the Okhrana became notorious for arbitrary arrests and torture, but it was not nearly as efficient and brutal a tool of oppression as the Cheka.

Ultimately, all secret police organizations in Russia and the Soviet Union trace their lineage back to Ivan IV, or Ivan the Terrible, who created the Oprichniki, or "men set apart." This elite bodyguard swore sole allegiance to the tsar and his family and were otherwise outside the law. Their sole purpose was to protect Ivan, who was in his person the state, and to torture and execute anyone disloyal to him. The Oprichniki were legendary (and notorious) in Russian history as hard, violent men who wore long black leather coats or tunics and rode black horses with a severed wolf's or dog's head attached to their saddles, a not-so-subtle reminder that their job was to sniff out the tsar's enemies and kill them.

The original Chekists during the Russian Revolution and Civil War adopted both the look of the Oprichniki—the black leather coats, if not the severed heads—and their methods. The Cheka did not enforce any law and was not bound by any law, and thus had unlimited power. The Chekists alone decided who was a threat to the revolution as a class enemy or worse; they also were executioners as well as judge and jury, imposing swift and brutal retribution for any perceived transgression. In the five years from its creation in December 1917 to 1922, the Cheka tortured and murdered a huge number of people, conservatively estimated to be in the many tens of thousands across Russia, in what became known as the Red Terror.

After the Cheka was dissolved in February 1922, its functions and culture were absorbed into successive secret police organizations in the Soviet Union and the Russian Federation, including the KGB and today's FSB. It was that secret police establishment and culture, nurtured and maintained by the Chekist "breed" over a hundred years, that came to form the core of Putin's power. What George Kennan, one of my predecessors as ambassador, observed about the Kremlin in 1946 was equally true when I arrived in Moscow: the "regime is a police regime par excellence, reared in the dim half world of Tsarist police intrigue, accustomed to think primarily in terms of police power. This should never be lost sight of."

It was a senior officer in the UK's Secret Intelligence Service, or MI6, who first told me that the only way to understand the contemporary Russian government is to view it as an "intelligence state." But it was a senior US intelligence official who educated me on the nature of the Russian government and the regime that Putin had created. We spent many hours every week discussing and analyzing how Russia is dominated by its security services and led by a president who is a self-proclaimed Chekist—personally identifying with those responsible for the Red Terror. In fact, Putin kept a statue of "Iron Felix" Dzerzhinsky in his office when he was the director of the FSB. Every year he enthusiastically celebrated the holiday on December 20, the date the Cheka was founded, to honor the Russian security services and known popularly as Chekist Day. Putin once joked that he and a group of fellow Chekists from the KGB were tasked to infiltrate the new Russian government and were "successfully fulfilling its task."

Putin is thus the preeminent Chekist of his generation, leading a small group of chosen men with the training, background, and disposition to defend Russian civilization from its enemies at home and abroad. Although never bound by law, the Chekist "breed" has its own code and rules, an omertà like that of an organized crime family. An important part of that code is loyalty—so once a Chekist, always a Chekist. As Putin himself has said, "There are no 'former' Chekists" and there is "no such thing as a former KGB man."

As ambassador, I drew several important conclusions about Putin and his government by viewing them through the historical Chekist prism. My confidence in these conclusions was bolstered by the fact that George Kennan had drawn the very same conclusions seventy-five years before me.

My first conclusion was that there was not, and had never been, a higher priority for Putin as a Chekist than maintaining the power of the state, whether in the person of the tsar, in the leadership cadre of the Communist Party of the Soviet Union, or in Putin himself as president of the Russian Federation. Indeed, in Russia it had always been thus, whether with the Oprichniki (Ivan IV), the Okhrana (Alexander III and Nicholas II), the Cheka (Lenin), the NKVD (Stalin), the KGB (Khrushchev, Brezhnev, et al.), or the FSB (Putin).

When I was the US ambassador to Russia, Putin *was* the Russian state. Vyacheslav Volodin, who served as chairman of the State Duma while I was stationed in Moscow, once famously said, "There is no Russia today if there is no Putin," and, as any good Chekist would declare, "any attack on Putin is an attack on Russia." Putin's power and the continuation of his rule were his only ends and, as Kennan observed about Russian leaders, "in seeking that security of their own rule they [are] prepared to recognize no restrictions, either of God or man, on the character of their methods."

My second conclusion was that in preserving the power of the state in the person of Putin, Russian leadership would shamelessly advance any position or argument, no matter how counterfactual or ahistorical, that was useful to support Putin (the state) at any given moment. Hence, there was no "truth" when defending Putin's power. According to Kennan, "[t]he very disrespect of Russians for objective truth—indeed, their disbelief in its existence—leads them to view all stated facts as instruments for furtherance of one ulterior purpose or another." In 2020, as in many prior years, that purpose was the protection of the state. And the state, in turn, was Putin.

My third conclusion was that there could be no independent sources of power in Russia beyond Putin and the Kremlin, and thus he required "the submission or destruction of all competing power." As was true for Russian leaders throughout history, under Putin no one else would be allowed to accrue power that was beyond his control. Thus, as Kennan noted about Stalin, that field of dominance included "the Russian Orthodox Church, with its foreign branches." I often said in sorrow to my embassy colleagues that there is nothing sacred in Russia. Putin and the FSB used the Russian Orthodox Church just as Stalin did during World

War II. Before that war, it was Stalin who had endorsed the persecution of priests and the Church; but after the German invasion in June 1941, he invoked the Church and its history to rouse the Russian people to defend their motherland and their ancient Christian civilization. Putin relied on the Church in the same way, as he promoted and defended a narrative of Russia and its civilization under siege by the decadent West. The Church was under his influence, to be sure (with rumors of undercover FSB officers studying at seminaries), and it had proven to be a useful tool for him, as for his predecessors.

That leads to my fourth conclusion, which was the continuing need for a menacing foreign enemy. Kennan invoked the "powerful hands of Russian history and tradition" when he wrote that the

> Kremlin's neurotic view of world affairs is [a] traditional and instinctive Russian sense of insecurity. Originally, this was insecurity of a peaceful agricultural people trying to live on [a] vast exposed plain in [the] neighborhood of fierce nomadic peoples. To this was added, as Russia came into contact with [the] economically advanced West, fear of more competent, more powerful, more highly organized societies in that area. But this latter type of insecurity was one which afflicted rather Russian rulers than [the] Russian people; for Russian rulers have invariably sensed that their rule was relatively archaic in form, fragile and artificial in its psychological foundation, unable to stand comparison or contact with [the] political systems of Western countries.

A sinister foreign power was used by Stalin, and similarly by Putin, as the rationale for suppressing internal dissent, and to maintain power and authority against the threat of the West. Indeed, for Putin, as Kennan observed for Stalin, "the menace confronting [Russian] society from the world outside its borders is founded not in the realities of foreign antagonism but in the necessity of explaining away the maintenance of dictatorial authority at home."

The idea of a foreign menace, combined with Russian insecurity about and lack of confidence in the worth or development, economically or technologically, of Russian society in comparison with the West, created a toxic brew of hostility and paranoia. All of this made it difficult for the United States to develop a productive relationship with Russia. There was always a sense of envy and distrust.

I thought it was uncanny how my own views on Putin and his government were reflected in Kennan's writings from seventy-five years ago—an American describing a Communist government led by Joseph Stalin in the last century. In some sense Kennan was my muse, as I kept dog-eared copies of his Long Telegram and X article on my desk at the embassy. It was hard for me to escape his presence, because my office had an attached conference room that the State Department had named after him, with a bookcase containing all the many books he had written over his long career.

But while he was my Russia muse in Moscow, Kennan also was a cautionary standard for me in a different way. This had to do less with his pointed observations about Russia than with the length of his tenure there as ambassador.

Kennan was appointed the US ambassador to the Soviet Union in 1952 by President Truman. After only five months in Moscow, however, he was declared persona non grata by Stalin—although not because of his prior critical commentary on the Soviet Union and its leaders and policies. In fact, Kennan was also a critic of US foreign policy under Truman. Ambassador Averell Harriman once said of Kennan, who had been his deputy chief of mission, that he was "a man who understood Russia but not the United States."

What raised Stalin's ire, when Ambassador Kennan spoke at a press conference in Berlin while on leave from his post in Moscow, was something that touched that most sensitive Russian nerve: World War II. Kennan, who served at the US embassy in Berlin before the war, was interned for almost six months in Nazi Germany after Hitler declared war on the United States in December 1941, and was finally repatriated with other US embassy officials because of their diplomatic immunity. At the September 1952 press conference, Kennan was asked to compare his treatment by the Soviets as ambassador with his treatment by the Nazis as an internee. Kennan made what Stalin considered an unflattering comparison with the Nazis, and the Soviet Union immediately declared him persona non grata and would not let him return to Moscow.

There were two aspects of this episode, a musty bit of diplomatic trivia, that stood out to me. First, how short the legendary Kennan's tenure was as ambassador. (I had my own little personal celebration when I passed my fifth month as ambassador and had not been expelled by Putin.) Second, how sensitive the Russians were and still are about the Second World War. I marveled at the ways the Russians are still captivated by the war and use the war and its aftermath to explain and justify their current conduct.

Kennan was not perfect, and he later acknowledged his mistake at the Berlin press conference. I found some of his criticisms of US policy in the late twentieth century unpersuasive and believed Ambassador Harriman's pithy assessment of Kennan might have had some validity. But there was no doubt in my mind—or Harriman's—about Kennan's insights on the Soviets and the Russians (terms that Kennan used interchangeably in the Long Telegram and X article). He had concluded that the "pursuit of unlimited authority domestically, accompanied by the cultivation of the semi-myth of implacable foreign hostility, [had] gone far to shape the actual machinery of Soviet power." I drew the same conclusion about Putin and his government seventy-five years later. This was not a new phenomenon in Moscow that the United States was confronting.

———————

Putin's drive for complete dominance within Russia was accelerating as I began my tenure as ambassador. The Kremlin announced major changes in government personnel and even more significant proposals to amend the Russian Constitution in January 2020. The constitutional amendments would allow Putin, who was term-limited under the existing constitution to two terms, ending in 2024, to continue to serve as president for two more terms that would end in 2036, when, if he lived, he would be eighty-four. In addition to the constitutional amendments, all elements of the Russian government and administrative state under Putin were engaged in a crackdown on what was left of the political opposition, independent media, and civil society in the country. All three categories of

changes—in personnel, the constitution, and statutes and regulations—
were patently designed to strengthen and extend Putin's control over the
government and the country.

The personnel changes, although a surprise, at least to the US government and its new ambassador, were the least impactful. Putin removed
Prime Minister Dmitry Medvedev, who had served as president from
2008 to 2012, when Putin was term-limited from serving a third consecutive term (he had served his first two terms from 2000 to 2008). Putin
had been prime minister during Medvedev's presidency, and in 2012 Medvedev deferred to Putin, who ran and won reelection as president. The
Russian Constitution had been amended to extend the presidential term
from four to six years, so Putin served until 2018. He appointed Medvedev
as prime minister at the start of his third term, and when he was reelected
to a fourth term, in 2018, he retained Medvedev.

The replacement of Medvedev as prime minister in 2020 was a significant but not a shocking development, because he was not perceived as an
independent, preeminent force in Russian politics as compared to Putin.
There were widespread rumors that Putin did not respect him, because
he thought Medvedev was weak, feckless, and an alcoholic. The most significant weakness for Medvedev, however, was likely that he was not a
Chekist. He was a lawyer and law professor by training, and although he
was from Leningrad and had worked closely with Putin for years in Saint
Petersburg and Moscow, he was not of the right "breed."

After removing Medvedev as prime minister, Putin appointed him
deputy chair of the Security Council, on which Putin was chair and Nikolai Patrushev was secretary (firm Chekist hands in control). As the new
prime minister, Putin appointed Mikhail Mishustin, a technocrat who
for the prior ten years had been the head of the Federal Taxation Service,
even further removed from the Chekist "breed" and no threat to Putin
politically. His appointment was viewed as an effort to install a competent
manager of the sprawling Russian administrative state. Mishustin was not
generally perceived as a presidential successor that Putin was grooming.

And presidential succession had been a lively topic of debate in Russia
because Putin repeatedly declared, after he was reelected in 2018, that he
would comply with the constitution's term limits, as he had in 2008, and

would not serve as president beyond 2024. That had obviously changed, however, and the debate over who would succeed Putin suddenly had less immediate relevance when, on January 15, 2020, Putin announced in a speech to the Federal Assembly—the State Duma (lower house) and the Federation Council (senate)—a series of proposed constitutional amendments. The most significant proposed changes to the constitution, and there were many changes, involved presidential term limits. All the amendments were drafted by a commission that Putin had appointed.

This was a surprising and shocking development. There were two principal changes to the constitutional article on presidential term limits. First, the limit on two terms was amended to drop the requirement of consecutiveness. Thus, the amendment would strengthen term limits by restricting a president to two terms, whether back-to-back or not. Putin relied on the consecutiveness requirement when he ran for two terms as president in 2012 and 2018, after he was elected to two terms in 2000 and 2004. But the concept of term limits would be rendered virtually nugatory with respect to Putin because another proposed amendment would negate, in applying the term limits article, any prior terms served by the current and former presidents (Putin and Medvedev). Putin could thus serve two full six-year terms as president, starting in 2024.

Some of the other proposed constitutional amendments were also important. One would provide that the Russian Constitution takes precedence over international law. Another, which I thought was very significant, would make it illegal to cede Russian territory to a foreign power. This amendment had major implications for the conflict in Ukraine after the annexation in 2014 of Crimea. This amendment would preclude any Russian leader from bargaining away Russia's claim to Crimea. It also would begin to lay some of the groundwork for the potential future absorption into Russia of the separatist Donetsk People's Republic and the Luhansk People's Republic in the Donbas.

In reporting on this provision to Washington, I noted that it was fortunate that Secretary of State William Seward had bought Alaska from Russia when he did in 1867 (Russian government officials were generally not amused when I thanked them for letting us take that property off their hands). But the proposed constitutional amendments were no laughing matter. Other amendments propagated Putin's historical narrative about the greatness of the Russian civilization, for example, by protecting the Russian language as the language of the state and religious faith as part of the Russian heritage. Russia was clearly headed in a bad direction if these amendments were adopted, guaranteeing as they did repression for people inside the country and danger for those beyond its borders.

Purporting to follow the procedure for amending the constitution (although some, like my friend Vladimir Kara-Murza, a well-known political activist and journalist, disputed the constitutionality of the process), Putin submitted the proposed amendments to the State Duma and the Federation Council for review in late January 2020. In March, the State Duma, the Federation Council, all eighty-five of the regional Russian legislatures, and the Constitutional Court of Russia approved the amendments. Putin also proposed a national referendum, not provided for in the constitution, on the proposed amendments in April.

Meanwhile, the State Duma, regulatory agencies, law enforcement bodies, and the security services were adopting, amending, and enforcing laws and regulations targeting civil society and any political opposition to Putin. Only the so-called systemic opposition—parties and politicians nominally opposed to Putin's United Russia party but ultimately supportive of the government—would be tolerated, and then only barely to maintain the veneer of democracy. Any person or organization that actually engaged in independent thought or advocacy, whether in the media, the academy, or the village square, would be stopped, because no one could be allowed to amass power and influence that would threaten Putin and the state.

The Russian government already had a sweeping array of laws and regulations to crush the nonsystemic opposition (i.e., genuinely opposed to Putin and United Russia), whether organizations or individuals. Most of the laws and regulations were premised on the illusion of fighting foreign influence. Domestic political opposition leaders have always been portrayed as the stooges of foreign governments and organizations hostile to Russia. For the Kremlin to silence an individual, all that was necessary was to designate him or her a "foreign agent." Organizations could be designated as "undesirable." Both individuals and organizations also could be designated "extremist" or, even worse, "terrorists." Earning one of those designations resulted in fines, lengthy imprisonment, or usually both for individuals.

There were also alternative means of silencing the opposition by selectively enforcing otherwise neutral laws or rules, for example by vigorously enforcing time, place, and manner restrictions on public assemblies—to avoid traffic congestion or to maintain access to public facilities—but not enforcing the same rules against state-sponsored or favored organizations or individuals. Then there was the old-fashioned Cheka way of extrajudicial killings, forced disappearances, and mysterious falls from high windows. This included the murder of leading journalists (Anna Politkovskaya) and political leaders (Boris Nemtsov) in this century, and notorious cases from the last (Leon Trotsky).

———————

Through personnel moves, constitutional reforms, and widespread legal and extralegal actions against civil society and any independent political opposition, Putin worked hard in 2020 to tighten his control. The question I wrestled with as I watched this unfold was why he went through all the effort to feign sham legality for his government's actions. The reason was not, as Putin said, that he had a law degree and was committed to the rule of law. Far from it, clearly the rule of law mattered not a whit to him. But why, I wondered, did he bother with elections? Why not simply declare himself president? (Some Russians would soon begin to say that they preferred the word "leader" because "president" was too Westernized, although I suspected they would not actually adopt that term, because of its echoes of the German term *Führer*, or "leader"—the title borne by Adolf Hitler, Russia's hated nemesis in the Great Patriotic War.)

I believed that the reason Putin insisted on this legal charade was that he craved legitimacy, which is why he would always have a legal pretense for any action he took. The tsars ruled by divine right. The Communists relied on ideology and the dialectic of the class struggle. Putin's only rationale for his rule was the support of the Russian people. He needed to show that they were behind him—whether they actually were or not.

Putin once was asked by a journalist why he should not be considered a twenty-first-century tsar, given how long he had served as president and might continue to serve. Putin responded that he was not a tsar, that he had worked hard for everything he had achieved. He did not inherit it, he earned it (or took it, depending on one's perspective) from the Russian people. The rub is that as a Chekist, he could not entrust his rule—the power of the Russian state—to something as erratic and unreliable as the will of the Russian people. That is why the Kremlin called its system of government a "managed" democracy. But just how the Russian people would be managed, or where their leader would steer them in the years to come, I could never have guessed when I arrived in Moscow as ambassador.

# CHAPTER 7

# ISOLATION AND TRANSITION

IN MID-FEBRUARY 2020, TWO WEEKS after my meeting with President Putin, I was scheduled to return to Washington for a gathering of all the US ambassadors from around the world, at the State Department, organized by Secretary Pompeo. Traveling home to attend the Global Chiefs of Mission (COM) Conference would give me an opportunity to convey in person to leaders from across the US government my initial impressions of our mission in Russia and our relationship with the Russian government.

As I prepared for the trip, Embassy Moscow began to consider whether there would be any significant impact on the operations of our mission from a novel coronavirus that had appeared in Wuhan, China, and was first reported by the World Health Organization (WHO) in early January 2020. I arrived in Moscow days after the WHO had confirmed the existence of Covid-19 on January 10. The first two cases in Russia were reported on January 31 and involved Chinese citizens in remote cities in Siberia and the Russian Far East. The Russian government had no significant comment on that development.

Bart Gorman, the deputy chief of mission, and I developed a routine, starting on my first day at post, of meeting daily to review operations at the embassy and the two consulates. In early February, at one of our daily meetings, Bart and I discussed how the mission might be affected by Covid-19 and what, if anything, we should do to prepare. We were fortunate to have as our regional medical officer at the embassy Dr. Sabrina Haas, who, in addition to serving as our general practitioner attending to the mission's medical needs, also happened to be an infectious disease specialist. Both Sabrina and Bart had gained experience earlier in their careers with severe acute respiratory syndrome (SARS) in Asia.

On their advice, I decided to hold a crisis management exercise (CME) on how we would respond in the event the few existing cases of the Covid-19 virus in Russia turned into something more significant. I presided over the exercise, but Bart and Sabrina led the discussion on the morning of February 12. We certainly hoped we would never have to lock down the mission in a serious pandemic, but we wanted to be prepared, particularly in a less than friendly host country where we believed we would be largely on our own. It was a very preliminary discussion, given what little we knew, but I left the exercise grateful to have such an experienced group on whom to rely in the event of an emergency at the embassy.

Following the CME, I spent the afternoon in a meeting that was one of the strangest I would have as ambassador in Moscow. I had been asked by Secretary Pompeo to meet with Igor Sechin, the CEO of PJSC Rosneft Oil Company, the giant state-controlled energy company, to discuss the support that Rosneft was providing to the illegitimate regime of the dictator Nicolás Maduro in Venezuela. The topic of the meeting was important, but I was skeptical that Sechin and Rosneft would diminish in any way their support for the Maduro regime, which after all was leading one of Russia's most important client states in Latin America. Sechin was a close personal ally of Putin from Leningrad and was widely acknowledged to have had a career in the KGB before working for Putin in Saint Petersburg in the 1990s. Among the most powerful of the *siloviki* in Russia, Sechin had been the CEO of Rosneft since 2012 and had been sanctioned by the United States in 2014 in response to the Russian seizure of Crimea and the military invasion of the Donbas. Rosneft also had been subject to certain US sanctions since 2014.

The meeting, hosted by the Russian MFA at the ministry's elegant Osobnyak guesthouse because I did not want to go to the Rosneft headquarters and the company's CEO did not want to come to the embassy, was one-on-one, with a translator whom Sechin brought with him. At the start, he gave me an unusual gift: an enormous, bright-red, leather-bound book with an old-fashioned lock and gold-leaf type for the title on the cover. It was a copy of Karl Marx's *Das Kapital,* in German. He smiled as he showed it to me. My immediate reaction was not to touch it, because I did not know what a gift like that, from someone with Sechin's background, might have inside it. But I had to admit that he had a sense of humor. He put the book aside and we sat down for the meeting.

Sechin began by passing across the table a deck of slides in English that was an overview of Rosneft's global operations. He gave a presentation to me as if I were considering an investment in Rosneft. Describing what a valuable and efficient enterprise it was, he concluded that the United States should lift its sanctions and allow US companies to work with Rosneft, which would be very profitable for them.

I told him that was impossible, considering what was happening in Ukraine. I said I was there to discuss only Rosneft's operations in Venezuela, which were supporting a dictator that was ruining the Venezuelan economy, and its oil industry in particular. I suggested that Rosneft's losses could be substantial if the Venezuelan economy collapsed completely, and I wanted to explore whether the United States could facilitate Rosneft's exit from Venezuela before that happened.

Sechin smiled and continued with his presentation on Rosneft and its global operations and prospects. He was intentionally talking past me and ignoring the issue I had raised. I had expected he would not be very interested in what I was proposing, but I wondered why he was wasting his time (and mine) with a presentation on what a great company Rosneft was, as well as his gift of the gaudy volume of *Das Kapital.* He knew in advance exactly why I had requested to speak with him, and it was not to discuss the merits of Rosneft's global business. Nonetheless, I used the rest of the meeting to get an education about Rosneft from its CEO.

I would be able to report fully to Secretary Pompeo on my curious meeting with Sechin while I was home in Washington for the Chiefs of Mission Conference. Before I left Moscow, however, I hosted a large event at Spaso House for hundreds of young Russian women and girls interested in science, technology, and engineering. The guest of honor was a famous retired NASA astronaut, Dr. Anna Fisher, who had the distinction of being the first mother in space when she flew on the Space Shuttle

*Discovery* in November 1984. The first woman in space was a Russian, Cosmonaut Valentina Tereshkova, in the Soviet Vostok program in June 1963. The event with Dr. Fisher was a fun and worthwhile evening for the young Russians in attendance. I planned to host many more large events like that at Spaso House when I returned.

My trip home allowed me to spend time with my family, whom I had not seen in almost a month. Grace and I were scheduled to travel back and forth between Washington and Moscow as frequently as we could. And beyond our regular telephone calls, we also developed a routine of Sunday night (Moscow time) family video calls. But they were no substitute for being home.

After arriving in Washington on February 19 and spending a few days with Grace, I made the most of my time professionally with a flurry of appointments during the week of February 24. In addition to seeing Secretary Pompeo and meeting with State Department and other executive-branch colleagues, I had numerous meetings with senators and members of Congress on Capitol Hill. I reached out to my friend Alex M. Azar, the secretary of Health and Human Services, for a meeting to get his insights on the pandemic and what I should be preparing for in Moscow. Finally, I met with the chairman of the Joint Chiefs of Staff, General Mark A. Milley, whom I had gotten to know when I was deputy secretary of state, to discuss Russia's military posture and the work of the defense attaché office at Embassy Moscow. General Milley is a fellow Bostonian and an intense hockey fan, like me, so I brought him an autographed Slava Fetisov Soviet national hockey team sweater emblazoned with the iconic CCCP across the chest (and Slava's "K" for captain), which he appreciated.

As I was preparing to depart Washington to return to Moscow, I ran into my colleague Ambassador Lewis M. Eisenberg at the State Department, who told me that he was having difficulty with his return flight to Rome, where he was the US ambassador. Lew said that the Covid-19 virus was having a significant impact on Italy and disrupting air travel. Fortunately, I did not have any issues with my return flights to Russia, but Lew's comment was ominous.

On March 3, on my way back to Moscow, I flew through Brussels and stopped in Mons, Belgium, to meet with General Tod D. Wolters,

NATO's Supreme Allied Commander Europe. When I entered General Wolters's headquarters, I received for the first time a fist bump in lieu of a handshake from one of the protocol officers, who apologized but cited the command's increased concerns with the Covid-19 virus. It was yet another signal that Covid-19 was going to change the world quickly and significantly.

When I got back to Embassy Moscow, Bart, Dr. Haas, and I had a series of meetings to discuss how we would adapt to the Covid-19 pandemic. A Russian citizen in Moscow had recently tested positive for the virus after a trip to Italy. The pandemic clearly was coming to Russia—in fact, it was already there, although the Russian government had made no official announcement—and we needed to prepare. The most pressing question I had to address was whether I would continue with the travel I had planned to the two US consulates in Russia during the month of March. My first trip was to Yekaterinburg, scheduled for March 15–16. The trip to Vladivostok was planned for the end of the month.

I decided that if the Russian airlines were still flying and Dr. Haas did not think it was too unsafe, I would make both trips. It was vital for me to visit the consulates operating under my authority and meet my colleagues in those important cities. Sonata Coulter and I flew to Yekaterinburg on March 15 and had dinner with Consul General Amy Storrow and her team, after we toured the Boris Yeltsin Presidential Center in the heart of the city. We had a busy schedule on the following day, meeting with, among others, Metropolitan Kirill of Yekaterinburg and Verkhoturye, an important leader in the Russian Orthodox Church. I visited the Church of All Saints (or the Church on the Blood), which was built on the site of the Ipatiev House—where Nicholas II, the last emperor of Russia, and his family were executed by the Bolsheviks in July 1918. I was impressed with the veneration of Nicholas and the royal family by the Russian Orthodox Church, although I could not help but wonder what the Russian political class thought of it.

In addition to being able to spend time with Amy to talk about Yekaterinburg, the region, and her consulate, I also met with each of the officers and staff at the post. They were doing impressive work for the United

States, representing our nation's interests in an understaffed consulate in an important Russian city. But I was disappointed that local government officials had declined to meet with me on my first trip to the region, which would have been typical for a visit by the US ambassador and which contrasted with my earlier reception in Moscow. Amy was not sure why, and I assumed that the message had been passed to local officials to decline meetings with me.

My flight back to Moscow from Yekaterinburg, on the evening of March 16, was the last time I would fly on an airplane or travel any significant distance for the next thirteen months. I was unable to visit the consulate in Vladivostok. The pandemic hit Russia hard, and I was stuck in Moscow, away from Grace and my family. But in a sense, I was lucky. My immediate family and I all survived the Covid-19 pandemic. So many others did not.

––––––––––

The Russian government's response to Covid-19 changed substantially during the month of March, as the virus continued to spread in the country. The first reaction by the Kremlin was to urge calm and to cite the lower infection rate in Russia as compared to other countries in Europe. Putin said on March 17, in a meeting with senior Russian government leaders, that "the situation is generally under control" and Russia "looks much better compared with other countries." Prime Minister Mishustin agreed, acknowledging that the global pandemic "remains challenging," but noting that in Russia "we have the situation with coronavirus under control."

Relying on Russia's lower infection rate, the Kremlin seized an opportunity to garner international goodwill—and to emphasize the health, strength, and generosity of Russia and its people, as compared to the decadent, unhealthy, and incompetent West—by shipping medical supplies, including much-needed ventilators, to a number of other countries. Russian medical personnel were also dispatched to some countries. The supplies were sent in boxes marked prominently in English with FROM RUSSIA WITH LOVE. International media gave extensive coverage to the equipment and personnel that Russia sent to Italy in March 2020, featuring videos of smiling Russians and Italians unloading boxes marked with the FROM RUSSIA WITH LOVE logo.

Putin extended the Russian goodwill campaign to the United States. In a phone call with President Trump in late March, he offered to send medical supplies, including ventilators, to the United States. Trump accepted and welcomed the gesture, offering to send two hundred American ventilators (which were then in short supply) later to Russia in return. The Russian supplies and forty-five ventilators arrived at JFK International Airport in New York on April 1. The American ventilators were sent in two shipments, on May 21 and June 4, to Vnukovo International Airport, outside Moscow. For each shipment from the United States, which arrived in a US Air Force C-17 Globemaster III transport aircraft, I went to Vnukovo to present the ventilators to a representative of the Russian government. I enjoyed observing the wide-eyed expressions on the faces of the Russians as they stared at a hulking US Air Force plane, which is obviously not a common sight in Russia. I also went aboard and enjoyed talking to the pilots and the crew before they had to turn the aircraft around and return to Germany. I joked with them that I needed to take a few deep breaths of freedom inside an American plane before I returned to my post, and they rewarded me with a squadron patch.

The delivery of Russian medical supplies to the United States was fairly criticized at the time by many in the US media as a "propaganda coup" for Russia. Adding insult to injury, the Russian ventilators sent to the United States were never used and were ultimately destroyed because they were revealed to be a dangerous fire hazard that caused fires at Russian hospitals in Moscow and Saint Petersburg, leaving several people dead. Russian health regulators soon suspended use of the ventilators, and the Russian propaganda coup lost its potency.

There was further embarrassment for the Russian "humanitarian" propaganda campaign on the international stage, when an Italian newspaper reported that in the creation of the Russian-generated video recordings of the delivery of medical supplies in Italy, "Italians were offered 200 euros for recording videos thanking the Russian authorities for their assistance." And the "assistance" to Italy was not what it seemed, since "at least

80 percent of the supplies were useless." More ominously, Italian media reported that among the "104-man-strong team" of Russian medics sent to Italy were "operatives from Russia's military intelligence service (GRU)." This was yet another example I would cite for the proposition that there was nothing sacred—even medical assistance in a global pandemic—to the Chekists in the Russian government.

Later in the spring and summer of 2020, the thrust of the Russian Covid-19 propaganda shifted to the international race to develop a safe and efficacious vaccine for the virus. The Russian government had been quick to announce in May 2020 that it was developing a vaccine, which would later become known as Sputnik V.

The virus, of course, was paying no attention to the Russian narrative about the extraordinary strength and resilience of a healthy Russia: infection and mortality rates rose quickly. The first Covid-19 death in Moscow was reported on March 19, and by March 24 the mayor of Moscow, Sergei Sobyanin, announced there were five hundred suspected cases in the city. Throughout the pandemic, no one—neither Americans at the US embassy nor Russians on the streets of Moscow—had any confidence in the public health figures released by the Russian government.

On March 25, Putin made the first announcement of a pandemic lockdown in Russia, but he did so in a counterproductive way, at least for purposes of trying to stop the spread of the virus. Apparently unwilling to convey a hard message to the Russian public, Putin said that the week beginning on March 30 would be a nationwide, paid "holiday for workers." Taking advantage of nice spring weather after a hard Russian winter, many Russians not surprisingly started to take advantage of the "holiday" on the weekend before March 30 by celebrating together and congregating in large groups. It was left to local officials to convey a serious health message and issue orders less pleasing to the public. On March 29, Mayor Sobyanin issued a stay-at-home order in Moscow that would start on the following day—the first day of Putin's "holiday." Many regional and local officials across Russia issued orders like Mayor Sobyanin's on March 30. That same day, the Kremlin closed the nation's borders. By April 3, the country was locked down in a "self-isolation regime."

I knew the Russian government was serious, at least initially, about dealing with the pandemic despite Putin's earlier tepid announcement on March 25, because in addition to declaring the "holiday," he also said that the promised referendum on the Kremlin's proposed constitutional amendments—a matter of huge significance to him—would be postponed. The public vote had been scheduled for April 22, and would be delayed. I also wondered how the pandemic would impact another event of singular importance to Putin, the Victory Day Parade, which was scheduled to be held on May 9. If Putin postponed *that* big event, it would underscore the seriousness of his pandemic response.

At the US mission to Russia, in any case, we did not wait for instructions from the Russian government to implement our response to the Covid-19 pandemic. By the time I returned from Yekaterinburg, on the night of March 16, the embassy had altered work schedules and adjusted operations to provide for as much social distancing as we could manage. But we could not simply mandate telework and order everyone to stay at home. A very large percentage of the Americans working at the embassy also lived on the compound, many with their families. The embassy compound thus was both home and work, and everyone needed access to the ground floor of the chancery to visit the commissary and the mail room. We closed the pub in the chancery, Uncle Sam's, but we kept the gym and pool open, with limits on how many people could use them at the same time. Following the examples of the NBA and the NHL, we tried to create our own bubble on the embassy compound. We restricted entry as much as possible by anyone from outside our community.

I continued to live at Spaso House and come to the embassy every morning. Our work needed to continue: the embassy had to be guarded; its systems and equipment had to be maintained; and Washington had to know from our reporting what was happening in Russia. We dispersed most of the Marine security guards out of their rooms in the Marine House at the embassy and into small clusters in other unoccupied living quarters on the compound so that no one marine could infect the entire detachment and wreak havoc with our security. In addition to protecting the embassy, the Marines also provided invaluable unofficial services to our community during the pandemic, from organizing activities for the children at the embassy to making their barber chair in the Marine House available for haircuts by Staff Sergeant Quinton Sloan, who, in addition to being a squared-away marine, had a talent for hairstyling (at least by USMC standards). The regular hair salon on the compound with Russian stylists was closed during the pandemic.

Bart and I, in consultation with Dr. Haas and the leadership of the embassy sections and agencies, had to make difficult decisions every day to keep the mission functioning without endangering safety. The most significant decision I made in March was to suspend operations at the US consulate in Vladivostok. The suspension was necessary because of the isolation of the post, which is over five thousand miles distant from Embassy Moscow. Consulate Vladivostok had traditionally relied on the US embassy in Seoul, which is less than five hundred miles away, in the event of an emergency or for management support. Anticipating that Russia would close its borders and severely limit air travel (which it soon did), I decided we could not risk having a small group of American diplomats stranded in the Russian Far East. It was safer to bring the consulate team to Embassy Moscow, where we had a medical staff and a greater capacity to address any health or other emergency. I decided not to suspend operations at the consulate in Yekaterinburg, because we had a plan for an overland evacuation to Moscow from there if that became necessary. It would be a long trip—one thousand miles—but worth the risk to keep an important diplomatic outpost in the Urals open. Amy Storrow and her consulate team agreed.

I met with Consul General Lou Crishock and his colleagues on March 24 after they had arrived from Vladivostok. They were not happy about having to leave their post and relocate to Moscow—no good diplomat would be—but they understood it was necessary for their safety. They were welcomed with enthusiasm by everyone at the embassy and were integrated as important new additions to our workforce, as we continued to try to do our jobs while also remaining safe.

Among the embassy's most important jobs during the pandemic was helping the thousands of American citizens in Russia and keeping them informed with accurate information. I posted regular video updates on the embassy's website to provide the latest information on travel and the pandemic. Many Americans wanted to leave Russia and return to the

United States but had difficulty making travel arrangements because of the numerous pandemic-related flight restrictions. To address this problem, the embassy chartered a special flight on April 9 that took hundreds of stranded Americans home. This sounds like a simple task, but it was a difficult and labor-intensive effort to coordinate with all the Americans from across Russia who wanted to leave and assemble them at the same airport in Moscow, at the same time, and with the right travel documents to get on the plane. The embassy's consular section under Cathy Holt had the lead, but because of the scale of the work it became a whole-of-embassy undertaking. A large group of us spent the night at the airport, processing passengers—there were few airport personnel available—until the crowded flight with no empty seats departed just before dawn.

As a rule, most of my work during the pandemic in 2020 became virtual; for example, telephone calls with the MFA and Deputy Foreign Minister Ryabkov and his colleagues; and biweekly videoconferences with representatives of the hundreds of US companies that were members of the AmCham. I made several exceptions to this rule, however.

Despite the risks of the pandemic, I continued to meet weekly in person with the ambassadors from the United Kingdom, France, and Germany. Referred to as the Quad, this group of myself and my three colleagues—Her Majesty's ambassador, Deborah Bronnert; Pierre Lévy, the French ambassador; and Ambassador Géza Andreas von Geyr of Germany—met every Thursday morning during my entire tenure as ambassador. We found the meetings extremely valuable, especially during the pandemic, as we discussed how our embassies were coping with the extraordinary developments that had already begun to unfold in Russia, and which would soon accelerate.

Another major exception I made was for the three Americans that we knew of (there may have been others of whom we were unaware) who were wrongfully detained in Russia: Paul Whelan, Michael Calvey, and Trevor Reed. I insisted on visiting each of them in person as often as I could and as the Russians would allow. Whelan's trial concluded on June 15, when he was sentenced to sixteen years in a labor camp. I attended the sentencing and gave a press conference on the steps of the courthouse in

Moscow, wearing a mask and gloves, to complain about the injustice of the secret trial and the evidence used to convict an innocent man.

Two months later, on September 22, I made my first trip to visit Paul at labor camp IK-17 in Mordovia, which is over three hundred miles and an eight-hour drive southeast of Moscow. I traveled in an SUV with my bodyguards, and more bodyguards followed in a trailing SUV. We stayed overnight at a hunting lodge (with fresh bearskin rugs) in a forest near the facility, and I saw Paul the next morning. Camp IK-17 was built before the Second World War, as part of Stalin's notorious Gulag system of prisons, and had housed German POWs during and after the war. It was known for hazardous work conditions, bad food, and frequent supplementary discipline—a euphemism for solitary confinement. The warden told me that I was the first US ambassador ever to visit that miserable place. Unfortunately, it was not my only trip there.

Trevor Reed's trial, which I followed closely, ended on July 30 with a conviction and sentence of nine years in a labor camp. My strategy of keeping a low public profile on his case had failed, and I tried to comfort his father, Joey Reed, who moved to Moscow to be near his son after Trevor was arrested in 2019. Unlike Paul Whelan, Trevor was not promptly transported to a labor camp after his sentencing. He remained in detention in SIZO-5 in Moscow throughout 2020, while his appeal was pending and I visited him there regularly.

As for Mike Calvey, he remained in home detention throughout much of 2020, awaiting trial. I visited him often to discuss his case and any support the US government could provide to him and his legal team. For the moment, he appeared to be the luckiest of the three—but in Russia's unpredictable legal system, that was little comfort for any of us.

I believed that my visits to the Americans wrongfully detained in Russia were important to reassure them that their country had not forgotten about them, and I hoped it might also have some positive impact, however slight, on their mental health in what were otherwise unbearably dreadful circumstances. I wished I could help them as an advocate to make the case for their release to an impartial tribunal, but, alas, there was no independent judicial system available to them in Russia.

I was also concerned about the mental health and well-being of my colleagues at Embassy Moscow. The usual social events at the embassy—gatherings that everyone looked forward to, like the annual July 4th party for which thousands would come to Spaso House, or the Marine Ball in November to celebrate the Corps's birthday—would not be possible for us to stage because of the pandemic. Because the community could not even meet for an in-person town hall, Bart scheduled regular "tele-town-halls" for us to convey information to, and answer questions from, all those affiliated with the mission. It was suboptimal, however, and although we were enduring the isolation far from home as best we could, I worried about the cumulative effect of the strain on our community. At least no one had become critically ill yet, I told myself.

My own spirits drooped when my strongest link to home, my ancient personal iPad, finally expired in late July 2020. I had been cautioned not to bring expensive new personal electronic devices with me to Russia, because they would be penetrated by the Russian security services and thus rendered worthless for personal use after I finished my tour and left Russia. I could use a personal iPad in my residence (or other nonsecure area), but I had to be aware that the Russians would monitor everything on it and could use it for audio and visual surveillance. When I departed post, I would have to leave it behind as an infected hazard. I had an old iPad, so, I figured, why waste money on a new one? That logic quickly fell by the wayside, however, when my old one died.

Despite the cost, I needed a new personal iPad to entertain myself and to have video calls with my family. So, I asked my bodyguards to take me to a large electronics store that had been recommended to me by an embassy colleague. I walked into the store unannounced on a Saturday morning and went to a counter that had a tall stack of iPad boxes on display. I saw the one that I wanted in the stack, but it was difficult to reach, so I pointed it out to a young store clerk. He took the box and went into a backroom off the sales floor. When he returned, he said that my iPad would be ready the following day.

I replied that I would much prefer to pay for the device now and take it with me. But the young man said that would not be possible, because the iPad was not ready.

Incredulous, but beginning to get the picture, I pointed to other customers who were getting similar boxes from the same stack, proceeding to the checkout counter, and walking out of the store with them. The clerk said sheepishly that I could pay for the device today, but he could not let me take delivery until tomorrow.

Realizing that this was going nowhere, I smiled at the clerk and said I understood. Someone needed to prepare the iPad specially for me before I could use it. I said I would come back.

It did not take enhanced training as a counterintelligence officer to understand the situation. I went to the embassy and reported my experience to Steve Sexton, our regional security officer, who laughed. There was not much else that I could do if I wanted a personal iPad; packages from the United States were taking months to reach the embassy in the pandemic.

So long as I kept the device in my residence—where, in accordance with the embassy's protocols, I would never have or discuss sensitive information—and so long as I used it only to watch videos and make family video calls, Steve said, there would not be an increased security risk. I was already using a personal iPad that was almost certainly compromised (remotely), and if the FSB wanted to know the movies and sports highlights I watched, they could have that information. Moreover, the risk of disclosing anything useful to the Russians on a video call was virtually the same as on a (monitored) phone call. I had to speak to my family; I just had to be careful and circumspect.

The episode illustrated the pressure to which everyone at the US embassy was subjected. We needed to be guarded in everything we said and did at every moment, because the Russians were always watching and listening. It was not a fun way to live one's life, but over time it started to become routine, as well as boring and lonely.

I went back to the store and bought the iPad that had been specially prepared for me, resolving to keep it quarantined and use it carefully. But I was disappointed in the FSB's tradecraft. I understood that they wanted to know what videos I was watching at night and what books Grace and I were reading, but I thought they could have accessed the US ambassador's personal electronic device in a more discreet way. I told Steve that I was reminded of a quote from William Peter Blatty's *The Exorcist*: "That's much too vulgar a display of power."

———————

Unfortunately, vulgar displays of power were becoming even more common in Russia as Putin's crackdown continued throughout the pandemic. The most heinous was the attempted murder by the FSB of Alexei Navalny, a very prominent nonsystemic political opposition leader and anti-corruption activist in Russia, on August 20, 2020. Navalny was poisoned in Omsk, Russia, with a dangerous Novichok nerve agent—the same type of chemical weapon used by the GRU in their attempt to kill Sergei Skripal in Salisbury, England, in 2018. As a group, Secretary Pompeo and the foreign ministers of the G7 (the United States, Canada, France, Germany, Italy, Japan, and the UK) condemned what they called the "confirmed poisoning" of Navalny. Not long after, in December 2020, the FSB plot to kill Navalny was documented in a remarkable report by Bellingcat, an investigative journalism group, along with other collaborators, including Navalny himself. He had miraculously survived the poisoning after being medically evacuated to Germany in a coma, through the intervention of Chancellor Merkel.

I thought a great deal about the value of life in Putin's Russia during the pandemic in the spring and summer of 2020. Covid-19 was tearing through the country, as it was virtually everywhere else. There was a severe shortage of hospital beds in Russia, and on April 29 Mayor Sobyanin announced that Moscow had begun constructing temporary hospitals to add ten thousand beds for Covid-19 patients. The next day, Prime Minister Mishustin announced that he had tested positive for the virus. There were several positive tests at the embassy, where the overworked staff in our medical unit was testing everyone as often as possible, but thankfully we had no serious cases yet. Anyone who tested positive on the compound had to isolate until they were cleared by a doctor—another necessary but unfortunate impact of the virus on the embassy's operations.

Putin was extremely cautious with his own health, which was likely a reflection of his age and his KGB-honed paranoia. He went to extreme lengths to isolate himself from the virus, with very few in-person meetings.

Those who were admitted to his presence had to endure long isolation in quarantine and then pass through disinfectant spray tunnels before they could see him. Photos and videos of his meeting with visitors in cavernous rooms, seated at elongated tables that separated him from his guests, were common. Putin has never had a wide circle of advisers whom he consulted, and his personal interactions were even more limited during his Covid-19 isolation.

Amid the uncertainty and danger of the pandemic, Putin announced on May 26 that the Victory Day Parade—which was originally scheduled for May 9 but which he was forced to postpone, just as I had suspected—would be held on June 24. A few days later, the Kremlin announced that the postponed referendum on the proposed constitutional reforms would also be held soon, on July 1. None of the medical experts that I consulted, including American, European, and Russian doctors, believed that it was possible to know at the end of May whether it would be safe to hold those large public events within the next month. Indeed, it seemed very unlikely, given the rate of infections. Nevertheless, on June 8, Mayor Sobyanin declared victory over the virus and announced that Moscow would lift its Covid-19 restrictions on the following day—just in time to begin preparations for the large parade on Red Square and the constitutional referendum. It was clear what value Putin ascribed to human life and public health when weighed against his political agenda.

The Victory Day Parade on June 24 presented a problem for me because President Trump expected a senior US government official to represent him at the event. I had two concerns: The first was the Covid-19 risk, which worried me because of the implications for the mission if I or someone with me at the parade were to get sick. The second was the appearance of participating in Putin's nationalist spectacle, which he clearly intended to use to support his gross abuses of power and imperial ambitions.

My reporting to Washington on how Putin would use the parade for propaganda and disinformation purposes was confirmed less than a week before the Victory Day celebration. On June 18, Putin published a lengthy article, "The Real Lessons of the 75th Anniversary of World War II," in which he reprised his familiar, ahistorical revisions to the record of the

Great Patriotic War. He equated Russia with the Soviet Union ("Russia is the legal successor state to the USSR, and the Soviet period—with all its triumphs and tragedies—is an inalienable part of our thousand-year-long history") and thereby laid claim to "an epic, crushing victory over Nazism [that] saved the entire world." He tried to whitewash the Secret Protocol of Stalin's nonaggression pact with Hitler in 1939, and outrageously dismissed the Soviet invasion, occupation, and annexation of the Baltic states (Lithuania, Latvia, and Estonia) in 1940 as being "implemented on a contractual basis, with the consent of the elected authorities."

It was a staggering weaponization of fake twentieth-century history to be used as a cudgel in Putin's twenty-first-century struggle against the West. I was vigorously opposed to any senior official from the US government supporting Putin's campaign by attending the Victory Day Parade. President Trump was not able to attend, and no other Western leaders were planning to come either. Regrettably, the issue of a stand-in for President Trump was still being debated in Washington, which gave me pause.

I was displeased when the White House, ignoring my advice, proposed that US Air Force General Tod Wolters, the NATO military commander, accompany me to the parade. I do not know where that proposal originated; it certainly was not from General Wolters. The image of a senior US military official in uniform—and the US military commander in Europe, no less—sitting in celebration with Putin, the person singularly responsible for the ongoing violence in Ukraine and undermining security in Europe, at a parade that would distort the history of World War II, was too far beyond the pale for me to accept. In reply, I said that it was a ridiculous idea and that I would not give my approval—the US ambassador's approval, known as country clearance, is needed for any US government official (other than the president and the secretary of state) to enter a country—for General Wolters to enter Russia.

In search of a solution, and seeking to assuage my unconcealed displeasure, my successor as deputy secretary of state, Steve Biegun, called me to say that General Wolters would not be required to attend the parade, but Steve asked whether I would go alone to represent the president. Worn down, and glad to have prevented an even worse outcome, I said that I would. On June 24, the UK ambassador, Deborah Bronnert, and

I sat together inconspicuously in the middle of one of the grandstands on Red Square to watch the parade, which turned out to be an impressive (at least to a civilian like me) military display. Thankfully, no photos of me at the parade appeared in any media. They certainly would have if General Wolters had been sitting with me. The Russian government and media would have had another field day, and the Chekists in the Kremlin would have smiled.

The day after the Victory Day Parade, electronic voting started in Putin's long-desired constitutional reform referendum. In-person voting was held on July 1, and the constitutional reforms endorsed by Putin were approved by 78 percent of those voting—a figure that was surprisingly high in some ways, but less surprising in others. Based on watching many elections in Russia, it appeared to me that voting percentages in the mid- to high 70s seemed to be the sweet spot for the political operatives in the Kremlin who were "managing" the Russian democracy. Any higher and the vote would appear to have been obviously rigged. Much lower would not show sufficient public support. A significantly lower margin also meant cutting it close and the required outcome (the election of a particular candidate or the passage of a referendum question) might not occur if there were technical malfunctions or other mistakes.

Putin might have been able to "manage" Russia's democracy, but he could not control Covid-19, and the pandemic remained a scourge in Russia, with high infection and mortality rates. Putin responded with propaganda and disinformation. The most important message, predictably, had to do with power—with signaling that the Russian government had a handle on the situation. Putin told the faithful on Orthodox Easter, April 19, 2020, amid widespread shortages of hospital beds and doctors across the country, that with regard to Covid-19 in Russia, "the situation is under full control."

The related false claim was that while Covid-19 might be a problem, the outlook was much better in Russia than in other countries. Repeating what he had said in March, Putin told Russian regional governors on September 24, 2020, that the Covid-19 situation in Russia "was far better than in some other countries." The only way he could justify that claim was by the Russian government's manipulation of its public health data, particularly on Covid-19 mortality rates. The statistics were indeed suspect from the beginning of the pandemic. A poll of Russian medical professionals in May 2020, according to Radio Free Europe/Radio Liberty, revealed that "more than a third of doctors working with coronavirus patients in Russia [had] received 'instructions' to manipulate statistics on the COVID-19 outbreak." This may help to explain why, in three separate incidents in late April and early May 2020, doctors "mysteriously [fell] out of hospital windows in Russia," as reported by CNN.

Numerous media and public health organizations were eventually able to document the manipulation of Covid-19 statistics by the Russian government. An analysis of mortality statistics by the *New York Times* showed that deaths in Russia during the pandemic in 2020 were 28 percent higher than in prior years and greater than the increase in the United States and most European countries. From its analysis, the *Times* concluded that Russia's true Covid-19 statistics "belie President Vladimir V. Putin's contention that the country has managed the virus better than most." And the *Times* went further to echo what I had been reporting to Washington: Russia was "more focused on the public-relations and economic aspects of the pandemic than on fighting the virus itself."

This was amply demonstrated in the Russian government's promotion of the Sputnik V vaccine, one of three vaccines produced in Russia. Putin announced with great fanfare on August 11, 2020, that Russia had registered the world's first coronavirus vaccine, Sputnik V. But for Putin to claim that title, the developer of the vaccine, the Gamaleya Research Institute of Epidemiology and Microbiology, in Moscow, had to rush Sputnik V to the market before completing the usually required studies and trials that other competing vaccines in the West were undergoing. Moreover, the Russians were suspiciously slow to share data with international regulators and other researchers, precluding emergency-use authorization by international regulatory bodies, including the WHO and the European Medicines Agency, which never approved Sputnik V. That did not prevent Russia from signing agreements to supply Sputnik V to countries, many in the Global South, that were desperate for any vaccines, whether they were fully investigated and tested or not. In the final analysis, the overriding interests of the Russian government in Sputnik V were public relations and economics, not public health.

This became painfully clear shortly after a meeting that I had with Russian health minister Mikhail Murashko, at his request, at the ministry on July 14, 2020, to discuss vaccines and the pandemic. The minister was a medical doctor from the Urals recently appointed to his position in Moscow. He sought my help in getting US government agencies and health regulators, as well as US pharmaceutical companies, to engage with their Russian counterparts to collaborate on vaccine research and other pandemic-related inquiries. On its face, his proposal was unobjectionable, even laudable. Who would decline to collaborate for the betterment of humankind?

But it was the Russian government making the request, and nothing was ever easy or straightforward with them. On July 16, two days after my meeting with Dr. Murashko, the BBC published a story with the headline "Coronavirus: Russian Spies Target Covid-19 Vaccine Research." The BBC reported that US, UK, and Canadian officials had warned that "hackers 'almost certainly' operating as 'part of [the] Russian intelligence services'" were "targeting organisations trying to develop a coronavirus vaccine in the UK, US and Canada." The New York Times on the same day described Russian hackers as exploiting "the chaos created by the coronavirus pandemic" to "steal intelligence on vaccines from universities, companies and other health care organizations." The Times quoted "American intelligence officials" as concluding that "the Russians were aiming to steal research to develop their own vaccine more quickly, not to sabotage other countries' efforts."

I had no reason to believe that the Russian health minister was specifically aware of the hacking activities of the Russian security services when he met with me on July 14—although I did note that before Dr. Murashko went to medical school, he had worked for the Soviet Ministry of Internal Affairs. In any event, we never spoke again.

———————

Weeks turned into months of isolation in Moscow during the pandemic for my colleagues and me at the embassy. I started to think about the upcoming US presidential election in November, which might have a significant impact on my status as the US ambassador in Moscow. Grace hoped that President Trump would lose, not only because she was (and had long been) politically opposed to him, but also because she believed that would mean I would be asked to resign and come home in January 2021 in a Biden administration. I had to agree with her about the likelihood of that happening if Biden won. I looked forward to being reunited with my family but, on the other hand, I had grown too invested in the mission to hope that I would be yanked out of Russia—and anyway, I had too much to focus on at the embassy in the fall of 2020 than to spend time making speculative plans for after the election.

The pandemic's adverse effects on operations at the mission were piling up as time went by. We had numerous Covid-19 infections, and several community members became sick. Our medical team at post did a terrific job of caring for everyone and bringing those infected and suffering back to health, with one exception. In November, a friend of mine, a senior officer who was very popular at the embassy, became infected and very sick, along with two members of his family. His family members recovered after a few days, but he could not shake his symptoms, which started to worsen. Our doctors advised that he needed to be medically evacuated to the United States.

We arranged for an air ambulance for our colleague through the State Department, and he was taken to a hospital in Washington, where he was admitted to the intensive care unit. He stayed in the ICU for weeks as his condition deteriorated. Eventually he rallied and recovered, but it was an emotionally stressful episode for his family, friends, and everyone at the embassy. Months later, like the resilient US diplomat that he was, he returned to Embassy Moscow, to a rousing welcome.

We were not as fortunate with a former Russian colleague who had worked at the consulate in Vladivostok until we suspended operations there. Yuriy Chernovol had worked at the US consulate for years and was a beloved member of that small team. In early December 2020, we learned that he was sick with Covid-19, and we were concerned because he had a comorbidity as a cancer survivor. It was a blow, particularly to the Americans who had worked with him in Vladivostok, when we learned that he had passed away later that month. The mission had a virtual memorial service for him on December 29, and we planted a tree in the spring at the embassy, with a plaque in his memory.

Considering the significant difficulties that the US mission in Russia faced in dealing with the pandemic, I was proud of our performance in protecting those who worked for us and their families, as well as the services we were able to provide to Americans in Russia. Many other US missions around the world had worse problems. Several had large numbers of medical evacuations and difficulty in getting American citizens out of the country and home.

Among the services that the US mission provided to Americans in Russia was information on, and assistance in, voting in the American presidential election on November 3. For me as ambassador, there was virtually nothing to do in connection with the election, other than to keep domestic politics out of our operations in Moscow. I had told my colleagues on my first day at the embassy that there would be no politics in our work at the mission. I let everyone know that if they had any concerns along those lines, including concerns about the relationship between the White House and the Russian government, or the relationship between Presidents Trump and Putin, they should tell me. I made it part of our ethos that just as we would not tolerate unethical behavior, we would not tolerate political behavior. Most of all, I kept a keen eye out for any inappropriate actions by anyone in the US government (or any American outside of government) regarding Russia.

On election day, because of the time difference in Moscow, I did not begin following the election returns until the early morning of November 4. Amid the uncertainty in the days immediately following the election, I monitored developments closely because I assumed that the outcome would determine whether I would be going home or not. As the days passed and it became clear that Joe Biden was the president-elect, I awaited instruction from Washington on the transition. None was immediately forthcoming. On the contrary, on November 10, Secretary Pompeo said in a press conference at the State Department, apparently in jest, that there would be a "smooth transition to a second Trump administration," which caused upset and confusion at the department.

As the established processes of the Electoral College unfolded in early December, however, there could be no further rational debate about who the president-elect was, and Secretary Pompeo clearly understood this; he designated a highly respected career ambassador, Daniel B. Smith, to head the transition for the State Department and work with the Biden team. I soon received an email from the White House Liaison at the State Department, the office that handles the appointment of noncareer officials and deals with the White House and the Office of Presidential Personnel; every political appointee was expected to prepare a letter of resignation for the president. I also received the paperwork necessary to process my resignation and return travel to the United States.

Shortly after I heard from the White House Liaison, I received a phone call from Ambassador Smith, who was the director of the Foreign Service Institute and someone I knew well from my time as deputy secretary. Dan said the Biden transition team wanted to know whether I would be willing to stay as ambassador in Moscow. I said I would, and asked whether I should continue to process the resignation paperwork and write my resignation letter to the president. Dan said I should, because the final decision to keep me in my post had not been made yet by the president-elect. I wrote a short letter of resignation, effective January 20, 2021, and returned it as instructed to the White House Liaison.

Later that night, in a phone conversation with Grace, I told her about the message from Ambassador Smith. She was incredulous, and very disappointed that we were not talking about my plans for coming home. But she noted that the idea of my being asked to stay in Moscow was a long shot, and I could not disagree when she declared, "There is no way Joe Biden is keeping anyone from the Trump administration, and certainly not Trump's ambassador to Russia." It was certainly my experience over many years in Washington that a new president replaces the political appointees of the prior administration, even if the incoming president is from the same party as the incumbent. In 2008, for example, I knew that if John McCain had won, he would have replaced me as the deputy secretary of commerce, even though I was a lifelong Republican and had served the department loyally and competently. In the case where a challenger beats an incumbent seeking a second term, as in 1992 when Governor Bill

Clinton beat President Bush, it is extremely rare for a political appointee to be held over.

Following Grace's advice, I did not count on remaining as ambassador in Moscow. Nonetheless, about a week later, I received another call from Dan Smith to tell me that the incoming administration definitely wanted me to stay in my position, but they were not prepared to announce that publicly. Thus, I had to continue to give the impression that I was resigning, including by preparing to move. That raised some complications for me, however. If I actually were leaving, I would have to give prior notice of my departure to the Russian MFA and the members of the diplomatic community. But I would lose future credibility if I gave notice and then promptly withdrew it when the incoming administration was prepared to announce that I was staying. I decided not to give notice of my departure to the MFA based on Dan's representation.

As the calendar turned to January 2021, however, I started to get a little anxious because I still had not been authorized to disclose that I was remaining as ambassador. I wondered whether the president-elect might have changed his mind. On January 8, I called Dan to check in. I said that if the incoming administration changed its mind at the last minute and I really had to leave, it would be undiplomatic, to say nothing of embarrassing, for the US ambassador to skip out of town on short notice. Dan understood my predicament and reassured me that I would be asked to stay—but he reiterated that I could not tell my embassy colleagues and had to continue to give the impression that I was leaving before President-elect Biden was inaugurated.

I was in the same position on Friday, January 15, five days before the inauguration on January 20. I had a reservation on a flight out of Moscow on Monday, January 18. My colleagues and I packed up my office in the chancery, and I was preparing to have my personal belongings packed at Spaso House over the weekend. At 8 p.m. on Friday night, Moscow time, Dan finally called to say that it was official and public that I was asked to remain as ambassador. I thanked him for the news and felt a great sense of relief that at least a decision had been made and I knew with certainty where I would be the following week.

I called Grace to tell her that I would not be coming home on Monday.

She had gone through the same ups and downs as I had over the last month. She was, as always, understanding, and said she was proud that the new president wanted me as his ambassador in Moscow. Neither of us was pleased that we would remain separated, and I knew she was, quietly, very disappointed about that fact. I was too, but I could not let my colleagues at the embassy see that.

With virtually every other Trump political appointee replaced, *Politico* reported that "Sullivan, though, was a rare exception." I was asked why I, as a Republican, stayed at my post to work for a Democrat in the White House. I responded that "it may be passé now, but I was taught that when a president asks an American to serve, only the most compelling excuse can justify a refusal with great remorse, . . . and I had no excuse, because I love my job, and I love working with my colleagues at Embassy Moscow."

I learned from subsequent media stories that my anxiety about whether I would be retained as the inauguration approached was unfounded: "'We knew from the start that we wanted Sullivan to remain in Moscow,' an unnamed senior State Department official said. 'He's the right person, and the post isn't one that we wanted to see vacant.' When pressed, the official insisted the decision had 'nothing to do with other candidates or lack thereof,' but that 'it was about him.'" It was reassuring to read those anonymous comments—although by then, I had much bigger concerns.

# CHAPTER 8
# MATTERS OF CONCERN

T HE VIOLENCE AND CHAOS AT the US Capitol in Washington on January 6, 2021, occurred in the middle of the New Year and Orthodox Christmas holiday week in Russia, when the entire country shuts down during the shortest and darkest days of winter—the sun rises at 9 a.m. in Moscow in early January and sets at 4 p.m. The US mission was thus closed for the week of January 4, but I was in my office every day, as were several of my colleagues. We followed the shocking and appalling developments at the Capitol on January 6 closely. I could not believe what I was watching. I thought back twenty-eight years, to November 4, 1992, when I stood on the South Lawn of the White House and watched the first President Bush demonstrate how a president, a patriot, and a man of honor should conduct himself after losing an election.

I issued public statements—mostly to reassure our mission and Americans in Russia—that the constitutional system in the United States was strong and time-tested over centuries, including during the Civil War, and that there would be a lawful transfer of power to President-elect Biden on January 20. But it was difficult to find something more constructive to say, and the Russian government did not need to work hard to exploit the situation. In fact, the most effective and painful commentaries by the Russian state-media quoted Americans on what was happening in Washington. *Sputnik* highlighted the statement by my former boss, President George W. Bush, that "this is how election results are disputed in a banana republic—not our democratic republic." Sadly, the former president said exactly what I was thinking as I sat in my office a long way from home. I knew that the Russians would use the stain of the January 6 riot as a political and rhetorical weapon against the United States at every opportunity.

The US mission returned to work on January 11, and as the Biden inauguration approached over the next week, the embassy in Moscow was plunged into a deep freeze. The temperature in the late morning of January 18 was −13°F (that was the actual and not the Western notion of "real feel" temperature, which was −24°F). I consider myself a hardy New Englander, but even I had to concede that it was cold. It was also, however, terrific weather for our outdoor hockey rink at the embassy, which Steve Sexton and several marines worked hard to set up and maintain on the large patio outside the Marine House. I was able to break out my hockey gear and skate in pickup games on the rink. My plans to play in a men's league in Moscow had been shut down by the pandemic the year before, so I welcomed the opportunity to get back on the ice, which in those temperatures in Moscow was hard and fast.

Another ice creation on the compound in mid-January 2021 was the outdoor "ice bar" in the parking lot behind the old chancery. Many people at the embassy, the ambassador included, were disappointed that our bar Uncle Sam's had to remain closed because of the pandemic. Meeting the obvious consumer demand and using the huge snow piles and drifts around the compound (it was a particularly snowy winter in Moscow), a group of rugged embassy officers, marines, and staff built a large (two-story) bar out of blocks of ice they made by putting snow in recycling bins and pouring water on the snow to freeze. Our embassy carpenter, Billy Groshan, used his tools and skill to shape the blocks into a real bar. The second story, known as the Champagne Lounge, was built on a snowbank next to the main bar, with stairs up one side and an ice slide down the other side as the exit. The "proprietors" put firepits around the bar to warm patrons.

I was pleased to be invited to preside at the opening of the ice bar on Friday evening, January 15, and even more surprised and honored when I found a sign on the bar naming it Sullivan's Post 5. The name was a play on the four guard posts at the embassy that the marines staffed, each one numbered for identification. I drank an ice-cold beer at the ground floor bar and then climbed the stairs to the Champagne Lounge for a sip of champagne before taking the exit slide. It was a fun, albeit frigid, night at the embassy and an example of the spirit and resilience of the Americans at the mission. I was immensely proud to serve with them. Because the temperatures stayed mostly at or below freezing every day until the middle of March, Sullivan's Post 5 remained available as a diversion for weeks, although I never used the slide again.

---

On Sunday, January 17, my attention was riveted on Moscow's Sheremetyevo International Airport, where Alexei Navalny arrived on his return from Germany. He had recovered from the FSB's poisoning in August after doctors at Charité Hospital in Berlin saved his life. He returned to Russia knowing that he would almost certainly be arrested by the government that had tried to kill him. As the most prominent Russian opposition leader and anti-corruption activist, Navalny had been investigated and prosecuted many times over the years. In January 2021, he was still subject to probation under Russian law from an earlier conviction and suspended sentence for fraud in 2014, which both the European Court of Human Rights and Amnesty International declared was arbitrary and unfair. Navalny was stoic in weighing the risks in the days before his return: "The question 'to return or not' never stood before me. Mainly because I never left. I ended up in Germany, having arrived in an intensive care box, for one reason: they tried to kill me."

As I expected, Navalny was arrested at passport control upon his arrival at the airport on January 17 and was charged with violating the terms of his probation by failing to report to the Russian probation service while he was in Germany. There was no mention or consideration of the fact that he had been in a coma and recovering in intensive care when he did not report to the probation service of the government that had tried to kill him. The absurdity of the situation was lost on no one. Protests over Navalny's arrest began in Russian cities almost immediately.

Two days after his arrest, Navalny's Anti-Corruption Foundation (known in Russia as FBK) released an extraordinary video narrated by Navalny that documented the vast corruption behind a lavish estate on the Black Sea owned by Putin and valued at over $1.3 billion. Almost two hours long, with detailed and compelling proof, the film was the number one trending video on YouTube in Russia and had over 100 million views worldwide by January 28.

Especially after this direct attack on him, Putin clearly felt that he could not allow Navalny, whose name he refused to mention publicly, to remain free. On February 2, a Moscow court ordered Navalny to serve the remainder of his suspended sentence—two-and-a-half years—in a labor camp for not checking in with the probation service while he was in a coma and later in intensive care. It was the beginning of Navalny's terminal descent into the Russian justice and penal systems that would see his incarceration extended until his death three years later in an Arctic penal colony.

The continuing public protests over Navalny's arrest and imprisonment were promptly crushed by the Russian security services. The government designated FBK as "an extremist organization," which meant that anyone affiliated with it could be prosecuted. The State Duma then passed a law making it illegal to support an extremist organization even if that organization had not been designated as "extremist" when the support was provided. In the face of that ex post facto criminal liability, most of the leadership and employees of FBK, as well as other prominent pro-Navalny activists, left Russia.

The Navalny protests in January 2021 were a last hurrah for civil society and public protests generally in Russia. In addition to rounding up well-known protest leaders and organizers, the security services arrested many ordinary people who dared to express their views on any topics the Kremlin deemed off-limits. Public health and safety regulations during the pandemic were strictly enforced to break up small public gatherings; even solo protesters were routinely arrested. Yet, large public gatherings not threatening to Kremlin, like patriotic events or traditional celebrations, were permitted or even encouraged. Meanwhile, the widespread designations of independent media organizations and journalists as "foreign agents" continued, which eventually drove almost all of them out of business or at least out of the country.

In response to criticism from me and other US government officials about the treatment of protesters, senior Russian government officials and their state media shills would invoke the January 6 "protests" at the

US Capitol and claim the United States was applying a "double standard" by arresting protesters at the Capitol while criticizing Russia for doing the same thing. In effect, the Kremlin attempted to equate its treatment of Navalny's supporters with the US treatment of the Capitol rioters. Foreign Minister Lavrov called the prosecution of the January 6 rioters a "persecution." Putin said of the January 6 mob, "These are not looters or thieves, these people came with political requests." When asked about the mass arrests of the Navalny protesters, Putin said in an NBC News interview, "You are presenting it as dissent and intolerance toward dissent in Russia. We view it completely differently." He asked, "Do you know that 450 individuals were arrested after entering the Congress?... They came with political demands."

Although the difference may seem patent, between violent rioters attempting to disrupt the peaceful transfer of power in the US Capitol and peaceful protesters objecting to the spurious arrest of a political opposition leader whom the FSB had tried to murder, it was not necessarily easy to convey that difference to the jaded and skeptical Russian audience I was trying to reach. This was among the many damaging legacies of the events of January 6: the riot's impact on America's image and influence abroad.

I expressed my views on the Russian crackdown on protests, independent media, and civil society, along with a variety of other issues, in several cables for the incoming administration. In return, I received two messages from the new Biden White House staff on Inauguration Day.

One message was to stand by for consultations tied to a new intelligence review that Biden was initiating. The president was charging the US Intelligence Community, led by the new director of national intelligence, Avril Haines, to investigate and provide him with an immediate assessment on four issues: first, Russia's alleged interference in the 2020 election; second, the use by the FSB of a chemical weapon (the Novichok nerve agent) in an attempt to assassinate Navalny; third, the alleged payment of bounties by the GRU in Afghanistan to have US military personnel killed, which had been reported in the US media beginning in June 2020; and fourth, whether the recent cyberattack on the federal government's computer systems through the SolarWinds software breach could be attributed to the Russian government. Once he had received the requested assessments, the president would consult in the coming weeks with his national security team, including me at Embassy Moscow, about the administration's response and overall approach to Russia.

Judging by the new administration's instructions, it seemed as though there would not be another feeble "reset" by an American president trying to improve relations with an adversarial Russian government that had no interest in changing its own hostile policies. An unnamed senior administration official was quoted in the *Washington Post* on January 21, forecasting that the Biden administration would "work to hold Russia accountable for their reckless and aggressive actions that we've seen in recent months and years."

The other message I received on January 20 was an order for action. President Biden had decided to extend the New START treaty on strategic nuclear weapons for five years, the maximum allowed under the terms of the treaty. In my prior discussions over several years with senior Russian government officials, including Deputy Foreign Minister Ryabkov, the Russians had sought an unconditional and full extension of the treaty, which is what the president was now proposing. My colleagues at the White House and the State Department assumed, therefore, that this news would be welcomed by the Russians and simple to implement in an exchange of diplomatic notes. I noted that the implementation had better be simple, because the treaty was set to expire on February 5, but I did not add my settled assumption that nothing is ever easy with the Russians. I should have.

I quickly called Deputy Foreign Minister Ryabkov with the news of the extension proposed by President Biden, and the Russians were, in fact, pleased and eager to extend the treaty. The deputy foreign minister and I had a meeting on January 26, at which we discussed the extension and how it would be legally documented and implemented. Biden had his first telephone conversation as president with Putin on the same day. The two presidents discussed, among other things, "both countries' willingness to extend New START for five years, agreeing to have their teams work urgently to complete the extension by February 5," as public statements by both the White House and the Kremlin later affirmed.

In subsequent telephone conversations with me, however, Ryabkov raised an issue that the Russians had not mentioned before. He said the State Duma and the Federation Council would need to ratify the treaty extension. I noted that the US Senate did not need to ratify the extension in the United States, because the text of the treaty the Senate had ratified in December 2010 contained the provision that authorized both governments to extend the treaty for up to five years. In effect, the US Senate had already approved the extension, subject to the future discretion of the president whether to use any or all of the five years. I asked why the same rationale would not apply to the State Duma and Federation Council. Ryabkov responded that lawyers in the Russian government opined that legislative review and approval were required. I asked how long that would take, because the treaty expired in a matter of days, and the extension needed to be approved and documented before then. Ryabkov said the review by the State Duma and the Federation Council could take weeks or months and would not be completed by the treaty's expiration date.

That was a very serious problem, I explained, because if the treaty expired on February 5, then the US president would not have authority to extend it without review by the Senate. Even if Biden and Putin agreed one day after the expiration that the identical terms of the treaty would continue to be binding for the next five years, the Senate would need to ratify that new agreement, because it was not an extension of the existing treaty. I could tell by the sound of Ryabkov's voice that as a diplomat with extensive experience in dealing with the US government, he understood how fraught that would be. The delay caused by the Senate ratification process alone would be substantial and problematic, in addition to the risk that the Senate would not ultimately approve the extension. He said he would consult with his leadership.

When Ryabkov called back, he insisted that review and approval by the State Duma and Federation Council were required, and there was no way to avoid those legislative processes. He proposed that Russia and the United States exchange diplomatic notes before February 5 agreeing to a "provisional" extension of the treaty subject to later review and approval by the Russian legislature. I said I would consult with the lawyers who were treaty experts in the Office of the Legal Adviser at the State Department, but that I was confident it would not be sufficient to avoid the need for ratification by the US Senate. The treaty provided for an extension, not a provisional extension for any purpose. I told Ryabkov that a "provisional" extension would, at minimum, put a serious legal cloud over the continuing validity of the treaty after February 5, which neither government wanted.

My report on these developments to the State Department and the White House was widely distributed, and no one was pleased by this turn of events casting doubt on the extension of the New START treaty. As I expected, the lawyers at the State Department were dubious at best on the lawfulness of a "provisional" extension. I had several more telephone calls with Ryabkov to make the case that the extension had to be finalized before February 5, otherwise the last arms control treaty between the United States and Russia would lapse, but Ryabkov was not optimistic.

Finally, Ryabkov telephoned me to report that Putin had submitted the treaty extension to the State Duma and the Federation Council with a request for expedited approval. Both legislative bodies gave their approval in less than a day. Each government had drafted diplomatic notes with the necessary language to extend the treaty for five years; I signed for the United States. Ryabkov and I met at the Russian Foreign Ministry on February 3 to exchange the documents. We were both relieved that the first very modest engagement between the new Biden administration and the Russian government had not gone completely off the rails.

As I returned to the embassy, however, I marveled that what should have been a simple agreement on a treaty extension, where both the United States and Russia wanted exactly the same thing, turned into a stressful exercise. I had my own suspicions as to why, focused on the reluctance of Putin's advisers to tell him at the last minute that he had to do something they had not anticipated—ask the State Duma and Federation Council for expedited review—because there was never any doubt in my mind that the Russian legislature would do exactly what Putin wanted. I could only speculate, but the episode confirmed yet again my conclusion that nothing is ever easy with the Russians—and foreshadowed many other, far more serious challenges ahead.

———————

In addition to discussing the New START extension and arms control in his first call with Putin on January 26, Biden raised the five most difficult issues involving Russia with which he was grappling. The first was the continuing conflict in Ukraine, instigated and propagated by the Russians, with which Biden was very familiar from his days as vice president. The discussion on this topic with Putin was brief, but Biden was clear in restating the United States' firm support for Ukraine's sovereignty.

Biden also raised the four "matters of concern" on which he had sought US intelligence assessments: the SolarWinds hack, GRU bounties in Afghanistan, Russian interference in the 2020 US election, and the Navalny case. The White House reported that Biden "made clear that the United States will act firmly in defense of its national interests in response to actions by Russia that harm us or our allies," and concluded that "the two presidents agreed to maintain transparent and consistent communication going forward."

The first and, in many ways, the easiest issue to be addressed by the new administration was the Navalny poisoning and arrest. The State Department, with input from me, had "publicly attributed the attack to the FSB in December." It did not take long, therefore, after the request from President Biden in mid-January, for the US Intelligence Community to conclude with "high confidence" that Navalny was poisoned with a dangerous Novichok nerve agent—outlawed under international law— by the FSB. Other governments, particularly in Europe, were ahead of the United States on this issue. The European Union in October 2020 had imposed sanctions on six senior Russian officials who were widely agreed to have been involved in the poisoning, including the director of the FSB, Alexander Bortnikov, and the director of a state research institute. The EU was preparing to impose new sanctions on Russia at the beginning of March 2021, following the arrest of Navalny on January 17, while the United States had yet to impose any sanctions related to Navalny. Biden wanted the United States to get in sync quickly with the EU on Russia sanctions.

Starting on February 12, the National Security Council staff convened a series of high-level meetings on the four "matters of concern" with respect to Russia, and the preliminary focus was on Navalny. I was invited to participate from Moscow by secure video teleconference (SVTC) in all the Russia meetings, which ranged in status from deputies committee meetings (known as DCs and consisting of deputy cabinet secretaries, chaired by the principal deputy national security advisor, Jon Finer), to principals committee meetings (known as PCs, with attendance by cabinet secretaries, chaired by the national security advisor, Jake Sullivan), and National Security Council meetings (the vice president and cabinet secretaries, chaired by the president). At the first principals committee meeting in February that I joined, Jake Sullivan jokingly introduced me as his "cousin" at Embassy Moscow. There were some participants in the SVTC who did not know me yet, and I could see they were a little confused. I wondered whether those who thought Jake was serious might surmise that is why the administration had asked me to stay in my position. Jake saw the confusion and said he was only joking.

The decision-making on the US response to Navalny's poisoning and arrest was straightforward. The declassified intelligence showed that the FSB had used a legally banned nerve agent to try to kill Navalny in August, and then arrested and imprisoned him without justification upon his return to Russia in January. In response, the United States, in coordination with the EU, imposed various economic sanctions and export controls that were announced on March 2. The new US sanctions, including the designation of the FSB and its director Bortnikov, brought them into line with the EU sanctions. The goal of the coordinated announcement was "a demonstration of transatlantic unity" to the Russians, a theme that would be repeated many times over the remainder of my tenure as ambassador.

The Russian response was predictable. They had vehemently denied from the very beginning that Navalny was poisoned in Russia and asserted that even if something unfortunate had happened to him somewhere (most likely Berlin), it was not by the actions of the FSB or the

Russian government. The Russians maintained that position, although their reaction to the March 2 sanctions was relatively mild, at least by Kremlin standards. Lavrov warned that Russia would respond, and his spokeswoman said the "response would be 'based on the principle of reciprocity, but not necessarily symmetrically.'" Putin's spokesman Dmitry Peskov said US sanctions were ineffective and "just making the bilateral relationship worse."

After the Navalny sanctions announcement, the NSC-led meetings continued with consideration of the other three "matters of concern" in the US-Russia relationship. The intelligence assessments were not as clear-cut with respect to some aspects of these issues, particularly the GRU's alleged bounties in Afghanistan, and the nature of the US response was subject to vigorous debate. While these discussions were ongoing, the president made a provocative (to put it mildly) and unscripted public statement about Putin in a March 17 interview with George Stephanopoulos of ABC News that upended US-Russia relations, at least briefly, and eventually led the Kremlin to invite me to leave the country a month later.

In the interview, Stephanopoulos asked about the report by the Office of the Director of National Intelligence, released the day before, on March 16, that concluded with "high confidence" about the 2020 election that "Russian President Putin authorized, and a range of Russian government organizations conducted, influence operations aimed at denigrating President Biden's candidacy and the Democratic Party, supporting former President Trump, undermining public confidence in the electoral process, and exacerbating sociopolitical divisions in the US." Biden said Putin would "pay a price" for Russian election interference. Stephanopoulos quietly asked the president if he thought Putin was a "killer," and Biden said tersely, "Mhmm. I do." Asked what price Putin would pay, the president demurred and said, "You'll see shortly."

I was dumbfounded when I saw the interview. This was not how the president's advisers—at least to my knowledge—were planning to recommend to him that we begin the rollout of the US response to Russia's malign activities. But as I was to learn, the president would often say in public exactly what he was thinking with no diplomatic filter, and the privilege to do that came with his election to office. My job, in addition to giving my best advice, was to implement the president's decisions and defend his statements. I expected the Russian MFA would summon me for a dressing-down and demand an apology. But I never heard from the ministry.

Instead, the most significant response by the Russian government to Biden's "killer" comment was Putin's immediate decision, on the same day the interview was broadcast, to recall his ambassador, Anatoly Antonov, from Washington for consultations in Moscow. This was a somewhat unexpected move. The public responses by Putin and his Kremlin spokesman Peskov, on the other hand, were more predictable. Expressing outrage on the day after the interview, Peskov told the press that Biden's comment was an unprecedented diplomatic insult: "There hasn't been anything like this in history." He described the remarks as "very bad statements by the president of the United States. He definitely does not want to improve relations with us, and we will continue to proceed from this." All of which was typical Russian diplomatic umbrage.

Putin's personal reaction was part Chekist nonchalance, with a dig at Biden's age and health, and part amateur psychology. On March 18, when first asked about Biden's comment, Putin said, at a press event on the seventh anniversary of Russia's annexation of Crimea, "What would I tell him? I would say 'stay healthy.' I wish him good health. I am saying this without irony or tongue in cheek. This is my first point." He then became more clinical, observing that "when we evaluate other people, or even other states and nations, we are always facing a mirror, we always see ourselves in the reflection, because we project our inner selves onto the other person." He continued, "I remember when we were children and played in the yard, we had arguments occasionally and we used to say: whatever you call me is what you are called yourself. This is no coincidence or just a kids' saying or joke. It has a very deep psychological undercurrent." In other words, Putin diagnosed that if Biden called him a killer, then Biden was really projecting his own "inner self."

Putin returned to the subject later in the same day, offering to debate Biden in a global showdown: "I would like to offer President Biden [the opportunity] to continue our discussion, but on condition that we'll do so what is called live, online. Without anything prerecorded, in an open and direct discussion. It seems to me, it would be interesting both for Russian people and for the US people, as well as for many other countries." This was more of Putin's Chekist bluster, showing his confidence in facing off against what he considered the elderly and weak American president.

Finally, on the evening of March 18, having made his aggressive points in response to Biden earlier in the day, Putin dialed back his rhetoric. He announced that he had directed his aides to arrange a telephone call with President Biden at some point in the future, because, as he put it blandly, "we can and we must continue to have relations." But he did not explain that those relations would be conducted, at least in the near term, without a Russian ambassador in Washington.

At the White House, the press corps was having a field day with the story. In response to the question whether President Biden regretted his "killer" comment, Press Secretary Jen Psaki said confidently, "No. The president gave a direct answer to a direct question." CNN reported that "when asked if the President's remarks might further escalate tensions with Moscow, Psaki noted that Amb. John Sullivan 'remains in Moscow' and is 'engaged.'" She concluded, "We continue to believe that diplomacy is the first step, . . . as we pursue all relationships—even with our adversaries."

No one in Washington ever suggested that I leave Moscow, and the thought never occurred to me. In fact, to emphasize the point that I was there to stay, I invited Ambassador Antonov, now home in Moscow, to join me for lunch at Spaso House on March 24. I knew Anatoly well from my years as deputy secretary of state. Over a long lunch, he told me that when he was instructed, with no prior notice, on March 17 to return to Moscow right away, he was not told why he was being recalled. He wondered whether he was going to be disciplined, because it was public knowledge that he and several members of his embassy staff had recently received Western Covid-19 vaccines in Washington. He said they had no choice, because the Foreign Ministry had not sent vaccines to their mission. It was only after he had landed in Moscow that he learned why he had been recalled: because Putin wanted to retaliate for Biden calling him a "killer."

I commiserated with Antonov about the challenges of conducting diplomacy in a pandemic, although I could not resist observing with pride that the State Department had done a remarkable job in sending vaccines to US diplomatic posts worldwide. That was no easy feat, considering the extremely cold temperatures at which the Pfizer and Moderna vaccines (both of which had been cleared for emergency use in December 2020) needed to be shipped and stored. I told the ambassador that I had received my first Moderna shot on March 19 at the Embassy Moscow medical unit.

Antonov also shared with me his views on the state of US-Russia relations. He warned there were elements in the Russian government that were pushing for a "very hard" response if the review currently underway in Washington resulted in more sanctions and other "hostile" actions against Russia. He said specifically that the Russian reaction would be "very hard" on my embassy in Moscow.

Struck by Antonov's comment, I asked whether he thought that Putin would sever diplomatic relations. Antonov said that he did not know whether it would come to that; much would depend on what the United States did with the results of the intelligence review. But he feared that the Russian response "would be bad" for the US embassy.

I tried to be a gracious host, but I was not buying the scare tactics of the ambassador. The Russians are masters at manipulating an adversary through threats and warnings to "self-deter," to avoid taking an action that "might" provoke a disproportionately hostile response by them. Their long-standing nuclear saber rattling was the most notorious example. I was determined to learn the lessons of history, and to continue to defend American interests, no matter the threat to the mission that I led.

---

In the deputies and principals committee meetings that continued through the end of March 2021, I advocated for a strong response to Russia's malign activities. If we believed what we said about the Russian government's behavior, then we had to take firm action. We needed the courage of our convictions, and I took that position as the head of an embassy that would likely bear the brunt of any Russian retaliation. At a National Security Council meeting on March 30, the president pushed his advisers to give him strong and credible measures in response to the three "matters of concern"—election interference, SolarWinds, and Afghan bounties—that he had identified at the start of his administration, in addition to the Navalny case.

The standard measures employed by the US government in these circumstances were, predictably, sanctions, export controls, and diplomatic expulsions. I had substantial experience with each of these tools. When I was the acting secretary of state in 2018, we expelled sixty Russian "diplomats" who were in fact undeclared intelligence officers. This was an easy and not entirely symbolic response to implement. Yet expelling Russian diplomats was not without its costs. The Russians would expel the same number of American diplomats from our mission in Russia, but we had a smaller number of diplomats, which would make any further cuts more painful to us.

The subsequent discussions in Washington in early April, in which I participated virtually from Moscow, sought to find the right balance of punitive and deterrent measures to match the hostile Russian actions that we could prove. That last point was problematic with respect to the Afghan bounties matter. The Intelligence Community was not able to collectively achieve a sufficient level of confidence to draw an actionable conclusion on the explosive allegation that the GRU had paid the Taliban bounties to kill American service members in Afghanistan. I had spent a considerable amount of time since early 2020 delving into the voluminous intelligence bearing on the question. I was disappointed at our inability to reach a consensus. I am not a trained intelligence analyst, but I found the proof persuasive.

What could not be disputed, however, was the dreadful way the matter was handled by the US government, starting with the leaks to the media of this classified intelligence the year before. President Trump called the report of GRU bounties "fake news" and denied that he had been briefed on the matter. His administration never took action in response to the intelligence other than to continue to investigate. Presidential candidate Biden seized on the issue politically, roundly criticizing Trump for refusing "to sanction or impose any kind of consequences on Russia for this egregious violation of international law." Perfunctorily acknowledging that the intelligence was not yet fully verified, Biden said he was "outraged by the [bounties] report" and promised that if he were elected, "Putin will be confronted and we'll impose serious costs on Russia" for the GRU's program.

The picture looked different once President Biden was in the Oval Office. The Intelligence Community was divided, and the US government ultimately decided to impose no costs on Russia, let alone the "serious costs" for the GRU's bounties program that candidate Biden had promised. Politicizing intelligence and sensitive national security matters is always fraught. In this case, our nation, and especially the men and women who had served in Afghanistan, some of whom were grievously wounded or made the ultimate sacrifice for their country, deserved far better from both Trump and Biden.

With the Afghan bounties matter removed from consideration, the remaining discussion among the president's advisers focused on imposing "serious costs" for the Russian government's 2020 election interference and the SolarWinds cyber intrusion. The Intelligence Community had already released its report on the 2020 election in March, as referenced in the Stephanopoulos interview. In April, the Intelligence Community also determined with "high confidence" that the SVR, Russia's foreign intelligence service, was "the perpetrator of the broad-scope cyber espionage campaign that exploited the SolarWinds Orion platform and other information technology infrastructures."

By April 13, the president had accepted his advisers' recommendations for a wide-ranging response to Russia's hostile actions. As later described in a White House statement on "Imposing Costs for Harmful Foreign Activities by the Russian Government," there were three principal components:

First, the president would sign a new executive order, providing additional authorities to "impose costs in a strategic and economically impactful manner on Russia if it continues or escalates its destabilizing international actions." Under the authority of this new order, the Treasury Department would prohibit US financial institutions from "participat[ing] in the primary market for ruble or non-ruble denominated bonds" issued by Russia, and from "lending ruble or non-ruble denominated funds" to

Russia. This was a new type of financial sanction, at least as applied to Russia.

Second, the United States would sanction dozens of Russian entities and individuals that supported the SVR's cyber program or were involved in the Russian government's attempts to influence the 2020 US presidential election. Also sanctioned were eight individuals and entities involved in Russia's occupation of and repression in Crimea. These were all standard sanctions determinations and surely were anticipated by the Russians.

Third, the United States would expel ten personnel from the Russian embassy in Washington. The White House noted in its later public statement that the expelled personnel "include representatives of Russian intelligence services." This action would have an impact on Embassy Moscow because the Russian government would automatically expel ten of my colleagues.

With the president's sign-off on this package, we agreed that it would be announced publicly on Thursday, April 15, and the rollout would begin with a telephone call from Biden on April 13 to give Putin the courtesy of notice that the United States was about to announce its response to Russia's hostile actions. The president would not go into detail about the response package, in part so as not to give the Russians an opportunity to prepare for and potentially undermine the White House announcement scheduled for two days later. The plan was for me to go to the Kremlin late on April 14 to provide more specifics shortly before the announcement in Washington early the next day.

Informed by reporting from Embassy Moscow, Biden's discussion with Putin went as we had expected and as reflected in the White House readout of the call. In addition to giving notice to Putin of the upcoming US actions, Biden raised several other issues, including his concern over the Russian military buildup near Ukraine. He told Putin that he wanted "a stable and predictable relationship with Russia," and toward that end he proposed a summit meeting with Putin in a third country later in the spring.

As soon as the phone call ended, well after 7 p.m. Moscow time, Yuri Ushakov, Putin's foreign policy adviser, called and asked me to come to see him in his office that night. It was an unusual request, and I was curious why he wanted to see me so urgently. He welcomed me into his conference room, where we typically met, and he greeted me, as usual, with a warm smile. He always had a friendly demeanor with a careworn air about him, often shrugging his shoulders or raising his eyebrows at difficult moments.

Ushakov gave me his assessment of the just-completed telephone call between the presidents. He thought it had gone well, and that he (which meant the Boss, Putin) was very pleased that Biden had proposed a summit meeting. The problem, he feared, was that the upcoming US actions to be announced in a few days would ruin the moment and the opportunity for progress in the relationship between Russia and the United States. He urged me to convey a message of restraint to Washington and pleaded that our actions "not be too hard." It was very similar to the message Ambassador Antonov had delivered over lunch three weeks before. I told Yuri that I would convey his message back to Washington but advised that there was substantial unfinished business between the United States and Russia that needed to be addressed before we could work on trying to improve the relationship. He and I agreed that we would reconvene on the following day, when I was authorized to provide a little more information on the US actions.

I met with Ushakov late in the afternoon of April 14 and provided an overview of the US actions, including the sanctions on Russian sovereign debt. I was asked by my colleagues at the Treasury Department to emphasize that the sanctions applied only to the primary debt market, not the secondary market. Yuri took careful notes and gave me a few eye rolls and sighs during my short presentation. He did not give me an official reaction, because we had not given the Russian government a formal statement of our actions, which I did the following day at the MFA. I met with Deputy Foreign Minister Ryabkov shortly before the whole package was announced in Washington on April 15 and gave him a list of all the sanctions designations as well as the names of the Russian diplomats who would need to leave the United States.

The Russians had a response ready the very next day. On Friday, April 16, Foreign Minister Lavrov announced that ten US diplomats would be expelled from Russia, and eight senior US government officials would be sanctioned, including FBI director Christopher Wray and the director of national intelligence, Avril Haines. But that was not all. Ambassador Ushakov asked to meet with me that afternoon. He told me that Putin would sign an order making it illegal for the US mission in Russia to employ any third country nationals. That was a significant escalation because, as Ushakov knew, it would require the United States to terminate hundreds of personnel and contractors who worked for us. The effect on the US embassy would be devastating. Ushakov gave me one of his careworn shrugs, as if to say, *Antonov and I warned you about the bad things that were going to happen if you Americans decided to play hardball.*

Then, in a casual comment with a barely audible voice, Ushakov said I should go home. I was not sure what he meant. He said I should leave Moscow. I asked whether he meant that I was being declared persona non grata and expelled. He said, "Oh God no," but that I should still leave. I asked why, and he just said it would be best. I replied that only President Biden decided when I come and go. He shrugged and repeated that it would be best if I left.

I called Deputy Foreign Minister Ryabkov to complain about the forthcoming presidential order that would make it illegal for us to employ third country nationals and also to get his view on the suggestion that I leave the country. He said the presidential order was finished, and I replied that forcing us to terminate hundreds of essential employees was the equivalent of hundreds of diplomatic expulsions. But Ryabkov said he could not change what Putin had decided. As for leaving the country, he advised that no one in, or affiliated in any way with, the Russian government would meet with me if I stayed. Putin said the same thing to Biden in a later phone call, recommending that he recall his ambassador because I would have nothing to do.

I consulted with my colleagues at the State Department and the White House over the weekend. My initial reaction was to stay in Moscow, and not allow the Russians to dictate to the American president the terms of service of his ambassador, unless they wanted to expel me the way Stalin had expelled Kennan. Unbeknownst to me, on Monday two unnamed sources leaked to *Axios* that "the United States ambassador to Russia is refusing to leave the country after the Kremlin 'advised' him to return home following new Biden administration sanctions." That news report apparently received high-level attention in Washington, and I had further conversations about the appropriate course of action. I made it clear that I was not refusing to leave and that if the president wanted me to come home, then of course I would.

While I was having those conversations on April 19, Jake Sullivan spoke by telephone on the same day with his counterpart Nikolai Patrushev, the secretary of the Russian Security Council, to stabilize the situation and discuss the prospect of a presidential summit between the United States and Russia. In announcing the US actions on April 15, President Biden had described them as "measured and proportionate" and he emphasized: "Now is the time to de-escalate. The way forward is through thoughtful dialogue and diplomatic process." I was advised by Washington to come home. The Russian MFA told our deputy chief of mission Bart Gorman that I should leave and not return until after a summit meeting of the presidents at which they would agree to return their ambassadors to their posts.

The issue of my departure was effectively moot because I was already planning to return home soon anyway. I had not seen Grace and my family for over thirteen months, and a visit with them was long overdue, particularly now that travel was easier in the second year of the pandemic. (I did not try to go home for the holidays in December 2020, because I was not sure at the time whether I would be staying in Moscow beyond mid-January under President Biden.) Another reason I wanted to return to Washington was that I had not met with the new senior appointees across the US government in Washington who had a stake in Russia policy. I knew many of them personally, including Secretary Blinken, but we had not met face-to-face since they had assumed their new positions.

I drafted a press statement combining both rationales to explain my forthcoming departure from Moscow that was cleared by the State Department and the White House and released on April 20:

> I believe it is important for me to speak directly with my new
> colleagues in the Biden administration in Washington about the
> current state of bilateral relations between the United States and
> Russia. Also, I have not seen my family in well over a year, and

that is another important reason for me to return home for a visit. I will return to Moscow in the coming weeks before any meeting between Presidents Biden and Putin.

I received my second shot of the Moderna vaccine at the embassy medical unit and departed for Washington on April 22, leaving behind what was described in the media as an "extremely tense situation." Bart Gorman would be the chargé d'affaires while I was in Washington, and we agreed that we would stay in close contact.

I was heading back to a country that had changed a great deal since I had last seen it, including in some refreshing ways. Just as it had signaled back in January, the Biden administration seemed intent on holding Russia accountable for its actions, but was doing so in a way that left open the possibility of constructive dialogue, if Putin was willing to engage in it. I looked forward to participating as a member of the administration in that effort.

Seeking a story, or at least a photo, Russian state media were at Sheremetyevo International Airport to cover my departure, which I had expected. During the long journey home, with a lengthy layover in London, however, I wondered whether the Russian state media based in Washington would be there to ambush me with a camera on my arrival looking haggard and disheveled after a twenty-hour trip. I resolved not to let them have that satisfaction. I phoned Grace, who was coming to Dulles International Airport to pick me up, and told her to be on the lookout for media in the arrivals area. I said I would call her later to see whether I needed to be prepared. After the plane landed at Dulles, I called Grace and she said there were two camera crews speaking Russian who were waiting for me.

I explained the situation to the flight attendants on my British Airways flight and, as the other passengers were deplaning, they graciously allowed me to go into the lavatory to clean myself up, shave, and put on a suit and tie with a fresh shirt—not my usual attire on a long flight. After I cleared passport control, collected my luggage, and entered the arrivals area, I cheerfully approached the Russian media and cameras to thank them for coming to welcome me home. I said I was sorry to leave Moscow during the beautiful spring weather we were having there, but it was more important for me to be home with my wife. Then I turned and walked toward Grace, who had saved me from embarrassment. It was always thus since I first met her in 1985: Grace coming to my rescue. We kissed, hugged, and walked out of the terminal arm-in-arm. It felt so good to be home and with her.

———————

Haunting me upon my arrival back in the States—and indeed lurking behind all the activity, engagements, and rhetoric in the US-Russia relationship during the first five months of the Biden administration—was the specter of Ukraine. While other issues occasionally rose to transitory prominence, Ukraine was the obbligato, the indispensable and unyielding issue that separated the two countries. It held that status because of the importance Putin put on controlling Ukraine as part of his imperial vision of the *Russkiy mir,* or Russian world. Ukraine was not a top priority for the incoming Biden administration, but Putin would not let it slip in importance. He would keep the pressure on and not allow the new administration to focus more attention on other more pressing matters, such as China.

In his first phone call with Putin, on January 26, 2021, President Biden recited familiar talking points on the United States' support for Ukraine's sovereignty, but the issue was folded into a long list of other "matters of concern." For Putin, Ukraine was his superseding "matter of concern," and within weeks after the first presidential call he made that clear by turning up the heat on the borders of Ukraine. The Russian Defense Ministry announced on February 21 the deployment of three thousand paratroopers to the Ukraine border. It was the first of many Russian deployments near Ukraine over the next two months that would eventually total many tens of thousands of troops. In addition, large amounts of weapons and equipment, as well as numerous fixed-wing aircraft and helicopters, were sent to support the deployed troops in a region that included Crimea, Rostov, Bryansk, and Voronezh.

Those deployment figures did not count the thousands of Russian military "advisers" in Ukrainian territory in the Donbas, which furthermore was occupied by separatists who were supported by Moscow. Violence escalated in the spring of 2021, before I left for the United States,

Signing documents after my ceremonial swearing-in as US Deputy Secretary of State, in the presence of Chief Justice John Roberts; Secretary of State Rex Tillerson; my wife, Grace; and our children Jack, Katie, and Teddy. June 9, 2017. (US State Department)

As the acting secretary of state, welcoming President Emmanuel Macron of France to the US Department of State with a toast before lunch, along with Vice President Mike Pence, on April 24, 2018. (US State Department)

Introducing the new secretary of state Mike Pompeo and his family at the State Department on May 1, 2018. (US State Department)

My departure from the State Department during a "clap out" after my ceremonial swearing-in as ambassador on January 10, 2020. (Author's personal collection)

With my wife, Grace, and son Jack on Old Arbat Street in Moscow on January 18, 2020. (Author's personal collection)

The Russian White House viewed from the Moscow River in a photograph taken by Grace on January 20, 2020. She was the family photographer. The US Embassy is directly behind this large Russian government building. (Author's personal collection)

Standing with President Putin at my credentialing ceremony in the Grand Kremlin Palace on February 5, 2020. Foreign Minister Sergey Lavrov looks on over my shoulder. (US State Department)

Posing with some of the Marine security guards at Embassy Moscow in front of the statue of President John Quincy Adams, a fellow native of the Commonwealth of Massachusetts who became the first US minister to the Russian Empire in 1809. (US State Department)

A US Air Force C-17 delivering ventilators in Moscow on May 21, 2020. (US State Department)

Standing outside labor camp IK-17 in Mordovia after visiting Paul Whelan on September 22, 2020. It is a grim and desolate place for hardened Russian criminals, let alone for an innocent American who cannot speak Russian, like Paul. (US State Department)

Sharing a laugh, at the Philadelphia Flyers' expense, with former Soviet hockey stars Alexander Yakushev and Slava Fetisov after a KHL game in Moscow on February 1, 2020. (US State Department)

Speaking with a Russian youth hockey team at a rink in Yaroslavl on December 3, 2021. (US State Department)

The expanded bilateral meeting between the US delegation, led by President Biden, and the Russian delegation, led by President Putin, in Geneva on June 16, 2021. (US State Department)

Sharing a light moment with President Biden after his meeting with Putin in Geneva and before his press conference on June 16, 2021. (US State Department)

Paying my respects to Mikhail Gorbachev in the Hall of Columns of the historic House of Unions in Moscow on September 3, 2022. (US State Department)

Grace and me in Belfast, Northern Ireland, on our last vacation together before I became deputy secretary of state—one of many happy memories from our thirty-plus years of marriage. Although a Mets fan from New York, she had the patience to indulge my Boston-Irish "tribalism." (Author's personal collection)

near the borders of the occupied portions of Donetsk and Luhansk, with mortar and artillery strikes across both sides of the line of contact. The Ukrainian military was alarmed, with the chief of the general staff estimating on March 30 that there were over sixty thousand Russian troops deployed to the border with Ukraine and more on the way. NATO allies, particularly in Eastern Europe, were equally alarmed. Many alliance intelligence experts concluded, based on an assessment of the troops and logistics capabilities deployed and—just as significant—not deployed, that the large Russian military buildup on the border of Ukraine was not likely intended for an imminent invasion of the country. That view was not unanimous and there was intense debate and some disagreement on the question in NATO capitals.

The Kremlin and the Russian Ministry of Defense took the position that the buildup was merely a set of ordinary military exercises. As a further justification, the Russians also said that the troop and weapons movements on Russian territory were a matter of national defense in light of NATO's large military exercise known as Defender Europe 2021, which began on March 16 in twelve countries with the participation of twenty-eight thousand troops from twenty-seven NATO members. Moreover, because the Russian troop movements were only on Russian territory, the Kremlin's view was that the entire issue was a matter of national sovereignty that other nations did not have standing to criticize.

It was in this context that President Biden, in his April 13 phone call with Putin, raised not only the United States' "commitment to Ukraine's sovereignty and territorial integrity," but also US concerns "over the sudden Russian military buildup in occupied Crimea and on Ukraine's borders." He "called on Russia to de-escalate tensions." Nerves were on edge as Western diplomats and intelligence experts continued to assess and debate whether Putin would further invade Ukraine, beyond the territory the Russians had already seized in Crimea, Donetsk, and Luhansk. I met frequently in Moscow with the other Quad ambassadors—from the UK, France, and Germany—to discuss the situation and pore over maps and updates on troop deployments. It was, as President Biden said in his call with Putin, a very tense time.

Finally, on April 22, the day I flew back to Washington, there was some modestly positive news. The Russian defense minister, Sergei Shoigu, announced that certain military exercises in the regions near Ukraine were winding down and some of the deployed troops would be returning to their garrisons by May 1. It was a positive sign, but not a reason to believe that the risk of a further invasion of Ukraine was greatly diminished. We would have to wait and see what troops, equipment, and matériel were removed and what remained in Crimea and southwestern Russia before we could draw any conclusions about Russia's plans for their neighbor to the west.

As it turned out, we would not have to wait long. Among the first appointments I had upon my return to Washington were meetings at the Pentagon on May 3. I saw Defense Secretary Lloyd Austin, whom I had not met before in person. Although he had an understated manner, the secretary was very interested in my perspective from Moscow on the Kremlin's thinking about Ukraine and arms control. I conferred separately with my friend Chairman Milley. The preliminary assessment of the recent developments on Ukraine's borders was not positive. Russia had sent only a few thousand troops back to their home garrisons, and eighty thousand troops remained deployed near Ukraine on May 5. This was an extraordinarily large number—not enough for an immediate full-scale invasion of Ukraine but huge by historical standards—and even many of the troops that were removed had left trucks and armored vehicles behind. More concerning was the infrastructure that was constructed, particularly in Crimea: fuel and arms depots, field hospitals, and communications stations.

The conclusion of the US government experts was that an invasion of Ukraine by Russia remained unlikely in the near term. But as Chairman Milley said to me, Putin had built the muscle and his military had the muscle memory to attack Ukraine when ordered by the Kremlin. It was a sobering thought as I joined (in person this time, not virtually from Moscow) in the preparations led by the White House for an expected meeting between Presidents Biden and Putin on a date to be determined.

# CHAPTER 9

# ELUSIVE SEARCH FOR STABILITY

I N THE FACE OF A serious expansion of the Russian military threat to Ukraine, the Biden administration in the spring of 2021 actively pursued a meeting with Putin "to stabilize" (or, to use another preferred phrase, "to provide guardrails for") our relationship with Russia. So eager was the administration for a meeting that the planning in Washington for a summit between Biden and Putin was underway long before there was even an agreement between the White House and the Kremlin on whether any meeting would take place and, if so, when and where it would happen. Following a traditional pattern, the more we sought the meeting, the less tractable the Russians became, at least publicly. Americans, unlike Russians, generally are not clever at disguising our desires and true motives from an adversary.

The first deputies committee meeting in which I participated to plan for the summit was on May 5, and I was confident the presidents would meet. Biden asked for the meeting, and Putin wanted and needed it more than Biden. But, consistent with his Chekist values and image, Putin could never let anyone sense that he craved the stature and attention accorded to any leader attending a summit meeting on a global stage with the president of the United States. As I predicted at the time, Putin's approach to the negotiations on the meeting was to strike a diffident pose; in effect, "Biden asked for this meeting, I didn't; I'll see if I can find the time."

Weeks went by as Washington and Moscow worked to come to an agreement on a presidential meeting. Simultaneously, the preparatory work at the White House and the State Department on the substance of the meeting was underway and focused, at least in part, on lowering expectations for the event. A threshold question was whether to refer to the meeting as a summit, which would seem to heighten its importance and add some more prestige to Putin's participation. The nomenclature question quickly became moot, however, because whether we wanted to call it a summit or not, the media insisted on using the term, and administration officials eventually followed suit.

Preliminary talks with the Russians indicated that they did not want me to return to Embassy Moscow before the summit took place. If I did, the MFA told Bart Gorman, I would be expelled. Thus, contrary to my statement upon leaving Moscow in April, I would not be back at my post anytime soon. The Russians proposed that the return of the two presidents' ambassadors—me to Moscow and Antonov to Washington—be a "deliverable" at the summit. If the meeting resulted in me and my Russian counterpart being able to resume our jobs, I thought, then at least it would have one positive outcome.

It was clear that I was going to be in Washington for an extended stay, so I resolved to make the best use of my time at home. It was not difficult to find senior officials with whom to meet. After all that had happened in the spring, the hunger for information on Russia and Putin was intense across the federal government. My most important meetings were with the new State Department leadership because, like any US ambassador, the department was my anchor in Washington. I needed to have a good working relationship with Secretary Blinken, whom I had succeeded as deputy secretary of state; with my successor, Deputy Secretary Wendy Sherman; and with our under secretary for political affairs, Ambassador Toria Nuland. I knew each of them personally and they were all extremely knowledgeable about the current challenges with Russia. They also, in their own way, helped me to get a fresh perspective on the country where I had been trapped for over a year.

I looked forward to seeing Secretary Blinken again. I have considered him a friend since we first met, in 2017, during my transition to become deputy secretary. He was a very experienced foreign policy professional, having worked in senior positions at the White House, the State Department, and on Capitol Hill over three decades in Washington—and for a large part of that time directly for Joe Biden. His manner is refined, understated, and intellectual, yet he has a terrific sense of humor and a knack for connecting with people of all stations. He is quite different in temperament and style from his predecessor, and my former boss, Mike Pompeo, who approached his work in a more aggressive and take-charge manner befitting his background as a former army officer and corporate CEO.

In our meeting on April 30, Secretary Blinken wanted my current impressions of dealing with Putin. I had previously put my thoughts and observations on the Russian president in classified cables to the department and the White House, and I struggled to find a new and pithy frame of reference. I was forced to revert to my long-standing comparison of Putin to a very savvy gangster, unbound by facts, law, morals, or truth, who presides over a corrupt system of *siloviki* and oligarchs. But he is more than that, because he is motivated not only by power and money, but also by the grandiose ambitions of the most powerful and fierce tsars in history. Lavrov is rumored to have said that Putin has only "three advisers. Ivan the Terrible. Peter the Great. And Catherine the Great." I tried to add some American color by invoking the name of a notorious gangster from my family's hometown of South Boston, James "Whitey" Bulger. I told Blinken to imagine a Slavic Jimmy Bulger leading the Kremlin. Dealing with someone so shrewd and brutal was not only difficult—it was dangerous.

I also met with people outside of the State Department, among them National Security Advisor Jake Sullivan, whom I saw at the White House on May 14. This was the first time I had met him in person, as opposed to over a secure video teleconference from Moscow. We covered the same issues about Putin that I had discussed with Secretary Blinken. I noted that Jake's younger brother, Tom, was the secretary's deputy chief of staff at the State Department, and I joked that we Sullivans were taking over. I said that he and Tom could become another one of the famous sibling combinations in US foreign policy and national security history, like John Foster Dulles and Allen Dulles, or Walt and Eugene Rostow. I could not resist the temptation to suggest they avoid the troubles of the Hiss brothers (Alger and Donald).

All the various components of the Intelligence Community—ODNI, CIA, DIA, and NSA—and their leadership similarly wanted to talk with me about Russia. I certainly learned more from these meetings than my Intelligence Community colleagues learned from me, but they appreciated hearing my perspective from Moscow. While I was at the CIA, I also met with Director William Burns, another predecessor of mine as deputy secretary of state (and as ambassador to Russia). There was no one in the US government more knowledgeable about Russia and Putin than Bill, whom I counted as a friend in addition to a valued colleague. We talked about the possible motivations behind Russia's alarming military buildup on Ukraine's borders, which could range from Putin dialing up pressure on the West to make concessions on Ukraine all the way to a full-scale Russian invasion. Neither of us was sanguine about the future of either Russia-Ukraine or US-Russia relations. It was good to speak with someone who understood Russia and Putin as well as Bill did. I was honored when he presented me with the agency's award as Ambassador of the Year.

Senators and members of Congress also were on my schedule, seeking to hear my views—and tell me theirs—on the difficult issues in our relationship with Russia, including the wrongfully detained Americans, Whelan, Reed, and Calvey. I was particularly gratified with the congressional interest in the details of the difficult operations of our understaffed embassy in Moscow, which was going to be subjected to more stress after the departure of ten more US diplomats, as ordered by the MFA in April, and the implementation of Putin's order prohibiting the United States from employing third country nationals in Russia. I testified in a classified hearing before the Senate Select Committee on Intelligence on May 11, and two weeks later I appeared before the Senate Foreign Relations Committee, again in a closed session. In between, I gave a classified briefing to the leadership of the House Foreign Affairs Committee.

The ten Americans expelled from Russia needed to leave the country before the end of May. The State Department chartered a flight for the departing diplomats and their families to take them from Moscow to Dulles Airport, in the Virginia suburbs of Washington, on May 19. Grace and I went to the private aircraft terminal to meet the flight on its arrival in the United States. I was allowed to board when the charter arrived at the terminal, along with US Customs and Immigration Service officers who helpfully expedited the processing of the immigration and customs paperwork. Although it was only ten individuals who were expelled, the inclusion of their spouses, children, and pets on the plane made it seem full. I exchanged warm greetings with everyone—colleagues and their family members whom I had not seen in almost a month. After a long flight, the passengers were ready to stretch their legs and embrace the family and friends who had come to Dulles to welcome them home. Grace and I hosted a brief reception in a large room set aside for us in the terminal, where I was able to thank my returning colleagues and their families for all they had done and endured for our country. Then the travelers gathered their luggage and went their separate ways for some well-deserved home leave.

The situation was less festive at Embassy Moscow, as the management team prepared to separate approximately 180 employees and an equivalent number of contractors who worked at the embassy and at our small consulate in Yekaterinburg. In follow-up conversations with the MFA after I departed, the Russians agreed to allow us until the end of July to comply with Putin's order that barred our employment of third country nationals. We would need that much time just to process all the necessary paperwork and clear the US government's bureaucratic hurdles to take so many personnel and contracting actions to terminate almost four hundred people. Not to mention the huge challenge of planning how the embassy would operate without them or the ten expelled American diplomats.

On May 19, the same day that Grace and I met the charter flight from Moscow, Secretary Blinken had his first meeting with Foreign Minister Lavrov on the sidelines of a gathering of the Arctic Council in Reykjavík, Iceland. The secretary and Lavrov discussed the proposed Biden-Putin summit, and both sides proceeded on the understanding that the presidents would meet, although there was no agreement on the date and location, which would be announced later. After the secretary's meeting with Lavrov, the State Department noted in a press release that in addition to planning for the summit, they discussed a wide range of issues, "as the United States sought a more stable and predictable relationship with Moscow." The White House continued to emphasize that "a normalization of US-Russia relations would be in the interest of both countries and contribute to global predictability and stability." This would be a recurring theme of the United States in connection with the summit.

On May 24, a few days after Blinken's meeting with Lavrov in Reykjavík, Jake Sullivan met in Geneva with Nikolai Patrushev, of the Russian

Security Council, to finalize the details for the summit. The following day, the White House announced that President Biden would meet with Putin in Geneva on the afternoon of June 16, and again emphasized that the "leaders will discuss the full range of pressing issues, as we seek to restore predictability and stability to the US-Russia relationship."

Summit preparation shifted into high gear after the May 25 announcement. There were many disparate and complex issues that President Biden could discuss with Putin in what would be a comparatively short period of time (when factoring in the need for translation) in a single afternoon. Ukraine was only one part of a crowded agenda that included arms control and strategic stability under the New START treaty extension and beyond; cybersecurity after the SolarWinds attack; wrongfully detained Americans; and embassy operations. The overriding goal, as the White House stressed repeatedly, was to minimize and contain the Russia problem while the administration focused on other priorities.

A new issue in which the Russians had a clear interest was Afghanistan, after the US focus had shifted from the ill-fated attempt to punish Russia for the alleged GRU bounties to ending completely the US military presence in the country. Biden had announced on April 14 that the United States would begin withdrawing its remaining military personnel from Afghanistan on May 1 and complete the withdrawal by September 11, the twentieth anniversary of the Al-Qaeda attacks on the United States. The Russians, along with many other countries, especially in Central Asia, were concerned about instability in Afghanistan after the US military left. Acknowledging the continuing terrorism threat from Afghanistan, the United States sought a new base in the region for its counterterrorism mission after it withdrew from its Afghan bases. This would be a topic for discussion at Geneva.

In preparation for the summit, I participated in extensive discussions with the president and his advisers covering all the foregoing potential agenda items and any other issues that Putin might conceivably raise. President Biden was an active participant in these meetings: he was always prepared, with a big binder of materials that he had plainly read, asking good questions and poking holes in arguments that I and others were making. In light of his decades of service in the Senate and as vice president, he approached the task of meeting with Putin, someone he had dealt with before, with an obvious advantage. We did not have to spend much time on background information. The president was a quick study: although he was undeniably elderly, I did not observe any of the debilitating effects of aging that later garnered so much media attention.

After a meeting at the White House on the evening of Sunday, June 6, the president asked me jokingly how it felt to be a "deliverable" for a US-Russia summit meeting. I said I was honored and very much looking forward to going back to my post.

President Biden did a double take. "Really?" His tone and facial expression suggested a little surprise that anyone in their right mind would seriously welcome a return to Russia in these circumstances. As I assured him that I was looking forward to returning to Embassy Moscow, I was reminded of my conversation two years earlier with his predecessor, who had also quizzed me incredulously about whether I really wanted to go to Russia. Trump and Biden, so different in so many ways, were at least on the same page about this.

---

The June 16 Geneva summit was added to the end of an unusually long, eight-day trip to Europe by President Biden. Before arriving in Geneva, the president would attend a meeting with G7 leaders in Cornwall in the United Kingdom, followed by a NATO leaders meeting in Brussels. I traveled directly to Geneva from Washington on June 14, and had dinner that night with Ambassador Robert Wood, the US representative to the Conference on Disarmament, who was based at the US Mission to the United Nations in Geneva. The weather was gorgeous and so we dined on the outdoor patio of a restaurant on Lake Geneva. This beautiful Swiss city was a perfect location for the summit, as it had been many times in history for important international meetings.

President Biden and his enormous traveling party arrived the following day. Anytime the president of the United States travels, even for short trips within the United States, it is an overwhelming logistical spectacle—and much more so for long international trips. Until one actually has seen all the various aircraft, limousines, staff and security vehicles, Secret Service and military personnel, White House staff, and accompanying members of the press, it can be difficult to visualize the scale of the undertaking. The White House took over the InterContinental Hotel in Geneva as its base of operations. I stayed at a separate hotel with State Department personnel traveling from Washington and worked out of an office at the nearby US Mission to the UN. One of the presidential limousines was parked at the mission, and I encouraged the mission staff to have their pictures taken next to the huge, armored vehicle, known as the Beast.

I met with the NSC staff on June 15 to discuss the final preparations for the summit the following day. There was a growing sense of anticipation: we had worked hard to prepare for the meeting, and we were eager for Biden finally to sit down with Putin, and to see how the discussion would unfold. We were told that most of the large Russian delegation had arrived separately from Putin, who would be flying into Geneva with only a small number of aides on his plane on the morning of the summit. We speculated that Putin's unusual travel pattern might be a further example of his Covid-19 isolation. I was curious to learn which Russian officials were in Geneva with the delegation, and who would make it into the room when Putin and Biden met.

The morning of June 16 dawned with more spectacular weather under a bright, sunny sky. I went to the InterContinental Hotel early to make sure I was included in the entourage that would travel with the president to the venue for the summit: Villa La Grange, which has been the setting for many important meetings and conferences over the years. The villa, an eighteenth-century manor house at the center of Parc La Grange, south of Lake Geneva, boasts lush gardens and a famous library of over fifteen thousand volumes. It was a fitting site for a summit meeting of the US and Russian presidents.

I tucked myself into a large black Suburban SUV in President Biden's motorcade, which wound through the streets of Geneva—an armored column, essentially, in a place where security was already very heavy. We arrived at the villa on time, shortly after 1 p.m. local time. Putin had arrived from the airport before Biden reached the villa, as was planned, but the fact that he was on time was itself noteworthy. In documenting his arrival, the media covering the summit correctly observed that Putin was notorious for being late to meetings with world leaders, including Presidents Obama and Trump and Pope Francis. Some wondered what Putin's on-time arrival might portend for the summit. I thought it might just indicate Putin's desire to get the summit done with and fly out of Geneva as quickly as possible.

Swiss president Guy Parmelin greeted Putin and Biden on the front steps of the villa. Flanked by the two visiting presidents, Parmelin briefly wished Biden and Putin a "fruitful dialogue, in the interest of your two countries, and the world," and then departed. Biden and Putin shook hands before turning and entering the villa for the summit, which would have two parts. The first was a "1+1 meeting" in which the presidents, accompanied by Secretary Blinken and Minister Lavrov, as well as two interpreters, would meet in the villa's library for an hour and thirty minutes. Following that meeting and a short break, the presidents and a larger group of their respective advisers would meet—an "expanded bilateral meeting," or "expanded bilat"—for up to three hours. I would participate in the expanded bilat.

The White House had set up a large air-conditioned white tent in the park near the villa for the use of US government officials and White House staff who were not in the meetings in the villa. There were tables, chairs, and multiple large video screens inside to follow the media coverage of the summit, as well as boxed lunches, snacks, and drinks. It was, at minimum, a nice place to keep cool out of the sun, as the temperature outside rose into the high 80s Fahrenheit. I found a comfortable place inside the tent as I awaited the conclusion of the 1+1 meeting. I had hoped there would be an opportunity to speak with the Russian officials who were not in the 1+1 meeting—I was told that Deputy Foreign Minister Ryabkov was in Geneva with the Russian delegation—but they were not available.

The first meeting ran a little over the planned ninety minutes. When it concluded, those of us participating in the expanded bilat went into the villa. The US delegation joining President Biden and Secretary Blinken for the expanded bilat consisted of Jake Sullivan, Under Secretary Nuland, myself, and the NSC senior director for Russia and Central Asia, Eric Green. While President Biden took a break, the rest of the delegation met with Secretary Blinken in a hallway to learn what had happened at the 1+1 meeting. There was a limit to what we could discuss, because of well-founded concerns about listening devices, but the secretary reported that the tone of the discussion had been respectful and businesslike. The two presidents had covered many issues, including strategic stability and arms control, cybersecurity, and wrongfully detained Americans. There was very little agreement, other than the prearranged decision that Ambassador Antonov and I would return to our respective embassies, but both presidents had expressed their positions without rancor, which was what I expected. The only drama was a brief scuffle between some reporters and security officials when the international press covering the start of the meeting in the library was asked to leave.

While inside the villa before the next meeting, I saw no sign of any senior Russian officials near us. The media had reported that the Russian delegation joining Putin and Lavrov for the expanded bilat might include Ambassador Ushakov; Kremlin press secretary Dmitry Peskov; the chief of the general staff of the Russian Armed Forces, Colonel General Valery Gerasimov; Deputy Foreign Minister Ryabkov; and Ambassador Antonov. They were reported to be in the villa but not making themselves available to anyone on the US side.

At the conclusion of the forty-five-minute break, the US delegation, led by President Biden, was invited first into the meeting room—as the nominal host, having asked the Russian president for the meeting—on the villa's ground floor. The room had ornate décor with fine art on the walls and a fireplace, but it was not large. The conference table took up much of the room. The US delegation stood on one side of the conference table, with the president at his place in the center. Moments later, the Russian delegation entered, led by Putin. He walked down the US side of the table and shook hands with each of us, and his delegation followed with handshakes for all. No one wore masks and Putin did not seem concerned about Covid-19 exposure. He looked just as I had seen him every time before: fit, relaxed, and nattily dressed in a black suit with a purple tie. He seemed to be in good humor, smiling broadly. Any ill will over Biden's earlier remark about him being a "killer" seemed to have been washed away, or at least very carefully hidden.

I had two immediate reactions. First, it was noteworthy that Ryabkov was not there. Each side was to have five advisers in addition to the president in the room, and apparently Sergei did not make the cut. Second, the

Russians included General Gerasimov in their delegation, even though there was no one from the US military in Biden's delegation. I sat directly across the table from the general and he appeared uncomfortable in that setting. He also looked tired and worn, with his hands showing a tremor that he tried to hide.

President Biden kicked off the discussion with the observation that he and Putin had covered many issues in the 1+1 meeting and so we might not need as much time for the expanded bilat as was scheduled. Speaking through an interpreter, Putin agreed with that assessment. The discussion moved to Afghanistan, with Biden making the case for the United States responsibly ending its twenty-year military mission there later in the summer. Putin expressed concern about instability in the region and the threat of terrorism from Afghanistan. In response to the US interest in seeking a counterterrorism base in Central Asia after its Afghanistan pullout, Putin mused with a grin that the Russian military might allow us access to its large and strategically important 201st Military Base in Dushanbe, Tajikistan, which is not far from the border with Afghanistan. As Putin chuckled, General Gerasimov's eyes widened. This clearly was an unscripted moment and an apparent effort at humor by Putin, because it was so utterly improbable, and indeed there was never any follow-up.

On Russia's militarization of the Arctic, an issue which Secretary Blinken raised, Putin dismissed our concerns as overstated. He said Russia was merely restoring Soviet-era infrastructure that had fallen into disrepair, not adding new facilities. At one point when Lavrov was speaking directly to Biden, Putin interrupted and advised Biden to be careful negotiating with Lavrov because he was half Armenian. Putin laughed at his own attempt at ethnic humor. It was another example of how loose and at ease he felt. He exuded confidence, which I believed was the message he wanted to convey.

The meeting adjourned after a little over an hour, having produced few notable moments. To my memory, Ukraine was not mentioned once in the expanded bilat, although it was raised briefly in the 1+1 meeting. I did not speak in the meeting and had not expected that I would, unless one of the principals had a specific question for me. Only the two presidents, the foreign minister and the secretary, and Jake Sullivan and Yuri Ushakov spoke. I was surprised at how short the meeting was and that

Ukraine was not a significant topic. The fact that Putin did not focus on Ukraine, which was obviously a prominent issue for him, puzzled me.

The two sides had agreed in advance that there would not be a joint press conference following the summit. Each president would meet with the media separately, with Putin going first. President Biden watched Putin's performance with a group of us in a workspace at the villa set aside for Biden to prepare for his press conference. It had been a long day at the end of a long trip, but President Biden was raring to go (after eating a couple of cookies as an energy snack) and interested to see what his Russian counterpart would say.

At the top, Putin began with a headline summary of the discussion at the summit as focused on "strategic stability, cybersecurity, regional conflicts, and trade relations. We also covered cooperation in the Arctic. This is pretty much what we discussed." He quickly turned, with no further elaboration, to the press for the first question from a Russian reporter, who asked about Ukraine, a topic the reporter described as "of great interest." Putin said Ukraine "was touched upon. I cannot say that it was done in great detail, but as far as I understood President Biden, he agreed that the Minsk agreements should be the basis for a settlement in southeastern Ukraine," which was accurate.

Putin offered "a general assessment" of the summit as "constructive." He said there "was no hostility at all. Quite the contrary." And he described Biden as "an experienced person, which is absolutely obvious," and a "very constructive and balanced person." Over the course of his remarks, Putin disclosed that there would be follow-up dialogues between the United States and Russia on strategic stability, cybersecurity, detainees, and issues involving the operations of our respective embassies, which he mentioned in connection with "the ambassadors returning to their stations."

There were, of course, substantial helpings of outlandish whataboutism in Putin's answers. He invoked the January 6 riot, the Black Lives Matter protests, and gun violence in deflecting criticisms of Russia and not answering questions about Russia by changing the subject to critiques of the United States. It was an obvious but nonetheless skillfully executed tactic. He was calm, confident, and in control of the room.

But three small, subtle points in Putin's answers stood out to me, beyond his typical Russian disinformation techniques. First, Putin could not resist emphasizing that it was Biden who wanted and asked for the meeting: "He also suggested that we meet—it was his initiative." Second, Putin gave a backhanded compliment to Biden's habit of invoking his mother's aphorisms: "He recalled some things about his family, about what his mother told him—these are important things. They do not seem to be directly related to the subject, but they still show the level and quality of his moral values." Putin was not-so-subtly mocking what he portrayed as the quaint musings of an old man. It was a signal of his confidence in himself and in his ability to deal with the American president. Finally, when asked whether it was possible to stop the deterioration in relations between the United States and Russia, Putin made the point that I had heard so often in my time in Russia: "It is hard to say, because all actions that led to the deterioration of Russia-US relations were initiated by the United States, not us."

As we watched Putin on the video screen in our workspace, I observed to President Biden that it was a standard performance by Putin, entirely predictable and with no surprises. The president seemed relaxed and took Putin's comments in stride. He never mentioned Putin's subtle mockery. Biden wanted to project his own confidence as he prepared to meet the media. It had been a long day already, but the president watched Putin's entire performance carefully.

By the time Putin was finished and Biden began his press conference, it was early evening. The venue near the villa was created for Biden (Putin's press conference was in another location) and was outdoors with Lake Geneva in the background. It was a magnificent setting, but the president's podium was on a stage under a bright sun, and it was hot. The advance team had visited the site multiple times, but each visit was earlier in the day when the stage was in the shade. Apparently, no one had accounted for the fact that the president would be standing under a glaring sun. The US officials who had participated in the expanded bilat were supposed to sit in the front row, to the right of the stage, but the sun was in our eyes and it was difficult to see the president. Only Secretary Blinken and I stayed in the heat and glare, rather than retreat to the shade.

In his opening statement, the president said he and Putin "share a unique responsibility to manage the relationship between two powerful and proud countries—a relationship that has to be stable and predictable. And it should be able to—we should be able to cooperate where it's in our mutual interests." He described his goal for the summit as laying down "some basic rules of the road that we can all abide by." The president then surveyed a wide array of subjects discussed at the summit: human rights issues, including the Navalny case and the wrongfully detained Americans, press freedom, strategic stability, cybersecurity, Syria, Iran, the Arctic, and Afghanistan. At the very end of this lengthy review, Biden made a fleeting reference to "the United States' unwavering commitment to the sovereignty and territorial integrity of Ukraine. We agreed to pursue diplomacy related to the Minsk agreement." He did not mention Ukraine again and did not receive a single question from the press about Ukraine.

At one point in the middle of the press conference, the president asked the indulgence of those in the audience as he took off his suit coat, because "the sun is hot." The secretary and I looked at each other as we broiled under the sun and shielded our eyes from the glare. We decided it was not a good look for us to retreat to the shade and leave our row completely empty in front of the president onstage, so we stayed there sweating.

Overall, Biden assessed that the tone of the summit was "good, positive." The ultimate test, however, would come in "six months to a year," after the start of the dialogues on strategic stability, cybersecurity, and detainees, when he would ask, "'Did the things we agreed to sit down and try to work out, did it work? Do we—are we closer to a major strategic stability talks and progress? Are we further along in terms of...' and go down the line. That's going to be the test." He denied that he had any trust in Putin: "Look, this is not about trust; this is about self-interest and verification of self-interest."

As the president was walking off the stage, a reporter yelled a question, "Why are you so confident [Putin will] change his behavior?" The president flashed an angry glance at the reporter and walked toward her, snarling, "I'm not confident he'll change his behavior. Where the hell—[why] do you do [that] all the time? When did I say I was confident?" It was an unbecoming end to the summit, and the president later apologized to the reporter at the airport, before boarding *Air Force One*. I attributed his outburst to the heat and to fatigue after a long day. As he was leaving the villa, the president pointed to me and said with a smile that he was sending me back to Russia for diplomacy and "not to paint walls," which was a reference to the frequent news stories about the staff cuts at Embassy Moscow and the "all-purpose duty" we had instituted to maintain the facilities. I said I would happily take that assignment.

I returned to our hotel in Geneva with Secretary Blinken and Under Secretary Nuland, where we discussed my return to Moscow and how long I would remain as ambassador. They were interested in having me stay at my post for as long as possible, because they were pleased with the job I was doing. I said I was willing to stay for another year, to June 2022, but that December 2022 would mark three years in the job for me, which was about the average tenure for recent American ambassadors in Moscow. They were grateful for my commitment to stay for at least another year after the sacrifices Grace and I had already made during the pandemic. I then flew home to Washington with the secretary while the under secretary flew to Brussels to brief our NATO allies on the results of the summit.

It seemed that both presidents had accomplished what they had set out to do at the summit. Just by accepting Biden's invitation and sharing the limelight with him, Putin had achieved his principal goal, which was to enhance his standing at home and abroad. He heard a US president describe him as the leader of a "powerful and proud" country that shared a "unique" relationship with the United States. The era of the Russian Federation as a "regional power," as President Obama famously described Russia in 2014, was over.

Biden laid down the "basic rules of the road" for Putin and established a diplomatic framework to test whether the two countries could come together to address challenging issues like arms control and cybersecurity. Moreover, he had sat across from Putin—universally acknowledged to be a very smart and exceedingly wily adversary—and handled the discussion with aplomb. There were no gaffes, no unforced errors, as some in the media had predicted when comparing Biden with Putin. All that was left was the "testing" that Biden sought from the dialogues he had set up with Putin.

---

After a few days at home with Grace, I flew back to Moscow on June 23. The work tasked out of and flowing from the summit was already underway. The United States and Russia released a joint statement after the summit that "reaffirm[ed] the principle that a nuclear war cannot be won and must never be fought" and announced a "bilateral Strategic Stability Dialogue . . . to lay the groundwork for future arms control and risk reduction measures." Deputy Secretary of State Wendy Sherman would lead the US representation at the dialogue and Deputy Foreign Minister Ryabkov would lead the Russian side, which mirrored the format of the prior dialogue in which I had led the US delegation as deputy secretary in July 2019. The cybersecurity dialogue with the Russians would be led by Anne Neuberger, the deputy national security advisor for cyber and emerging technology at the NSC. I would lead the discussions with the Russian government on wrongfully detained Americans.

I met with Ambassador Ushakov on June 25, and with Deputy Foreign Minister Ryabkov on July 1, to discuss the dialogues on which the presidents had agreed, as well as the other meetings that were planned or proposed after the summit. For example, former secretary of state John Kerry, the president's special envoy for climate, visited Moscow for three days in mid-July to discuss climate change issues with the Kremlin. His visit included a phone call with President Putin, who was in Sochi at the time. The US special envoy for Iran, Robert Malley, visited for two days in September to meet with Deputy Foreign Minister Ryabkov on issues related to the Joint Comprehensive Plan of Action, known informally as the Iran nuclear deal. And a high-level delegation from NASA came to Russia in November for meetings with the Russian space agency, Roscosmos.

I had a brief sense, in the summer after the June summit, that US-Russia relations were no longer in a precipitous free fall, with the presidents no longer trading insults and expelling diplomats. It appeared that our relationship had stabilized—in an overall wretched state, to be sure, but at least more stable than before the summit, which was Biden's principal goal. The two delegations in the Strategic Stability Dialogue met twice in July and September, with future meetings planned, and the cybersecurity dialogue was progressing. Despite my substantial doubts to the contrary, it might just become a "normal," while very hostile, diplomatic relationship between two adversaries, more akin to the relationship between the United States and the Soviet Union at certain points during the Cold War. That was the best I thought we could hope for, at least during my tenure as ambassador.

As the lead for the United States on our engagement with the Russians on detainees, much of my attention in this period was focused on the three wrongfully detained Americans in Russia: Whelan, Reed, and Calvey. I attended the court hearing on Reed's appeal on June 28, and, like everyone else, was not surprised when the appeal was denied. Reed was moved to a labor camp near where Whelan was incarcerated, in Mordovia.

I traveled to visit each of them on September 21 and 22, making the eight-hour drive from Moscow. The IK-12 facility in which Reed was held was smaller than the Stalin-era IK-17 camp in which Whelan had been an inmate for over a year, but equally depressing and dilapidated. Both men were holding up remarkably well, considering what they had suffered. I was able to speak with each of them for over an hour without a guard present, although we were certainly being monitored. I brought books and other items that they had requested. I did my best to reassure them that the US government was doing everything it could to secure their release. Whelan and Reed also had specific concerns about their treatment in their respective camps—for example, excessive punishment in isolation cells, denial of phone calls, delayed mail, lack of medical care— that I raised with the respective wardens.

The Calvey case was different. After several months of pretrial detention and subsequent forms of house arrest, the charges against Calvey were changed to embezzlement, and he was convicted in a Moscow court on August 6, 2021. Most significantly, he received a five-and-a-half-year *suspended* sentence, which was a surprise. He came to visit me at Spaso House a few days later, relieved that he had not received a sentence of further imprisonment. He told me how his American and Russian friends had reacted differently to the conviction and sentence. Americans contacted him to commiserate and offer their sympathy and concern over the fact that he was wrongfully convicted of a serious crime, embezzlement. His Russian friends, on the other hand, were ecstatic that he had achieved a rare "victory" in the Russian judicial system by not being sentenced to further incarceration. In any event, he was in much better shape than Whelan and Reed, who were languishing in labor camps in Mordovia.

I met with Ushakov and Ryabkov in July to explore how we would structure the discussion about detainees, on which the presidents had agreed in Geneva. Ushakov told me that President Putin had put one of the FSB's highest-ranking officers, Colonel General Sergey Beseda, in the lead for the Russian government on all matters involving detained Americans. As one of the FSB's most senior leaders, General Beseda had led the Fifth Service (Operational Information and International Relations) since 2009. Known colloquially as the Baron, Beseda was heavily involved in the Russian operations in Ukraine from 2014 to 2015 and was sanctioned by the EU and UK as a result. I asked for a meeting with Beseda as soon as possible.

Ryabkov called me later to say that he would host a meeting for me and Beseda at the MFA on Friday, July 23. I asked why the meeting would be at the MFA, if the FSB was in the lead, and Ryabkov said that was how the FSB wanted to proceed. I prepared for the meeting by reviewing all the ideas that had been discussed in the prior administration for a trade for Whelan and Reed. An interagency team had reviewed every Russian individual in US custody, as well as other actions that the United States could take that might interest the Russian government enough to release the innocent Americans they were detaining.

My review focused on a tenuous proposal in October 2020 by the former national security advisor to Trump, Robert O'Brien, which involved trading certain Russians convicted in the US criminal justice system for Whelan and Reed. This was rejected by the Russian side, which at the time was led by Patrushev. The Russians did not respond to a slightly revised proposal by O'Brien in late 2020, after the election. In my meeting with Beseda, I would review what had transpired in the prior year and try to get his reaction to the unanswered proposal, which I would suggest might still be open.

I arrived at the MFA in mid-afternoon and was escorted to the large conference room that Ryabkov often used for meetings with me. The Russians were already seated on one side of the table, and it was a large contingent from both the MFA and the FSB. Ryabkov introduced me to Beseda, who greeted me with a large smile and firm handshake. It was immediately clear why he was known as the Baron. Tall and trim, in his midsixties, Beseda looked like an investment banker in an expensive suit. He carried himself in a self-confident but not overtly threatening manner. He did not have to pose; everyone knew who he was and what he represented.

Beseda did not speak English; his second language was Spanish, and he had spent time in Cuba and Central America earlier in his career with the KGB. Ryabkov was the host and very deferential to his senior guest from the FSB. He spoke in Russian to accommodate Beseda, which was a change because he and I usually spoke English in our meetings and phone calls. Ryabkov said Biden had asked for this meeting and I was his representative, so the Russians looked to me to guide the discussion.

I directed my remarks to General Beseda, reviewing the proposals that had been discussed in the prior year and the interest of the United States in exploring whether any of them, including the last proposal to which the Russians had not responded, could form the basis for a negotiation that would lead to the release of Whelan and Reed.

Ryabkov asked some questions about my characterization of the scope of the prior discussions between O'Brien and Patrushev, and whether I was renewing the final proposal made by O'Brien. Beseda was mostly silent, staring at me with an interested but not fully engaged countenance. I said I was there to start a discussion and not to make a final offer. We went back and forth over the serious nature of Whelan's alleged crime (espionage). They objected to my use of the word "alleged," because Whelan was already convicted, as was Reed. Beseda continued to say very little and began looking at his watch.

After approximately half an hour, Beseda announced that he regretted that he had to leave for another meeting, but that Ryabkov and I could continue the discussion. As he walked out the door with his entourage, Beseda said to Ryabkov and me that there was no need to update him on what we discussed after he left: "I'm FSB. I'll know what you talked about." I laughed, as did Ryabkov, although his was more of a nervous laugh. I appreciated the Chekist humor.

The discussion on detainees effectively ended after Beseda left, and we had accomplished nothing. I had no more idea of what the Russians might be willing to consider for the release of Whelan and Reed than I did before the meeting. Ryabkov and I moved on to other matters involving the operations of the US embassy. As our discussion finished, Ryabkov said I would hear from them later about the issues we had discussed with General Beseda.

On Monday, I received a message that Ambassador Ushakov wanted to meet with me on the following day to discuss the American detainees. When we met, I told Ushakov that I was disappointed that Beseda would not engage with me. Ushakov said there was a problem because the FSB did not want to negotiate with the American ambassador. It was not how they operated; they wanted to speak with senior officials from the CIA or the FBI or both. I told Ushakov that President Biden had designated me as the person to speak on his behalf about detained Americans, and it was not the FSB's role to decide who would speak on behalf of the American president. Ushakov said he understood my point, but that he had worked hard to get the Russian government to move on this issue and that the FSB's leadership would play a key role in the negotiations. It was vitally important that they be included, and they would not negotiate with an ambassador; they would negotiate only with their counterparts from the US Intelligence Community. I said I would need to consult with Washington.

I went back to the embassy and called Ambassador Roger Carstens, the special presidential envoy for hostage affairs and a decorated former US Army Special Forces officer. Roger was an old friend and one of the other rare holdovers from the Trump administration. The message from Ushakov was yet another problem to layer onto the already hard and complicated matter of wrongfully detained Americans in Russia. We needed to consult with the White House and the leadership of the CIA and the FBI to find a solution.

———————

As we pressed forward with the discussion about American detainees in Russia, we were simultaneously conducting a diplomatic campaign to shore up the operations of our embassy in Moscow. In this effort, I worked closely with Chris Robinson, an experienced Russia hand who served as the deputy assistant secretary of state for Russia after he was expelled by the Russians in 2017 as the political counselor at Embassy Moscow.

Chris and I shared the lead for negotiations with the Russian MFA on two related problems: First, we not only had to fire all our local staff (employees and contractors) by the end of July under Putin's April order, but we also had to find replacements for those local staff who were performing indispensable tasks. That would require the approval of the MFA. Second, we had to get visas for Americans who were needed to maintain our facilities. Again, we needed help from the MFA. To put it mildly, I was not happy that we were so dependent on the Russians.

The negotiations with the MFA in the summer of 2021 focused most intensely on the first problem. We needed contracts for some essential services, which included the security provided by my bodyguards and our Local Guard Force. When I first arrived at the embassy, in January 2020, I was astounded to learn how much the State Department relied on the Russians who were employed as my bodyguards and also the Russians who worked as contract security guards to provide continuous coverage at the entrances to the embassy compound and at Spaso House (these were in addition to the Russian Interior Ministry officers, who stood outside the walls). The Local Guard Force supplemented the security provided by the Marine Security Guard detachment and the Diplomatic Security officers assigned to the embassy. All our security personnel—American and Russian—were subject to the authority and direction of the embassy's regional security officer (RSO), a senior US diplomatic security officer.

The US government seemed confident about the security provided by the Russian employees and contractors, but I thought the situation was absurd on its face and that we were far too dependent on Russians who could be coerced by their government to undermine our security. One of the most confounding features of the entire arrangement was that Elite Security, the Russian company that provided the local guards under contract, was owned by a retired KGB officer. I said this was embarrassing and could not stand. Thus, long before Putin made it illegal for us to employ Russians, I forged a plan to substitute Americans for the Russian bodyguards and the Local Guard Force, but the plan was expensive and would take time and the cooperation of the Russian MFA to implement. In the interim, we needed an arrangement with the MFA to continue to contract for the local guards and to employ my bodyguards. After many hours of discussions over many weeks, the Russians finally agreed to this temporary arrangement until the spring of 2022.

As these negotiations were ongoing, the safety and security of Embassy Moscow was also threatened by our inability to get visas for American technicians and engineers to maintain essential systems on the compound. The most acute problem was the failure of the water pump in the basement of the chancery. We needed experienced technicians to come to Moscow with new parts to fix the pump, which supplied water to the fire suppression system (sprinklers) throughout the building, but we could not get visas from the MFA unless we gave visas to Russian "diplomats" who were assessed to be undeclared intelligence officers.

It was the same problem we had been confronting for years, except in this case there was a major safety risk for the United States. The embassy had already had two recent (small) fires in the chancery that were fortunately discovered and extinguished before there was any serious damage or the failing fire suppression system was triggered. One of these was an electrical fire near my office that was discovered by the smell of wires smoldering. We organized an old-fashioned twenty-four-hour-a-day fire watch and had numerous random fire drills to make sure everyone was prepared for the worst. I complained loudly to the MFA. And I reminded my colleagues back in Washington that Embassy Moscow had an unfortunate history of disastrous fires over the years. Among the most notorious was in 1977, when Moscow "firefighters"—some of whom were actually KGB officers in new and ill-fitting turnout gear—were allowed into the old chancery that was on fire and made off with an undetermined amount of classified information and documents. In 1991, KGB officers again showed up to fight a fire at the US Embassy wearing turnout gear. The tell this time was the dress shoes they wore (poor tradecraft).

We discussed the issue in a country team meeting at the embassy, and I said it was my intention not to allow any Russian "firefighters" onto the compound in the event of a fire in the chancery, which was an office building (not a residence) that had a large amount of highly classified information and valuable security systems in controlled-access areas. I would rather let the building burn to the ground than potentially give the Russians access to all of that. I said our approach would be like the old

'70s song "Disco Inferno," by the Trammps ("Burn, baby, burn"). Eventually, after many months and an even larger number of snap fire drills, we finally got visas for American technicians to come to Moscow to fix the chancery's fire suppression system.

Despite frustrating problems like this, I was determined to do all I possibly could to "normalize" our relationship with the Russian government and, especially, the Russian people. In July, I finally took my first trip as ambassador to Saint Petersburg, a visit that had been delayed for almost a year and a half because of the pandemic. Over several days, I met with academics, lawyers, art historians at the State Hermitage Museum, and business leaders. I had lunch with members of the American Chamber of Commerce in Saint Petersburg. US businesses comprised some of the last major connective tissue between Russia and the United States, which made it that much more essential to support them.

It was a good trip and long overdue. I had arrived as ambassador with plans to travel frequently across Russia, but those plans were upended, like so many other things, by the pandemic, which continued to impact our activities at the embassy. For yet another year, we could not have the traditional July 4th party at Spaso House with hot dogs and hamburgers for thousands of guests. Instead, we had a small party outdoors on the embassy green for the American mission community, which did not have the public diplomacy impact that a large celebration of America with hundreds of Russian guests would have had. It was a fun party, nonetheless. Billy Groshen's band Persona Non Lada (a wordplay on diplomatic expulsion—the Latin *persona non grata*—and the Russian Lada automobile) performed, and Bart Gorman, our staid deputy chief of mission and a Russia expert, dressed up in an Uncle Sam costume. The Russian security services were kind enough to participate by flying a surveillance drone low over the green during the party.

Under Secretary Toria Nuland was an enthusiastic supporter of my efforts to "normalize" our diplomatic relationship with the Russian government. She was very experienced in Russia, having served at Embassy Moscow as a junior foreign service officer. Later, after serving as the US ambassador to NATO and then as spokesperson of the State Department, she was the assistant secretary of state for European and Eurasian affairs during the Revolution of Dignity in Ukraine in 2014. She was well known to the Russians, and she and I shared similar views on the difficulties of dealing with a hostile Kremlin.

A normal diplomatic relationship, even between adversaries, includes occasional meetings with and visits by senior diplomats to survey and discuss all relevant issues, not merely separate dialogues on single topics, no matter how important. So, we proposed a visit by Under Secretary Nuland to Moscow in October, in the hope of encouraging a pattern of reciprocal visits by senior diplomats once or twice a year. The Russian MFA was interested, but there was a legal issue that they needed to address. Under Secretary Nuland had been sanctioned by the Russian government for her service as assistant secretary during the Ukrainian revolution, and the Russians had to suspend that sanction while she served as under secretary to allow her to enter the country. The MFA subsequently notified me that they had made the necessary legal adjustments to permit Nuland to travel to Russia, but the sanction was only suspended and would continue to apply after she left her position at the State Department. Undeterred, we arranged for her to travel to Moscow for meetings in mid-October— another minor win, as far as I was concerned, in our effort to get US-Russia relations back on something resembling a normal footing.

---

Amid all the dialogues, discussions, and meetings with the Russians in the four months after the Geneva summit, the one thing we were not talking to them about was Ukraine. But Putin was certainly thinking, talking, and writing about it himself. At his June press conference in Geneva, the first question from the Russian state media was on Ukraine. This was not a question asked by a disinterested journalist exercising independent editorial judgment. This was a question from the Russian government through its state media on the first matter "of great interest" that Putin wanted to talk about. He returned to the topic of Ukraine later in the press conference, when he condemned the Zelensky government for allegedly failing to comply with the Minsk agreements.

He also rejected criticism of Russian troop movements threatening Ukraine. He described them as "military exercises" that should not be subject to international scrutiny because "we conduct them on our territory, just like the United States conducts many of its exercises on its territory." In short, the United States should mind its own business. Indeed, he went further and accused the US military of moving close to the borders of the Russian Federation in a threatening manner. "So, the Russian side, not the American side, should be concerned about this, and this also needs to be discussed, and our respective positions should be clarified."

Immediately after the summit, the White House was sensitive to criticism that it was not doing enough to support Ukraine. On June 18, White House press secretary Jen Psaki issued a statement, responding to Republican criticism in Congress, in which she denied that the administration had "held back security assistance to Ukraine." She asserted that "in the run-up to the US-Russia Summit" the United States had "provided a $150 million package of security assistance, including lethal assistance," to Ukraine. But there was no organized discussion with the Russian government on its campaign to undermine Ukraine and expand and make permanent Russia's seizure of Ukrainian territory in 2014.

On July 12, Putin issued his own extraordinary "statement" on Ukraine in the form of a lengthy article, "On the Historical Unity of Russians and Ukrainians," a purported historical narrative surveying well over a thousand years of history dating back to ancient Kyivan Rus and "the princes of the Rurik dynasty." Putin sought to establish that Ukrainians and Russians "are one people," united by a common language and religion, who "have developed as a single economic system over decades and centuries." The article was universally scorned by a wide variety of scholars as "bad history," in the words of Yale history professor Timothy Snyder. Interestingly, for a Russian president who routinely excoriated the European empires in Africa and Asia, the article glossed over the massive and bloody imperial expansion by Russia, particularly in the seventeenth and eighteenth centuries.

The real significance of the article, however, was not as bad history but as a political statement by Putin. He identified an "anti-Russia concept which we will never accept" in Ukraine, which he attributed to "radicals and neo-Nazis" in Kyiv who were "systematically and consistently pushed" by the United States and the EU. To make his point, Putin used overwrought, emotional language: "Russia was robbed, indeed." Russia was not treated "with respect!" The treatment of Russians by Ukraine is a "despicable thing."

Putin's article concluded with an ominous warning. "All the subterfuges associated with the anti-Russia project are clear to us. And we will never allow our historical territories and people close to us living there to be used against Russia. And to those who will undertake such an attempt, I would like to say that this way they will destroy their own country."

To be sure that no one missed or misinterpreted his strongly held views on Ukraine, the Kremlin published an interview with Putin the day after his article was released. Putin described his written work as "more than just an article" in which he laid bare the "anti-Russia agenda." In a revealing moment of paranoia, he described the "anti-Russia project" as having started "a long time ago, during the Middle Ages." Toward the end of the interview, Putin asserted that

> it does not matter to us how a neighboring state—in this case, Ukraine—will shape its foreign policy and its roadmap. What matters is . . . that nobody creates problems or threats for us. What we see, however, is that military development of this territory is starting, which is worrying. I have expressed my opinion about this issue multiple times. And I think that our concerns will eventually be heard by those involved. After all, it is not Ukraine's doing. It is happening on Ukrainian territory and people are being used. I really do hope that our concerns will be taken seriously.

I believed that before long, the United States was going to have to face Putin's "concerns" about Ukraine. His rhetoric showed he would not let the situation continue indefinitely on a slow boil. Ukraine was his highest priority, and we were going to have to reckon with it or he would turn up the heat. I hoped that the visit of Under Secretary Nuland in October would give us the opportunity to discuss Ukraine constructively with senior Russian officials. I could not have imagined that by the time of her visit, the flames would already be beginning to grow.

PART III

# THE MARCH TO WAR

# CHAPTER 10

# RUMORS OF WAR

THE MOST IMPACTFUL EVENT IN US-Russia relations in the busy summer of 2021 occurred not in Washington or Moscow but in South Central Asia: the calamitous and tragic American withdrawal from Afghanistan. In fact, this was the only event during my entire tenure as ambassador that prompted ordinary Russians to express to me personally their contempt for the United States. It was not the January 6 riot; nor the George Floyd murder and protests; nor our political, cultural, and legal conflicts over LGBTQ or abortion rights. Not even the ongoing investigations within the United States into Russia's various forms of interference in our elections or our civil society. Rather it was the Afghanistan debacle that really resonated with the Russian government and people. Part of the explanation for that resonance was certainly the Soviet Union's equally disastrous history in Afghanistan in the 1980s and final withdrawal from the country in February 1989. But whatever the reasons, the impact of our withdrawal from Afghanistan on our relationship with Russia soon proved to be significant.

The end of the American presence in Afghanistan unfolded quickly after the mid-June Geneva summit between Biden and Putin. An offensive initiated by the Taliban at the beginning of May gradually built momentum and swept across the country. On July 2, the US military abandoned its huge air base at Bagram, with no advance notice to the Afghan security forces, and the facility was immediately ransacked by looters. As intense fighting continued between the Taliban and the Afghan government, *Al Jazeera* reported that the Taliban was advancing quickly and would soon be "at the door of Kabul." President Biden announced on July 8 that the conclusion to the US war in Afghanistan would be on August 31.

In explaining his decision to withdraw US troops, Biden said he trusted "the capacity of the Afghan military, who is better trained, better equipped and...more competent in terms of conducting war" than it had been to resist the Taliban. But after the withdrawal of American support, the Afghan security forces were promptly routed by the Taliban in a matter of weeks. On August 15, Kabul fell and Afghan president Ashraf Ghani fled the country. The United States was left with a harried and dangerous evacuation of personnel and Afghan contractors and allies from Hamid Karzai International Airport in Kabul.

The Kremlin watched all of this closely and drew a direct connection to Ukraine. Four days after Kabul fell, Patrushev said in an interview with *Izvestia* that the United States would eventually desert Ukraine as it had forsaken its ally in Afghanistan. "Kyiv is obsequiously serving the interests of its overseas patrons, striving to get into NATO. But was the ousted pro-American regime in Kabul saved by the fact that Afghanistan had the status of a principal US ally outside NATO? (No). A similar situation awaits supporters of the American choice in Ukraine." Patrushev predicted that like Afghanistan, Ukraine would be left to "the whim of fate."

On August 19, the same day that Patrushev spoke to *Izvestia,* I met with Deputy Foreign Minister Igor Morgulov, who had responsibility at the MFA for Afghanistan. He said that Russia would not close its embassy in Kabul, but neither would it recognize a new Taliban government. The Russians had received assurances from the Taliban about the security of their embassy. Nevertheless, Morgulov was concerned about the threat of terrorism and the safety of Russian diplomats in the country. His concerns were justified a year later when an Islamic State suicide bomber killed two diplomats at the Russian embassy in Kabul.

The United States suffered a more immediate and grievous loss in a terrorist attack by the Islamic State on August 26, during the Kabul airport evacuation. Over 180 people, including thirteen US service members, were killed in a suicide bombing and the resulting chaos. The United States compounded the tragedy by targeting a vehicle on August 29 a few kilometers from the Kabul airport. The US was tracking Islamic State

terrorists, but a drone strike on this vehicle mistakenly killed ten innocent civilians, including seven children, and no terrorists. The ignominy
for the United States as this horror unfolded was palpable.

I was running along the Moscow River very early one morning in late
August with my bodyguards when an older gentleman out for a walk recognized me as the US ambassador—not an uncommon event. He pointed
at me and chanted, laughing, "Afghanistan! Afghanistan!" My bodyguards
(one running with me and one on a bicycle) looked at me and shrugged. I
did not feel threatened; I was simply embarrassed. Russians would tell me
that at least the Soviet Union was able to leave Afghanistan with a planned
evacuation and a final column of troops and vehicles processing over the
Hairatan Bridge into the Uzbek SSR. But not the United States. Like our
infamous evacuation of Saigon at the end of April 1975, we had terrified
civilians seeking to get on our aircraft fleeing Afghanistan. These Afghans
were so desperate that some clung to the wheel well of a departing C-17
transport and fell to their deaths as the plane rose above Kabul.

Kremlin propagandists did not need to embellish what happened to
the United States in Afghanistan in August 2021. The blow to American
credibility and standing was in some ways immeasurable. How does one
calculate that type of damage? When I was deputy secretary of state, a
senior diplomat from a very close US ally, and an individual with great
affection for the United States, told me that in his opinion, our country
never had recovered fully from the reputational wounds inflicted by the
WMD fiasco in Iraq and by President Obama backing down from a "red
line" he had declared on chemical weapons use by the Assad regime in
Syria. Our chaotic, deadly, and dishonorable withdrawal from Afghanistan ripped open those wounds. And while Americans were debating
loudly among themselves who was at fault—Trump or Biden or both—the
Russians were making their own assessments and planning accordingly.

As the initial furor over the humiliating US withdrawal from Afghanistan began to subside in September, the Russian parliamentary elections
that month would become the most important political event of the year
for the Kremlin, and I followed them closely. At stake were the 450 seats
in the State Duma, where Putin's United Russia party had held a supermajority of 343 seats since 2016. Putin signed a decree on June 17, 2021, the

day after the Geneva summit, calling for new elections over three days in mid-September. Voting over multiple days was a change authorized by Russian law in 2020, during the Covid-19 pandemic. The September 2021 elections also featured remote electronic voting in certain regions, including Moscow. Both voting "innovations" raised concerns among independent election observers about the increased ease of vote fraud and manipulation by the Kremlin.

But Putin was not worried about the concerns of election observers, since there were not going to be any independent observers of this election. For the first time since 1993, the Kremlin declined to allow the OSCE to send a full election observer mission for a Russian election. In addition, the Russian government designated Golos, the country's only independent election monitoring organization, as a "foreign agent," which rendered it unable to observe the election. At the end of the day, the September 2021 State Duma elections were overseen only by the Kremlin, just as it oversaw all other aspects of Russia's "managed democracy."

The Kremlin's management included arresting, forcing into exile, or removing from the ballot all credible opposition leaders, including Alexei Navalny and anyone associated with him through his Anti-Corruption Foundation, which the Russian government had previously designated as an extremist organization. Those few opposition candidates who remained on the ballot were often targeted by "doppelgänger" candidates for the same office—candidates who were recruited to run to create voter confusion because they physically looked almost exactly like the true opposition candidate and had the same surname. This low-tech method of disrupting the vote was worthy of the best nineteenth-century ward heelers of Tammany Hall in New York.

In a high-tech move that implicated US interests and companies, the Russian government targeted an internet-based voting strategy created by Navalny and his Anti-Corruption Foundation called Smart Voting. Under this scheme, the Navalny organization would designate a single opposition candidate (often from among many) in each race, enabling voters to consolidate their votes in support of that candidate and in opposition to the candidate of Putin's United Russia party. Smart Voting had shown some promise in opposing United Russia candidates in Moscow city elections in 2019. The Kremlin would not let that happen again.

In early September 2021, a Moscow arbitration tribunal enjoined Google and Russian internet search giant Yandex from providing search results for the query "Smart Voting" in response to a lawsuit by an agricultural wholesaler that only months before had coincidentally (i.e., wholly implausibly) decided to register Smart Voting as a trademark. Simultaneously, the Russian government's media regulator and censor, Roskomnadzor, blocked access to the Smart Voting website and warned Apple and Google that they would be fined for interference in the election if they did not remove the Smart Voting application from their app stores, which they did on September 17, the first day of voting.

When voting concluded on September 19—amid widespread allegations of fraud, ballot-stuffing, and electronic voting chicanery, and in the absence of any credible election observers—Putin's United Russia party unsurprisingly had maintained its supermajority in the State Duma with 324 seats. Even though United Russia had lost almost twenty seats from its prior total, the Kremlin was seemingly satisfied with the overall results in an election with 52 percent turnout. There would be plenty of time to work out the kinks in the new system combining both multiday and electronic voting before Putin stood for reelection in 2024.

Indeed, with a chill in the air as the calendar turned to fall, 2021 was shaping up to be "a pretty good year for Vladimir Putin," as Russia scholars Eugene Rumer and Andrew S. Weiss concluded in an article published in November. Putin had met with the US president as an equal and "worthy adversary" on the global stage in Geneva, presiding over a rebuilt military and a resilient economy that had withstood Western sanctions since 2014. On the other hand, Biden and the United States had been revealed to be weak, unreliable, and incompetent in Afghanistan. Domestically, Putin had further solidified his political standing with fully implemented constitutional reforms and a dominant victory in the State Duma elections, having crushed what was left of the opposition. It was entirely reasonable to conclude, as Rumer and Weiss did, that from Putin's perspective "Russia's house [was] in order." But the title of their article highlighted the single issue that would soon shake Russia's house to its foundation: "Ukraine: Putin's Unfinished Business."

———————

Following the Russian elections in September, Embassy Moscow began preparing for the visit of Under Secretary of State Toria Nuland in October. We arranged a busy schedule that included separate meetings for the under secretary with Deputy Foreign Minister Ryabkov and Ambassador Ushakov, in addition to gatherings with international correspondents in Moscow, business leaders from the AmCham, and Russian alumni of US educational exchange programs.

The last—but what I believed would be the most important—meeting on the proposed schedule for Nuland was with Dmitry Kozak, one of Putin's key aides. Kozak had served as Putin's deputy chief of staff since January 24, 2020, and before that was the deputy prime minister of Russia, from 2008 to 2020, and he had the lead for the Kremlin on negotiations about Ukraine. Meeting with Kozak would give the United States an opportunity to engage with the Russians in a meaningful way on Ukraine, something that had not happened in years.

The first two days of Under Secretary Nuland's visit, October 11–12, saw little progress on our aspirational plan to try to "normalize" our diplomatic relationship with the adversarial Russian government. She covered a wide variety of issues, including the operations of Embassy Moscow and the ongoing strategic security dialogue, in her meetings with Deputy Foreign Minister Ryabkov and Ambassador Ushakov, but there was virtually no agreement on anything other than that we should keep talking. From my parochial perspective as ambassador, among the most valuable aspects of her visit was having a senior leader from Washington meet with embassy staff, participate in our country team meeting, and hold a town hall for the entire community. This was a morale boost at a post that had been isolated in a hostile country for a long time during the pandemic, with little direct engagement from the department's leadership.

We also used the occasion of the under secretary's visit to host a wonderful dinner on her last night in Moscow, for a half dozen prominent Russian journalists at Spaso House. The gathering included Dmitry Muratov, a cofounder and the editor-in-chief of *Novaya Gazeta*, who days before had won the Nobel Peace Prize, and Alexei Venediktov of Ekho Moskvy. The conversation was uninhibited and covered the full scope of US-Russia relations. The mood was decidedly pessimistic about the future of Russia under Putin's rule, but the discussion also covered topics unflattering to the United States. Dinners like that were once common at Spaso House, and I wondered whether we would ever return to that routine—or was this the last hurrah for an era that was ending?

Before she departed for the airport the next day, Under Secretary Nuland and I met with Kozak in his office on Staraya Square, near the Kremlin. I had not met Kozak before but was familiar with his personal background: born in Kirovohrad in Soviet Ukraine, he served as a young man in the *spetsnaz* (special forces) of the Soviet military's GRU (Main Intelligence Directorate). He moved to Leningrad after leaving the military, got a law degree, and worked as a prosecutor. When Leningrad became Saint Petersburg, following the collapse of the Soviet Union, Kozak joined the city government in the 1990s, eventually working alongside, and developing a close relationship with, Vladimir Putin.

After Putin moved to Moscow and was elevated to prime minister, Kozak joined him as his chief of staff. He stayed with Putin when he assumed the presidency in 2000, serving as deputy chief of staff in the office of presidential administration. In various roles over twenty subsequent years, Kozak became one of Putin's most trusted lieutenants. He was not a Chekist—he had never served in the KGB. Yet Kozak was part of a small group from Saint Petersburg (which also included former president Medvedev and Alexei Miller, the CEO of Gazprom) who, although not part of that feared elite, were able nonetheless to maintain close connections to Putin.

Kozak was a technocrat with a reputation for getting hard jobs done. He was described to me by one Russian observer of the Kremlin as Putin's assistant for "special assignments," of which he had many over the years. In 2004, he headed Putin's successful reelection campaign for president. Ten years later, Putin made Kozak responsible for insuring the success of the Winter Olympics in Sochi. And after the Olympics, Kozak was charged with integrating Crimea, newly seized from Ukraine, into the Russian Federation.

Kozak's role in the Ukraine conflict expanded considerably in early 2020. He left his position as deputy prime minister to return to Putin's office of presidential administration as deputy chief, a position he had held twenty years before. But this time he had an expanded portfolio with a mandate from Putin to oversee Russian policy on Ukraine. This included negotiations with the new Ukrainian government of President Volodymyr Zelensky, who had defeated Petro Poroshenko in Ukraine's presidential election in April 2019.

Zelensky had campaigned on a pledge to prioritize efforts to achieve peace in the Donbas, without conceding Crimea to Russia but giving it a lesser priority. In furtherance of this effort in the second half of 2019, the Ukrainians and Russians took a few modest steps toward de-escalation in Donetsk and Luhansk, with prisoner exchanges and some limited disengagement of forces on the line of contact. The faint hope for peace was grudgingly acknowledged by Putin, who said in 2019 that Zelensky was "sincere" in trying to settle the conflict.

This was the complex situation that Kozak inherited when he was designated by Putin as the lead negotiator on Ukraine, replacing Vladislav Surkov, a long-serving Putin adviser who had been the ideological architect of the conflict in the Donbas. The substitution of the "technocrat fixer" Kozak, himself born in Ukraine, for the "hard-liner" Surkov was viewed by me and many others at the time as a faintly positive sign. Consistent with that view, in February 2020, as I was settling in as ambassador, Kozak and Zelensky's chief of staff, Andriy Yermak, began a series of discussions to address the ongoing conflict in the Donbas, where there remained a persistent backdrop of violence.

The Kozak-Yermak negotiations led to an agreement in March among Ukraine, Russia, and the OSCE, the so-called Trilateral Contact Group, to establish a multiparty negotiating framework—an "advisory council"—for the conflict that would include representatives of the government of Ukraine and of the unrecognized "people's republics" in Donetsk and Luhansk. The agreement was extremely unpopular with most Ukrainians, however, as it represented a form of recognition of the two occupied regions of Ukraine and the Russian military presence there. Because of the hostile reaction of the Ukrainian people to this apparent surrender of sovereignty, the agreement later had to be repudiated by the Zelensky government.

Despite this setback, Kozak and Yermak continued their discussions, which led in July 2020 to a cease-fire agreement for the Donbas. But like prior cease-fires, this one did not hold. As a result, Zelensky was beginning to be viewed by Putin and the Kremlin as an unreliable counterparty in negotiations, as someone who could not deliver on his commitments. The Zelensky government's manifest desire to end the conflict by considering unpopular compromises like the advisory council was met by Putin's resolve to end the conflict only on his terms. This was Kozak's mandate from Putin, not to negotiate peace but to achieve victory. Zelensky, on the other hand, was bound by popular sentiment against any compromise with Russia that involved surrendering sovereignty over the Donbas.

In the final analysis, Putin proved to be unyielding. Since 2014, he had been committed to reversing the Ukrainian Revolution of Dignity and the country's westward movement toward NATO and EU membership. These developments were anathema to him and entirely inconsistent with his historical and imperial vision of Russia, of which Ukraine was an essential and undeniable part. In his mind, and as he had laid out in his long historical article in July 2021, Russia and Ukraine were not two separate countries but rather constituent parts of the *Russkiy mir,* or Russian world. Russians and Ukrainians were one people, one nation, and should have one leader. It had been so for over a millennium, so who was Zelensky to resist what Putin considered the immutable tide of history?

Crucially, Putin was willing to have Russia endure Western opprobrium and sanctions to achieve his imperial goals. The importance of those goals to Putin and his vision of the *Russkiy mir* was worth those sacrifices or even greater ones in the future, to such an extent that it was difficult for Westerners to assess how far he was willing to go. He had no interest in a compromise that allowed the Zelensky government—an illegitimate usurper, in Putin's view, which was now cracking down on Russian oligarchs and interests in Ukraine—to regain control over the occupied portions of Donetsk and Luhansk. At a minimum, those regions needed to have autonomy from Kyiv (Putin was not yet demanding their legal absorption into the Russian Federation), and ultimately Ukraine needed to be independent of the West (and never affiliated with NATO).

Thus, although the Kozak-Yermak discussions continued, there was no progress in resolving the conflict in the Donbas. The Russians had been satisfied to wait to achieve Putin's objectives through negotiations with the Zelensky government, but their patience was wearing thin by 2021, because they believed that Zelensky could not or would not deliver what Putin wanted. The Russians were also finished engaging with the French and German governments in the Normandy Format to implement the Minsk agreements and negotiate a final resolution to the conflict. They were going to turn up the heat on Ukraine and the West.

The emerging Russian strategy was to force the Zelensky government to negotiate directly and exclusively with the separatist leaders of Donetsk and Luhansk by applying pressure through a military buildup on Ukraine's borders and increased violence in the Donbas. By threatening a war in Ukraine, which Western leaders so obviously (and rationally) wanted to avoid, Putin also sought to push those leaders to compel the Ukrainian government to negotiate and compromise with the separatist leaders.

This was the Russian policy being coordinated by Kozak when Under Secretary Nuland and I met with him on October 13. Known as the Cheshire Cat since his Saint Petersburg days for his wide smile and often inscrutable ways as a political operator and fixer behind the scenes, Kozak was an intense figure and heavy smoker. We met at a conference table in his office rather than a conference room, which was a change in protocol from how virtually every other senior Russian government official had received me. For example, I had never seen the offices in which Patrushev, Ryabkov, and Ushakov worked; and, for that matter, I never met with a Russian official in my office—for security reasons—when I was the deputy secretary of state. Kozak brought us into his office, as though he were taking us into the Cheshire Cat's lair, and spoke in Russian with an interpreter from the Kremlin.

Kozak's message from the very start of the meeting was that Kyiv needed to deal with the separatist leaders in the Donbas. Under Secretary Nuland raised the Minsk agreements, to which Russia was a signatory, and the Normandy Format negotiations on implementing the agreements led by the German and French governments with the Russians and Ukrainians. She said the United States did not want to interfere with or substitute for what the French and Germans were doing, but that we wanted to be helpful and provide support for a process that would lead to a peaceful resolution in the Donbas.

Kozak was not interested in discussions that involved the French and the Germans. He said they had not been productive for years. Moreover, he made it clear that although he was still in frequent communication with Yermak in Kyiv, Russia did not consider itself a participant in the conflict—despite the fact that it had signed the Minsk agreements. Russia would no longer engage in dialogue directly with the Zelensky government about peace. A solution in the Donbas was something that needed to be worked out between Kyiv and the representatives of the breakaway areas of Donetsk and Luhansk.

When Nuland pointed out the obvious Russian role (including of its military) in the conflict, Kozak pushed back, saying the only productive step the United States could take was to persuade its clients in Kyiv to come to a reconciliation with the separatists in the Donbas. The history of Russia's military intervention in the Donbas and the continuing presence of Russian troops, military equipment, and advisers there was not something he would debate. Under Secretary Nuland took that message back to Washington when she left Moscow that evening.

The Kremlin's views on negotiating with Ukraine were clearly hardening in comparison with its approach in 2020, when Kozak and Yermak negotiated over the failed advisory council and the short-lived cease-fire. The Russians were now focused on pressuring the United States and the West to force the Zelensky government to make concessions to the Russian proxies in the Donbas. The Russian military buildup on the borders of Ukraine was just part of that pressure campaign—for now.

In another effort to achieve "normalcy" in my tenure as ambassador to Russia, I scheduled a trip home for leave with Grace in late October. After our thirteen-month separation from 2020 to 2021 during the pandemic, my trip home earlier in the year, after the Russians asked me to depart, was not really a vacation. Much of the time was spent managing the embassy from afar in Washington and preparing with the State Department and the White House for the Geneva summit in June. Grace and I did not have a chance to take a vacation together.

I resolved to change that and to try to lead a more typical life as an ambassador with regular home leave. Grace and I planned to travel to one of our favorite warm places in the United States after I got home. Somewhere like the famous Fontainebleau Hotel, in Miami Beach, where we had stayed many times, including on our honeymoon in 1988, or the equally famous Hotel Del Coronado, in California, where we were also frequent guests over the years. A warm, comfortable, and familiar locale was just what we needed.

Because there were no direct flights between Washington and Moscow, I would connect through one of a few airports in Western Europe, and I would follow my routine of stopping to visit NATO leadership in Brussels and SACEUR (the Supreme Allied Commander Europe, General Wolters) at his headquarters in Mons, as I had done in March 2020—the trip on which I had received, in the form of a fist bump, an ominous indication that Covid-19 would soon shut down our world. Now, a year and a half later, I was relieved to have something resembling a normal routine. For my travel home to Washington in late October 2021, I added two additional stops, in Naples, Italy, where I met with the leadership of the US Navy in Europe, and in Stuttgart, Germany, for separate meetings with the US military's European Command and Africa Command. Thus, from October 17 to 21, I met with the entire senior military leadership of the United States responsible for Europe and Africa. It was a rare opportunity to take the pulse of the experts who were following and analyzing all of Russia's military moves carefully.

My discussions with US military leaders over those five days in October covered many subjects, including Russian threats to European security, the ongoing strategic stability talks between Russia and the United States, and the dangerous influence of Yevgeny Prigozhin, the career criminal who had befriended Putin years before in Saint Petersburg, and his private military organization, the Wagner Group, in Africa and

Syria. I offered my views on Putin and the political situation in Russia. And, most important, we all shared our assessments of Russia's prior military buildup near Ukraine and Putin's plans for the ongoing conflict in the Donbas. There was a concern among all of us about the real potential for a further Russian military intervention in Ukraine, although we were not yet anticipating an imminent Russian invasion. The discussion about Ukraine was at the top of the agenda, in short, but it was not the entire agenda.

Following my last meeting in Stuttgart, I boarded a train for the two-hour trip to Munich and a flight to Washington. I was joined by two of my colleagues from Embassy Moscow who were taking a separate flight from Munich to Moscow. I sat in a window seat and Jeff Sillin, a young political officer at the embassy, put his backpack in the overhead rack above us and sat next to me. The train was crowded, with every seat taken and people standing in the aisle. As we approached the Munich airport station, Jeff stood up to get his backpack and was startled to see that it was gone. We searched near our seats, and a woman sitting behind us said that two men speaking Russian (a fact she volunteered and of which she was certain) had put their coats on the overhead rack covering the backpack and when they took their coats to leave the train at a prior station, they must have taken the backpack with them. We knew immediately that this was not an ordinary theft.

Jeff lost some personal belongings and his personal, but not his diplomatic, passport. Fortunately, there were no sensitive documents in the backpack and Jeff never would have traveled with classified material. It was a lesson, however, that we were subject to surveillance, scrutiny, and harassment by the Russian security services even when we were outside Russia. When we got to the Munich airport, Jeff reported the incident to diplomatic security at the State Department. Because he still had his diplomatic passport, he was able to fly back to Moscow. I flew home to Washington.

Grace met me at Dulles Airport on Thursday night, October 21, and we spent a three-day weekend relaxing and planning our vacation, which would start on Friday of the following week, October 29. During the first four days of that week, I had meetings scheduled with the secretary and other senior leaders at the State Department and with the national security advisor and the NSC staff at the White House. I was also scheduled to give remarks at a leadership summit at NSA and had several meetings with senators on Capitol Hill. It seemed that everyone wanted to talk about Putin and Russia, but I was not going to miss the most important thing for which I came home, which was my time away with Grace. Or so I thought.

---

The week of October 25, 2021, changed everything in my life, both personal and professional. I was summoned to an unscheduled meeting with the secretary that turned into a secure videoconference with the NSC, the Defense Department, and the Intelligence Community. I listened as the secretary was briefed on consolidated reporting from across the Intelligence Community. The message was shocking.

The Russian military and security services were undertaking a massive aggregation of forces on the border with Ukraine in ways that gave strong indications they were actually going to invade. Not only were the number of forces significantly larger than earlier in the spring, but so were the logistical preparations necessary to support a full-scale military operation against Ukraine. The confidence among the intelligence professionals was high that Putin was putting in place all the personnel, equipment, fuel, and other resources that could start a major war in Europe at his command and with no notice.

The only question remaining appeared to be, would he do it? Would Putin invade Ukraine, or could we deter his aggression? The president was briefed on the situation and decided to send CIA director William Burns to Moscow to tell Putin and the Kremlin what we knew of Russia's preparations for an invasion of Ukraine, as well as to convey a message describing the significant response the United States and the West would have to such a blatant act of violent aggression. In sum, the message Burns would deliver on behalf of the president would be, "We see what you are planning to do and, if you do it, the response by us and our allies will be devastating to Russia."

After the Kremlin agreed to admit Burns to the country and allow him to speak with Putin, I was told by the department that I would accompany the director on his trip to Moscow. The plan was for Burns to leave on Sunday night, October 31, arrive on Monday for meetings, stay overnight at Spaso House, have meetings on Tuesday, and return to Washington that night. I would attend the meetings with Burns and return with him to Washington. What happened after that would depend on our assessment of the meetings in Moscow.

I had to break the news to Grace that our vacation plans would have to be postponed, which made neither of us happy. I told her there was a serious situation that needed to be addressed and that I was asked to accompany Burns on a trip to Moscow for meetings with Kremlin leadership. I apologized and said I had no choice in the matter. She agreed that having accepted the position of ambassador, I could not back out of my responsibilities when it was inconvenient, but that did not alleviate her disappointment. All we could do was plan to reschedule our vacation, and hope that the rain date would coincide with a calmer moment in US-Russia relations.

As the time for the Sunday night flight to Moscow approached, and I digested the intelligence reporting that had prompted the trip, I was struck by the fact that the information had come together so quickly and was presented with such confidence by the Intelligence Community. Just a week before, I had met with the senior US military leadership in Europe, and no one had raised an alarm about an imminent invasion of Ukraine by Russia. Being able to obtain the forewarning so quickly was a testament to the strength and talents of our Intelligence Community. And putting the intelligence to use by confronting the Russians, without revealing protected sources and methods, was a strategy the Biden administration would employ successfully in the future.

As I left my home in Bethesda on Sunday evening to get into the car taking me to Joint Base Andrews, children in trick-or-treat costumes were swarming my neighborhood on Halloween. The "spooky" atmosphere was a fitting send-off for the trip I was about to take. Grace remained at home to dispense the candy, which had always been my responsibility in our marriage.

The flight to Moscow on the CIA plane was delayed en route because of ground fog and bad weather at our destination. We were forced to divert to Riga, Latvia, where we spent Monday night. The US embassy in Riga did a terrific job in scrambling to accommodate our traveling party, which included a large security detail for the director, with no prior notice.

Burns and I had the opportunity to talk at length on the flight and the overnight stay. We were friends and fellow former deputy secretaries of state, but he held a more exalted office now and also had the ear of the president, a potent combination. I was there to support him, although he did not need much support. A retired career ambassador, Burns was a legend in the Foreign Service. A large auditorium in the State Department headquarters was named after him. Quiet and cerebral, with a PhD from Oxford, he was extremely influential. Everyone, including the president, wanted to know what Burns thought about an issue. The fact that Biden had given him the mission of meeting with Putin on Ukraine was a testament to his stature.

Our traveling party departed Riga on Tuesday morning after the weather had cleared in Moscow and arrived at midday. Burns and I went straight from the airport to our first meeting, which was with Patrushev. We were escorted into his conference room to wait for him. He entered with a smile and a friendly greeting for Burns, whom he had known for many years. As the host, Patrushev started the discussion after he sat down on his side of the table. He spoke in Russian through an interpreter as he read from notes in front of him. Patrushev surely had some sense of the message Burns was coming to deliver, yet he started the meeting with a bland review of the terrible state of US-Russia relations and the steps taken since the Geneva summit to try to improve the relationship that the United States had tried to destroy over several years. It was a typical Russian lament about American malevolence and betrayal.

Burns was brief and direct in his response. He said he was asked to come to Moscow by President Biden to deliver a message about what the United States had learned concerning Russia's recent extraordinary military buildup near Ukraine. It appeared that Russia was actively preparing to invade Ukraine. If Russia followed through on that threat, the United States and its allies would respond decisively and the consequences for

Russia would be severe—much more significant than the sanctions imposed from 2014 to 2015 over the illegal annexation of Crimea and the separatist violence directed and supported by Russia in the Donbas.

Patrushev, as a well-trained Chekist, betrayed no visible reaction. He folded his notes, put them to one side, and looked Burns directly in the eye while speaking extemporaneously in a firm, confident voice. He acknowledged that the Russian Federation was not an economic colossus like the Soviet Union and that the United States was much more powerful economically, but, Patrushev said, the Russian military was different now. It had been rebuilt and modernized with weapons that even the United States did not possess. He went so far as to say that Russia had equaled or even surpassed the United States in military strength.

As for the problems in Ukraine, Patrushev observed that Russia could handle any difficult issues in its geographic neighborhood. He scoffed at the idea of Russia invading Ukraine but did not deny it had the plans and capabilities in place to do so. His demeanor exuded confidence bordering on arrogance. I interpreted his message to us as saying: Ukraine is part of our ancient homeland and we can manage the problems there as we see fit. We have the capacity to do so, and you have neither the capacity nor the will to stop us. It was a chilling message that confirmed, at least in my mind, the intelligence reports that I had read the week before.

The Patrushev meeting concluded with a renewal by Burns of the American warning. At the very end, the small talk with Patrushev on our way out the door of his conference room turned incongruously, given the subject of the meeting, to a topic that Patrushev cared about deeply: volleyball (he had served previously as the head of the Russian Volleyball Association). Perhaps this was another sign of how relaxed and confident he felt.

Burns had two other meetings on his schedule before he would speak with Putin the following day. Alexander Bortnikov and Sergey Naryshkin, the directors of the FSB and SVR respectively, asked to see him separately. It appeared to be a matter of spy protocol that each wanted to meet with the CIA director while he was in Moscow. Another aspect of that protocol, as I had learned from Colonel General Beseda of the FSB, is that ambassadors (particularly American ambassadors) are unwelcome in such meetings, so I did not accompany Burns on his visits to the FSB and the SVR. He later reported that the discussions with Bortnikov and Naryshkin were entirely consistent with our discussion with Patrushev, which was not surprising, given Patrushev's very close relationship with Putin, his current position at the Kremlin, and his stature as the former FSB director who had succeeded Putin in that role.

The final meeting on Burns's trip was with Putin the following day, but it would not be in person. We learned that Putin was in Sochi, the Russian city on the Black Sea where the Olympics had been held several years before, and would speak with Burns by videoconference. We were instructed that Burns should go alone to Ambassador Ushakov's office near the Kremlin to access the video link. Putin, always circumspect in the reporting of his whereabouts, was especially sensitive about the large amount of time he spent in the mild climate of Sochi, particularly when the weather was cold and snowy in Moscow. It was widely acknowledged that he had rooms at his "billion-dollar palace" on the Black Sea configured to look like rooms at the Kremlin (or at his residences near Moscow) so that video coverage of him at work would give the impression that he was in the capital when he was actually in Sochi.

Burns returned to the embassy after the Putin videoconference in the early afternoon of November 3 and gave a brief report on the conversation with Putin, which again was very similar to the prior conversation with Patrushev. One thing that Putin had said that I found revealing in his discussion of European security with Burns was his observation, as he sat looking out his window at the Black Sea, that his intelligence advisers told him that over the horizon was an American warship carrying missiles that could kill him in a matter of minutes. He was obsessive about his security and very paranoid. Many world leaders, whether sitting in the Oval Office or at 10 Downing Street, could make the same point about missiles targeting them but do not personalize their discussion of national security like Putin.

As we departed the embassy for the return flight to Washington after the Putin debrief from Burns, I was reminded of his prior quip that dealing with the Russians had given him all of his gray hair. It was clear that the risk of a Russian invasion of Ukraine had risen dramatically since the Geneva summit in June.

On the flight home, Burns drafted a memorandum for the president and prepared to brief him on the response by the Russians to the warning from the United States. Our assessment of the Russian position was that they were extremely confident in their ability to invade and conquer Ukraine swiftly and were actively preparing to do so. We did not know whether Putin had made the final decision to launch an invasion, which might come without warning at the most tactically advantageous moment for the Russians, based on considerations as varied as politics and the weather. The one thing we knew after the meetings on this trip was that if Putin *did* decide to launch the invasion, he was convinced that Russia would prevail. That confidence and the attitude of the Russian leaders we saw, combined with the military preparations already underway, made me think an invasion was likely, but only time would tell.

The plane stopped to refuel at Shannon, Ireland. The traveling party deplaned, and I used the opportunity to buy some cans of Guinness for my colleagues and me to enjoy on the final leg of the trip. I offered a can to Bill, from one Irishman to another, and he gratefully accepted.

---

My return home was brief. The real threat of war meant that I was expected to be at my post in Moscow to deal with any contingencies and convey messages in both directions to and from Washington. There would be no vacation for me and Grace in the near future. I was not even sure whether I would get home for Thanksgiving, a cherished family event. If a war started, I did not want to be on the wrong side of the Atlantic.

When I told this to Grace, she was as upset and angry as I had ever seen her. I had missed Thanksgiving the year before, which was unavoidable because of the pandemic and the quarantine rules. To miss our family holiday gathering for a second straight year, however, was just too much. I did not have a good answer for her understandable reaction, other than to blame the threat of imminent war. Grace thought I must be exaggerating, because it was difficult for anyone in the West to believe that after the bloody history of the last century, any country would choose to start a major war in Europe in the twenty-first century.

But Russian statements and actions were confirming our concerns almost daily. Former Russian president Medvedev, now the deputy chair of the Security Council, published an inflammatory article in mid-October in the mainstream newspaper *Kommersant* entitled, "Why Contacts with the Current Ukrainian Leadership Are Meaningless." Citing Putin's article from July, Medvedev invoked all the vicious Russian tropes about Ukraine and its leaders and people. He described the "cognitive dissonance" of a Jewish president of Ukraine manipulated by Nazis leading the "absolutely dependent" Ukrainian people "under direct foreign control" by the United States and the West in a "confrontation with Russia, total containment of our country, and the creation of what was aptly named 'Anti-Russia.'" It was a bizarre and only semi-lucid rant (he referred at one point to "the Jewish intelligentsia in Nazi Germany, for ideological reasons, . . . [being] asked to serve in the SS"), but his conclusion was unmistakably clear: negotiations with Ukraine and its democratically elected government "are absolutely pointless."

If the Russians were not going to pursue a diplomatic resolution to the conflict with Kyiv, then the fact that their military was massed on the Ukrainian border, with only the command from Putin needed to launch an immediate full-scale invasion of the country, took on an even more insidious appearance. The next few months, if there was that much time left, would test whether America could muster the resolve, and rally its allies and partners, to deter Putin from choosing war.

# CHAPTER 11

# A GUN ON THE TABLE

NOVEMBER 2021 WAS AN UNUSUALLY tense month in Moscow. When I returned to the embassy after my trip with Director Burns, my priorities as ambassador had narrowed dramatically. No longer was I giving as much thought to cultural exchanges and the other usual programming of an American embassy; now I spent much of my time focused on the conflict in the Donbas and trying to do anything I could to lessen the risk of an imminent Russian invasion of Ukraine.

Back in Washington, the Biden administration was doing the same. After briefing allies and partners following the Burns trip, the US government released declassified information in mid-November documenting the extraordinary Russian military buildup on the Ukraine border. The German and French governments reached out to the Russians, seeking further engagement in the Normandy Format. Angela Merkel, who in a few weeks was leaving office after sixteen years as Germany's chancellor, was keen to try to bring Putin back from the brink of war. The anxiety in diplomatic circles in Moscow was rising fast.

I was skeptical, based on prior discussions in October with Kozak, that the Russians had any interest in further meetings with the Germans and the French on Ukraine, particularly if they included the Zelensky government in the Normandy Format. On November 17, the Russian Foreign Ministry breached diplomatic protocol by publishing twenty-eight pages of private correspondence between Lavrov and the French foreign minister, Jean-Yves Le Drian, and the German foreign minister, Heiko Maas. It was an effort by the Russians to try to show that the French and the Germans were misrepresenting the Russian position on negotiations about Ukraine.

The dispute boiled down to whether Lavrov was willing to meet with his German, French, and Ukrainian counterparts in the Normandy Format. The French had claimed publicly that Russia refused to accept a ministerial meeting. The Russian MFA disputed this contention and published these private diplomatic letters purporting to show that Lavrov had not declined the meeting, but merely was unavailable on the date proposed. The French and Germans complained about the breach of "diplomatic rules and customs," as described by the French Foreign Ministry spokesperson. And no meeting was ever held.

There were, from my perspective, two noteworthy aspects of this otherwise minor diplomatic contretemps involving other countries. First, the published documents included a proposed statement on the Donbas conflict, drafted by the Russians, that described it as an "internal Ukrainian conflict." The draft statement was completely contrary to the facts on the ground, where the Russian military and security services were firmly entrenched in the occupied portions of Donetsk and Luhansk, and therefore the draft was completely unacceptable to the Ukrainians, the French, and the Germans. But the draft statement was entirely consistent with the message Kozak had conveyed to Under Secretary Nuland and me. The Russians would not engage in any negotiations with the Ukrainians, because they claimed that Russia was not a party to the civil conflict in Ukraine. Moreover, the Russians were not interested in negotiations in the Normandy Format, which is why they published this private diplomatic correspondence: to poison the atmosphere and successfully scuttle a meeting with the French, German, and Ukrainian foreign ministers.

The second notable aspect of this row over diplomatic correspondence involved the United States and me directly. Kozak asked to meet with me at the Kremlin, and I assumed the meeting would be about Ukraine. When I arrived at his office on November 29, he told me that he wanted to share some documents and information with me. He handed me the stack of leaked documents, as well as other documents that had been generated in connection with prior meetings of the four Normandy Format countries. He told me, in what I thought was a patent embellishment, that

President Putin had asked him to give these documents to me personally and to explain their significance. Kozak said the files I now held would demonstrate that the French and the Germans were unreliable counterparties for the Russians in talks about Ukraine. Repeating his now familiar slogan, he said only the United States could bring pressure to bear on its client Zelensky to negotiate with the separatist leaders in Donetsk and Luhansk. That was the only way to solve the problems in the Donbas.

While we were speaking, the phone on Kozak's desk rang. He got up from the conference table and answered it. I could not hear what he said, and the call ended after a few moments. Kozak returned and said the call was from the Boss, who wanted to know whether he had given the documents to me. I asked, incredulously, "President Putin just called you?" He smiled and nodded. I found that hard to believe, but it was a remarkable moment whether Putin had been on the line or not. I thought the most likely scenario was that Kozak went through the ruse of a fake Putin call to try to convince me of the importance of the documents and the message he was conveying to me. I suppose it was conceivable that the Russian president had time on his hands and nothing more important to do than to call his deputy to find out whether he had, as instructed, handed the American ambassador some papers—but the odds of that seem vanishingly small.

The meeting ended shortly after the alleged phone call from the Boss, and I took with me the stack of documents Kozak had provided. I sent copies of the documents to Washington, along with a cable describing my unusual meeting with Kozak, including the phone call. The documents themselves were unremarkable and did not change anything about my assessment of the Russian role in undermining Ukrainian sovereignty in the Donbas, let alone the illegal Russian annexation of Crimea. But the meeting in which the documents were conveyed was itself an unusual signal of Russian intent to resolve the conflict in Ukraine, and through more nefarious means than the standard negotiations with Ukraine, France, and Germany.

Amid the Ukraine drama created by the Russian government, I still had to prioritize some of the usual business of the US embassy. I traveled to Mordovia again to visit Paul Whelan and Trevor Reed at their respective labor camps on November 23 and 24. It was important to reassure them and their families that I was doing all I could to look out for their interests. The best way to do that was to make the eight-hour drive over poorly paved and snowy roads to see them and meet with the warden at each camp to advocate for their proper treatment. The United States was no closer to getting them released, but at least I could bring them mail and personal items sent by their families to let them know that they were not forgotten.

I also continued to try to make personal connections with ordinary Russians, particularly outside Moscow. I planned a trip to Yaroslavl, an ancient city on the Volga about 160 miles northeast of Moscow, on December 3 and 4. The city has many cultural attractions, including a UNESCO World Heritage site, and is a hotbed of Russian hockey with many amateur teams and a well-known KHL team, Lokomotiv. In fact, the city had suffered a great tragedy ten years before when the Russian plane carrying the Lokomotiv team to its first game of the KHL season in Minsk, Belarus, crashed on takeoff from Yaroslavl and everyone associated with the team was killed. With players and coaches on board from many countries besides Russia, including Canada, Sweden, Germany, Ukraine, Latvia, Slovakia, Belarus, and the Czech Republic, as well as several former NHL players on the roster, it was a disaster not just for Russia, but for the entire hockey world.

During my visit to Yaroslavl, in addition to the standard cultural and political events, the embassy arranged for me to skate with youth hockey teams at two different rinks in the city. I was looking forward to the trip and brought my skates, gloves, and stick, along with a USA Hockey sweatsuit and a big bag of hockey pucks embossed with the US embassy logo to give to the young players on the ice. But as soon as I arrived in the city, it was apparent that someone in Moscow had advised the leadership of the city of Yaroslavl that it should not cooperate with my visit. My meetings with city administrators were canceled and I was advised that because of the Covid-19 pandemic I could not go into any hockey rinks in the city, even though the rinks were open and all teams at every level were practicing and playing.

I tried to make the most of my time, visiting two museums and touring many of the historical sites in Yaroslavl. While I was doing so, there was an apparent rebellion by local hockey coaches and parents against the edict that I could not visit any rinks in the city. Several local residents apologized to me and eventually I was allowed to meet with players in each rink, but I could not go on the ice. I stood on the bench while the players and many parents gathered on the ice in front of me. Some of the youngsters had decals on their helmets or patches on their sweaters commemorating the Lokomotiv team. We talked about our favorite players—Alexander Ovechkin was the consensus—and the players asked me questions about hockey in the United States. I am sure the highlight from their perspective was that they each got a souvenir puck, always popular with hockey players everywhere of any age.

At a large dinner that evening, I was able to speak about the tenth anniversary of the Lokomotiv team tragedy and what a loss it had been for the city and for hockey generally. I recalled that the head coach of the team, Brad McCrimmon, had been drafted by the Boston Bruins in the first round of the NHL draft in 1979 out of Brandon, Manitoba, when I was living in New England, and what a terrific player he had been over his NHL career. There were toasts to the players and coaches lost in the crash, and a current executive with the team approached me later to thank me for my remarks. He said that there was a Russian film in production on the tragedy and he wondered whether I could connect him with people in the United States and Canada who might be interested. I said I would be happy to make inquiries.

My trip to Yaroslavl was my last as ambassador to a Russian city outside Moscow. The pace of events involving war and peace in Ukraine, combined with an increasingly hostile attitude by the Kremlin toward interaction with me by public officials, made further travel inside Russia impractical. I was disappointed because I always enjoyed my engagement with the Russian people and those whom I met seemed to be pleased to meet with me. I suppose that was an unwelcome problem for the Kremlin.

———

Winter was approaching, and in addition to hardening its views on negotiations over Ukraine, the Kremlin was broadening the scope and increasing the urgency of its security demands in Europe. A key signal of this shift was a speech by Putin to the leadership of the Foreign Ministry on November 18, which was a *tour d'horizon* on the "implementation of Russia's foreign policy and priority tasks for the future."

In his speech, Putin focused on "Ukraine's internal crisis [as] among the most pressing and sensitive issues for" Russia but turned quickly to a criticism of Germany and France for "indulging the current [Kyiv] leadership's course on dismantling" the Minsk agreements, which "has led the talks and the settlement itself into a dead end." In fact, Putin said, it was "Western partners" that were "exacerbating the situation by supplying [Kyiv] with modern lethal weapons, conducting provocative military exercises in the Black Sea and other regions close to our borders." This was, in turn, part of "NATO's eastward expansion," of which "there have been several waves." He summarized the placement of NATO military infrastructure on Russia's borders that "can easily be put to offensive use" in "only minutes." Yet Russia's "concerns and warnings regarding NATO's eastward expansion have been totally ignored" by the West and, as a result, "tensions have arisen."

He warned NATO not "to stage some kind of conflict on our western borders which we do not need, we do not need a new conflict." But Putin also advised that he would defend Russia by providing "a proper response to NATO's military activity." And he charged the Foreign Ministry, and the Foreign Minister personally, with bolstering Russia's defenses: "Mr. Lavrov, it is imperative to push for serious long-term guarantees that ensure Russia's security in this area, because Russia cannot constantly be thinking about what could happen there tomorrow."

Two weeks later, on December 1, in a speech at the Grand Kremlin Palace, Putin expanded on Russia's immediate demand for "reliable and long-term security guarantees" from the United States and NATO. He complained that "Russia's legitimate security concerns were ignored, and they continue to be ignored," even as the "threat on our western borders is really growing, and we have mentioned it many times." To address this threat, Putin sought a "dialogue with the United States and its allies," in which Russia "will insist on the elaboration of concrete agreements that would rule out any further eastward expansion of NATO and the deployment of weapons systems posing a threat to us in close proximity to Russia's territory." Just as he had charged Lavrov two weeks earlier, Putin declared, "We need legal, juridical guarantees."

The stridency and urgency of his remarks led to an obvious question: why had Putin not raised these issues with President Biden in Geneva in June? It would have been the perfect forum in which to do so. What had created the existential "crisis" he described, and the immediate need for legal security guarantees, in the few months since Biden and Putin had met? The answer, of course, was nothing—except the massive Russian military buildup on its border with Ukraine, which Putin tried unsuccessfully to dismiss as military exercises on Russian territory and as "adequate military and technical measures" by Russia in response to the existing US military and NATO presence in and around Ukraine.

This "crisis" was, in short, manufactured entirely by the Russians— and they would discuss it only with the United States.

Putin got a small measure of relief a few days later, in the form of a two-hour video teleconference with President Biden on December 7. In the month since Burns's warning in Moscow, the Russian military had continued to amass more military personnel and resources targeting Ukraine and made further logistical arrangements for an invasion, including the preparation of field hospitals and ammunition stockpiles. It was a menacing response to the message Burns had conveyed to Putin and the Kremlin in early November.

President Biden, in renewing the American commitment to Ukrainian sovereignty and territorial integrity in his December video teleconference with Putin, also reissued the Burns warning. As Jake Sullivan later recounted to the media, Biden told "Putin directly that if Russia further invades Ukraine, the United States and our European allies would respond with strong economic measures." In addition, the United States would provide "defensive matériel to the Ukrainians above and beyond that which we are already providing, and we would fortify our NATO allies on the eastern flank with additional capabilities in response to such an escalation."

Putin's response was to pivot from Ukraine to NATO. The Kremlin statement after the call, in describing the discussion of the threat to

Ukraine raised by Biden, said that "Putin warned against shifting the responsibility on Russia, since it was NATO that was undertaking dangerous attempts to gain a foothold on Ukrainian territory, and is building up its military capabilities along the Russian border." For this reason, Putin repeated his assertion that Russia was "eager to obtain reliable, legally binding guarantees ruling out the eventuality of NATO eastward expansion and the deployment of offensive strike weapons systems in the countries neighboring Russia."

The two presidents were talking past each other, with Biden focused on the immediate military threat to Ukraine and Putin focused on his larger and longer-term security concerns with NATO. Putin was leveraging his ability to invade Ukraine to confront the United States about NATO's presence in Eastern Europe and talks to admit Ukraine, a redline for the Russians. Biden was looking to deter Putin from starting another war in Europe. The only thing on which the two men could agree was that officials from both countries would follow up in future meetings.

Sensitive to the urgency of the situation, Washington wanted those future meetings to take place immediately. The US assistant secretary of state for European and Eurasian affairs, Dr. Karen Donfried, accompanied by senior NSC staff, would come to Moscow the following week for talks. Assistant Secretary Donfried was an expert in European affairs and the former president of the German Marshall Fund. She also had worked previously at the State Department and the NSC. We were personal friends because her husband, Alan Untereiner, was my former law partner for many years at Mayer Brown.

Dr. Donfried and her traveling party arrived on the evening of December 14 and stayed with me at Spaso House for the evening. We had two meetings with familiar Russian figures scheduled for the following day. The first would be with Deputy Foreign Minister Ryabkov and the second with Deputy Chief Kozak in the office of presidential administration. The assistant secretary and I were prepared to talk about issues ranging from security in Europe, and Putin's new quest for legal guarantees, to the Russian military buildup on the border with Ukraine, which was growing by the day.

---

The meeting with Deputy Foreign Minister Ryabkov on the morning of Wednesday, December 15, began at the Foreign Ministry with a statement by him that in response to a request from President Putin, the Russian MFA had drafted two proposed treaties, one between Russia and the United States and the other between Russia and NATO. He gave copies of the two draft treaties to the assistant secretary and me and said that the MFA wanted to begin negotiations with the United States on these documents in two days, on Friday, December 17, in Geneva. Finally, whether the United States agreed to meet with the Russian delegation in two days or not, the MFA would release the two drafts to the public on that date.

The presentation by the Russians of two draft treaties at the meeting was unexpected: we had not come for that purpose. I looked at the two documents I held in my hands and realized immediately that this was not a serious proposal but a propaganda stunt bordering on the absurd. This was evident at a glance: the two drafts were in Russian, and no English translations were provided. The usual protocol for a document presented by the Russians to me was for the official version to be in Russian and a courtesy translation to be provided in English. Similarly, any official document I presented to the Russian MFA was in English with a courtesy translation provided in Russian. Under the schedule for the Geneva negotiations Ryabkov had proposed, we had less than forty-eight hours to prepare for the meeting, but it would take several hours alone just to have the two drafts translated.

Furthermore, even if we had been given translated drafts, it was ludicrous to think that the assistant secretary and I could brief the senior leadership of the US government, up to and including the president, on these extremely complex and sensitive subjects in time for the United States to formulate a negotiating position, put together a negotiating team, and have that team travel to Geneva in less than two days. I said as much, and asked Ryabkov: Why the rush? Why had this become a crisis? He did not have a good answer, other than repeating Putin's claim that the security of the Russian Federation was at stake based on threatening moves by NATO. Dr. Donfried politely said that we would have to review the draft treaties after they were translated, consult with Washington, and get back to the MFA with a response to the proposed meeting in Geneva, although it was very unlikely we could proceed on the Russian schedule.

Ryabkov plainly was not expecting the United States to be prepared to meet with a Russian delegation on Friday in Geneva. His presentation to us was a pretext for the Russians to make public their draft treaties—containing the legal guarantees Putin sought—with an accompanying statement of regret that the United States had declined to negotiate over the documents on the schedule proposed by Russia. I was tempted to call their bluff and ask Ryabkov, why wait until Friday? If there was indeed a crisis, we should begin negotiations right now. But I quickly thought better of it, because the only ones who would have been as flustered by that idea as Ryabkov would have been my colleagues in Washington.

The meeting with Ryabkov continued, but there was little we could productively discuss about European security, because we had not read the draft treaties he had just handed us. We shifted the conversation to Ukraine, but Ryabkov had a dodge for that issue. He said that the MFA was not authorized to speak with us about Ukraine; only Dmitry Kozak in President Putin's office could have that discussion, and we were meeting with him later in the day. Thus, other than receiving the draft treaties and the message about proposed negotiations in Geneva in less than two days, which could have been transmitted without a meeting, it was a frustrating morning with Ryabkov.

One thing Ryabkov said, however, did get my attention. As we talked about the United States and Russia engaging to discuss security in Europe, Ryabkov said that was vital for world peace because as nuclear superpowers the situation could quickly spiral into a nuclear standoff like the Caribbean Crisis, which is what Americans and the rest of the world call the Cuban Missile Crisis. It always amazed and appalled me how quickly my Russian interlocutors could invoke the threat of nuclear war—often with just a hint or a suggestion, but occasionally with outright nuclear blackmail—to support their position and hijack a discussion about a subject that had nothing to do with nuclear weapons or war. Our conversation with Ryabkov on the morning of December 15 should have been about peace in Ukraine and the terms and implementation of the Minsk agreements. Instead, he was invoking nuclear war between the United States and Russia to heighten the sense of crisis and put the United States on its back foot.

This was a common Russian tactic dating back many decades into Soviet history, and it was one they would use with increasing frequency in the months ahead in connection with Ukraine. I said publicly as ambassador that if I ever casually invoked nuclear war in a negotiation, as the Russians did, my president would recall me immediately, fire me, and in doing so suggest that I have my head examined. It was that dangerous and crazy, because no sane person wants nuclear Armageddon, and that includes Putin. But the Russians were nonetheless willing to say anything, including invoking nuclear war, to achieve the objectives of the state in the person of Putin.

Dr. Donfried and I left the MFA disappointed by the discussion with Ryabkov and skeptical that we would hear anything more encouraging from Kozak in the afternoon. We stopped at the embassy to drop off the draft treaties to have them translated into English. It was too early in the morning in Washington to brief anyone at the State Department or the White House by phone on what had happened with Ryabkov, so we wrote email updates for our colleagues back home and prepared to depart for Kozak's office.

The Cheshire Cat was his smiling and inscrutable self during our meeting, blowing smoke from his gold-filtered cigarettes into the face of the assistant secretary and launching into long soliloquies about the evil and perfidious regime in Kyiv. He had nothing new to offer, repeating his previous admonition that the United States needed to step in and direct its "vassals"—his word and a favorite among senior Russian officials—in Kyiv to negotiate with the separatist leaders in the Donbas. The only new development that I observed was that when the discussion inevitably veered to a topic beyond the precise borders of Ukraine, Kozak would stop the conversation and declare that he could not continue because he was not authorized to discuss European security, which was the exclusive province of the MFA.

It was a classic case of bureaucratic misdirection and not a serious effort at good faith diplomacy. The notion that Ukraine and European security could be divided into two separate silos and not discussed together in one meeting was factually, legally, and politically ridiculous, and completely at odds with Russia's oft-stated commitment to the "indivisible security" of Europe, which of course includes Ukraine. But it was a tool for them to avoid actual negotiations while trying to give the public appearance of engaging in diplomacy. Dr. Donfried and I left the meeting with Kozak as frustrated as we had been with the earlier meeting with Ryabkov. Moreover, Kozak's long-winded diatribes against the government in Kyiv had caused the assistant secretary to miss her flight out of Moscow.

We returned to the embassy in the late afternoon and finally had time to read the now-translated draft treaties that Ryabkov had presented to us. Each document was short; the draft treaty with the United States was a little over three pages and had eight articles. The first three articles articulated platitudes that would commit the two countries to the "principles of indivisible, equal and undiminished security," with a pledge not to "undertake actions nor participate in or support activities that affect the security of the other Party," whether "individually or in the framework of an international organization, military alliance or coalition."

Article 4 of the draft treaty with the United States got to the heart of Putin's pursuit of security guarantees by gutting a key provision of the North Atlantic Treaty that created NATO. This draft article would commit the United States "to prevent further eastward expansion" of NATO and "deny accession to the Alliance to the States of the former Union of Soviet Socialist Republics." In addition, the United States would be prohibited "from establishing military bases in the territory of the States of the former Union of Soviet Socialist Republics that are not members" of NATO, using "their infrastructure for any military activities or develop[ing] bilateral military cooperation with them."

The next article in the draft treaty would dramatically curtail US military deployments worldwide, including in support of NATO treaty obligations and in defense of treaty allies like Japan and South Korea. Article 5 of the draft prohibited the United States "from deploying [its] armed forces and armaments, including in the framework of international organizations, military alliances or coalitions, in the areas where such deployment could be perceived by the other Party as a threat to its national security." This would include a prohibition on "flying heavy bombers equipped for nuclear or nonnuclear armaments or deploying surface warships of any type, including in the framework of international organizations, military alliances or coalitions, in the areas outside national airspace and national territorial waters respectively, from where they can attack targets in the territory of the other Party."

Articles 6 and 7 sought to limit the deployment of nuclear weapons by the United States and covered the extended deterrence of its "nuclear umbrella" in defense of Japan, South Korea, and every NATO ally. The draft treaty prohibitions would preclude the United States from deploying "ground-launched intermediate-range and shorter-range missiles outside [its] national territories, as well as in the areas of [its] national territories, from which such weapons can attack targets in the national territory of the other Party." More broadly, the United States would be prohibited from deploying any "nuclear weapons outside [its] national territories" and would be required to "return such weapons already deployed outside [its] national territories" to the United States, which would undo decades of US nuclear defense policy.

The draft treaty with NATO was a little shorter but had nine articles and was virtually identical in substance and tone to the draft treaty with the United States. Article 4 of the draft NATO treaty declared that Russia and the members of NATO, "as of 27 May 1997,...shall not deploy military forces and weaponry on the territory of any of the other States in Europe in addition to the forces stationed on that territory as of 27 May 1997." Draft articles 6 and 7 precluded NATO enlargement, "including the accession of Ukraine as well as other States," and prohibited NATO "military activity on the territory of Ukraine as well as other States in Eastern Europe, in the South Caucasus, and in Central Asia."

Read together, the two draft treaties that Ryabkov had delivered would have completely undermined the US defense relationships with, and military support for, its treaty allies around the world. The Russians essentially were proposing to rewrite the North Atlantic Treaty to eviscerate the bedrock mutual-defense commitments in that historic agreement adopted more than seventy years ago, during the Truman administration, in the aftermath of the war. For example, there could be no US military deployments on the territory of NATO allies that Russia "perceived" as threatening, no bomber training missions, and no port calls by US Navy ships. The draft treaties also would have eliminated NATO's "open door" policy enshrined in Article 10 of the North Atlantic Treaty under which NATO allies "may, by unanimous agreement, invite any other European State in a position to further the principles of this Treaty and to contribute to the security of the North Atlantic area to accede to this Treaty."

The cumulative scale of the proposed changes to long-standing US defense policies established after World War II was breathtakingly broad. No US president would ever agree with many if not most of the proposals in the draft treaties, and the Russians clearly knew that. These were not serious drafts to be negotiated by diplomats and military experts. These were unreasonable public demands to be used solely for misdirection and disinformation. The *New York Times* later quoted Samuel Charap, a Russia expert at the RAND Corporation, on the draft treaties released publicly by the Russian MFA: "Diplomacy requires compromise and flexibility. It usually entails avoiding public ultimatums. Basically, this is not diplomacy. It's the opposite of diplomacy."

After Dr. Donfried and I had read the two drafts, we arranged for a secure call with our colleagues at the State Department and the White House to describe the meetings with Ryabkov and Kozak and to provide our thoughts on the proposed treaties. My view was that the sum of the contrived crisis atmosphere, the preposterous schedule for the meeting proposed by Ryabkov in Geneva, the shell game played by Ryabkov and Kozak in abjuring authority to negotiate on different aspects of an indivisible problem, and the outrageously excessive security guarantees in the two draft treaties combined to make the Russian engagement with the United States on this matter insultingly unserious. I resorted to a profane colloquialism and said Putin had just given President Biden the finger and told him to perform an unnatural act on himself. It was "the opposite of diplomacy."

The United States would not meet with the Russians on their proposed schedule in less than forty-eight hours to review their draft treaties. Instead, we suggested alternative meetings in three different fora to discuss Ukraine and European security in mid-January. President Biden spoke with Putin on December 30 and the White House reported that in addition to "urg[ing] Russia to de-escalate tensions with Ukraine," Biden "also expressed support for diplomacy, starting early next year with the bilateral Strategic Stability Dialogue, at NATO through the NATO-Russia Council, and at the Organization for Security and Cooperation in Europe."

The intervening Christmas and New Year holidays were relatively somber for me and my colleagues at the embassy. I was compelled to stay at my post because of the pace and seriousness of events related to Ukraine and our engagement with the Russians. It was the second consecutive Christmas I would not spend with my family and neither Grace nor I was happy about it. But I had little time to brood, because the Russians had agreed to the three meetings that Biden had discussed with Putin, and preparations for each were already underway.

The first meeting was in Geneva on January 10, 2022, as a follow-up to the US-Russia Strategic Security Dialogue in the standard bilateral format begun after the Geneva summit, with Deputy Secretary Sherman leading the US delegation and Ryabkov leading the Russian delegation. Two days later, the NATO-Russia Council met in Brussels, and the United States was again represented by Deputy Secretary Sherman, while the Russians were led by Alexander Grushko, the Deputy Foreign Minister responsible for NATO in the MFA. Grushko was a seasoned diplomat who had served previously as the Russian permanent representative to NATO. Finally, on January 13, the US and Russian representatives to the OSCE participated in a meeting of the Permanent Council of that organization in Vienna.

Three meetings in three different fora with three different senior Russian diplomats, and unfortunately the outcome of each meeting was the same. No progress: the talks were at an impasse. At each meeting, the Russians would read their talking points and would not engage in any real back-and-forth dialogue, because they were not authorized to do so (although they would not say that publicly). They would say they were awaiting written responses to the two draft treaties the MFA had provided. Putin had set forth his security demands in those drafts and his diplomats were not going to retreat from them. Yet for the United States and other NATO members, many of the key provisions in the proposed treaties were absolute nonstarters. There was the further problem of the unwillingness of the United States and NATO to negotiate anything about Ukrainian security without Ukraine being represented in the negotiations.

Overarching all these difficult issues was the dilemma of conducting any negotiations under the threat of a Russian invasion of Ukraine. Would the West reward Russia's belligerent threats with concessions on security in Europe? The UN Charter, to which the Russians professed they were committed, clearly prohibited "the threat or use of force against the territorial integrity or political independence of any state." How could the United States, or any other country for that matter, allow one of the five permanent members of the UN Security Council to violate blatantly a basic provision of international law underlying world peace?

Although the United States would continue to stay engaged in diplomatic discussions with the Russians in the vain hope of deterring war, we also were coordinating closely with our allies and preparing sanctions, export controls, and military, economic, and humanitarian support for Ukraine in the event of a Russian invasion, which seemed increasingly likely. By mid-January there were well over a hundred and fifty thousand Russian troops poised on the border of Ukraine, along with mobile missile systems, and strike aircraft, and the deployment of numerous Russian warships, including troop-carrying landing ships, in the Black Sea. Among the most telling developments was the movement of Russian troops into Belarus beginning on January 17, nominally for military exercises, but at levels rarely if ever seen before.

President Biden addressed this dangerous situation in a late-afternoon White House press conference on January 19 to mark his first year in office. He was asked several questions about the Russian threat to Ukraine, including why he thought anything the United States had said or done would give Putin pause in planning his invasion of Ukraine. Biden responded,

Well, because he's never seen sanctions like the ones I promised
will be imposed if he moves, number one.

Number two, ... the idea that NATO is not going to be united,
I don't buy. I've spoken to every major NATO leader. We've had
the NATO-Russian summit. We've had other—the OSCE has
met, et cetera.

And so, I think what you're going to see is that Russia will be
held accountable if it invades. And it depends on what it does. It's
one thing if it's a minor incursion and then we end up having a
fight about what to do and not do, et cetera.

I was at Spaso House, watching the press conference on the television in the small upstairs dining room after eating a late dinner. As soon
as I heard the president say "minor incursion," I knew that his remarks
had created a problem with which we would have to reckon. Zelensky
tweeted in response, "We want to remind the great powers that there are
no minor incursions and small nations." I could only imagine how Putin
and the Kremlin leadership interpreted the remark. Not only did it signal
a lack of resolve to confront Russian aggression on any level, but it also
called into question our commitment to our principles and values, and
our will and ability to resist a "major invasion" by Russia. As viewed by
the Russians in the immediate aftermath of the Afghanistan debacle, it
was further proof that the United States would "go wobbly," to borrow
a famous expression of Margaret Thatcher's, if push came to shove over
Ukraine.

In the same press conference, President Biden further emboldened
Putin and undermined Ukrainian morale when he endorsed Russia's military prowess and unquestioned ability to conquer Ukraine: "They'll be
able to prevail over time, but it's going to be heavy, it's going to be real,
and it's going to be consequential.... Militarily, they have overwhelming superiority, and on—as it relates to Ukraine. But they'll pay a stiff
price—immediately, near term, medium term, and long term—if they
do it." Many people agreed with that assessment, including myself, but I
would never have said it publicly. It is one thing for a senator to hold forth

expansively on global affairs, as Biden did for decades. It is quite another for the president of the United States to speak loosely from the White House without filtering his words through the strategic interests of the nation.

The White House staff and the president himself tried to clarify his remarks in the following days, but there are no do-overs or "mulligans" in a situation like that as the pace of events inevitably overtakes any effort to correct the record. Secretary Blinken met with Foreign Minister Lavrov in Geneva on January 21, two days after Biden's press conference. Again, there was no progress on the substantive disagreements between the United States and Russia over Ukraine and security in Europe. In his post-meeting press conference, Blinken obliquely addressed Biden's "minor incursion" remark by declaring that "if any Russian military forces move across Ukraine's border, that's a renewed invasion," which would "be met with swift, severe, and a united response from the United States and our partners and allies."

Blinken also addressed the Russian complaint that neither the United States nor NATO had responded in writing to the draft treaties Russia had prepared. This was the common reason offered by the Russians in the prior meetings for not engaging in substantive discussions on the issues raised in the drafts. Blinken told Lavrov that following consultations with allies and partners in the coming days, "we will be able to share with Russia our concerns and ideas in more detail and in writing next week. And we agreed to further discussions after that. We agreed as well that further diplomatic discussions would be the preferable way forward." Lavrov said he was pleased that Russia had finally "ended up with an agreement that we will receive written responses to all our proposals next week."

The work on the US written response began long before the January 21 meeting in Geneva, and I joined many colleagues from across the US government in reviewing and editing the document. Meanwhile, the preparations for war continued—with the United States now racing to brace itself and its allies for a Russian attack. The United States announced a new $200 million security aid package for Ukraine, and on January 24 NATO put troops on standby and sent warships and military aircraft to strengthen its eastern flank. The following day, Russian military exercises with more than six thousand troops and sixty military aircraft commenced near Ukraine.

Watching these developments from Embassy Moscow, I was becoming convinced that war was inevitable because the Russians were not negotiating in good faith while their military was making every preparation for a full-scale invasion of Ukraine. Of course, this did not relieve me or the United States of our obligation to continue work to stop it, but Putin and his government were not going to relent unless President Biden made compromises that no American president has ever made or would ever make.

On January 26, the written response of the United States was finished; NATO would submit its own similar response by letter. The State Department sent the final version of the US document to the embassy, and I was to present it to the Russian government. The note from Washington accompanying the document instructed me to submit the response as is, without changing a single thing. I thought the tone of the transmittal document was slightly condescending—I had never received an instruction like that in all the years I had served as deputy secretary or ambassador. I certainly knew that I was not free to edit an important document that had been cleared by so many senior officials. There was no need to remind me of the obvious, but I let the matter go.

Despite the admonition from Washington, the lawyer in me could not resist rereading the response one more time to make sure it was perfect. In the middle of the document, I found a word missing—and not just any word. The word "not" was missing from a sentence and its omission changed completely, as in 180 degrees, and harmfully the meaning of the sentence, and in some ways the meaning of the whole submission. It was an obvious typographical error that I otherwise would have corrected without a moment's hesitation, but I had received a written instruction not to change the document in any way. I probably just should have made the edit, and no one would have noticed or cared. But I got my Irish up and decided to send a pointed message to Washington seeking permission on behalf of the ambassador to insert the missing word "not" in the appropriate place. My embassy colleagues were amused by the groveling apology and profuse gratitude expressed in the immediate reply authorizing the change.

The final document was not to be made public and, in fact, was classified with an exception for its release to Russia. But the position of the United States and NATO, as expressed in their responses, was entirely consistent with prior statements by Secretary Blinken and other senior leaders in Washington (and later would be disclosed by the Russian government). The United States and NATO rejected any limitation on the "open door" policy of Article 10 of the North Atlantic Treaty, and specifically rejected the Russian demand that Ukraine never join NATO. On the other hand, the United States and NATO were willing to discuss with Russia future nuclear arms control negotiations and potential measures regarding the status and deployment of conventional military forces and exercises, including reciprocal restrictions on certain military deployments by the United States and Russia on the territory of Ukraine. There were also proposals to improve communications and increase transparency in military and security matters. Both the US and NATO responses made clear, however, that no progress in any discussions with Russia was possible so long as Russia was threatening a military invasion of Ukraine. We could only hope that the Kremlin was still interested in continuing to talk.

———————

I arranged for a meeting at the MFA to deliver the US response to the draft treaties at approximately 7:30 p.m. Moscow time on January 26. The ministry reported that Deputy Foreign Minister Grushko would meet with me and accept the response. It was overcast, snowing, and 21°F when I arrived at the ministry. There was ice on the steps leading to the main entrance of the building, which was now closed and dark. A large group of media with cameras were standing nearby, waiting for my arrival. Many cameras flashed as I got out of the car and walked with two of my colleagues into the ministry. The only thought racing through my mind was a prayer to God to please not let me slip and do a pratfall on the ice in front of the gathered media. The FSB would have loved that photograph.

A security guard let me into the ministry, which was an imposing building—one of the historic Seven Sisters built by Stalin and completed in 1953. The ministry never had a welcoming presence even on a sunny summer day. On a dark, cold, snowy night in January, with a war looming, the building, with all the lights out, felt downright sinister.

I was escorted to a conference room on an upper floor to meet with Grushko, who was joined by four MFA associates. I handed Grushko multiple copies of the US response, which was several pages in length, with the original version in English and courtesy copies translated into Russian. I expected to engage in a dialogue with Grushko that evening about the response after he had read it.

The deputy minister and his colleagues took their time reading both the original and translated versions of the document carefully, and they noted a few minor corrections in the translation. When they were finished, Grushko smiled and said he could respond by reciting his usual talking points that I had heard many times before, but because the hour was late, he would spare both of us. Once again, there would be no substantive, give-and-take discussion with the Russians. They would respond in writing in due course. The meeting at the MFA ended after less than an hour and I exited into the snow and ice of a Moscow winter evening to return to the embassy.

A photograph of me arriving at the Foreign Ministry with the US response circulated widely overnight in the international media. When Grace saw it, she called me to say that the weather looked miserable and that I was lucky I did not slip and fall on my rear end in front of the assembled cameras. I laughed and told her of the prayer I had offered as I walked into the ministry. Even after being apart for so long, we still thought alike.

Foreign Minister Lavrov replied quickly to the US and NATO written submissions in a letter to Secretary Blinken on January 28. Lavrov complained that both documents mischaracterized "the principle of equal and indivisible security, which is fundamental to the entire European security architecture." Lavrov cited some prior OSCE agreements to which the United States, NATO members, Russia, and Ukraine had subscribed—the Charter for European Security (1999) and the Astana Declaration (2010)—and on which the United States and NATO had relied for the "right of each participating State to be free to choose or change its security arrangements, including treaties of alliance, as they evolve."

Lavrov argued that the "collective West," as the Russians referred to the United States and its allies, erred in relying on this "right" to assert that Ukraine could make its own independent decisions on national security and choose to join NATO. Lavrov argued that the "right" stated in the OSCE agreements was conditioned directly by "the obligation of each State not to strengthen its security at the expense of the security of other States." This was Lavrov's principle of "indivisible security." In his view, if Russia was made insecure—in its own subjective estimation—by a security decision by another European country or group of countries, then that decision was illegitimate and impermissible.

But there were insuperable problems with Lavrov's legalistic construct of "indivisible security," which he said stood for the proposition "that there is security for all or there is no security for anyone." That cliché could not eliminate or undermine the sovereign right of a nation to make decisions for its own national security. If it did, then there would be chaos. Any country could cite its own subjective insecurity to object to a decision by another country. Moreover, the Russians would never allow another country to apply that standard to Russia. Would Lavrov agree that Ukrainian or Polish or Romanian or Danish or Spanish insecurity would give any one of those countries standing to object to a security decision by Moscow? Of course not. Ukraine had clearly communicated its understandable insecurity caused by Russia's decisions and actions. Did that cause Russia to change its belligerent posture? Of course not.

Lavrov's January 28 letter was diplomatic obfuscation interposed only for delay and to avoid real negotiations and diplomacy. Lavrov demanded a clear answer to the question of how "our partners understand their obligation not to strengthen their own security at the expense of the security of other States on the basis of the commitment to the principle of indivisible security." It was pure sophistry. Imagine if Lavrov had been asked how Russia planned to comply with its obligation not to strengthen its security at the expense of the security of Ukraine. He would scoff because he would consider the question absurd. But without an answer to his question—"without having full clarity on this key issue," according to Lavrov—further negotiations were going nowhere. Lavrov said he needed to "understand the extent of the ability of our partners to remain faithful to their commitments, as well as the prospects for common progress toward decreasing tensions and strengthening European security."

On the same day that the Russians delivered Lavrov's letter to Blinken, I participated in a virtual press conference organized by the State Department's Brussels Media Hub. I described the "extraordinary" Russian military buildup on Ukraine's borders, including the unusual deployment of Russian military personnel and equipment in Belarus. In commenting on the ongoing negotiations with the Russians, I observed that they were creating a crisis atmosphere by their military buildup and that by coming to the negotiating table amid such a military threat, they were putting "a gun on the table." After the press conference, which seemed routine and uneventful to me, I finished my schedule for the day and returned to Spaso House.

While I was relaxing with a bucket of popcorn and a beer that Friday night, I turned on the news and saw John King of CNN introduce an alarming segment on the increasing likelihood of war in Ukraine. He said in amazement, listen to what the US ambassador in Moscow said today, and there I was on the television screen saying that by their massive military deployment threatening Ukraine the Russians were negotiating by putting "a gun on the table." It was a surreal moment as I sat alone in a huge mansion wondering why anyone in the United States would find what I had said unusual or newsworthy. It was simply a statement of fact from my perspective. But then I realized that my perspective had changed: I was now behind the lines in Moscow on the eve of war.

# PART IV

# CONFLAGRATION

# CHAPTER 12

# AGGRESSIVE WAR

THE ATTEMPTED DIPLOMACY BY THE United States with the Russians in the six weeks after they had presented their draft treaties did nothing to lower the risk of war. If anything, the risk rose as Russian officials continued fomenting a crisis atmosphere while making wildly unrealistic demands of the United States and NATO. In meeting after meeting, they read without variation from standard talking points that amounted to ultimatums. There was not even a half-hearted attempt by the Russians to feign to negotiate, which—combined with the Russian military's continued troop deployments, movements of ships and aircraft, and large-scale logistical preparations—just reinforced my conclusion that a Russian invasion of Ukraine was virtually inevitable.

As a result, my priorities in February 2022 shifted from the increasingly futile efforts to negotiate with the Russians to warning anyone who would listen that war was imminent. I had maintained my practice, begun during the pandemic, of regular video teleconferences with the members of the AmCham in Moscow. It was important for me to stay in close contact with US business leaders in Russia, a key constituency for any US ambassador that was even more critical in my case because commercial relations were one of the few connections left between the United States and Russia. On our video teleconference on February 4, I was blunt in warning AmCham members about what I thought was going to happen. I cited the huge Russian military buildup, including troop movements into Belarus, the lack of good-faith diplomacy by the MFA, and the gradual withdrawal of Russian diplomats from Ukraine that began in January. I told the AmCham members that they needed to be prepared for war, citing President Biden's recent public assessment that Putin "will move in. He has to do something."

My audience of almost two hundred AmCham members, many of whom had decades of experience operating in Russia, was skeptical and their comments and questions to me during the video teleconference and in subsequent phone calls with individual members reflected their doubts. A common view was that Putin was only threatening war for leverage in negotiations over Ukraine and NATO expansion, and the threat had to be credible, which is why it only looked like the Russians were going to war. But an actual invasion of Ukraine, from this viewpoint, would not happen because it would be irrational, and Putin was a rational if ruthless leader. The damage to Russia and its people from a war over Ukraine would far exceed any further potential gains in Ukrainian territory; the enormous cost to the economy alone would be staggering. Several AmCham members urged me not to overstate the risk of war, lest I cause businesses to take unnecessary actions out of unwarranted fear.

Those AmCham members were not entirely wrong. When viewed from the perspective of a rational Western business leader, an expanded war in Ukraine would be irrational, undermining the very security that Russia ostensibly sought. It was the same reason that Grace thought I was exaggerating the risk of war when I had returned to Moscow in November.

The basic error in that analysis, regrettably, was the belief that Putin thought and acted like a rational Western leader. He most certainly did not. He was a Chekist whose imperial ambition for Russia in the post–Cold War world was difficult for Westerners to understand. The rational cost-benefit analysis, for him, led to a different conclusion on the question of war and peace than it did for most Western observers.

On the same day that I had the Moscow AmCham video teleconference, Putin arrived in Beijing to meet with his "dear friend" President Xi Jinping of the People's Republic of China. In February, the PRC was hosting the XXIV Winter Olympic Games, a very important event for the country and for Xi personally. Putin traveled to attend the start of the Olympics and received a lavish welcome. His visit was notably highlighted by the PRC because many Western leaders had declined to attend the games, following a diplomatic boycott over the PRC's human rights record, a measure announced by the United States in early December. While in Beijing, Putin had a lengthy "summit meeting" and lunch with Xi, in addition to watching the opening ceremony.

In the week preceding Putin's visit, the PRC supported Russia's position on Ukraine. During a phone call with Secretary Blinken on January 27, Foreign Minister Wang Yi parroted Russian talking points, insisting that "the security of one country should not be at the expense of the security of others, and regional security should not be guaranteed by strengthening or even expanding military blocs." He told the secretary that "Russia's 'reasonable' security concerns" needed to be "taken seriously and resolved" by the United States. Four days later, the PRC joined Russia as the only members of the UN Security Council to vote against a council meeting organized by the United States to discuss Russia's military threat to Ukraine. Although the Russians had worked hard for months to create a "crisis" atmosphere over Ukraine, they said the US effort to organize a Security Council meeting on the subject was nothing more than "whipping up tension."

Following the Putin-Xi meeting on February 4, Russia and the PRC issued a lengthy joint statement on their bilateral relationship and international relations generally. In this unusual document, the two countries declared that "the new inter-State relations between Russia and China are superior to political and military alliances of the Cold War era. Friendship between the two States has no limits." I, along with diplomats around the world, read with great interest the joint statement, which was littered with the usual factual distortions and disinformation that I had come to expect from both governments. Parts of the joint statement were simply preposterous. I laughed out loud when I learned that "Russia and China...have long-standing traditions of democracy." That would have been news to the Romanovs, Lenin, Stalin, Khrushchev, Brezhnev, Andropov, and Chernenko.

But the joint statement was not merely propaganda. Russia and the PRC staked out detailed common positions on the most important global security issues and on Ukraine in particular. Both countries "oppose[d] further enlargement of NATO and call[ed] on the North Atlantic Alliance to abandon its ideologized Cold War approaches, to respect the sovereignty, security and interests of other countries," i.e., Russia. The PRC emphasized the point by announcing in the joint statement that it was "sympathetic to and supports the proposals put forward by the Russian Federation to create long-term legally binding security guarantees in Europe." Obliquely invoking both Ukraine and Taiwan, the joint statement also declared that "Russia and China stand against attempts by external forces to undermine security and stability in their common adjacent regions, [and] intend to counter interference by outside forces in the internal affairs of sovereign countries under any pretext."

It was not clear how much of his planning for action on Ukraine Putin disclosed to Xi in their February meeting at the Olympics. Whatever the scope of that nonpublic briefing by Putin, the PRC's public support for Russia in its standoff with Ukraine was unqualified—there were "no limits." Bolstered by this embrace by Xi and the PRC, Putin returned to Moscow and continued to ratchet up the pressure on Ukraine and finalize Russia's preparations for war.

The pressure included increased cyberattacks, which had started in Ukraine in mid-January. The attacks were first directed at Ukrainian government websites and servers, and later accelerated to a wider array of targets. On February 15, major cyberattacks attributed publicly by the White House to the Russian GRU hit the Ukrainian Ministry of Defense and the two largest banks in Ukraine, PrivatBank and Oschadbank. While Kremlin spokesperson Dmitry Peskov denied that Russia was responsible for any of the attacks, the increased cyber activity complemented the Russian military buildup, which continued unabated.

On February 10, Russia and Belarus announced ten days of military exercises in Belarusian territory. Over thirty thousand Russian troops were participating in the largest deployment of Russian military personnel to Belarus since the Cold War. The sense of war fever was building. President Biden warned Americans in an interview with NBC News, following the announcement of the massive Russian military deployments in Belarus, to leave Ukraine: "American citizens should leave. Leave now. We're dealing with one of the largest armies in the world. This is a very different situation, and things could go crazy quickly."

The Russian government continued to deny that it would invade Ukraine. To support this public position, the Russian Ministry of Defense announced on February 14 and 15 that certain military exercises in southwestern Russia had concluded and that some troops were returning to their bases away from the border with Ukraine. That was outright disinformation, however, and NATO secretary-general Jens Stoltenberg said on February 16 that "we have not seen any de-escalation on the ground. On the contrary, it appears that Russia continues the military buildup."

The Russian MFA again called the warnings by the United States and NATO "anti-Russian hysteria," although the facts on the ground in Ukraine told a different story: further military intervention by Russia was coming. In addition to increased cyberattacks, shellfire increased on February 17 along the line of contact in the Donbas. The separatist leaders of Donetsk and Luhansk, under careful guidance from Moscow, also announced that they would begin evacuating residents of their territories to Russia. On February 15, the State Duma overwhelmingly passed a resolution asking Putin to recognize the independence from Ukraine of the Donetsk People's Republic and the Luhansk People's Republic. This coincided with an intensification of the Russian government's rhetoric accusing Ukraine of brutally mistreating ethnic Russians and Russian speakers in the Donbas.

The accusation that the Ukrainian government persecuted Russians was a familiar staple of Kremlin propaganda since 2014, justifying the illegal annexation of Crimea and occupation of the eastern Donbas. In their diatribes against Kyiv, Russian nationalists would often invoke the specter of genocide. When Ukraine sought to isolate the separatists in the Donbas and cut off gas supplies in 2015, Putin himself said, "Imagine these people will be left without gas in winter. Not only that, there is famine.... It smells of genocide." In December 2021, Putin renewed that loaded accusation in an interview with Russian media: "You and I know what is happening in Donbas. It certainly looks like genocide."

Now, two months later, Putin's rhetoric had shifted slightly but significantly. He no longer equivocated by saying that Ukraine's actions "smelled like" or "looked like" genocide by the Ukrainian government against Russians. Putin had reached a firm conclusion when he declared on February 15 that "what is happening in the Donbas today is genocide." This inflammatory denunciation was amplified by Russian state media, which broadcast frequent reports alleging that innocent Russians in the Donbas were fleeing violence directed at them by Kyiv.

President Biden quite rightly and emphatically pushed back: "Russia state media also continues to make phony allegations of a genocide taking place in the Donbas and push fabricated claims warning about Ukraine's attack on Russia without any evidence." But the president's statement missed a crucial detail: it was not just Russian state media making these "allegations." It was Putin himself, the president of the Russian Federation, stating his definitive conclusion that Ukraine was engaged in genocide. Russian state media often made wild, unsubstantiated allegations that were ignored by most of the rest of the world. The unqualified official statement on genocide by the president of Russia, on the other hand, was of a fundamentally different character and would soon have significant consequences.

At this point in mid-February, the question with which I wrestled was not whether Putin would invade Ukraine, but rather how he could *not* invade after his genocide declaration, combined with the escalating violence orchestrated by the Kremlin in the Donbas, and all that Russia had invested in preparing for a further military intervention. How would the Chekist defender of the *Russkiy mir* explain his failure to act in this dire (if self-made) crisis? As President Biden said earlier, Putin had to do something. We could only watch and wait for him to make his move.

---

The faint embers of diplomacy were finally extinguished after a flurry of fruitless telephone calls and meetings in the first three weeks of February 2022. President Macron traveled to Moscow on February 7 for a five-hour, one-on-one meeting with Putin that produced a bizarre image of the two presidents seated at either end of an absurdly long white table (because of Putin's extreme Covid-19 precautions), but no tangible results to advance peace in the Donbas. Macron nevertheless would doggedly continue his pursuit of diplomacy in numerous telephone calls with Putin until the very end.

President Biden had his own telephone call with Putin on February 12 during which, as the White House later reported, the president warned (once again) that in response to a further Russian invasion of Ukraine, the United States and its allies and partners would "respond decisively and impose swift and severe costs on Russia." The president "reiterated that a further Russian invasion of Ukraine would produce widespread human suffering and diminish Russia's standing." Biden's warnings about sanctions, suffering, and standing had no more effect on Putin than all the similar warnings given by the United States over the prior three months. The more they were repeated, the weaker the warnings seemed.

In another telephone call with Lavrov days after the two presidents had spoken, Secretary Blinken offered the Russians a last clear chance at what the State Department called "a diplomatic solution to the crisis Moscow [had] precipitated." Lavrov in turn said that Russia would provide a formal written reply to the document that I had delivered to the MFA in late January responding to the draft Russian treaties. On the afternoon of February 17, I was summoned to the Ministry and handed what was styled as Russia's "written reaction to the US response concerning security guarantees." This document would constitute the Russian government's final written word on the future of war and peace in Ukraine and Europe.

The reply from the MFA asserted that the United States had "failed to give a constructive response to the basic elements of the Russia-drafted treaty with the US on security guarantees." The US response was not constructive because it failed to agree with the Russian demands for: the "renunciation of NATO's further expansion, the revocation of...prospective NATO membership for Ukraine and Georgia, and desisting from the creation of military bases on the territory" of states that were once part of the USSR and were not members of NATO, "including the use of their infrastructure to conduct any kind of military activity, as well as the return of the NATO military potentials, including strike capabilities, and NATO infrastructure to their status as of the year 1997." In the absence of US agreement to the Russian demands to rewrite the North Atlantic Treaty and turn the clock back twenty-five years, "Moscow [would] have to respond, including by implementing certain military-technical measures."

The MFA reply specifically disclaimed that an invasion of Ukraine was among the "military-technical measures" under consideration (emphasis added): *"No 'Russian invasion' in Ukraine* [something officials in the United States and their allied countries have been predicting since last autumn] *is happening or being planned,"* read the reply that I was given that day. Thus, the MFA put in writing on February 17 what senior Russian officials had been saying repeatedly since the Burns meetings in Moscow in early November. Not only would Russia not invade Ukraine, but it also had no plans to do so. Of course, Russia's massive military movements and many other actions like cyberattacks since November completely belied that assertion. It would not take long to see whether Russia would keep its written word.

On the larger question of security in Europe, the MFA reply made clear that the Russian demands were not negotiable. "Russia's proposal is a package deal and should be considered in its entirety, not item by item." Indeed, like the draft treaties they presented in December, the "package deal" was a public ultimatum by Russia. It was the opposite of diplomacy. In my mind, the die was cast.

President Biden agreed. At a press conference on Friday, February 18, the day after the MFA handed me Russia's reply, he was asked whether he thought Putin had made the decision to invade. He replied, "As of this moment, I'm convinced he's made the decision. We have reason to believe that." Yet Biden was still willing to allow diplomatic talks with the Russians to continue up to the point when Putin launched the war, saying "until he does, diplomacy is always a possibility." Secretary Blinken accepted an invitation from Lavrov to meet on February 24, unless the war started before then.

The secretary called me from the Munich Security Conference on Saturday, February 19, to check in and share thoughts on what was going to happen. I told him that I believed we were on an unalterable course to war in Europe, and it would be an aggressive war by Russia without justification—like the war that Germany started with its invasion of Poland in 1939. The only question was when it would start.

I included myself among those who believed that Putin would not start the war until after the Winter Olympics in Beijing had concluded on Sunday, February 20. I thought he would be loath to distract global attention from such an important event for his "dear friend" Xi, on whom he was becoming more dependent. But not everyone agreed. On February 11, Jake Sullivan had said at the White House that "we continue to see signs of Russian escalation, including new forces arriving at the Ukrainian border," and that the invasion could start "during the Olympics," which meant possibly over the weekend—including while the secretary and I were speaking. In the event, the Olympics concluded without the start of another war in Europe.

Predicting a date for the invasion with any surety was difficult, as the intelligence assessments were changing quickly. Nevertheless, the United States was able to put what solid information it did have to good effect. The use of declassified intelligence reporting by the Biden administration, indeed, played a key role in keeping the American public and the world informed about what Russia was planning to do in Ukraine. There was skepticism, of course, because of prior American intelligence failures, but the use of declassified intelligence by the Biden administration would prove to be an innovative and effective strategy. It also was time-consuming and not easy to implement, because of the requirements of the declassification process to protect the sources and methods by which the United States collects intelligence.

The use of declassified intelligence was more than just the release of information describing military movements. The reporting included disclosure of Kremlin plans for staged provocations or false-flag operations targeting Russians on either side of the border with Ukraine that could be used to justify an invasion. The public disclosure in advance of those operations disrupted their implementation by and utility to the Russians. Secretary Blinken was interviewed on CNN on Sunday morning, February 20, and described the continuation of Russia's military exercises and massing of troops on Ukraine's border, concluding that "all of this, along with the false-flag operations we've seen unfold over the weekend, tells us that the playbook that we laid out is moving forward."

As the pace of events leading to war quickened over the weekend of February 19–20, President Macron had a final series of telephone calls with Putin and Biden, seeking to broker a summit meeting between the two presidents, to be followed by larger meetings to negotiate new security arrangements in Europe. In the end, Macron's diplomacy was in vain. It was too late and, more significantly, Putin and the Kremlin had never been interested in diplomacy or negotiations. The Russians had demands that either would be met by the United States and NATO or would be achieved by other "military-technical measures."

The last full week of February 2022 was physically and emotionally draining for me, as the war of which I had been warning for months appeared to finally be arriving. At the embassy, my colleagues and I were monitoring and reporting to Washington around the clock on developments in the Russian government, and the embassy's Emergency Action Committee (EAC) met regularly to assess our security and operations. In Moscow, the weather early in the week was relatively mild by Russian standards and traffic on the streets of the city was busy as Muscovites went about their daily routines. Taking a walk or a drive beyond the walls of the embassy compound, one would never know that a major war would be starting in a matter of hours.

---

The execution of the Russian plan to invade Ukraine began with an unusual meeting of the Russian Security Council in an ornate Kremlin hall on Monday, February 21. The meeting was convened by Putin and broadcast (purportedly live, although detailed scrutiny of the watches worn by some of the participants suggested it had been filmed earlier) on state television. The agenda was to consider whether to recognize the independence of the self-proclaimed "people's republics" in the occupied parts of Donetsk and Luhansk.

The State Duma had previously recommended that Putin do so, and the separatist leaders Denis Pushilin and Leonid Pasechnik, in requesting recognition for their "people's republics," proposed treaties with Russia that included military cooperation. Making the connection with Russia even closer, over seven hundred thousand Ukrainian residents of the two separatist regions in the Donbas had been given Russian citizenship and passports since 2019 (many against their will, under duress) in a process decried as "passportization" that further undermined Ukrainian sovereignty.

Putin presided over the Security Council meeting from behind a large white desk on one side of the great hall, with each of his senior security officials—including, among others, Medvedev, Patrushev, Lavrov, Kozak, Prime Minister Mishustin, FSB director Bortnikov, and Defense Minister Shoigu—seated in chairs arranged on the other side of the cavernous room, which was ringed with tall white columns. The setting was reminiscent of Putin's Covid-19 isolation. Each official was summoned to a small white podium and asked to provide Putin with an answer to the question whether Russia should recognize the independence of the two "people's republics" in the Donbas. The unanimous response was a scripted *yes.*

This was not a dialogue. Only one answer was acceptable. Looking tired and occasionally bored, as he drummed his fingers on the desk at which he sat, Putin flashed his anger at SVR director Sergey Naryshkin, who bungled his response to the question presented when he said he "will support" the recognition of the two "people's republics." Putin interrupted, "Will support, or do support? Tell me straight." As a flustered Naryshkin tried to answer, Putin barked at him, "Speak directly!" That made Naryshkin even more nervous, and he misspoke again by saying that he supported absorbing the two "people's republics" into the Russian Federation. A frustrated Putin corrected him, "We're not talking about that. We're talking about whether to recognize their independence or not." In full humiliation, Naryshkin finally stammered his affirmative response on the question of recognition and Putin let him sit down.

The proceedings of the Russian Security Council on February 21 were a form of theater organized by Putin to establish and record the collective responsibility of the officials present for the decisions on Ukraine that Putin would announce after the meeting. Later in the day, Putin signed two decrees recognizing the independence of the Donetsk People's Republic and the Luhansk People's Republic, as well as treaties with them "on friendship, cooperation and mutual assistance." Russia then announced it was sending "peacekeepers" into the two new "republics," allegedly to protect civilians from the Ukrainian government's violence against them.

That night, Putin broadcast an address to the Russian people to explain what he had decided based on the "situation in Donbas, [which had] reached a critical, acute stage." For almost an hour, a weary and visibly angry Putin repeated his usual arguments and grievances against Ukraine, the United States, and NATO. Between heavy breaths and occasional sighs, he began with his discredited alternative history of Ukraine, which he maintained was not a country independent of Russia. In his mind, Ukraine existed as a separate nation only because of the "Bolsheviks' policy, and can be rightfully called Vladimir Lenin's Ukraine." He seethed with contempt for ungrateful Ukrainians who have since "overturned monuments to Lenin in Ukraine. They call it decommunization." He threatened portentously, "You want decommunization? Very well, this suits us just fine. But why stop halfway? We are ready to show what real decommunization would mean for Ukraine."

Ultimately, it was another Russian Communist, Mikhail Gorbachev, who in Putin's view committed the "fatal" error that separated Ukraine from its rightful place in the *Russkiy mir*. In 1989, the Central Committee of the Communist Party of the Soviet Union under General Secretary Gorbachev approved a policy declaring that the republics of the USSR, including Ukraine, "shall possess all the rights appropriate to their status as sovereign socialist states" and that each "shall have citizenship of its own, which shall apply to all of its residents." The result was an independent Ukraine—now under the control of "radical nationalists," "neo-Nazis," and corrupt oligarchs and public officials—that Putin claimed was an existential threat to Russia. "As we know, it has already been stated today that Ukraine intends to create its own nuclear weapons," he intoned, and "Ukraine's Western patrons may help it acquire these weapons to create yet another threat to our country."

The real villains in Putin's twisted history were "Ukraine's Western patrons" in NATO:

All the while, they are trying to convince us over and over again that NATO is a peace-loving and purely defensive alliance that

268

poses no threat to Russia. Again, they want us to take their word for it. But we are well aware of the real value of these words. In 1990, when German unification was discussed, the United States promised the Soviet leadership that NATO jurisdiction or military presence will not expand one inch to the east and that the unification of Germany will not lead to the spread of NATO's military organization to the east. This is a quote.

Contrary to those alleged promises, Putin bitterly observed, NATO expanded eastward, issuing "lots of verbal assurances, all of which turned out to be empty phrases." The United States told "us that the accession to NATO by Central and Eastern European countries would only improve relations with Moscow." But "the exact opposite happened. The governments of certain Eastern European countries, speculating on Russophobia, brought their complexes and stereotypes about the Russian threat to the Alliance and insisted on building up the collective defense potentials and deploying them primarily against Russia."

The current crisis, as Putin laid it out for the Russian people on that Monday night, was that NATO was on the verge of absorbing Ukraine and moving its "military infrastructure" even closer to Russia's borders. Meanwhile in Kyiv, "the aggressive and nationalistic regime that seized power" would not "recognize now any solution to the Donbas issue other than a military one." For those reasons, Putin concluded, it was "necessary to take a long overdue decision and to immediately recognize the independence and sovereignty of the Donetsk People's Republic and the Luhansk People's Republic."

The actions by Putin and his speech on February 21 were a major escalation that put a final stake through the heart of diplomacy. The next day, Secretary Blinken canceled his meeting scheduled for February 24 with Lavrov. The United States, along with NATO and the EU, condemned Putin's recognition of the two "people's republics"; and the United States and the EU announced sanctions focused on those territories.

Yet Putin's gambit, while fatal to diplomacy, was not nearly at the scale of the Russian operation that I had predicted. It was either merely the first step in a larger military campaign, or it would be more like the "minor incursion" about which President Biden had mused in January. There was no doubt that moving Russian "peacekeepers" into the separatist regions of Donetsk and Luhansk further violated Ukrainian sovereignty, but that alone was not the major land war in Europe that I had confidently told Secretary Blinken was coming.

Any fleeting uncertainty in my mind about what was going to happen was removed when the Federation Council voted unanimously on February 22 to grant Putin's request for authorization to deploy the Russian military outside the country to support the separatists in the Donetsk People's Republic and the Luhansk People's Republic. The next day, Kremlin spokesperson Peskov said that the leaders of the two separatist republics had requested Russia's help "in repelling the aggression of the Ukrainian armed forces." By February 23, the MFA had removed all Russian diplomats from Ukraine and the Russian flag no longer flew over the embassy in Kyiv.

---

As the night of February 23 turned into the early morning of Thursday, February 24, I was at Spaso House and found it hard to sleep. I was waiting for a phone call from Admiral Phil Yu, the defense attaché at the embassy, with the Schwarzenegger-inspired code that would alert me if (or rather, when) Putin's war started.

The fateful call came a few hours after midnight as I was dozing, and I proceeded to my office in the chancery, where, before 6 a.m., I watched Putin's address to the Russian people announcing the "special military operation" he had launched against Ukraine.

Repeating many of the same themes from his address on February 21 after the recognition of the two "people's republics," Putin's speech was a call to war based on the perfidy of the United States (an "empire of lies") and NATO: "They have deceived us, or, to put it simply, they have played us," seeking to "destroy our traditional values and force on us their false values that would erode us, our people, from within." Putin charged that the United States would accomplish its goals of "containing" and "destroy[ing]" Russia by the "expansion of the North Atlantic alliance's infrastructure" via a "military foothold" in Ukraine.

The intolerable result of this expansion for Putin was that in Ukrainian territory "adjacent to Russia, which I have to note is our historical land, a hostile 'anti-Russia' is taking shape. Fully controlled from the outside, it is doing everything to attract NATO armed forces and obtain cutting-edge weapons." For Russia, this was "a matter of life and death, a matter of our historical future as a nation. . . . It is not only a very real threat to our interests but to the very existence of our state and to its sovereignty." Putin vowed that Russia would eliminate this existential threat and not wait until it was too late: "We are acting to defend ourselves from the threats created for us and from a worse peril than what is happening now."

He assured the nation that Russia was fully capable of defending itself, because "even after the dissolution of the USSR and losing a considerable part of its capabilities, today's Russia remains one of the most powerful nuclear states." In fact, just as Patrushev had told Burns in November, Putin said Russia was stronger than its adversaries, with "a certain advantage in several cutting-edge weapons. In this context, there should be no doubt for anyone that any potential aggressor will face defeat and ominous consequences should it directly attack our country."

Turning to the critical problem of "the situation in Donbas," Putin emphasized the persecution of Russians there by the government of "far-right nationalists and neo-Nazis" in Kyiv, which "became impossible to tolerate." Russia "had to stop that atrocity, that genocide of the millions of people who live there and who pinned their hopes on Russia, on all of us. It is their aspirations, the feelings and pain of these people, that were the main motivating force behind our decision to recognize the independence of the Donbas people's republics."

It was in "this context, in accordance with Article 51 (Chapter VII) of the UN Charter, with permission of Russia's Federation Council, and in execution of the treaties of friendship and mutual assistance with the Donetsk People's Republic and the Luhansk People's Republic, ratified by the Federal Assembly on February 22," that Putin made the "decision to carry out a special military operation." He declared:

The purpose of this operation is to protect people who, for eight years now, have been facing humiliation and genocide perpetrated by the [Kyiv] regime. To this end, we will seek to demilitarize and denazify Ukraine, as well as bring to trial those who perpetrated numerous bloody crimes against civilians, including against citizens of the Russian Federation.

Putin also included a menacing warning to "those who may be tempted to interfere" in the "special military operation." "They must know that Russia will respond immediately, and the consequences will be such as you have never seen in your entire history....I hope that my words will be heard." It was the first rattle of his nuclear saber—by "one of the most powerful nuclear states"—and a tactic that Putin would repeat in the future.

While I watched Putin speak, tens of thousands of Russian troops, tanks, aircraft, and missiles were attempting to envelope Ukraine from three directions: moving south from Belarus, west from Russia, and north from Crimea. A massive, coordinated invasion was underway, which the Russian government less than seven days before had proclaimed was not going to happen and was not even being planned. The war, Russia's war, was on.

———————

Confident though I had been that Putin would launch a major war in Europe, I was equally confident that Ukraine would be unable to resist the Russian invasion for long. That was the consensus of the military and intelligence experts I had consulted inside and outside the US government over many months. The Russian leadership, from Putin through Patrushev, and on down, was equally confident about their ability to subjugate Ukraine. And there were undeniable facts to support their position. The enormous size of Russia and its military (as Biden had said, "one of the largest armies in the world") compared to Ukraine and its military was such an overmatch that I could not imagine that Zelensky and the democratically elected government in Kyiv would survive.

I expected an outcome like Operation Danube—the Warsaw Pact's invasion of Czechoslovakia ("fraternal assistance," in the Soviet parlance of the day) on August 20, 1968—that ended the Prague Spring. Soviet premier Leonid Brezhnev had ordered hundreds of thousands of troops and thousands of tanks—at the time, the largest military action in Europe since World War II—to invade and reverse the liberal reforms introduced under Czech leader Alexander Dubček. I thought the best that could be hoped for Zelensky personally was the fate of Dubček, who was arrested and sent to Moscow for "negotiations" before being returned to Prague and eventually banished to Bratislava for work in the state forestry agency. Zelensky should be so lucky, was my view. The Russian military was targeting him and his government with a large, armored column of tanks moving south from Belarus and an airborne assault to capture Kyiv.

Seated in my office at Embassy Moscow on February 24, hundreds of miles to the northeast, I was safe behind the front lines of the conflict. My colleagues at the US mission to Ukraine, who were on the other (far more dangerous) side of the front lines, had all finally been evacuated to Poland days before the invasion began. Although I was carefully following the astonishingly horrific developments in Ukraine, my first responsibility was the security of the US mission in Russia—so it was to that pressing matter that my attention now turned.

After watching Putin's speech and reviewing the cable traffic to and from Washington overnight, I convened an emergency action committee meeting with the senior leaders of the embassy at 9:30 a.m. to review our operations and threats to the mission and to Americans in Russia. The situation felt tense inside the embassy. There was less friendly banter and more concern about the families and children living on the compound. I was keenly focused on our security posture, although there were no demonstrations outside the compound or other unusual activity directed at us beyond the usual scrutiny and harassment by the FSB. We resolved to remain alert and convene regularly in the days ahead.

It was not long before the embassy began to receive requests from American citizens for help in leaving Russia. We had issued the latest security alert for Americans in the country about heightened threats on February 20, and the shock of the war starting motivated some who had been hesitant to leave. One member of the AmCham, who had expressed skepticism about my earlier warnings on the likelihood and scale of a further war in Ukraine, called me on his way to the airport to tell me that he was leaving Russia for the foreseeable future. I felt no satisfaction when he told me that I had been right. The situation was just too dreadful, and my mind was racing with all I needed to do and all the terrible things that still could happen and for which I needed to be prepared, like attacks on American citizens or American diplomats, violent protests outside the embassy, or my expulsion as ambassador.

The EU ambassador to Russia, Dr. Markus Ederer, invited me and all the ambassadors of the EU member countries in Moscow, as well as the UK ambassador, Deborah Bronnert, to a meeting at his embassy at 3 p.m. It was a large group of almost thirty ambassadors that had not met collectively before in my tenure. The emotion and anger in the cramped conference room about what Putin and Russia had done was palpable. I and every other ambassador spoke, some with tears in their eyes, expressing outrage that Russia, a permanent member of the UN Security Council, had chosen to start a war of conquest in Europe after the staggering scale of death and suffering on the continent during the last such war. A few speculated that Putin's Covid-19 isolation had increased his paranoia and megalomaniac ambitions, but who could say what really drove him to this outrage. I left the meeting confident that Europe would stand firmly united against the egregious Russian violence and aggression against another European country.

I returned to the embassy to catch up on developments and was invited to participate in a secure video teleconference organized by the NSC at the White House that would start at 4:30 p.m. eastern time, which meant 12:30 a.m. in Moscow. It was then I realized that I could not continue to live at Spaso House. The understandable demands on me from my colleagues in Washington every day at any time meant that I had to be at the embassy around the clock to be accessible via secure channels. I moved into an empty and spacious three-story townhouse on the compound the following day and never returned to the beautiful mansion in which I had lived for over two years.

During the opening days of the war, I established a regular routine of internal EAC meetings with embassy leadership on security and operations; town halls with the entire embassy community to provide updates and reassurance to everyone—diplomats, marines, employees, contractors, and families—who lived on the compound; and daily (often multiple times a day) SVTCs with Washington. I also had twice-a-week meetings with the other Quad ambassadors (UK, France, and Germany) in secure settings, and a once-a-week secure meeting with the other ambassadors of the so-called Five Eyes intelligence alliance (UK, Canada, Australia, and New Zealand). It was important for us as the ambassadors of close allies to provide mutual support, including on logistical matters, as all our embassies were under pressure from the Russian MFA, and to share information and our perspectives to remain tightly aligned in our operational decisions and public statements.

My close relationships with the ambassadors from NATO and EU countries in Moscow were, in part, a reflection of the unity displayed by those multilateral organizations in fierce opposition to Putin's "special military operation." NATO members (except Turkey) and the EU imme-diately imposed harsh economic sanctions and export controls on Russia at the start of the war. The EU sanctions were stronger and were imposed more quickly than I had imagined possible. Countries outside the EU also imposed sanctions, including Switzerland (a surprise to the Russians), Japan, South Korea, Singapore, and Taiwan. The ability of Western coun-tries to act fast in imposing sanctions was the result of months of leader-ship and hard work in advance by the United States.

The overwhelming Western opposition to Putin's war in the days after February 24 went beyond heavy sanctions and export controls. There was a pervasive sense of a break with the past and the failed efforts to accommodate a hyperaggressive and dangerous Russia. The moment was captured by German chancellor Olaf Scholz in a speech to the Bund-estag on February 27. In what became known as the *Zeitenwende* speech (the German word for turning point), the chancellor said the "special mil-itary operation" was a "watershed," and

the world afterwards will no longer be the same as the world before. The issue at the heart of this is whether power is allowed to prevail over the law. Whether we permit Putin to turn back the clock to the nineteenth century and the age of the great powers. Or whether we have it in us to keep warmongers like Putin in check.

With those rousing words hanging in the room, the German chancellor announced a major increase in defense spending, with a €100 billion fund to modernize the Bundeswehr, and a new willingness to provide Ukraine with military equipment and support.

The principal reason for the decisive actions by Germany and the other Western countries on sanctions, defense spending, and support for Ukraine was, of course, the scope and brutality of the Russian invasion. Another reason was the brave resistance by Ukraine and its people. President Zelensky addressed EU leaders by video on the night of February 24, pleading for support and concluding that "this might be the last time you see me alive." Instead of trying to flee, he was staying in Kyiv while the full might of the Russian military was bearing down on him, and ballistic and cruise missiles exploded across the city. The media reported that in response to a US offer of assistance to evacuate, Zelensky declared, "The fight is here; I need ammunition, not a ride."

There was later debate on whether Zelensky actually said those words, which became legendary, but his physical presence leading Ukraine's defense in his soon-to-be-iconic olive-green sweatshirt and cargo pants, not to mention every one of his public comments, were completely consistent with that epic statement. Zelensky displayed remarkable courage and patriotism in standing up to the Russians and staying in Kyiv when virtually everyone (including the US ambassador in Moscow) thought he had no chance to survive. The man and the moment met, inspiring Ukrainians, as well as leaders and ordinary people across the West, to oppose Russia's aggression.

In a larger sense, Zelensky's actions were a reflection of the heroism of millions of Ukrainians, who chose to fight against the Russian invasion and not surrender their country to Putin. A widely publicized event in the early hours of the war occurred when the Russian navy's Black Sea flagship, the cruiser *Moskva*, warned outgunned Ukrainian soldiers on Snake Island by radio to surrender. One of the Ukrainian border guards on the island responded, "Russian warship, go f**k yourself," which instantly reminded me of US Brigadier General Anthony McAuliffe's historic response—"NUTS!"—to the German general demanding the surrender of the 101st Airborne Division at Bastogne in December 1944.

The early heroic tales of resistance across Ukraine showed a nation rallying and uniting in its defense. I was impressed by a viral YouTube video on February 25 that epitomized Ukrainian resolve and opposition to the invasion. It showed an unarmed Ukrainian woman, identified by some in the media as a grandmother, confronting heavily armed Russian soldiers on the first day of the invasion in Henichesk, a Ukrainian city on the Sea of Azov, just north of Crimea. She asked them, "What the f**k are you doing in our land?" She shouted, "You're occupants, you're fascists," and then she offered the soldiers a fistful of sunflower seeds to put in their pockets, "so that they will grow on Ukrainian land after you die."

It was an unforgettable scene, and an incredible act of bravery considering what the world would subsequently learn about the Russian military's willingness to commit war crimes, including the murder of unarmed civilians. I asked others at the embassy to come into my office to watch the video. I remarked that if all Ukrainians responded to the "special military operation" in the way the woman in the video did, then Putin would have a much more difficult task in overpowering Ukraine. His plans were based on many Slavic brothers and sisters in Ukraine accepting his offer of Soviet style "fraternal assistance." That assumption was one of many Russian mistakes in the planning and execution of the "special military operation" that would be revealed over time.

———————

The reaction of most governments in the world to Putin's war was almost as hostile as the Ukrainian woman's reaction in Henichesk. The United Nations was the most appropriate venue in which to express that opprobrium, although action on Ukraine in the Security Council was blocked by Russia's veto power as a permanent member. On March 2, the UN General Assembly approved a resolution on "Aggression against Ukraine," with the support of 141 of the 193 UN member states. The US mission to the UN, led by Ambassador Linda Thomas-Greenfield, worked skillfully to garner that overwhelming support.

The UNGA resolution, invoking Article 2 of the UN Charter, which outlaws the "use of force against the territorial integrity or political independence" of any nation, "condemn[ed]" the Russian "special military operation," and "deplore[d] in the strongest terms the aggression by the Russian Federation against Ukraine in violation" of the UN Charter. The resolution "demand[ed] that the Russian Federation immediately cease its use of force against Ukraine" and "withdraw all of its military forces from the territory of Ukraine." It described the "special military operation" as being "on a scale that the international community has not seen in Europe in decades," for which "urgent action is needed to save this generation from the scourge of war."

The large number of countries voting for the resolution, including many outside NATO and the EU, was a stunning censure of Russia. Only four countries (Belarus, Syria, Eritrea, and North Korea) voted with Russia in opposition. Thirty-five countries declined to support Russia and abstained, including the PRC, Iran, and Cuba, and twelve countries did not vote. Unfortunately, unlike Security Council resolutions, the resolutions of the General Assembly were not legally binding. It was a symbolic rebuke that as President Biden had predicted, "diminish[ed] Russia's standing," but would not stop the large-scale killing and massive destruction in Ukraine. Putin simply did not care.

The resolution was marginally useful in establishing a factual predicate for addressing related important issues in the future, including war crimes. Thus, the resolution expressed "grave concern at reports of attacks against civilian facilities such as residences, schools and hospitals, and of civilian casualties, including women, older persons, persons with disabilities, and children." The resolution also condemned the "decision by the Russian Federation to increase the readiness of its nuclear forces" and deplored the February 21, 2022, "decision of the Russian Federation related to the status of certain areas of the Donetsk and Luhansk regions of Ukraine as a violation of the territorial integrity and sovereignty of Ukraine," in violation of the UN Charter.

The United Nations continued its repudiation of Putin's war with a decision on March 16 of the International Court of Justice (ICJ), which is the judicial organ of the UN based in The Hague. The ICJ responded to an application by Ukraine contending "that the Russian Federation [had] falsely claimed that acts of genocide [had] occurred in the Luhansk and Donetsk Oblasts of Ukraine" and that in response, Russia had "implemented a special military operation against Ukraine with the express purpose of preventing and punishing purported acts of genocide that have no basis in fact." Ukraine sought relief from the ICJ under the 1948 Convention on the Prevention and Punishment of the Crime of Genocide.

The fifteen judges on the ICJ voted 13–2 in favor of Ukraine. The Court found that it was "not in possession of evidence substantiating the allegation of the Russian Federation that genocide has been committed on Ukrainian territory." Moreover, even if there were such evidence, "it is doubtful that the Convention...authorizes a Contracting Party's unilateral use of force in the territory of another State for the purpose of preventing or punishing an alleged genocide." Therefore, the Court ordered the Russian Federation to "immediately suspend" the "special military operation."

This was another symbolically significant loss for Russia. The two dissenting judges were from Russia and the PRC. Among the majority of thirteen judges voting for Ukraine were seven from countries that were not members of NATO or the EU: Brazil, Somalia, India, Uganda, Jamaica, Lebanon, and Morocco. But like the General Assembly, the ICJ had no enforcement authority independent of the Security Council, where Russia had a veto to block action against it.

---

After reading the ICJ opinion, I took the time to go through the mental exercise of reviewing and critiquing Putin's rationales for waging war, and to try to find historical precedents. There were principally two overarching justifications by Russia for the war, one focused on the Ukrainian government and the other on the United States and NATO. Neither had any basis in fact or law.

The Ukrainian justification was premised on Putin's claim that the "special military operation" was launched to "protect people who, for eight years now, have been facing humiliation and genocide perpetrated by the [Kyiv] regime" and to "demilitarize and denazify Ukraine, as well as bring to trial those who perpetrated numerous bloody crimes against civilians." The ICJ decision, as well as the prior UNGA resolution supported by 141 countries, obliterated Putin's outrageous charge that a "genocide of the millions of people" in the Donbas had been committed by a Nazi government in Kyiv. There was no genocide, and when Russia was presented with the opportunity to submit evidence to prove the allegation, it did not, and could not, do so. Saving Ukrainians from genocide was not a justification for waging war against Ukraine.

Defending Russians was the second justification for the war, based on Putin's long-standing allegation of an existential threat to Russia from NATO and its expansion eastward, led by the United States. This rationale stemmed from the lie—pure disinformation—that the United States broke a solemn promise to "Soviet leadership that NATO jurisdiction or military presence [would] not expand one inch to the east and that the unification of Germany will not lead to the spread of NATO's military organization to the east."

There was no such promise. The two people who led the negotiations over German reunification in 1990 for the United States and the Soviet Union, former US secretary of state James A. Baker III and former general secretary Gorbachev, have each categorically denied that the Soviets got any assurance that NATO would never expand to the east. Baker publicly called the argument "ridiculous," and said so again privately in a conversation with me, decades after the negotiations. I never had the opportunity to ask Gorbachev directly about the matter while I was serving in Moscow, because of his declining health during the pandemic. Nevertheless, he agreed with Baker and was quoted on the record in 2015 denying there was a promise: "The topic of 'NATO expansion' was not discussed at all, and it wasn't brought up in those years."

All of which made perfect sense, because there was no writing that reflected an alleged understanding by either the United States or the Soviet Union on NATO expansion. The "Treaty on the Final Settlement with Respect to Germany," under which East and West Germany were reunified, did not mention the issue. How could the parties negotiate for months to reach agreement on a written treaty and not include such an important provision that would rewrite the North Atlantic Treaty? As Secretary Baker said in an interview, "It just doesn't make sense." Was it a secret side agreement? Even the notorious Secret Protocol of the Molotov-Ribbentrop Pact of August 1939 was put in writing.

No, the only relevant promise with respect to Ukraine that was breached was the Russian commitment in the Budapest Memorandum, an international agreement signed by the leaders of the Russian Federation, Ukraine, the United Kingdom, and the United States in December 1994. Under this agreement, in return for Ukraine relinquishing its nuclear weapons and joining the Treaty on the Non-Proliferation of Nuclear Weapons as a non-nuclear-weapons state, Russia, the United States, and the UK pledged "to respect the independence and sovereignty and the existing borders of Ukraine," and to "refrain from the threat or use of force against the territorial integrity or political independence of Ukraine." That written promise by Russia regrettably did not factor into Putin's decision to invade Ukraine.

What did factor into the decision was Putin's view of NATO's "eastward expansion" as a threat to the very survival of Russia. My view was that NATO remained, as always, a defensive alliance and that the Eastern European countries that had joined in the prior twenty-three years—starting in 1999 with the accession of Poland, Hungary, and the Czech Republic—were motivated by their own security concerns, mostly about their large neighbor to the east, the Russian Federation, after four decades of Soviet domination during the Cold War. NATO did not conquer those countries or compel them to join; they applied for admission to NATO. It was not NATO expanding to the east, so much as the people and the elected governments of Eastern Europe looking to the west to join a defensive alliance.

Yet that was not the end of the discussion. There was ample room for debate, diplomacy, and serious negotiations. The United States was prepared to discuss with the Russian government all aspects of NATO's military presence in Eastern Europe that it found threatening. Indeed, that was the point of the US response to the Russian draft treaties. What was not open to debate was either a wholesale revision of the North Atlantic Treaty, which had endured for over seven decades as a pillar of Western security, or an agreement that Putin could make security decisions for the Ukrainian people—as he put it, to protect and assuage "their aspirations, the feelings and pain of these people." Under the UN Charter, Russia could not make decisions for a sovereign Ukraine.

Unfortunately, that was exactly what Putin wanted to do, and his position was nonnegotiable. He tried to create a sense of urgency and crisis after Burns's November visit put a spotlight on his plans, but there was no crisis. If there had been, Putin would have raised it with Biden in Geneva or in subsequent phone calls. Instead, he quietly prepared in the fall to launch a war of choice. He made the decision without any credible justification, as there was no merit in his arguments about saving Ukrainians or defending Russians.

Instead, Putin's decision-making and statements about the "special military operation" in February 2022 were a reincarnation of the old Brezhnev Doctrine, which the Soviet leader had developed in the latter half of 1968 to justify the Warsaw Pact's invasion of Czechoslovakia. In a speech on November 13, 1968, Brezhnev stated that while socialist countries "should have freedom for determining the ways of advance," no decision by them "should damage either socialism in their country or the fundamental interests of other socialist countries." If a socialist country erred in its "approach to the question of sovereignty," the Soviet Union and its socialist allies would correct that error. In the case of Czechoslovakia, the Soviet Union and the Warsaw Pact countries, "discharging their international duty toward the fraternal peoples of Czechoslovakia, . . . had to act decisively and they did act against the antisocialist forces in Czechoslovakia."

The new Putin Doctrine was a direct descendant of the Brezhnev Doctrine: every country on Russia's periphery that was formerly a part of the Soviet Union, while nominally sovereign, could not "damage either [security] in their country or the fundamental [security] interests of [the former] socialist countries" of the USSR, especially Russia. If, in the exclusive judgment of the Russian Federation, a country subject to the Putin Doctrine erred in exercising its sovereignty and made Russia feel "insecure," then Russia would discharge its "duty toward the fraternal peoples" of that country and "act decisively" to correct the error. That was the rationale for Putin's invasion of Ukraine; and the mimicry of Soviet oppression extended to the use of a euphemism for war: "special military operation," rather than the old-fashioned "fraternal assistance" of the Soviet era.

While it shared the heritage of the Brezhnev Doctrine, Putin's war was in a way even more sinister because at least Brezhnev and his Soviet comrades were ostensibly animated by a shared Communist ideology. Putin, on the other hand, had no ideology other than hypernationalism in his quest to regather the Russian lands into an empire worthy of the *Russkiy mir.* The "special military operation" was at its core an "aggressive war," as that term was used by the Allies in 1945 and 1946 in establishing the International Military Tribunal at Nuremberg and prosecuting the high-ranking officials of Nazi Germany who were responsible for the invasion of Poland on September 1, 1939. History, I felt sure, would judge Putin and his henchmen just as harshly.

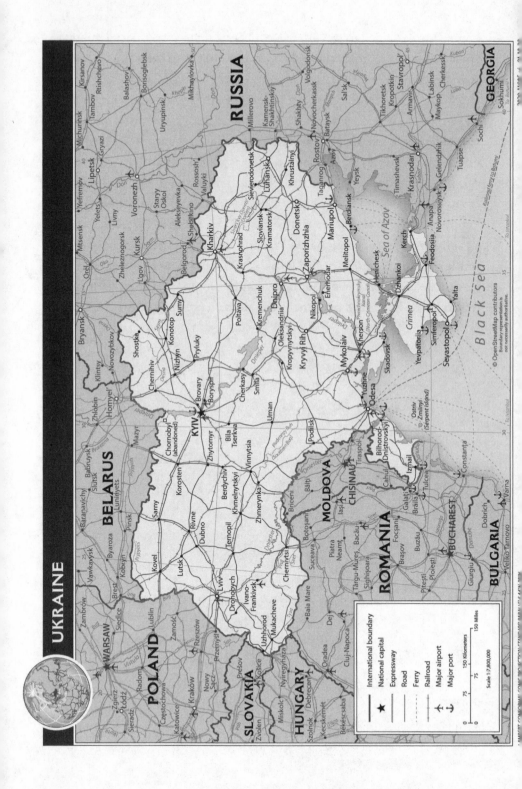

UKRAINE

# CHAPTER 13

# NO EASY DAYS

**D**ESTROYED RUSSIAN TANKS AND ARMORED vehicles, smoking hulks along the roads leading to Kyiv, were the lasting images I had of the opening month of the invasion of Ukraine, which I followed hour-by-hour from Embassy Moscow. The massive attack started while Putin was announcing the "special military operation" before dawn on February 24, with Russian ballistic and cruise missiles striking targets across the country, and explosions rocking the historic cities of Kyiv, Kharkiv, and Odesa. It was a Russian attempt at "shock and awe" that targeted critical infrastructure and command centers. The intentional targeting of civilians would not become clear until later.

At the same time, Russian military units moved simultaneously from their staging areas in Russia, Crimea, and Belarus with the immediate goal of enveloping the eastern half of Ukraine. Most important, the Russian security services—principally the FSB, whose Fifth Service was heavily involved in preparing for the invasion—would have a key role in implementing the plans for regime change in Ukraine that Putin demanded. In support, the Russian military's *spetsnaz*, or GRU special forces, were alleged by Zelensky to be operating in the country, including inside Kyiv itself, and he declared martial law after formally breaking diplomatic relations with Russia and ordering a general mobilization of Ukrainian men.

The armed forces participating in the Russian invasion also included unconventional elements controlled by the Kremlin, which—combined with the enhanced role for the FSB—signaled to me the particular, and particularly brutal, type of war that Putin would wage. Part of the Russian order of battle were the militias and irregular troops of the Donetsk People's Republic and Luhansk People's Republic in the occupied portions of the Donbas. Ramzan Kadyrov, the fiery and violent leader of the Chechen Republic in Russia, announced that the Kadyrovtsy—Chechen paramilitary units loyal to him with a well-deserved reputation for lawless outrages—would be deployed to fight in Ukraine. There also were reports that assassins from the Wagner Group had slipped into Ukraine to kill Zelensky. All of this indicated that Putin's war of aggression would not be a conventional conflict fought under the constraints of international law or with concern for civilized norms and the protection of innocent life.

In monitoring the start of the invasion, my attention was riveted on north-central Ukraine. The battle for Kyiv in February and March was the strategic focus of Putin's campaign to "denazify" and demilitarize the country and would be decisive for the future course of the war. Capturing the Ukrainian capital and decapitating the Zelensky government (and perhaps Zelensky himself) would, according to the Russian plan, disorient and disrupt the command and control of the Ukrainian military. That would, in turn, sap the Ukrainian will to resist nationwide and ease the formation of a regime in Kyiv, as well as local governments, particularly in the eastern and southern parts of the country, that could be controlled by the Kremlin through leaders already identified and vetted by the FSB. The tasks of weakening the Zelensky government and preparing new leadership aligned with Moscow were among the important roles of the FSB in Putin's war.

The principal land route for the Russian attack on Kyiv was a 140-mile advance south from the Belarusian border through the Chernobyl Exclusion Zone, a thousand-square-mile closed area surrounding the Chernobyl Nuclear Power Plant, which had suffered the infamous and catastrophic explosion of a nuclear reactor in April 1986. The Russians captured the plant and the abandoned cities of Chernobyl and Pripyat on the first day of the invasion. An armored column over forty miles long traveled from Belarus along the existing road network, and a recently paved highway, to attack Kyiv from the western side of the Dnipro River. Creating a pincer, the Russian forces also moved southwest from Russia and Belarus toward

Chernihiv, a city ninety miles northeast of Kyiv on the Desna River, and west from Russia through the Ukrainian border city of Sumy.

A key component of the plan to sack Kyiv was an air assault by the Russian Airborne Forces (VDV) on Antonov International Airport near Hostomel, less than ten miles northwest of Kyiv. Seizing the huge airfield quickly with paratroopers and swarms of helicopter-borne VDV troops would allow the Russians to establish an "air bridge" and move large numbers of soldiers and their equipment, vehicles, and heavy weapons directly from Russia and Belarus to the doorstep of Kyiv. The Russian armor and soldiers traveling overland from Belarus would support the VDV and the troops and equipment ferried into Antonov Airport, and other airports in the region, in the final attack on Kyiv. Russian troops moving southwest from Chernihiv and west from Sumy would complete the encirclement of the capital and cut off the sizable Ukrainian military formations in the east on the existing line of contact in the Donbas.

The Russian plans were premised on speed, like the American military victories over the Iraqi military in February 1991 and March/April 2003. Russian planners expected Kyiv to fall in days and for the major combat portion of the "special military operation" in Ukraine to be completed in less than two weeks. A noteworthy difference from the prior American experience, however, and a critical impediment to the success of the Russian military plans from the very start, was the failure of the Russian Aerospace Forces (VKS)—despite an overwhelming numerical advantage over the Ukrainian military—to achieve dominance in Ukrainian airspace. The Russians lost an unexpected number of VKS aircraft to Ukrainian air defenses and their own friendly fire in the opening days of the war. As a result, VKS pilots and air crews became reluctant to loiter above Ukraine.

The battle for Kyiv was ultimately decided by fierce Ukrainian resistance and staggering Russian incompetence, which completely unraveled the Kremlin's plan to capture the city. It took two days, rather than a few hours, for the Russian armed forces to wrest control of Antonov Airport from the Ukrainians, but the destructive battle for the airfield rendered it unusable as an air bridge. The Russian armored column from Belarus crept slowly toward Kyiv, plagued by bad planning and organization, a lack of fuel, faulty equipment, and frequent ambushes. Disabled armored vehicles and tanks (some blown up and others just out of gas or needing mechanical assistance) blocked roadways and further delayed the movement south. Videos of the debacle appeared on YouTube, which I watched with no small amount of Schadenfreude while eating dinner alone in my townhouse on the embassy compound.

The armored column stalled by mid-March and never advanced closer than twenty miles from the center of Kyiv. Just as Russian soldiers finally reached the outskirts of the city, they met the tenacious opposition of the Ukrainian military and paramilitary groups, which rolled back the Russian advance in a series of battles for the small cities and towns surrounding Kyiv, such as Makariv, Hostomel, Irpin, Brovary, and Nova Basan. The Russian military suffered heavy casualties fighting an adversary they had grossly underestimated, and they never took the capital.

The Russian defeat in the battle for Kyiv was total. In Moscow on March 29, the Ministry of Defense announced publicly that it would "fundamentally ... cut back military activity in the direction of [Kyiv] and Chernihiv." I was mildly surprised by the statement because the Russian government under Putin rarely hinted that one of its programs or undertakings, particularly one as important to Putin as the "special military operation," had gone awry. On the other hand, the facts on the ground could not be hidden.

By April 2, the Ukrainian government declared that all Russian armed forces had withdrawn from Kyiv Oblast (the big province surrounding the capital, which extends through the Chernobyl Exclusion Zone all the way north to the Belarusian border). The Russian armed forces also withdrew completely in early April from the sprawling Chernihiv and Sumy Oblasts, without capturing either of the besieged cities in those oblasts that had been targeted at the start of the invasion. A huge swath of northeastern Ukraine was thus liberated.

Kyiv, Chernihiv, and Sumy—along with many nearby smaller cities, towns, and villages that the Russians had managed to occupy briefly until forced to abandon them—survived but were devastated with heavily damaged and looted buildings, homes, schools, and infrastructure. As they fled, the Russians left behind their dead, substantial amounts of destroyed and abandoned military equipment, and dangerous mines and booby traps that would continue to inflict casualties on Ukrainians long into the future. They also left compelling evidence of the terrible war crimes they had committed and of their own strategic and tactical mistakes in executing the plan to capture Kyiv.

The sizable number of dead civilians (men, women, and children) in the Ukrainian territory abandoned by the Russians in late March and early April 2022 was among the most damning evidence of their war crimes. More than a few dead bodies were just left lying in the streets; others were found in bunches with their hands bound, each shot in the back of the head. There was a mass grave in Bucha with the bodies of hundreds of civilians who had been executed. Over time, the accumulation of witness testimony, photographs, videos, and other evidence proved that Russian soldiers had intentionally shot countless unarmed civilians throughout the region in places like Hostomel, Peremoha, and Nova Basan. The Russians also used hundreds of civilians as human shields, forcing them into Russian military sites to deter Ukrainian fire, in one instance in the village of Yahidne for almost an entire month, during their attack on the city of Chernihiv.

The extensive and incontrovertible proof of war crimes led the UN Human Rights Commission subsequently to find, during the "first phase of its investigations," focused on events in February and March 2022, that "war crimes and violations of human rights and international humanitarian law have been committed in Ukraine since 24 February 2022. Russian armed forces are responsible for the vast majority of the violations identified." In a shocking finding, the UN concluded that "children have become the victims of the full spectrum of violations investigated by the Commission, including indiscriminate attacks, torture, and rape, suffering the predictable psychological consequences."

As unconcerned as Russian military leaders were with the international law of armed conflict and their legal and moral obligations to protect civilians, especially children, they equally were unprepared to support the troops they were sending into battle. Widespread shortages of food, fuel, and ammunition among the Russian armed forces in Ukraine baffled me because, as I knew well, the Russians had been preparing for the invasion for a long time. This was not a contingency operation cobbled together on short notice.

I had trouble understanding how they had failed to plan properly for the logistics of Putin's war, especially when I saw the first, astonishing reports of Russian soldiers suffering frostbite from a lack of cold weather gear. Of all the militaries in the world, how could the Russian army—the self-proclaimed heir to the Red Army of the Great (and frigid) Patriotic War—not be prepared for the cold? It was only one of a number of head-scratching moments as I followed closely Putin's aggressive war in Ukraine.

Another was the Russian military's movements and conduct in the Chernobyl Exclusion Zone, which became apparent after their defeat outside Kyiv. In the ensuing evacuation to Belarus, Russian military convoys and armored vehicles churned up the irradiated soil in the exclusion zone and predictably increased radiation levels, yet Russian soldiers did not wear protective gear in the zone. Even more disastrous, Russian soldiers were ordered to dig trenches and foxholes in the irradiated soil. The subsequent reports of acute radiation sickness among Russians deployed in the exclusion zone, therefore, should have been expected.

How could the Russian military not have been prepared for the radiation hazard at Chernobyl? Just as fighting a war in Ukraine in February required cold weather gear, so too fighting a war in the Chernobyl Exclusion Zone required caution and special gear (and should have been avoided in the first place). The only conceivable explanation was that the military's leadership was unconcerned about debilitating frostbite and radiation sickness among its personnel. It brought to mind my conclusion from two years before, during the pandemic, that the Russian government was much more concerned with public relations than with public health. Except now, Russian lives were being traded for Ukrainian turf.

---

The opening month of the war, culminating in the Russian withdrawal from its failed offensive against Kyiv, revealed a great deal about Putin's "special military operation." In announcing the withdrawal at the end of March, the Russian Defense Ministry did not refer to its crushing defeat at the gates of Kyiv, but instead cited a desire to "increase mutual trust and create conditions for further negotiations" with Ukraine. This was a reference to the desultory talks in March between Russian and Ukrainian representatives in Turkey after unsuccessful earlier rounds in Belarus. The Zelensky government sought a cease-fire and guarantees for its security, in return for surrendering its ambition to join NATO, but would not cede territory, including Crimea. That was a nonstarter for Putin, who would never surrender land that Russia claimed as its own, especially Crimea— and who indeed had bound his own hands in this regard. (Recall the 2020 revision to the Russian constitution that made it illegal to cede Russian territory to another country.)

The discussions between Russian and Ukrainian representatives continued into early April. I had a meeting on April 1 with Ambassador Ushakov to review issues involving US embassy operations, and I used the opportunity to raise with him the status of the negotiations with Ukraine. He was doubtful there would be a settlement. I thought the prospects for "mutual trust" leading to a cease-fire were vanishingly slim—and that was before the scale of the Russian war crimes against Ukraine became more widely known. After those atrocities, particularly the mass grave in Bucha, were revealed with greater clarity in April, and the rapacious Russian invasion ground on unabated in eastern and southern Ukraine, the concepts of "mutual trust" and "cease-fire" were simply not viable.

The body count of civilians executed by the Russian armed forces during the failed Kyiv offensive was rising, with new graves and victims discovered almost daily. I started to become desensitized to the regular, anodyne, and impersonal reports summarizing the violence unleashed by the Russian armed forces on innocent Ukrainian civilians. Sitting in my office in Moscow, hundreds of miles removed from the scenes of savage destruction in Ukraine, Russian brutality was becoming almost routinized. That was, until a deadly missile strike on a train station in Kramatorsk, a small city on the Ukrainian military's side of the line of contact in northern Donetsk in eastern Ukraine, finally crystallized for me the unspeakable horror of Putin's aggressive war. My views on his war would never be the same.

At midday on April 8, I received an email from my colleague Kristina

Kvien, the chargé d'affaires at US Embassy Kyiv, alerting me that she was going to send a subsequent email with disturbing images of a Russian missile attack in Donetsk that had just occurred. She sent the alert because the images were so gruesome. I had never received an email warning like that, and I already had seen extremely graphic images from the war in Ukraine. By early April, Russian shelling, VKS bombing, and missile attacks on apartment buildings, schools, hospitals, and other civilian targets had killed thousands of innocent Ukrainians.

Many Russian attacks caused mass casualties, like the March 16 bombing of the Donetsk Academic Regional Drama Theater in Mariupol, in which the basement had been used as an air raid shelter by up to twelve hundred civilians, including children. As the UN later found, the theater had "signs clearly marked CHILDREN, visible from the sky." Estimates of the number of bodies removed from the bombed theater ranged into the hundreds. Other Russian attacks had more symbolic significance, such as the deadly March 1 missile attack on Kyiv that damaged the Babyn Yar Holocaust Memorial Center, the most hallowed memorial to the Holocaust in Ukraine. Then there were towns like Borodianka, north of Kyiv, which was shelled and bombed into ruins and occupied by the Russian armed forces during its offensive against Kyiv. After the Russians withdrew from Borodianka in early April, hundreds of civilian bodies were found in the wreckage of demolished apartment buildings and in graves dug by local residents during the occupation.

I kept careful track of the atrocities committed by the Russians in Ukraine and was accustomed to seeing explicit photographs and videos of the consequences of their violence. So, I had to wonder what Kristina was sending and how bad the images could be. Once I opened the follow-up email and saw what was attached, I understood her prior warning. The Kramatorsk incident was different because of where the victims were (massed civilians outdoors) and the weapons used against them (antipersonnel). This missile attack was meant only to kill large numbers of people, not to destroy buildings that happened to have people in them.

The files emailed to me had photographic and video evidence of the carnage caused by two Russian missiles, each loaded with cluster munitions, that struck near the Kramatorsk train station at approximately 10:30

a.m. on a sunny spring morning. Thousands of people (the Ukrainian government later estimated up to four thousand) were waiting at the station, almost all of them crowded together outdoors, to board trains to escape shelling from the advancing Russian armed forces in the region. Kramatorsk was among the easternmost cities in Donetsk that still had train service westward to relative safety and had become a daily hub for evacuations. Like the thousands of civilians at the train station on April 8, millions of Ukrainians had been driven from their homes by the Russian invasion and turned into refugees, fleeing to other countries, or internally displaced persons, living in cities like Kyiv, Chernivtsi, and Lviv in central and western Ukraine.

Among the travelers at the Kramatorsk station when the cluster munitions exploded were numerous families with young children. There were no units of the Ukrainian military present or military trains at the station. The final toll from the strike was 63 people killed, among them 9 children, and another 150 wounded, including 34 children. Dry statistics alone do not convey what the cluster munitions did to those innocent people. Shattered corpses, gore, and body parts were mixed with bloody luggage, backpacks, stuffed animals, and baby strollers to create an unimaginably horrific scene. There were no destroyed buildings in the wake of the strike, with dead bodies buried under the rubble, as I was used to seeing. There were only dead and mangled civilians, forty-three of them children. The grotesque images of the aftermath of the attack were searing and unforgettable.

International condemnation was immediate, and the Russian government flatly denied responsibility, as it always did in such situations. I was reminded of George Kennan's warnings from the past about Russian "duplicity" and the "disrespect of Russians for objective truth—indeed, their disbelief in its existence"—which "leads them to view all stated facts as instruments for furtherance of" the interests of the state. The Russian state interest in the aftermath of the Kramatorsk atrocity was to avoid responsibility by spreading disinformation about the attack. This included a "fake video with BBC News branding"—which the broadcaster had to disavow—that falsely asserted Ukraine was responsible for attacking its own citizens in Kramatorsk. The actual forensic and circumstantial evidence told a different story that placed the blame squarely on the Russian armed forces. The United States and the EU, among others, joined the Ukrainian government in holding the Russians responsible.

---

The horror in Kramatorsk, following the Russian withdrawal from the Kyiv, Chernihiv, and Sumy Oblasts, shifted my attention fully to the front lines of the war in eastern and southern Ukraine, where the Russian invasion was unrelenting. What was left of the Russian troops, equipment, and weapons that had survived the Kyiv offensive were being redeployed to the east. The Russian Ministry of Defense spokesperson, Major General Igor Konashenkov, said with a straight face on March 30 that the goals of "the Russian armed forces in the Kyiv and Chernihiv directions" had "been met" (yet another example of Russian leaders' disdain for the truth), and that therefore Russian forces were being regrouped to "intensify operations in priority areas and, above all, to complete the operation for the complete liberation of Donbas."

In fact, the Russians achieved mixed results in three regions in eastern and southern Ukraine during the opening months of the war. First, they attacked across Russia's western border on February 24, and headed toward the major urban center of Kharkiv, the second largest city in Ukraine, located less than twenty miles from the border. Second, the Russians concurrently moved north from Crimea in an offensive that split east toward Melitopol and Mariupol, a valuable port in southern Donetsk on the Sea of Azov, and west toward the port cities of Kherson, Mykolaiv, and Odesa. Third, along the original line of contact in the Donbas at the start of the invasion, the Russians moved north to occupy the rest of the Luhansk Oblast that borders Russia and link with the Russians approaching from the Kharkiv campaign. They also moved southeast to occupy part of the Donetsk Oblast on the Sea of Azov, encircle the port of Mariupol, and link with the Russians approaching from Crimea.

The most intense battle at the start of the Russian war in the east was for the city of Kharkiv, which was similar to their failed attack on Kyiv. The Russian armed forces moved quickly to try to encircle the city and overwhelm it with artillery fire, VKS bombs, and missiles. The brutal fighting extended into the city itself, although the Russians were never able to conquer it. Instead, they bypassed Kharkiv, while combat operations inside it were ongoing, and occupied significant portions of the surrounding oblast, including the cities of Kupiansk and Balakliia, approaching the borders of the Luhansk and Donetsk Oblasts. On April 1, the Russians captured the city of Izium, in the Kharkiv Oblast, only fifty miles north of Kramatorsk in Donetsk. The Russian advance caused fear and panic among the civilians in the region, many of whom sought to flee by train from Kramatorsk, leading to the crowded station on April 8.

As in the battle for Kyiv, the Russian assault on Kharkiv was finally defeated in May by persistent and effective Ukrainian resistance that drove the Russians completely from the city and its surrounding area. A Ukrainian offensive begun later in the summer would expel the Russians from almost all of the remainder of the Kharkiv Oblast. And as in the aftermath of their failed Kyiv offensive, when the Russians withdrew from Kharkiv Oblast they left behind undeniable evidence of their war crimes against civilians. On September 15, for example, Ukrainian officials found a mass grave near Izium that had over 440 bodies. The location had changed, but not the ghastly criminal tactics of the Russians.

In southern Ukraine, unlike the battles for Kyiv and Kharkiv, which were decisive defeats, the Russians achieved some, but not all, of their objectives. From Crimea, the Russian armed forces attacked three vital port cities, Kherson, Mykolaiv, and Mariupol. The northwestern spur of the campaign first targeted Kherson, an important commercial center on the Dnipro River with access to the Black Sea, which was captured on March 2 and was the only oblast capital (Kherson Oblast) Russian forces were able to occupy in 2022.

After the fall of Kherson, the Russian forces continued their advance northwest to the outskirts of Mykolaiv, another key port, on the Southern Bug River with Black Sea access, where Ukrainian resistance stiffened, and the Russians were stopped before they could capture the city. On April 8, Ukrainian officials announced that all Russian forces had been pushed back from Mykolaiv and its surrounding region, although the Russians maintained control of Kherson. (It was only months later that Ukraine would recapture Kherson from Russian occupation.)

By not seizing Mykolaiv in the spring of 2022 and never getting close to capturing historic Odesa—the third largest city in Ukraine and the westernmost port on the Black Sea, as well as a UNESCO World Heritage Site—the northwestern spur of the southern campaign failed to achieve two of its main objectives after Kherson. The northeastern spur of the campaign, by contrast, was more successful. The Russian armed forces captured the city of Melitopol on March 1 and secured the Ukrainian coastline along the Sea of Azov, including the city of Berdiansk, leading to Mariupol, where they combined with elements of the Russian military in Donetsk that were surrounding that city.

The siege of Mariupol was the bloody and destructive capstone of the first three months of Putin's aggressive war, from February 24 until May 20, when the final Ukrainian defenders of the last redoubt in the city, the huge Azovstal Iron and Steel Works, surrendered. The capture of Mariupol completed a strategic victory for Putin in connecting Russia by land with Crimea. Tragically, the cost of that victory was beyond measure. The UN high commissioner for human rights, Michelle Bachelet, who is a former president of Chile, concluded that in March and April 2022 Mariupol was "likely the deadliest place in Ukraine. The intensity and extent of hostilities, destruction and death and injury strongly suggest that serious violations of international humanitarian law and gross violations of international human rights law have occurred."

The final civilian death toll of the siege was never determined with any precision and the estimates ranged from many thousands, at a minimum, to tens of thousands. The UN found that 90 percent of the residential buildings in Mariupol were damaged or destroyed, and that three hundred and fifty thousand people were forced to leave the city to escape the Russian violence. The visual evidence I saw of the siege of Mariupol and its aftermath was apocalyptic. The city looked like Stalingrad in January 1943 or Berlin in May 1945. I found it hard to fathom, eight decades later, that a European government, and a permanent member of the UN Security Council, had inflicted that measure of death and destruction again on another European city.

After the surrender of Mariupol, there were no further large-scale movements or territorial gains by either Russia or Ukraine for the next several months in the war. Military operations nonetheless continued at a deadly pace. The Russians focused on extending and solidifying their control over the Donetsk and Luhansk Oblasts. There were fierce battles for the cities of Sievierodonetsk, Lysychansk, and Rubizhne in Luhansk, with great losses on both sides, as the Russians consolidated their control of the oblast. Meanwhile, the Donetsk Oblast remained divided between the Ukrainian and Russian armed forces.

On July 7, Major General Konashenkov of the Russian Defense Ministry announced that Russian forces in Ukraine would rest and regroup in a pause of undetermined length. That did not mean that Russia would stop all military activities, however, and the Russian armed forces continued small-scale ground operations and deadly shelling, bombing, and missile strikes across Ukraine after the July 7 announcement. The Ukrainians did their best to try to answer in kind, while promising a counteroffensive later in the summer.

In the midsummer of 2022, I considered Putin's aggressive war against Ukraine to be a failure, at least to that point, because the Russians had not achieved their objectives on the timeline they had planned and forecast. The Kyiv and Kharkiv offensives were soundly defeated, and fighting continued furiously for control of Donetsk and Luhansk in the Donbas. The southern campaign had established a Russian land bridge to Crimea, but the greater goal of capturing Odesa and the entire Black Sea coast of Ukraine to create a much lengthier land bridge to the west with Transnistria, a Russian-occupied breakaway republic in Moldova, was never within reach. Moreover, the extremely modest Russian gains from the "special military operation" had come at an astronomically high cost in lives and treasure.

Reliable casualty figures were always difficult to find on both sides of the conflict. The best estimate of the Russian casualties (dead, wounded, and missing) that I could find (provided by the Center for Strategic and International Studies) was approaching two hundred fifty thousand for the first year of the war. The total combat fatalities likely were between sixty and seventy thousand, and that was a conservative estimate. To provide perspective, sixty thousand dead Russians would exceed the total number killed in all the conflicts of the Soviet Union and the Russian Federation from the end of World War II to February 24, 2022—including in Syria, the Donbas, and the Afghanistan and (two) Chechen wars—combined. It would exceed in one year the total number of US personnel killed in the Vietnam War from 1965 to 1975. The butcher's bill among the Russian armed forces for Putin's aggressive war was high indeed.

In addition, the losses in Russian military hardware—tanks, armored vehicles, air defense systems, helicopters, fixed-wing aircraft, and ships—were equally huge and debilitating. The Russian Ministry of Defense announced a pause on major combat operations in July not by choice but by necessity because of the attrition in personnel, weapons systems, and ammunition.

One high-profile loss was both militarily significant and downright humiliating. On April 14, 2022, two Ukrainian anti-ship missiles sank the flagship of the Russian navy's Black Sea Fleet, the guided missile cruiser *Moskva*. The *Moskva* had participated in the highly publicized attack on Snake Island at the start of the invasion. It was the first Russian flagship sunk by an enemy since the Russo-Japanese War in 1905, and the ignominy was too much for the Kremlin to concede what had happened. The Russian government denied that Ukrainian missiles had sunk the ship, and claimed it was lost in stormy seas after an onboard fire had caused munitions to explode. Even that patently false explanation did not reflect well on the Russian military, but it was better from the Kremlin's perspective than acknowledging that the Ukrainians had sent a Russian flagship named after the capital of the *Russkiy mir* to the bottom of the Black Sea.

Putin himself had to admit privately that his war was not the success he had envisioned. As the *New York Times* later reported in part of its Pulitzer Prize–winning coverage of the conflict, Putin acknowledged—during a March 2022 meeting with Israeli prime minister Naftali Bennett—that the Ukrainians were "tougher 'than I was told,'" and "this will probably be much more difficult than we thought." It could not have been easy for Putin, the leading Chekist, to confess to something approaching weakness or defeat, even in private. And he could never admit that publicly to the Russian people.

There were countless breakdowns that combined to doom the opening months of Putin's war. Some were strategic, like the failure of the Russian cyber campaign before the war to undermine the Ukrainian economy and government; the inability of the VKS to dominate the skies over Ukraine after combat operations began; and the failed implementation by the Russian armed forces of the modern military doctrine of combined arms warfare by using infantry, armor, artillery, missiles, drones, aircraft, and satellites synchronously to attack an enemy. Russian troops at the start of the invasion still fought in various ways like the Red Army of the mid-twentieth century and died in large numbers like their predecessors in the Great Patriotic War.

Other Russian shortcomings were more prosaic, but equally disruptive and deadly, like the logistical problems that beset the Russian advance on Kyiv, problems that were repeated across Ukraine, or the lack of up-to-date maps for military commanders, which made targeting and combined movement difficult. Russian soldiers, including senior officers, breached operational security by continuing to use cell phones on the battlefield, which allowed the Ukrainians to geolocate them for targeted strikes. A number of Russian generals were killed as a result. Finally, there was the old scourge of corruption in procurement and other areas that sapped the readiness of the Russian armed forces.

In the final analysis, the Russian military erroneously planned and was provisioned for only a short campaign against Ukraine, which was slowed by logistical and related deficiencies. The longer the campaign took, the worse the impact of the planning and logistical problems, which in turn slowed the campaign even more. It was a vicious cycle that caused morale among Russian troops to plummet. Senior Russian officers went to the front lines to motivate or threaten (or both) their troops, which exposed more of them to Ukrainian fire and resulted in more of them killed.

This was not the military performance that Putin and Patrushev had confidently expected when they met with Bill Burns in November 2021. The effect on the psyche of the senior leaders of the Russian armed forces in Ukraine must have been profound. These were men who had been advised just before the war started to bring their dress uniforms with them to Ukraine for victory celebrations. Instead, a number of them were coming home from Ukraine in body bags. The Russian nationalists who were planning on a World War II Victory Day parade on May 9 in Kyiv were bitterly disappointed.

---

Yet, as bad as its performance was, the Russian military was not the most culpable participant in the planning and execution of Putin's war. That distinction belonged to the FSB, which I believed was more responsible for Russia's inability to achieve the goals of the "special military operation" in 2022 than any other branch of the Russian government. It was a two-pronged failure: first, inadequately preparing the battlespace in advance for the invasion by the Russian armed forces; and second, misinforming the Kremlin of the true prospects for accomplishing Putin's stated war aims of "denazifying" and demilitarizing Ukraine.

The FSB, through its Department for Operational Information and its Department for International Relations, known collectively as the Fifth Service from its KGB days, had been operating in Ukraine for decades, including during the Revolution of Dignity in 2014. The FSB had inherited from the KGB's Fifth Service the responsibilities for intelligence, espionage, and related covert and clandestine activities in the countries of the former Soviet Union, Russia's "near abroad." The head of the FSB's Fifth Service for well over a decade was none other than Colonel General Sergey Beseda, with whom I had engaged briefly after the 2021 Geneva summit on the cases of wrongfully detained Americans in Russia, until he declined to negotiate with an American ambassador.

The FSB officers in Beseda's Fifth Service in Ukraine had a broad mandate to restore Kyiv's allegiance to Moscow and undermine the Zelensky government by any means, to include increasing economic pressure (disrupting coal and gas supplies), sowing political discord, co-opting officials and institutions, and generally fomenting unrest. In 2021, the Fifth Service's Department for Operational Information significantly expanded its activities in Ukraine and formed a unit of almost two hundred more officers in the 9th Directorate, as described by the Royal United Services Institute in the UK, an old and venerable think tank on defense and security issues with excellent sources among intelligence services worldwide.

In the year preceding the war, the hundreds of FSB officers in Ukraine were specifically tasked with expanding the existing Russian network of agents to: provide intelligence from within the Ukrainian government (especially the military and security services); assess the Ukrainian will to resist a Russian invasion (using, among other means, polling); and identify and recruit potential leaders to replace existing national and local government officials (as well as identify for elimination those Ukrainian leaders opposed to Russia). The results of the FSB's work were fed into the Russian military's planning.

On the eve of the invasion, the FSB and its network of agents began to take "direct action" in support of the Russian military. These measures included destroying facilities or infrastructure important to the Ukrainian military and, vice versa, protecting facilities or infrastructure (for example, bridges and airfields) necessary for the movement of Russian troops and equipment once the invasion began. The 9th Directorate coordinated its activities with the Russian armed forces, which was not typical of the historical relationship between the FSB and the Ministry of Defense. The coordination was close enough that FSB officers were present with the spearhead Russian military units that sought to capture major cities like Kyiv and Kharkiv in late February 2022.

In addition to direct support of the military campaign, the FSB also established "filtration camps" for Ukrainians in the territories occupied by Russia. In these ghoulish-sounding camps, the FSB would: (1) screen individuals to determine their status (civilian, military, or other); (2) register and interrogate them; and, based on the screening and interrogation, (3) detain or release them. The Russian filtration camps became another source of war crimes and human rights abuses with widespread reports of torture and extrajudicial killings taking place within these facilities.

The FSB's multiple roles in the invasion were pervasive and fed into the Kremlin's seriously flawed planning for an abbreviated "special military operation" against Ukraine. That planning was premised, first, on an overestimated ability of the FSB to weaken Ukraine's defenses and resistance to the invasion, and thereby to lessen the burden on the Russian military, allowing it to proceed with fewer troops and equipment than it might otherwise have employed. Second, the Russian planning was pervasively misinformed by the advice that Putin received from the FSB that most Ukrainians did not have the will to fight for their country against Russia. The FSB largely failed in executing the first premise and was wrong on the second.

The only region in which the Russian armed forces achieved some success during the invasion in 2022 was southern Ukraine, where the FSB and its network of agents was most effective. It was in the south, for example, where key bridges necessary for the Russian military to advance quickly out of Crimea were not destroyed, as the Ukrainian government had previously planned. Zelensky complained about the lack of effective resistance in the region, and senior officers in the Security Service of Ukraine (SBU), the Ukrainian counterpart to the FSB, were charged with treason, including the head of the SBU in Kherson. Zelensky subsequently fired the director of the SBU, Ivan Bakanov, after the arrest of Bakanov's adviser Oleh Kulinich, who had been the head of the SBU in Crimea. Ukrainian prosecutors charged that Kulinich had colluded with the Russians before the war and had blocked timely dissemination of intelligence that the Russian armed forces in Crimea were mobilizing for an attack in the south.

The FSB did not have the same level of success elsewhere in undermining Ukraine's defenses, however, and that adversely impacted the performance of the Russian military. If the FSB had been as effective across the rest of Ukraine as it was in the south, the "special military operation" might have achieved more of the Kremlin's goals or, at a minimum, Russian losses might have been reduced. That is far from certain, however, because there was a bigger problem undermining the Russian invasion that also was attributable to the FSB: overconfidence leading to underpreparation and a lack of resources for the enormous scale of the war.

The FSB embraced and amplified the narrative, promulgated from the top of the Russian government, that most Ukrainians would welcome the "fraternal" intervention of Russia, or at least were not prepared to resist it forcibly. Some in the FSB actually might have thought that, and others simply were saying what Putin wanted to hear because that is what they always did. But with hundreds of trained officers on the ground in Ukraine before the war, the FSB was uniquely positioned to advise Putin accurately on this critical issue and it failed him spectacularly.

I am convinced that this breakdown was, to a significant degree, because the FSB was in a difficult, conflicted position. It was not merely a question of groupthink or unwillingness to tell Putin what he did not want to hear. It was more complicated than that. Telling the truth would have been a confession of error or worse. Putin had given the FSB huge sums of money (in the billions of dollars) and ample personnel over eight years to weaken Ukraine and render it susceptible to Russian suasion, influence, and intervention. Telling him what he later learned the hard way—that the Ukrainians were "tougher" than he had imagined, and the war would "be much more difficult" than he had thought—would have been an admission that the FSB could not do, or had not done, what Putin had ordered. A confession of that nature and magnitude would have required a tall order of courage and strength from individual FSB officers and from the Russian system in general, virtues that were lacking in this case.

I assumed there would have to be a reckoning for misguiding Putin on such an important subject. The questions were obvious: what happened to all the money spent to weaken Ukraine, and what had the FSB been doing for all these years? Sure enough, there were multiple news stories in a variety of media starting in mid-March 2022 that General Beseda had been arrested. Some reported that he was in home detention; others that he was in Lefortovo Prison. Some reported that he was arrested for providing misleading intelligence before the war; others that he was charged with corruption or embezzlement.

The gist of the reports on accountability and punishment for Beseda, if not the exact details, sounded completely plausible to me and to be expected in the wake of such a high-profile debacle—until they were contradicted by Beseda himself weeks later. He appeared at a nonpublic meeting with foreigners present and again demonstrated his Chekist sense of humor by putting a Russian spin on Mark Twain's famous quip that reports of his demise were greatly exaggerated.

I struggled to assess how Putin's system could function. No senior official—the minister of defense (Shoigu), the chief of the general staff (Gerasimov), the director of the FSB (Bortnikov), or the Kremlin staff (Patrushev or Kozak)—appeared to be held accountable for the calamitous errors in the war. Not even the senior official who seemed to be most culpable, the head of the FSB's Fifth Service (Beseda). To be sure, some lower-ranking generals and admirals, at least those who were still alive, were replaced in commands in Ukraine, and there were reports of mid-level FSB officers being relieved. But no senior official was fired, even though Putin—by his own admission—had been seriously misinformed if not intentionally misled on the most important issue involving Russian national security: the planning for his aggressive war.

It made no sense to me. If no one was held accountable, how could the grave mistakes and shortcomings revealed in the "special military operation" be corrected? If any of the embarrassing setbacks suffered by the Russian military (for example, radiation sickness among its troops from reckless actions in the Chernobyl Exclusion Zone) had happened to the American military, I knew from experience that heads would have rolled at the Pentagon. And if the US commander in chief were unwilling to hold leaders accountable for their decisions and actions, then Congress and the American people would demand it.

A leading explanation for the contrary approach in Russia was that there was a shortage of potential replacements from Putin's perspective. The number of officials and advisers that he trusted, his inner circle, had shrunk considerably over the years. As a result, there were very few people whom he would allow to hold the most senior positions in the national security establishment.

Equally challenging was the fact that Putin could not discipline a single high-profile official like Shoigu, Gerasimov, Patrushev, Bortnikov, or even Beseda, without contradicting the consistent public line from the Kremlin that the "special military operation" was going according to plan—the Kyiv offensive had accomplished its goals, Russian losses were minimal, the *Moskva* was not sunk by Ukraine, the Bucha massacre was staged, the Ukrainians were responsible for the Kramatorsk atrocity, and so on.

To fire or prosecute a senior official would have been an admission that the war was not a success, and the truth had never been valued by any government in Moscow. Worse, it would be seen as a confession of weakness and failure, which Putin could never abide. There was no recognition in Moscow that the inability or unwillingness to admit and correct mistakes was an even greater weakness that would cause even more disasters in the future.

At the end of the day, the faults in the "special military operation" were singularly attributable to Putin himself. It was his system—designed to keep him in power without subjecting him to an "unmanaged" democratic election—that had produced a badly planned and under-resourced war. A war in which his military could not fight competently or efficiently and his security service, whose very existence formed the basis of his Chekist identity, could not advise him properly on the risks of, and prospects for, the fight.

---

Putin's role in the war was one of the issues on which I engaged with the Russians after February 24. When the Russian military was in extremis on the outskirts of Kyiv, and the United States and its NATO allies were aligned in imposing substantial economic sanctions on Russia and increasing the flow of weapons and military support to Ukraine, Putin responded with his outrageous (albeit familiar) nuclear saber rattling. He publicly announced at the end of February that he had ordered the Ministry of Defense "to transfer the deterrence forces of the Russian army to a special mode of combat duty." His stated rationale was that "Western countries aren't only taking unfriendly actions against our country in the economic sphere, but top officials from leading NATO members made aggressive statements regarding our country."

The United States, which always carefully tracked Russia's nuclear weapons posture, subsequently announced that there did not appear to be any change in the status of the Russian nuclear arsenal. Moreover, the language Putin used, "special mode of combat duty," was not part of the detailed Russian nuclear weapons doctrine that had been revised and published in an executive order, signed by Putin in June 2020, on the "Fundamentals of Russia's Nuclear Deterrence State Policy." Putin's announcement thus appeared to me to be threat and bluster, not a substantive military order, but on a subject that should never be used for such purposes.

Indeed, Putin's statement was extremely dangerous, irresponsible, and escalatory, and was described publicly as such by the White House, in a briefing by Press Secretary Jen Psaki, and by NATO secretary-general Jens Stoltenberg. I conveyed the same message to the Russian MFA. The US government went beyond public statements and diplomatic démarches, however, and on March 2 announced the delay of a long-scheduled and routine test of a US Minuteman III intercontinental ballistic missile, which would ensure the readiness of our own nuclear deterrent forces. The Pentagon's rationale for extending the suspension was to show that the United States and Russia must "bear in mind the risk of miscalculation and take steps to reduce those risks." I was skeptical that Kremlin leaders, who obsess about strength, abhor weakness, and regularly rely on explicit nuclear blackmail, would bear anything like those worthy sentiments in mind.

My opportunities for follow-up conversations with Russian officials to gauge their reaction to the United States' announcement, and generally to learn their thinking as the war progressed, were limited because the policy of the United States after February 24 was that there would no longer be "business as usual" with the Russian government. Meetings with Russians everywhere, in Washington, Moscow, and around the world, were restricted to essential business and there would be no official participation in social events with them. As a result, I had far fewer interactions with government officials in Russia.

I did continue to have meetings at the MFA and was summoned on March 21 to meet with Ambassador Alexander Darchiev, Ryabkov's deputy and the director of the MFA's North American department. I knew Darchiev from my meetings with Ryabkov, but I had never dealt with him directly before. In ordinary times, I might have sent someone else from the embassy to take the meeting, but these were not ordinary times. I welcomed the opportunity to get inside the MFA and have a conversation with Russian diplomats, even if they were not the most senior leaders of the ministry. It turned out to be the most contentious meeting of my entire tenure as ambassador to Russia.

Darchiev had been tasked with admonishing me over President Biden's comment five days before, on March 16, when, in responding to questions about Putin and the conduct of the Russian military toward civilians in Ukraine, he said of Putin, "I think he is a war criminal." Describing Biden's statement in high dudgeon, Darchiev lectured me and charged that was no way for one head of state to speak about another head of state, and that the United States and Russia could not conduct diplomacy if the American president used such language to insult the Russian president. Darchiev must have thought I was just going to sit there and take it, because he seemed surprised that I had a firm rejoinder.

Why waste an opportunity, I figured, to demonstrate that the United States was not weak and that its ambassador was not a punching bag? I also knew this was not an important message from the Russians—otherwise Darchiev would not be delivering it, and they would not have waited five days to summon me—so I did not mince words out of fear of inciting a diplomatic incident. But neither did I lose my cool. Rather, channeling Kennan's advice that American diplomats should always maintain their composure, I calmly recited the facts establishing Russian war crimes in Ukraine and the overwhelming votes against Russia and its "special military operation" in the UN General Assembly and the International Court of Justice. I concluded by suggesting that if President Putin did not want to be called a war criminal, he should stop his military from committing war crimes and withdraw his troops from Ukraine as directed by overwhelming majorities in the United Nations and the International Court of Justice. I stopped short of noting that Putin, as a Chekist in the tradition of Dzerzhinsky, may well have been flattered by Biden's accusation.

As I was speaking, Darchiev's face turned bright red. While he let me speak, he was visibly enraged. When I finished, he started screaming at me in a profane tirade that I should not come into the ministry with such a belligerent attitude. He became further unglued when I said quietly that I was not belligerent and that it was he who was screaming and swearing. As Darchiev started to rise from his chair, my colleagues Bo Palmer and Andrew Freeman, who attended the meeting with me from the embassy, later said they thought he was going to take a swing at me. I wondered whether he was going to lunge across the table or storm out of the room. As it turned out, he did neither. He sat down and tried to compose himself while I sat across from him stone-faced and his Russian colleagues looked nervously at each other.

Remarkably, Darchiev calmed down enough that we could continue our discussion on another topic involving the operations of the US embassy, and we concluded the meeting with a handshake. As Bo, Andrew, and I drove back to the embassy chancery, we marveled at what had happened and how Darchiev had dialed back his frothing anger. I questioned whether, after my statement, he had to put on a show of outrage for the benefit of his colleagues sitting on the Russian side of the table, at least one of whom likely was an SVR officer. It could not be easy, I mused, to work as a diplomat in an intelligence state run by a KGB man.

Later that night, when I called into the Operations Center at the State Department in Washington to get some information from the watch officer on a completely different subject, she thanked me. I asked her what she was talking about, and she said that the cable (written report) on my meeting earlier in the day with Ambassador Darchiev had raised spirits back home as evidence that we were standing up to the Russians. Her expression of gratitude meant more to me than any award I received for my service.

Ironically, the most important subject I discussed with Darchiev on March 21 was not Biden calling Putin a war criminal; it was the persistent problem I had in getting more visas from the MFA for Americans to work at Embassy Moscow. I continued to raise the issue in virtually every meeting I had with Russian officials, before and after the war started. Unfortunately, the problem had become frustratingly complex, involving US and Russian law, the Vienna Conventions on Diplomatic and Consular Relations, the UN Headquarters Agreement, and the conflicting interests of the various law enforcement and intelligence agencies on both sides. The intransigence of the Russian MFA, as a front for the FSB and SVR, made it all worse.

The issue could be boiled down to its simplest terms as my insisting on reciprocity (equal numbers and terms of visas on each side) and the Russians insisting, despite their professed desire for reciprocity, on maintaining their numerical advantage in personnel (more Russians in the United States than Americans in Russia). I could never overcome that gap, and the security, health, and safety risks that plagued Embassy Moscow in my first year only got worse in subsequent years, because we could not increase our staffing and because key personnel were expelled by the MFA. The most experienced officer at the embassy, Bart Gorman, the deputy chief of mission, had been declared persona non grata by the Russians and left the country in mid-February, shortly before the war began. Dave Simons, our highly capable management chief, stepped into the role of acting DCM until I could get a visa for Bart's successor, which usually took months or longer.

In our contentious meeting on March 21, Darchiev described the MFA's position as an "exsanguination" strategy. I chuckled at his use of the term, which means death from blood loss, to describe the Russian approach to diplomatic negotiations with the United States. It was a perfect metaphor on two levels. First, it showed (as if I needed further proof) that the Russians would never relent in keeping their advantage in diplomatic numbers, even if it meant trading diplomatic expulsions with us until we reached zero (bled out) first, because we started the process with fewer personnel.

Second, it showed (as if I needed further proof) the type of hostile government with which the United States was dealing. Concepts of reciprocity and compromise were completely alien to the Russians, as Kennan once noted. In fact, when Darchiev spoke of exsanguination, I was reminded of Kennan's description of the hallmarks of Russian foreign policy: "the secretiveness, the lack of frankness, the duplicity, the wary suspiciousness, and the basic unfriendliness of purpose." I repeated ad nauseam to my US embassy colleagues that what was true in the 1940s continued to be true in the 2020s.

---

The Russian government had an equal "unfriendliness of purpose" in its treatment of American citizens wrongfully detained in Russia. Paul Whelan and Trevor Reed were still languishing in labor camps when I met with Darchiev in March 2022, and I continued to advocate for their proper treatment. Two more Americans had been arrested by the Russians in August 2021 and February 2022 in circumstances that immediately raised concerns about whether they also were wrongfully detained. The first was Marc Fogel, a popular teacher at the Anglo-American School of Moscow, who was returning for the school year and was arrested at Sheremetyevo International Airport, with a small amount (17 grams—a little over half an ounce) of medically prescribed "marijuana and hash oil" in his luggage. He was held in pretrial detention in Moscow and charged with "large-scale drug smuggling." Characterizing the possession of half an ounce of medicinal marijuana as "large scale" drug dealing seemed like a fairly good signal to me of wrongful detention by the Russians.

The second American arrested was Brittney Griner, the WNBA star and Olympic gold medalist. On February 17, 2022, she was detained at the same airport as Fogel and on similar charges: possession of one gram (an even smaller amount) of medically prescribed hash oil in her luggage. Contrary to consular relations law and practice, the Russians did not notify the US embassy of Griner's arrest until weeks later. When I was informed, I knew instantly that her case was a prize for the Russian security services because of her background as a popular American athlete and Olympian. Griner was charged with drug smuggling and cannabis possession and remained in pretrial detention in Moscow.

While my colleagues and I at Embassy Moscow were focused on the treatment of all the wrongfully detained Americans in Russia, negotiations between the US and Russian governments—through intelligence service channels, as required by the FSB—continued to focus on potential deals for the release of Paul Whelan and Trevor Reed. In early April 2022, it appeared that the only deal the Russians would make was to trade Reed for Konstantin Yaroshenko, a Russian pilot serving a twenty-year sentence in the United States after being convicted in federal court in 2011 of a large drug conspiracy. The proposed deal was not universally popular within the US government, because we would be releasing a major Russian narcotics trafficker in return for an innocent American and leaving Whelan in Russia.

It was a tough call, and I was glad I did not have to make it. We had serious concerns about Reed's health in IK-12 because he had been exposed to an inmate who had died of tuberculosis, and he was not being treated for symptoms of the disease that he was exhibiting. How could the president turn down an opportunity to get an innocent former marine out of that perceived danger? On the other hand, the Department of Justice had expended enormous resources to extradite Yaroshenko from Liberia and convict him of a very serious crime. Moreover, releasing Yaroshenko would inevitably encourage the Russians to detain more Americans without cause. And we would be leaving behind an innocent American who had been imprisoned longer than Reed.

In all the vigorous debates in which I participated, there was never an easy answer to the question whether to make the trade. After all the arguments were aired, the issue was presented to the president for his decision. He decided to get Reed safely home and release Yaroshenko to the Russians. The logistics of the physical transfer, which would occur on Wednesday, April 27, in Turkey, did not involve Embassy Moscow. The deal was that the Russians were obliged to get Reed to Ankara, where the United States would present Yaroshenko for the exchange.

On Monday evening, April 25, I had just finished dinner in my townhouse when I received a call from one of my embassy colleagues asking me to return to my office because an FSB officer from IK-12 was calling and wanted to speak with me. I knew it must involve Reed, but I had no idea why the FSB was calling me. When I spoke to the officer, he said that Reed was refusing to sign a document necessary to release him and that if he continued to refuse there would be no prisoner exchange.

I asked what the document was, and the FSB officer said it was an acknowledgment that Reed had committed the crime of which he had been convicted—in effect, a guilty plea or confession. I observed that Reed had consistently refused to admit guilt or to sign a confession since he was arrested. I asked whether anyone had told Reed why he was being asked to sign the document tonight, and the answer was no. Incredulous, I said, *You have not told him that he needs to sign the document now to get released in two days?* The FSB officer again said no. I told him that was unhelpful and not calculated to lead to the trade that his president and my president both wanted. The FSB officer asked me if I would speak to Reed, and I agreed. He asked me to stand by to be connected.

When Reed got on the line, I asked whether he knew what was going on. Trevor said that he did not. The Russians had presented, without explanation, another draft confession to him, which he had always refused to sign. I told him they were asking him to do so now because there was a deal for his release to be executed in less than two days. He was completely unaware of that. I said the Russians were making his signature on the confession a condition of his release. He asked me why they had not told him that, and I had no answer. We talked about whether the Russians would get his signature on the document and then back out of the deal. I told him that was extremely unlikely, and that if he signed the document he would almost certainly be released. Reed said in that case he would do so. He thanked me, and I wished him good luck and Godspeed.

After Reed signed, the FSB took him from IK-12 to Moscow, where he was held until he was put on a plane to Turkey on Wednesday morning in FSB custody. In Ankara, my friend Roger Carstens, the special presidential envoy for hostage affairs, greeted Reed on the tarmac and brought him home to freedom in the United States. It was a wonderful moment of joy and relief for the entire Reed family.

I was happy for them, but two things continued to gnaw at me. First, I told the US embassy team that it was even more important for us now to focus on Paul Whelan and our advocacy for his proper treatment until his release. It was a hard blow for him and his family to hear the news that Trevor Reed was released while he remained locked up in IK-17. I wanted to make sure that we did everything we could to support Whelan and his family, including his elderly parents in Michigan. It was not easy to endure what the Russian government was putting them through, and we owed it to them to not rest until Paul was back home, too.

Second, experiencing the final hurdle in getting Trevor Reed released was the latest confirmation of my mantra—one that I had been saying for over two years now—that nothing was ever easy with the Russians. It was not a joke or a pithy observation; it was gospel. Nothing was ever easy with them, even when we both wanted the same thing, like the extension of the New START treaty or Reed's release. That idea had to be built into the planning for everything we did with them. The Navy SEALs have a famous expression that "the only easy day was yesterday." For American diplomats in Moscow, there were no easy days.

# CHAPTER 14

# TWO FUNERALS

SINCE 1933, WORKING AS A US diplomat at Embassy Moscow has never been a soft assignment, and true to form, in my almost three years as ambassador the Russians did everything they could to make it even more difficult for us than it should have been. In a peculiar way, though, the severe challenges and restrictions that the Russians imposed on the US mission before February 24, 2022—the fact that our diplomatic relations with Russia were already so bad—meant that the war itself did not have as significant an impact on our operations as one might have expected. From Putin's perspective, he had been in a hybrid conflict with the West for years ahead of his aggressive war against Ukraine.

We were vigilant about our security at the embassy, of course, but the threat level did not increase materially after the war started, because we were already smothered by the FSB, and the massive, bloody violence unleashed by the Russians in Ukraine seemed to be a long way off, at least geographically. In the early months after the invasion, it appeared unlikely that the Ukrainians would be able to attack Moscow successfully and thereby impose a risk of collateral damage to our mission (although that risk assessment would change with the passage of time and the subsequent use of armed drones by Ukraine against targets in Moscow).

Moreover, the local threats against our embassy were not substantially heightened by the start of the "special military operation." There were occasional protests outside our gates, but they were not large, spontaneous, lengthy, or menacing. A few dozen protesters would appear at the same time with signs denouncing the United States, often on a weekend afternoon, arrange themselves to be recorded by their accompanying videographer, and then disperse in under an hour. It was a performance organized or at least approved by the FSB, which would never allow an unauthorized protest like that in Moscow.

Harassment of US embassy personnel did increase slightly after Russia's war began. In one case, the Russian security services followed an American who was driving from the embassy to the grocery store in her white automobile. While she was in the store, they taped a large black "Z"—a symbol used by Russian military units in Ukraine that came to represent Putin's entire war effort—to the roof of her car. When she returned to her vehicle, she did not notice the "Z" or the overhead drone videotaping her as she drove back to the embassy compound with the Russian symbol on the roof of her car. The video was released and became a source of amusement for Russian nationalists on social media. I wondered how many people and hours of planning it took to organize that operation, and to what end. Because it did not adversely affect our morale; if anything, it strengthened our resolve. We were a feisty and resilient outpost of Americans.

Life at the embassy in wartime continued much as it had previously. The children left on school buses every weekday morning for classes at the Anglo-American School. I hosted a dinner every Saturday night in my townhouse for a rotating group of a half dozen or so of my mission colleagues, then went to a Roman Catholic mass at 9:30 a.m. each Sunday morning in a community room in a building on the compound. The mass was celebrated by a remarkable Irish priest who had been living in Moscow and coming to the embassy every Sunday for decades. His movements and his homilies were monitored by the Russian authorities.

Those Sunday masses for a small group of us in an unadorned, windowless room—in an embassy surrounded by a threatening country that had a long history of hostility (at best) toward its tiny Roman Catholic population—were as meaningful to me as any of the masses I had attended at St. Peter's Basilica in Rome, the Cathedral of Notre-Dame in Paris, or Saint Patrick's Cathedral in New York. We were not exactly in the catacombs of ancient Rome, but the dismal and oppressive setting at Embassy Moscow did provide for a greater sense of connection with the origins and meaning of our faith.

Uncle Sam's, the bar on our compound, had reopened after the lifting of pandemic restrictions, to rave reviews from its clientele, the ambassador included, which also eliminated the need to rebuild Sullivan's Post 5 outdoors in the cold. Our community liaison officer (the person generally responsible for, among other things, morale, welfare, and recreation) organized sightseeing trips for US embassy personnel and their families. I joined an embassy outing for a tour of Saint Basil's Cathedral on Red Square on April 3, and later visited Lenin's Tomb and the Kremlin Wall Necropolis on June 4 with another embassy group. It was fun to get off the compound for a break with my colleagues and walk around Moscow to feed my hunger for Russian history and culture.

I still enjoyed engaging with Muscovites, under the watchful gaze of my bodyguards, and almost all the people I met were polite and respectful, if not admirers of the United States. Those engagements in Moscow, combined with my drives and walks around the city and my official meetings and activities, also gave me a limited opportunity to assess the impact of Putin's war. It was limited because Moscow was not, and had never been, representative of Russia—many Russians view Moscow in the same way many Americans (and especially we Bostonians) view New York. In any event, what city or region would be entirely representative of a country as huge as Russia? But after being cooped up in the embassy compound, I welcomed the chance to take the pulse of the Russian people.

My impression in the early spring of 2022 was that the war was out of sight and out of mind for many Muscovites. It was sometimes difficult to tell whether there was any kind of military operation, special or not, underway a few hundred miles to the southwest of Moscow. One sign of the changed times was that luxury stores and car dealerships with Western brands had shut down right away when the war started, leaving the lights on and discreet notes on their locked doors informing customers that they were temporarily closed. There also was a feeling of anxiety among Muscovites concerned about the economic sanctions and export controls imposed on Russia by the United States and its allies and partners.

The financial sanctions did have an immediate impact on Russia, causing the ruble to drop to a record low of almost 130₽ to the dollar in March. The Central Bank of Russia (CBR), led by its highly regarded governor,

Elvira Nabiullina, responded by imposing strict controls to prevent capital flight, raising its key interest rate to 20 percent, reducing bank regulations to try to ease credit, and shutting down the Moscow Exchange. Those actions stopped the slide of the ruble, which gradually regained value over several months to under 60₽ to the dollar, a seven-year high.

The CBR itself was the target of Western sanctions, including an asset freeze on the $630 billion it held in foreign-exchange reserves. Russia's prodigious wealth in natural resources, however, meant that export revenue, principally from oil and gas sales, remained high. Meanwhile, inflation surged in April to almost 18 percent. There were spot shortages of goods and supply-chain issues caused by a lack of imports from the West. The CBR lowered its key interest rate to 14 percent on April 29, as producers tried to address their supply-chain problems. At the time, Nabiullina described the Russian economy as being in a "zone of colossal uncertainty."

The purpose of the Western economic sanctions was not to hurt the Russian people, and certainly not to damage the global economy, but to target those individuals and institutions responsible for Putin's aggressive war against Ukraine and to undermine the Kremlin's ability to continue to fight that war. Export controls on Western-produced technology were an important part of that effort and a longer-term threat not only to the Russian economy but also specifically to the nation's defense industrial base. The Russians scrambled to find alternative sources of equipment and technology, including from the PRC and Iran, while the effectiveness of Western sanctions and export controls was constantly debated.

The Kremlin worked hard to try to shield the Russian people from the effects of the country's isolation from the West. There were shortages of some staple products, and inflation was eating at the average Russian's purchasing power, but the economic situation eventually stabilized later in 2022 with extensive government intervention and the support of huge oil and gas revenues. The Russian people also could recall a long history of dealing stoically with economic dislocation and deprivation. They went about their daily lives without seriously questioning the brutal war against Ukraine launched ostensibly on their behalf, which was exactly how the Kremlin wanted it.

To shape and cow public opinion, Putin and senior Russian leaders refused to call their invasion of Ukraine a war or to tolerate anyone who did. With no sense of irony and with a euphemism that would make even George Orwell blush, they insisted that everyone call the war a "special military operation." The Russian government went so far as to criminalize the use of terms like *war, assault, invasion, attack,* or any other synonym to describe what the Russian armed forces were doing in Ukraine. It was the latest step in the Russian government's enhanced suppression of civil liberties that had begun years before.

The Kremlin appealed to Russian patriotism and insisted on unity during wartime (or rather, "special military operation" time). Protests against the war, and there were some, were crushed immediately by the Russian security services, just as the Navalny protests had been crushed in the prior year. Anyone who voiced an opinion critical of the "special military operation" could be subject to a fine or incarceration, or both. Those who dared to engage in public protests with signs, even blank ones, were often rousted by the police and during their arrest might receive a "wood shampoo" (head blow from a nightstick) for their troubles. The Russian security services created a climate of fear by tirelessly ferreting out even the mildest forms of dissent from the war. I recall a particularly egregious case in which a Russian prosecutor brought criminal charges against an individual for writing "special military operation" in quotation marks. Punctuation as a crime was Orwellian censorship on stilts.

The justifications for Russia's aggressive war—a Ukrainian genocide against Russians and NATO aggression against Russia—were equally absurd and had been rejected overwhelmingly by the United Nations and the International Court of Justice. But these preposterous justifications were what the Russian people heard repeated and endorsed by their government every day. It was difficult for independent or foreign news to penetrate the government's censorship and reach ordinary Russians, particularly those outside Moscow and Saint Petersburg. There were technical means to access uncensored news via the internet, such as with a VPN, but that was risky and required both a dedicated effort to seek independent sources of news and technical competence that was often beyond the means of most, particularly elderly, Russians. Above all, the search for uncensored news required Russians to maintain an open mind after being flooded for years with propaganda and disinformation demonizing Ukraine, the United States, and NATO.

On May 25, I visited a prime source of that propaganda and disinformation when I returned to the TASS offices for another meeting with the editorial board and journalists from Russian state media. This was not a friendly audience, as I had learned more than two years previously when I first arrived as ambassador. The mood of the group this time was somber. The common question to me was, "When will things go back to the way they were with the United States before February 24?" Many, especially the younger ones in the group, were clearly discouraged by my answer of "Not anytime soon." I assumed they all supported (at least publicly) Putin's war, but they were not pleased with the huge breach the war had caused with the United States.

Their attitude seemed to be that Putin had done what he had to do with Ukraine, which after all was in their neighborhood—*and when is the United States going to get over it because we all need to get on with our lives?* I told them that the United States was not going to get over Putin's aggressive war or the Russian military's widespread war crimes; that the war had killed thousands of innocent people and driven millions more from their homes as refugees and displaced persons; and that the war had been denounced by the UN and the ICJ. The response of the United States and the West in harshly sanctioning Russia and resolutely supporting Ukraine was politically, legally, and morally necessary, and would be enduring. My audience, unsurprisingly, was not convinced and they remained somberly defiant.

It was nonetheless obvious to me that sanctions, export controls, the closure of Western ports and airspace to Russian ships and aircraft, and the limited availability of visas were all contributing to these insiders' sense of anxiety and isolation. To be clear, this was not a group of typical Russians; although they worked for Russian state media and reflected only the Kremlin's viewpoint in their news reporting and commentary, some of them had visited the United States, and a few had studied or had relatives there.

One of the people at the meeting approached me discreetly afterward to inquire about the possibility of getting a US visa; I referred them to the State Department's visa application process. What the future had in store for applications from Russian citizens, I could not know—but I did know that travel from Russia was one form of protest that the Russian government did not, or could not, stop. Hundreds of thousands of Russians, many of whom were young and highly educated, were fleeing the country after the war started. Putin described them and any other Russians who did not support his "special military operation" as "scum" and "traitors." He advised true Russians to "spit them out like a midge that accidentally flew into [our] mouths." Chillingly, he added a few words worthy of the twentieth-century fascists he purportedly despised: "I am convinced that this natural and necessary self-cleansing of society will only strengthen our country, our solidarity, cohesion and readiness to meet any challenge."

Despite the crackdown on dissent and Putin's ominous rhetoric, a handful of high-profile Russians opposed to the war made the difficult and courageous decision to stay in the country and risk almost certain arrest. On March 19, my friend Vladimir Kara-Murza, a well-known journalist who was a protégé of assassinated Russian opposition leader Boris Nemtsov and a vocal opponent of Putin and the war, stopped by the embassy to meet with me. I talked to him about how dangerous it was for him to stay in Russia, but he insisted that he could not leave his homeland while it was being led to ruin by Putin. He was arrested on April 11, and was later convicted and sentenced to twenty-five years in a "strict regime" penal colony for, among other crimes, treason. I had never witnessed such a pure act of patriotic self-sacrifice.

---

By the end of May 2022, I needed a break. Despite my vow in the prior October to have a more "normal" life as ambassador and to travel home more frequently, I had not been home or seen Grace or my family in person since November. For that matter, I had not had a day off since then either. It was not healthy, as Grace would remind me frequently. Putin's war, like the pandemic before it, had again turned my life upside down.

It also had been almost a year since my conversation with Secretary

Blinken and Under Secretary Nuland in Geneva about the length of my tenure in Moscow as ambassador. I had not spoken to either of them about the issue to set a firmer date after we had discussed my staying for at least another year; so much had happened and it seemed so long ago. Although I would be approaching three years in the job—about the average length of tenure for prior ambassadors to Russia (Jon Huntsman served two years, Bill Burns served two years and nine months)—the war had changed my thinking. In line with my revised view, I had heard through unofficial channels that the president was disinclined to change his ambassador in Moscow during a war. My instinct was to keep my mouth shut and, to quote the legendary former head coach of the New England Patriots Bill Belichick, do my job.

Home leave was another matter, and that I definitely needed after more than six months away from my family. Plus, I had a professional reason to return to Washington. The secretary had scheduled a Global Chiefs of Mission conference for all ambassadors at the department during the week of June 20. The problem was that the Russian MFA still had not granted a diplomatic visa to Elizabeth Rood, an experienced senior officer who would be the embassy's new deputy chief of mission, succeeding Bart Gorman, who had been expelled by the Russians in February. The embassy was so shorthanded that I did not believe it would be responsible for me to leave my post until Elizabeth arrived.

There was certainly plenty of work to do while I stayed in Moscow. The US and international news media were always looking for an interview. US businesses with investments in Russia wanted advice to factor into their decision-making on whether or how to exit the market. Some businesses, like the National Hockey League, had more attenuated but still significant interests in Russia; in the case of the NHL, it was the many Russian players in the league. I gave a briefing to Commissioner Gary Bettman and representatives of the league on the long-term impacts of Putin's aggressive war.

In that connection, I considered it one of the major perks of serving as the US ambassador in Moscow that I got to know Lou Lamoriello, the general manager of the NHL's New York Islanders, and a hockey legend (an Honoured Member of the Hockey Hall of Fame in Toronto) from Rhode Island.

Lou had been a leader in bringing Soviet players into the league when he was the general manager of the New Jersey Devils in the late 1980s. When one of my embassy colleagues saw that I had a phone message from a Mr. Lamori- ello, he asked who that was. I exclaimed in my thickest Boston accent, "Who is Lou Lamoriello? He is a [expletive] hockey god." When I later told Grace that story, she said she was embarrassed for me, because I apparently had no shame. I attributed her reaction to more of her still inexplicable anti-Boston prejudice.

In June, after difficult negotiations with the Russians (there are no other kind), Elizabeth Rood finally got a visa from the MFA. She arrived in Moscow in time for me to return to Washington on Friday, June 17, in advance of the secretary's conference the following week. Because of sanctions and the airspace closures in Europe to Russian aircraft, the trip home took longer than it had in the past. I had to fly through Dubai, and even with flights that were on time, the trip door-to-door took over twenty-four hours. I arrived at Dulles and was met by Grace, who as always picked me up on my return from Moscow. There were no Russian camera crews waiting for me this time.

As we were driving home to Bethesda on that beautiful Friday morn- ing, Grace told me that she had to go to her doctor. She had just found a lump in her abdomen. My heart sank and I thought of the awful day ten years earlier, in May 2012, when she told me that she had found a lump on her breast, which turned out to be cancerous. She had successful surgery then, and I had thought her cancer was long behind us after ten years had passed. And now this news. Maybe it was something benign—but I could not shake the awful feeling that her cancer had returned. We agreed in the car that we would not tell anyone until she had more information from her doctor.

Over the next two weeks, after multiple visits to different doctors and various tests, Grace was diagnosed with uterine cancer. She did not look ill, and—always a very strong as well as a very private person—she did not want to tell anyone how sick she was. She was going to handle this matter in the same way she had successfully handled her prior breast cancer. We agreed that I would tell the State Department leadership that I needed to stay in Washington for a medical issue involving my wife and that I would not be able to return to my post in Moscow for an undetermined length of time. The secretary and my department colleagues, as I expected, were very understanding, and told me to take as much time as I needed.

I was afraid for Grace, but I also had enormous confidence in her, and I thought that if anyone had the physical and emotional strength to overcome cancer again, she did. One of my favorite stories about Grace dated back to the time after she was first diagnosed with breast cancer. Her surgeon tried a lumpectomy to see if he could avoid performing a mastectomy (which eventually was necessary). I took her to the hospital in the morning for the outpatient lumpectomy and brought her home that afternoon. She had a follow-up appointment with her doctor in seven days. She recovered very quickly, looked fit and healthy, and by day six said she felt like going for a run, which she did. The next day, Grace's doctor was amazed by her recovery. He said that if she kept that up, she could be back running in a couple of weeks. "I guess I shouldn't have gone for a run yesterday," Grace replied, ironically. He looked at her and said, "Oh, you're one of *those* people." She truly was, and I always knew she was, which gave me hope and confidence as we confronted this new illness together.

Grace's surgery was scheduled for July 28, a little over a month after my return from Moscow, and we spent the interim together in nervous anticipation. She continued her law practice from our Bethesda home, and I remained in daily contact with the embassy and drove to the State Department when necessary for secure phone calls with Elizabeth Rood and the embassy leadership team, or to review classified documents.

Grace and I also worked on a project together. Some months earlier, we had decided to buy a second home to enjoy after I finished my service in Moscow and she retired from her law practice. Having found a home we liked in Westport, Connecticut (closer to the Mets than to the Red Sox, but marriage is about compromises), we spent hours picking out furniture and preparing for the closing on the purchase of the property in August.

I took Grace to all her medical appointments in the weeks before the surgery and drove her to Sibley Memorial Hospital in Washington early on the morning of July 28 to check in with the surgical unit. I waited for a report from the surgeon on the operation, which took over four hours. The report was positive, but it was a major operation and Grace would be in the hospital for five days. I stayed with her in her room, and as was typical of Grace, she recovered faster than the doctors had expected. She was in pain, but she tried to get out of bed as soon as she could. I was there as her assistant. When she asked for coffee, I got her preferred Starbucks brand (even though it hurt my Dunkin' pride). I was not surprised when she was released from the hospital a day early, on August 1.

I got Grace a wheelchair and set up our house for her recovery. Within days, she was on the phone with her clients and colleagues at King & Spalding, most of whom did not know that she was recovering from cancer surgery. I drove her to all her follow-up medical appointments. She felt well enough to insist that I leave her and go to the closing on our Westport house on August 8. I went up to Connecticut and back by train on the same day. Buying that house gave us something to look forward to—something for which we could plan. We had a lot to talk about, besides, and a lot to catch up on.

We discussed my job as ambassador. I said I was finished because I had a full-time job now, and that was helping her. I told the secretary, who informed the president. I was pleased but not surprised that everyone in the US government was extremely gracious and understood the changed circumstances in my life that required this move, despite the ongoing war in Ukraine. I said to my department and embassy colleagues that if I could, I would return to Moscow briefly at some point to pack and conclude the diplomatic protocols that usually accompany the departure of an accredited ambassador. I was assured by them that it would be nice if I could do that, but it was not necessary.

As the month of August passed, Grace's condition stabilized. We knew she had a dangerous cancer, and we were planning for months of difficult chemotherapy and radiation treatments, with which we had experience after her breast cancer ten years before. Despite that grim prospect, Grace continued to work from home, and on August 13 she took a photograph of herself in our backyard in Bethesda that was remarkable. Looking at that picture, it was not possible to tell what she recently had been through. She was mentally strong and determined to regain her health, and I would be there with and for her full-time, which gave real purpose to my own life.

We agreed that I would get my brief return trip to Moscow out of the way as soon as possible, and close that chapter in our lives. I planned to leave at the end of August, after our wedding anniversary, to pack up our belongings (including Grace's clothes that she had brought with her to Moscow before the pandemic), to say goodbye to my embassy and diplomatic colleagues, and to perform the other rituals associated with an ambassadorial departure, including a final meeting with Deputy Foreign Minister Ryabkov at the Russian MFA.

While I was away, our children, Jack, Katie, and Teddy, came to stay with her, as did Grace's mother and sister. Grace and I, along with members of our family, had dinner at our home to celebrate our thirty-fourth wedding anniversary on Saturday, August 27. The next day, I kissed Grace goodbye and flew to Moscow for the last time.

---

I had been gone for over two months, but when I returned to the embassy at the end of August, it felt as though I had never left. Partly that was because I had received regular briefings while I was at home and had continued to participate in embassy decision-making, but it was also because nothing had meaningfully changed (at least for the better) in US-Russia relations. It was also because the embassy was a self-contained little world in which it was easy to get reacclimated. I resumed my usual routine, but my time horizon in Moscow was now measurable in days, rather than months.

I arrived on Monday evening and went into my office early on Tuesday morning, August 30. I received a lengthy briefing on the wrongfully detained Americans in Russia, and the report was as bad as I could have imagined. Paul Whelan—who had been arrested in Russia long before I arrived as ambassador and, tragically, would still be detained when I departed my post—remained at IK-17 with no serious prospect for his release. Marc Fogel had been sentenced in June to fourteen years in a labor camp; and Brittney Griner had received a nine-year sentence on August 4, after pleading guilty to narcotics smuggling.

The fact that Fogel and Griner were given such lengthy sentences for possessing trace amounts of medicinal marijuana and hash oil was further proof that they had been targeted by the Russians only because of their status as American citizens. I was filled with contempt and disgust for a government that would do that to my fellow Americans, but I also had to acknowledge that the Russian government treated many of its own citizens as unjustly and cruelly as it was treating Whelan, Fogel, and Griner. That did not make it right, or reduce my anger and outrage, but it put the situation in context. Americans and Russians alike were dealing with a loathsome government in the Kremlin.

I spent the rest of my first day back in the office meeting the few new embassy personnel who had arrived while I was away and filling out paperwork for my departure and retirement from public service—I was old enough and had worked for enough years in the federal government, starting with my law clerkship for Judge John Minor Wisdom in 1985, to retire. I also started making appointments for final calls with other ambassadors in the diplomatic corps and with the friends I had made in Moscow. In the evening, I went back to my townhouse for dinner, started sorting and packing Grace's and my belongings, and checked in by phone with Grace, who was continuing to work from home while I was gone.

Historic news emerged in Russia that night: Mikhail Gorbachev had died at Moscow's Central Clinical Hospital after a lengthy illness. He was ninety-one years old and had been in declining health for several years. I had tried to meet with him during my tenure as ambassador and had lunch with a representative of his foundation, who said the former president was interested in meeting me, but his age, ill health, and Covid-19 precautions made that impossible. Now I would never get the chance.

Gorbachev—the general secretary of the Communist Party of the Soviet Union from 1985 to 1991, and the first and only president of the Soviet Union, elected in 1990 as the party was losing influence and stature—was lionized in the West. The Norwegian Nobel Committee awarded him the 1990 Nobel Peace Prize "for his leading role in the process which led to the peaceful ending of the Cold War." The committee cited the "dramatic changes" he wrought in the "relationship between East and West." Under Gorbachev, confrontation was "replaced by negotiations. Old European nation states...regained their freedom." In the Soviet Union, there was "greater openness" that promoted "international trust." And the UN began "to play the role which was originally planned for it in an international community governed by law."

The impressive record of achievements by Gorbachev, which was lauded by the West, was reviled by Putin and the vast majority of Russian nationalists. Putin specifically blamed Gorbachev for the difficult problems Russia was having in subjugating Ukraine in 2022. In his speech on February 21, announcing the recognition of the Donetsk People's Republic and the Luhansk People's Republic, Putin cited prominently Gorbachev's "fatal" mistake in 1989 when he recognized Ukraine as a "sovereign socialist" state. That act was the culmination, in Putin's view, of decades of Communist policies that unnaturally separated Ukraine from its rightful place in Russia's orbit, the *Russkiy mir*. In his mind, Gorbachev had fundamentally betrayed Russia. The fact that Westerners had awarded him the Nobel Peace Prize was just further proof to Putin of the righteousness of that conclusion.

Gorbachev represented everything that Putin despised: liberal weakness in the form of glasnost (openness) and perestroika (restructuring) that allowed the Russian empire, in the form of the Soviet Union, to crumble. When the Soviet Union collapsed, the internal boundaries that separated the fifteen former Soviet republics became international boundaries separating sovereign nations. What had been a colossal empire governed from and by Moscow became in late 1991 the Commonwealth of Independent States—smaller, weaker nation-states, including the Russian Federation, Ukraine, and Belarus. That mammoth international development, which brought self-determination and freedom to millions of people, was the "greatest geopolitical catastrophe of the century," according to Putin. In his view, it was a "genuine tragedy" for the Russian people, as "tens of millions of our fellow citizens and countrymen found themselves beyond the fringes of Russian territory."

It was not the demise of Soviet Communism, however, that upset Putin; he did not regret that in the least. In another quote from more than two decades ago, he repeated approvingly the expression common among former Soviet citizens that "anyone who doesn't regret the passing of the Soviet Union has no heart. Anyone who wants it restored has no brains." Rather than the loss of the Communist system, the catastrophe for Putin was the loss of an empire gathered and controlled by Moscow. It became Putin's singular personal mission, the overriding goal of his presidency, to correct the mistakes that Gorbachev had made and to restore the Russian empire to greatness on the world stage.

The former leader's death was therefore an extremely symbolic, complicated event for Russia and Putin. I planned to attend Gorbachev's funeral on behalf of the United States. I wondered whether Putin would also attend. But there would be neither a state funeral nor any official days of mourning to honor Gorbachev and his legacy. This despite the fact that every Soviet or Russian leader in the last one hundred years, except Khrushchev, had received a state funeral and official days of mourning: Lenin, Stalin, Brezhnev, Andropov, Chernenko, and even Yeltsin, who was not popular with many Russians when he died in 2007 after the tumult of his years in office during the 1990s. Yeltsin, however, unlike Gorbachev, had the man he had handpicked as his successor, Putin, in office as the president of Russia deciding whether the nation would honor him with a state funeral and a day of mourning, which Putin ultimately approved. Gorbachev also had never been the president of the Russian Federation.

And so, just as Brezhnev did not honor Khrushchev when he died in 1971, Putin would not honor Gorbachev. On the other hand, Putin would not sully himself with statements overtly critical of the former Soviet president. He would seek to be a magnanimous leader, reluctant to speak ill of the dead, but nonetheless damning Gorbachev with faint praise and leaving it to others to provide more explicit negative commentary. This approach reminded me of Putin's conduct during the Covid-19 pandemic, letting other officials announce unpleasant news and restrictions.

On Wednesday, August 31, Putin released a carefully worded personal statement of condolence—a telegram to the Gorbachev family—on the death of the former president. Putin called him "a politician and statesman who had a huge impact on the course of world history," and who "led our country during a period of complex, dramatic changes"—without specifying whether either the impact or the changes were positive. Putin's statement further observed that Gorbachev "deeply understood that reforms were necessary" in the Soviet Union, and "offer[ed] his own solutions to urgent problems," again without saying whether Gorbachev's reforms or solutions were good or bad. In fact, Putin previously had made abundantly clear that he thought many of Gorbachev's "solutions" were "fatal" to Russia. Finally, like any benevolent leader, he offered his "sincere words of sympathy and support" to the Gorbachev family, and complimented "the great humanitarian, charitable and educational work" of Gorbachev's late wife, Raisa.

The Kremlin's response to the death of Gorbachev, by contrast, took a different approach. Spokesman Dmitry Peskov said that while Gorbachev was an "extraordinary" statesman destined "always [to] remain in the country's history," he had a naïve and "romantic" view of the West: "Gorbachev gave an impulse for ending the Cold War and he sincerely wanted to believe that it would be over and an eternal romance would start between the renewed Soviet Union and the collective West." Unfortunately, his "romanticism turned out to be wrong. There was no romantic period, a 100-year honeymoon did not materialize, and the bloodthirsty nature of our opponents showed itself. It's good that we realized this in time and understood it." That sounded closer to the true Chekist view of Gorbachev and his legacy, rather than Putin's flaccid telegram.

It was also left to Peskov to announce that Putin would not attend Gorbachev's funeral. On Thursday, September 1, Putin privately visited Gorbachev's body at the hospital and a video later was released showing him laying flowers at the open casket. Peskov subsequently announced: "Regrettably, the president's working schedule wouldn't allow him to" attend the Gorbachev funeral on Saturday, "so he decided to do that [visit] today." Peskov added that although there would be no state funeral or day of mourning for Gorbachev, the government was helping to organize the funeral ceremonies, which would include some "elements" of a state funeral, such as a public viewing in the Hall of Columns in the House of Unions in Moscow, where Soviet leaders had lain in state after their death (and which was memorably depicted in the movie *The Death of Stalin*).

On Thursday evening, as I was planning what I would do and say at Gorbachev's funeral on Saturday, I received news from my family that Grace's health had suddenly deteriorated. I needed to return home immediately. I could scarcely process what I was hearing: Grace had seemed so strong when I left home. Now, just a few days later, and after all of her feats of strength and resilience, after all of our hope and optimism, our worst fears were being realized.

It was still difficult to get flights out of Moscow, because so many people were trying to leave the country; and there were even fewer flights, because of sanctions and airspace closures. The first flight on which I could get a seat (the last one) departed late on Saturday night and took me via a connection in Istanbul to Dulles. I alerted the department, canceled all my future appointments, which had extended into the middle of the following week, and packed what I could take with me on the trip home. The rest of Grace's and my belongings would be shipped to us later.

It was a hectic and disorderly way to depart my post, but it seemed ironically appropriate in light of how I had started my first day as deputy secretary of state years before: scrambling with hurried preparations for a deputies committee meeting on the US nuclear posture review. Because of the delay before my flight departed, I was able to attend Gorbachev's funeral and, after that, host a dinner for some of my embassy colleagues in my townhouse before I left for the airport that night. I telephoned as many people as I could in Washington and Moscow to tell them of my change in plans, and of course I kept in touch with Grace and my family. Somehow, Grace was still working from home on Thursday. She really was one of *those* people.

On Saturday, I arrived at the House of Unions well before noon, as the Russian MFA had instructed me. The doors had been opened hours earlier to the public, and there was a continuous stream of mourners filing past Gorbachev's open casket in the Hall of Columns, flanked by two soldiers and surrounded by flowers. Thousands of people stood outside in a lengthy line winding down the street and out of sight around the block, waiting to enter the hall and pay their respects to the former president. I entered the House of Unions through a separate door, but my entrance into the Hall of Columns was delayed while Hungarian prime minister Viktor Orbán, the only foreign leader to attend the viewing, was inside in an area close to the casket and the Gorbachev family.

After Orbán departed, I entered the hall and laid flowers at the foot of Gorbachev's casket. I was escorted to meet Gorbachev's family, his daughter Irina, and granddaughters Anastasia and Ksenia. Other family members and friends sat with them on the right side of the casket. I stood with Gorbachev's close friend, Nobel Peace Prize laureate Dmitry Muratov, whom I had hosted several times at Spaso House and the embassy. Gorbachev had donated money from his own Nobel Peace Prize to help Muratov in 1993 cofound *Novaya Gazeta,* the last independent newspaper in Russia. In March 2022, after the "special military operation" began, the newspaper had been forced to suspend publication. Two days after Gorbachev's funeral, *Novaya Gazeta*'s license to operate in Russia was permanently revoked. Muratov remained in Moscow.

The plan for the funeral was that the public viewing would conclude shortly after noon, and the proceedings would continue with a graveside ceremony in Moscow's famous Novodevichy Cemetery, where many illustrious Russians are buried, including Yeltsin and Khrushchev. Gorbachev's will provided for him to be buried next to his wife, Raisa, who was interred there in 1999. I planned to follow the Gorbachev family and the crowd to the cemetery after the public viewing ended.

The funeral plan was upended, however, by the enormous number of ordinary Russians who turned out to pay tribute to Gorbachev during the public viewing. The crowd seeking access to the Hall of Columns was so much larger than anticipated that the viewing was extended for more than two hours. I stayed inside the hall near the Gorbachev family and watched the mourners file past the casket as they were urged to move along quickly to accommodate the big crowd. Even when the doors to the House of Unions were finally closed, there were still thousands of people outside who were not able to get in.

When the ceremony finally shifted to the Novodevichy Cemetery, the procession carrying the coffin to the grave site was led by Muratov, who was holding a large, framed photograph of Gorbachev. A crowd formed for the final service, which was held not far from Khrushchev's grave. I did not notice any senior Russian government officials present, nor had I seen any in the Hall of Columns, although I learned later that former president Medvedev, the current deputy chair of the Russian Security Council, had attended the funeral.

I did not see Medvedev on Saturday, but after the funeral he published an unhinged social media statement that caught my attention, linking the collapse of the Soviet Union in 1991 under Gorbachev with Putin's aggressive war in Ukraine. Medvedev's rant aptly captured the worldview of the Kremlin. He asserted that the West had plans to "take advantage of the military conflict in Ukraine to push our country to a new twist of disintegration, do everything to paralyze Russia's state institutions and deprive the country of efficient controls, as happened in 1991." He called those plans "the dirty dreams of the Anglo-Saxon perverts, who go to sleep with a secret thought about the breakup of our state, thinking about how to shred us into pieces, cut us into small bits." Not missing a chance to rattle Russia's nuclear saber, he concluded, "Such attempts are very dangerous and mustn't be underestimated. Those dreamers ignore a simple axiom: a forceful disintegration of a nuclear power is always a chess game with Death, in which it's known precisely when the check and mate comes: doomsday for mankind."

In departing Moscow, I was not going to miss spending time with Russian officials who thought and spoke that way. As I left the funeral, I gave my last interview on camera as ambassador to Fred Pleitgen of CNN, standing on a Moscow street outside the Novodevichy Cemetery. After I returned to the embassy, I had a final dinner with a group of my colleagues. I then loaded my suitcases into the SUV, and my bodyguards drove me to the airport for my flight home.

---

Grace was admitted to the intensive care unit of Sibley Hospital on Friday, September 2, the day before my flight home. Her surgery had not been the success that it had first seemed: unbeknownst to us, her cancer had spread rapidly through her abdomen and attacked vital organs, eventually causing them to begin to fail.

I landed at Dulles on Sunday, and my son Teddy picked me up and drove me straight to the hospital, where family members were gathering. I spent the rest of the day and night with Grace in her room, along with our family.

Grace died on Labor Day, September 5, 2022. In retrospect, I was lucky to have made it back to Washington to be with her before she died, although lucky was about as far as possible from what I was feeling as I tried to process the enormous loss. I resisted thinking about what would have happened, or how I would have felt, if I had not made it home in time. It was bad enough that I had spent so much time away from her during my service as ambassador in Moscow, because of the pandemic and Putin's war. Serving alone and away from Grace turned out to be a much greater sacrifice than I could have realized at the time. She and I thought we would have many years together after I was finished as ambassador. Instead, we had one final day.

After Grace died, I left the hospital and went to our home in Bethesda, where we had lived for thirty years. After dragging my suitcases inside, I sat down on a couch in our living room and took a deep breath to try to clear my head before thinking about the plans for Grace's funeral. As I sat there, exhausted, I took out my cell phone, which I had not looked at since before landing at Dulles the day before. I scrolled through the voice, text, and email messages I had received.

I froze when I saw a text message to me from Grace. Then I looked at the date and time. She had sent it early on Sunday morning before I had arrived at the hospital. She had been in a lot of pain and asked our son Jack to get her phone so that she could send me a final message in the event she passed away before I made it back to her. She wrote: "Nothing working. End is near. Love you and our family."

Receiving that message from Grace after she died was an incredible and overwhelmingly emotional experience. It was as if she were speaking to me from beyond. I marveled at the strength and courage she exhibited in her final days. A friend of ours told me that she had shown everyone the right way to face death. I was stricken with grief for all that I had lost in her and would never get back, including the time I could have spent with her—now lost, among so many other things, to Putin's war.

---

After her funeral mass at the Catholic church where we were married, St. Pius X, in Fairfield, Connecticut, Grace was buried on Tuesday, September 13, close to our new home in Westport. I would remain as ambassador for another month, until I retired in October, but did not return to

Moscow. I resolved to remain in touch with my colleagues at the embassy and to continue to support the mission.

Secretary Blinken asked me to consider staying in government service part-time after my retirement, in the newly created position of US special representative for Ukraine's economic recovery. I was honored by the secretary's offer and his confidence in me. But after all that had happened, I was spent and could not give the position the intense focus it required. Regretfully, I had to decline. The former secretary of commerce, Penny Pritzker, was later appointed to the role.

It pained me to turn down the opportunity to continue to serve in the State Department, whose mission and people are so important to me, and that prompted thoughts about service and sacrifice. Throughout my career while I was in government, well-meaning family members, friends, and strangers had thanked me for my service, and it always made me feel uncomfortable when they did so. I had not done anything to deserve their thanks. I had derived far more pleasure from my time in government than the value of any service I had rendered.

What is more, I knew from my father and uncles, and their friends, all World War II combat veterans, what constitutes profound sacrifice in service to our nation. They had survived the war, but some of their friends, classmates, shipmates, and comrades had not. They understood why President John F. Kennedy, a man of their generation (in fact, almost exactly their age), in his 1961 inaugural address, had urged his fellow Americans to "ask not what your country can do for you—ask what you can do for your country." That exhortation may sound trite today, but it resonated in my family at the time of Kennedy's inauguration and far beyond. Only through the sacrifices of countless Americans over many generations—and not just in war or in the military—has our nation made the progress it has since its founding.

I have served with women and men, civilians and military members, in the United States and abroad, who have made sacrifices worthy of thanks from a grateful nation. My thoughts always return to my former colleagues at the US mission to Russia, each of whom sacrificed to serve in difficult circumstances where their country needed them. They served during the perils and dislocations of the pandemic; some were separated from their families; others had family members die back home while they were in Moscow. A few had serious health emergencies that were made more challenging by being in Russia. And all were subject to harassment from the Russian government.

I was honored to serve with them, many of whom would move from one hardship post to the next. Our deputy chief of mission, Bart Gorman, and his wife, Donna, along with their four children, were prime examples. Bart and Donna were on their third tour in Moscow, enduring every hardship one could imagine, and were the bedrock of our mission. I learned a lot about service and sacrifice from them.

Losing Grace, after spending the better part of three years away from her, did not put me in the league of those who have made great sacrifices for the United States, by any means. Indeed, it was Grace herself who sacrificed more, by bearing the burden of separation from her spouse and taking care of our family alone during the pandemic, without the pleasures, satisfaction, support, and status I enjoyed as an American ambassador.

No one ever thanked Grace for her service and sacrifice, but they should have. She earned that recognition by quietly joining the ranks of those worthy of our nation's gratitude. Now, when people thank me for my service, I feel a little more comfortable accepting those kind words on behalf of Grace and myself.

# CHAPTER 15

# A CRIME AGAINST PEACE

SEPTEMBER 2022 WAS A TERRIBLE whirlwind for me. The sudden end of my tenure as the US ambassador in Moscow preempted my plan to have a series of final meetings with Russian officials before my departure. I had not expected to see Foreign Minister Lavrov again, which would have been the typical protocol before the war but was unlikely given the abysmal state of US-Russia relations after the February 24 invasion of Ukraine. In any event, I had no great desire to meet with him, considering his emphatic commitment to Putin's aggressive war. Although I had listened tactfully to his didactic critique of my Senate confirmation hearing testimony in November 2019, I was not going to submit, without vigorous objection, to a tendentious lecture by him in September 2022 about a fictional Nazi genocide against Russians in Ukraine or the horror of NATO's imaginary war against Russia.

I had hoped to meet with Deputy Foreign Minister Ryabkov, one of the few senior Russian government officials whom I continued to respect after all that had happened in the last three years. He was a serious professional with an engaging personality, but most of all he was a Russian patriot with whom I always thought I could at least have a rational conversation. We did not often agree, yet I still believed that if he and I had been allowed to negotiate freely we could have solved, based on reciprocity, the visa impasse that so hobbled the US embassy in Moscow. Unfortunately, Ryabkov was not empowered to negotiate with me. In the Russian system that the Kremlin oversaw, he had to answer—unofficially but completely—to the FSB and SVR, neither of which would agree to reciprocity with the United States.

I regretted not having a chance to say goodbye to Ryabkov before I left Moscow. After I departed, the embassy returned my diplomatic *kartochka* to the MFA, symbolically terminating my relationship with Russia. I left the country with no hope of ever coming back, in any capacity, official or personal, which was another regret, given my lifelong interest in Russia and respect for its history, culture, and people. It was a matter beyond my control, however, the consequence of Putin's decision to invade Ukraine and start a devastating land war on the European continent for the first time in eight decades.

Although I was no longer in Moscow after September 3, I continued to serve as ambassador until October from Washington and stayed in contact with my colleagues at Embassy Moscow. Unfortunately, Putin's war was beginning to have more of an impact on the operations of the embassy, which I had observed during my brief return at the end of August. The Moscow city government had refurbished the sidewalk and a small strip of grass next to the corner of the embassy wall across the street from the Russian White House and named it Donetsk People's Republic Square, in a move intended to provoke the United States. It was a common practice in some countries, including the United States (although not promoted or sanctioned by the State Department), for government authorities (in the United States, it was usually the municipal government, and often with congressional prompting) to name the street in front of the embassy or consulate of an unpopular or hostile country in a provocative way.

Putting an offensive name on the little plot at the corner of Embassy Moscow was of no real concern to me. It was, in fact, a tit-for-tat response by the Russians after the District of Columbia in 2018 designated the main street outside the Russian Embassy in Washington as Boris Nemtsov Plaza, after the Russian opposition leader who was assassinated in 2015. In the 1980s, during the Cold War, the same street was named Andrei Sakharov Plaza, after the famed nuclear physicist turned human rights advocate. I was a little surprised that the Russians waited as long as they did before responding in kind. The name change in Moscow had no effect on our operations, any more than naming the corner Ambassador Sullivan, New York Yankees Fan Square would have had. It was insulting, but with no practical impact.

I would not make things easy for the Russians, though. The city had originally proposed in the spring to name the corner at the embassy Defenders of the Donbas Square. That was until I issued a public statement noting that the United States would welcome a square dedicated to the brave Ukrainians who were expelling Russian invaders from the Donbas. Forcing a change in the name of the "square" was no real accomplishment, only a tiny moral victory that lifted spirits at the embassy and reminded the Russians that we were not passive targets.

My instinct was to give as good as I got as ambassador to Russia, but to try to do so in a smart and principled way and without unnecessary rancor. Russian leaders respected that attitude. What they disliked and disrespected was weakness, people who would not or could not competently defend themselves. My friend Senator Dan Sullivan of Alaska had once described me to the Senate Foreign Relations Committee years before as a pugnacious Irishman, which I noted in jest to him at the time was not always a shining attribute for a diplomat. In Russia, as it turned out, diplomatic pugnacity often came in quite handy.

The Russians characteristically took the square-naming issue one step too far, and it was illustrative of how they operated and the increasing pressure they brought to bear on Embassy Moscow. The Russian MFA informed me that the mailing address for the embassy had been changed to Donetsk People's Republic Square and that no mail would be delivered unless that precise address was used. Any mail sent to our prior, well-known street address would be held or returned to the sender. This may seem like a small matter, but it was a real problem for the operations of the embassy, as it would be for any institution or business to not receive mail.

The Russian response to my complaint was utterly disingenuous, citing reciprocity for the naming of Boris Nemtsov Plaza in Washington. But the United States had not changed the street or mailing address of the Russian Embassy, which was still listed on Wisconsin Avenue, as it had been for decades, and we would not change that mailing address, because of the obvious effect it would have on the embassy's operations. Moreover, even if we had, we would not refuse to deliver mail that used the prior address or that was clearly intended for the embassy. The Russians paid no heed to my argument, dismissing it as logistical bellyaching. That was how they operated—one small example among the many with which I had to contend as ambassador every day.

The Russians also changed the address of the UK Embassy, to Luhansk People's Republic Square. Her Majesty's ambassador to the Russian Federation, Deborah Bronnert, and I used to joke about which of our countries was more disfavored by our Russian hosts. I maintained to Deborah that between us "Anglo-Saxon perverts," to quote former Russian president Medvedev, the UK was more disfavored, but the competition was very close. I gave the edge to the UK because I believed the Russians considered them more clever, and therefore more challenging, as opposed to the lumbering giant from North America. Dark humor was common among Western diplomats and expatriates in Moscow.

The number of protests outside Embassy Moscow started to increase in the late summer, and the Russians began projecting huge video images at night onto the side of a tall building across the street from the compound and the new Donetsk People's Republic Square. Again, this was similar to what was happening at the Russian Embassy in Washington. The difference was that unlike the Russian government, the US government neither organized nor endorsed the effort in Washington. I watched the video show in Moscow briefly on the night before I left in early September. It was like looking at an old drive-in movie screen, with large text criticizing the United States and its wars in Vietnam, Iraq, and Afghanistan, accompanied by graphic images highlighting the brutality of those wars. The public messaging, mostly to the Russian people, was that the warmongering United States was again at war, this time against Russia in Ukraine.

Out-of-control rhetoric from influential Russian nationalists, which bore no connection to reality, also increased; and it was not merely the paid media shills of the Kremlin and their disinformation warriors who debased themselves. Former president Medvedev again led the charge, declaring on November 4, 2022: "We are fighting against those who hate us, who ban our language, our values, and even our faith, who spread hatred toward the history of our Fatherland...a bunch of crazy Nazi junkies...and a large pack of barking dogs from the Western kennel."

This from a man who, when he was president of Russia from 2008 to 2012, was thought to be a potential liberal reformer.

I attributed the distinct shift in the Russian government's public treatment of Embassy Moscow and the United States over the course of the summer and fall of 2022 to the further embarrassing defeats that Russia was suffering on the battlefield in Ukraine. By the end of August, Ukraine had begun a counteroffensive against the overextended Russian military, which was defending large parts of Kharkiv Oblast in the east and Kherson in the south. In a startling collapse, the Russian military was rapidly driven out of Kharkiv Oblast by early October, except for a small pocket on the border of the Kharkiv and Luhansk Oblasts. The Russian losses in territory, personnel, and equipment were debilitatingly large.

The Ukrainian counteroffensive around Kherson moved more slowly but made steady progress, inflicting more casualties on the Russian military and regaining territory that had been seized at the start of the "special military operation." On November 11, the Ukrainian military recaptured the city of Kherson. They drove the Russians to retreat across the Dnipro River to the left bank in Kherson Oblast. In a public relations debacle for Putin, Ukrainian troops were welcomed as liberators by cheering residents of the city of Kherson, which Putin had said on September 30 would be part of Russia "forever."

Defeats and losses farther from the battlefield in Ukraine also shook Russian confidence in the fall of 2022. On September 26, explosions severely damaged the Nord Stream I and Nord Stream II pipelines under the Baltic Sea that connected Russian gas fields with European markets via their termini in Germany. This was a significant geopolitical development, even though the Russians had, weeks before, shut down gas exports through the only operating pipeline of the two (Nord Stream I) to threaten Europe with energy blackmail, and the Europeans had pledged to eliminate their reliance on imports of Russian gas in the future.

The perpetrators of the Nord Stream attack were not initially identified, although early suspicion (including my own) focused on the Russians themselves, despite the Kremlin's vigorous denials. The consequence of the Russians having utterly no respect for the truth was that no one ever believed their denials, even when they might occasionally be true.

No definitive finding was reached on who had conducted the operation, as more credible suspicion later turned to the Ukrainians. The effect of the attack, however, was to further sever, literally and figuratively, Russia from the West.

In another unsettling development for the Kremlin, Ukraine used a powerful truck bomb on October 8 to severely damage the Kerch Strait Bridge, a vital (and the only) direct connection between Russia and Crimea, across the strait that separates the Sea of Azov from the Black Sea. On May 14, 2018, Putin had celebrated the opening of the twelve-mile-long bridge by driving a truck across it. The successful Ukrainian attack on such a critical component of Russian infrastructure was a symbolic blow to Putin.

It also was a logistical setback to the Russian military, which used the bridge for truck and rail traffic to resupply its substantial presence on the Crimean peninsula, which in turn supported Russian troops on the front lines in southern and eastern Ukraine. The attack, combined with Ukraine's success on the battlefield, raised hopes in Kyiv and Western capitals that Ukraine might actually be turning the tide against its invaders.

---

Waves of Russian missile and drone strikes on Ukrainian cities and infrastructure continued throughout this entire period, but the "special military operation" clearly was not going "according to plan," as the Russian government had been insisting since February 24. Putin's war plans were in such disarray—with an already staggering number of casualties and the Russian military collapsing in the Kharkiv Oblast—that even the Kremlin, with its legendary disdain for the truth, could no longer blink at reality and continue to lie to the Russian people. Thus, in September the Kremlin shifted its policies and rhetoric to adjust to the significantly changed circumstances.

First, because of the enormous Russian troop losses in Ukraine, Putin was forced to announce a partial mobilization of military reservists in a prerecorded speech on September 21. The official decree he signed, however, did not limit the mobilization to reservists (the decree referred to the "conscription of citizens for military service for mobilization in the

Armed Forces of the Russian Federation") and did not specify the number of civilians without prior military experience who would be conscripted. Defense Minister Shoigu announced that three hundred thousand Russians would be mobilized, but it was widely rumored that a nonpublic, classified part of the decree authorized up to 1 million Russians to be conscripted, which Peskov denied. Conscription and even the related (and slightly less drastic) measure of mobilization were very unpopular in Russia, and Putin had avoided taking this step for as long as he could until Russian losses proved too great.

Second, Putin announced in his mobilization speech that the "parliaments of the Donbas people's republics [Donetsk and Luhansk] and the military-civilian administrations of the Kherson and Zaporizhzhia regions" would hold referenda on whether to seek to join the Russian Federation. The result of the vote in the four partially occupied Ukrainian oblasts was a foregone conclusion, as Putin himself said in his pre-referenda speech on September 21: "We know that the majority of people living in the territories liberated from the neo-Nazis, and these are primarily the historical lands of Novorossiya, do not want to live under the yoke of the neo-Nazi regime."

After the "sham" votes (as Biden described them) in the war zone favoring absorption by Russia, Putin signed "accession treaties" on September 30 that claimed to annex territory in the four Ukrainian oblasts. The Kremlin could not answer whether the annexed territory included the entirety of the four oblasts or only those portions that the Russian military still occupied. The key point was that Ukrainian territory was now Russian territory and, under the amended Russian constitution, could never be alienated from the fatherland.

The UN General Assembly voted on October 12 to condemn the purported annexation—what the UK ambassador to the UN denounced as "the largest forcible annexation of territory since the Second World War"—and called on member states not to recognize it. The vote adopting the resolution, like the prior UNGA votes in the spring of 2022 against Russia, was lopsided, with 143 countries in favor, five (Russia, Belarus, Syria, North Korea, and Nicaragua) against, thirty-five (including the PRC) abstaining, and ten (including Iran) not voting.

Third, Putin identified a scapegoat. By annexing Ukrainian territory in oblasts where his military was still losing territory and taking heavy casualties, Putin was doubling down on his until-then-unsuccessful "special military operation." In doing so, he had to have an explanation for the patent Russian failures to date that did not include crediting Ukrainian courage, competence, patriotism, or resistance. He needed what Kennan had described as a "menacing" foreign enemy that "is founded not in the realities of foreign antagonism but in the necessity of explaining away" the lack of success of the "special military operation." The easy answer, Kennan's faux foreign enemy, for Putin was the United States and the West, and this was reflected in the increased harassment and targeting of Embassy Moscow.

In his narrative for the Russian people in the September 21 mobilization speech, Putin said it was the United States and its NATO allies that had initiated the conflict in Ukraine in a bid to destroy Russia: "The goal of the West is to weaken, divide and ultimately destroy our country. They are openly saying that they succeeded in breaking up the Soviet Union in 1991, and now the time has come for Russia to disintegrate into a great many regions and areas bitterly hostile to each other." To accomplish this nefarious global plot, Putin claimed, the West "turned the Ukrainian people into cannon fodder and pushed them into a war with Russia."

The United States and NATO continued to "pump" weapons into Ukraine and support and guide the Ukrainian military. According to Putin, Russia was not merely fighting Ukraine, it was also fighting the combined might of NATO: Ukraine, he said, was "flooded with weaponry. The Kyiv regime deployed gangs of foreign mercenaries and nationalists, military units trained to NATO standards and under the de facto command of western advisers. Today our Armed Forces are . . . confronting not only neo-Nazi units, but in fact the entire war machine of the collective west." In this larger (imaginary) context, of course, it was understandably difficult for the Russian military to make advances and achieve the goals—denazification and demilitarization of Ukraine (the former factually impossible and the latter practically impossible)—of the "special military operation." The Russian failures and setbacks thus were not an adverse reflection on Putin or his government, or signs of success by a smaller, weaker enemy. A

Chekist leader could never admit that Ukraine had successfully stood up to Russian aggression.

Putin tried to reassure the Russian people that despite the challenges posed by an existential war initiated by the United States and NATO against their country, the Russian military would ultimately prevail against the brutish might of the West assembled in Ukraine: "To attack it head-on would result in heavy casualties, so our units . . . are operating in a planned and competent manner, using combat vehicles, saving personnel and freeing the land step by step, clearing towns and villages of neo-Nazis and helping people whom the [Kyiv] regime has turned into hostages and human shields." Even a chronicler of the culture of Kremlin prevarication like Kennan would have been astounded by the many falsehoods and bits of disinformation compressed into that one sentence.

To buttress his message of reassurance, Putin concluded by invoking his now hackneyed threat of nuclear war, telling his fellow Russians: "I'd like to remind you that our country also has various means of destruction. And, in some areas, more advanced than those of NATO countries. If the territorial unity of our country is threatened, in order to protect Russia and our nation, we will unquestionably use all the weapons we have. This is no bluff." The more he repeated that warning—saying, in effect, "I really mean it this time"—the more he degraded the psychological potency of the threat from Russia's nuclear arsenal. That in itself was a dangerous phenomenon both as a sign of weakness and in lessening the fear of nuclear war.

It was all to no avail, because Putin's nuclear blackmail could not improve the Russian military's performance on a conventional battlefield against a determined enemy defending its own territory. After the Russians fled the city of Kherson in mid-November and armed Ukrainian drones increasingly targeted military bases and infrastructure deeper inside Russia, Putin canceled his annual televised press conference in December. He acknowledged publicly on December 7 the "slow process of the special military operation," calling it a "long-term" undertaking. Nonetheless, he insisted that it had accomplished "significant results" for Russia with the addition of "new territories," and observed that the "Azov Sea [had] become an internal Russian sea. Even Peter I [the Great] had fought for access to the Azov Sea."

Putin later had to concede the obvious, however, in stating on December 21 that the "situation in the Donetsk and Luhansk People's Republics, in the Kherson and Zaporizhzhia regions, [was] extremely difficult." He would not concede the further obvious point that it was his aggressive war that had caused that "difficult" situation. No Chekist worth his salt would ever confess to that.

One day later, he set the international media abuzz with the comment that Russia's goal in Ukraine was "not to spin this flywheel of a military conflict, but, on the contrary, to end this war." Western commentators and journalists interpreted his remark as a concession that he had started a war, as indicated by his use of that illegal term to describe the "special military operation." This was a serious misinterpretation, because Putin actually was referring to the imaginary war—of Kennan's faux foreign enemy variety—started by the United States against Russia in Ukraine. The "special military operation"—and it was still illegal to call that "operation" a "war"—was, in Putin's lexicon, the Russian defensive response to overt (albeit fictional) American military aggression. As I learned early in my tenure as ambassador, absolutely everything was the fault of the United States in Russia's eyes—even Putin's war.

---

When calendar year 2022 concluded, more than two months after I retired, the war had settled into a winter stalemate. Russian missiles and drones continued to pound Ukraine and kill innocent people, and the Russians pressed their assault—on a vastly smaller scale—on the Ukrainian defense of what was left of the settlement of Soledar and the small city of Bakhmut, a little over twenty miles southeast of Kramatorsk in Donetsk. Elements of the Wagner Group, which had gradually increased its participation in support of Putin's war in Ukraine in the second half of the year, were heavily involved in this vicious combat, which the participants on both sides called a "meat grinder." (So much, I thought, for Putin's boast about "saving personnel.")

The casualty rates for Russian troops in Ukraine continued to be ghastly, and the Russians needed more bodies in uniform than the expected yield from the new round of "partial" conscription and mobilization ordered by Putin. To fill the gap, Wagner had begun recruiting "volunteers" in Russian prisons in the summer of 2022 under its leader, Yevgeny Prigozhin, himself an ex-convict. In return for fulfilling contracts (usually of six months' duration) to serve in Wagner units in the war in Ukraine, Russian inmates—including murderers, rapists, and other violent criminals—would be pardoned by Putin. Tens of thousands of prisoners participated in this Wagner program to bolster the Russian ranks in Ukraine.

The Wagner prisoner recruitment program was simply astonishing and far beyond the pale. It brought to mind a memory from my childhood in 1965, when I had relatives serving in southeast Asia and members of the Hells Angels had volunteered to President Johnson to go to South Vietnam to fight for the United States. Their offer was, of course, not accepted, and even my six-year-old mind knew it was crazy (though I did appreciate at the time the underlying sentiment of support for our US personnel in harm's way). Yet what the Russians were doing through Wagner was so much worse and on a far larger scale.

I found it difficult to believe that a civilized people would condone and facilitate the Wagner prisoner recruitment scheme. What modern country—and what permanent member of the UN Security Council, no less—would empty its prisons to field a rogue army to fight a war in a neighboring country that it had invaded? What group of people in any nation would be less likely than the prison population to follow the law of armed conflict and not engage in criminal violence against innocent civilians or captured enemy prisoners of war? Each of the Wagner "prisoner-volunteers" had already been judged to be unable to follow the law and many, if not the large majority, were demonstrably (criminally) violent. It was a recipe for more war crimes, and further evidence that the Russian government had no concern about that outcome.

The Wagner prisoner-volunteers were themselves subjected to cruelty, abuse, and worse in Ukraine. Military "justice" was often administered in Wagner units with summary executions (and, in at least a few cases, reportedly by means of a sledgehammer crushing the accused's skull). A sizable percentage of the Wagner prisoner-volunteers were untrained militarily and simply slaughtered on the battlefield in human-wave assaults on entrenched positions.

The sheer brutality of the whole enterprise was stunning. Nonetheless, the Kremlin endorsed it. Putin signed pardons for each of the convicts who survived their service with Wagner and sent them home to their cities, towns, and villages, where they might run across the victims of their prior (and now pardoned) crimes.

There were times when I thought I had seen it all, and the outrages of the "special military operation" could not get any worse. Then I would discover something like the full depravity of the Wagner prisoner-volunteer program and would have to recalibrate my scale of abominations. The experience led me, even before I had retired as ambassador, to channel my thoughts and emotions into a reflection on war crimes, accountability, and justice.

Perhaps it was because of my legal education or my prior service early in my career at the US Department of Justice or as a senior lawyer at the US Department of Defense, but I could not resist the urge to consider the need for justice. No matter how the war would conclude in the future, with a victory (under any definition) for Russia or Ukraine, or with a long-term stalemate as on the Korean Peninsula, there would be an overriding obligation to assess and assign responsibility for how the war had begun and how it was conducted. History, on behalf of the millions of Ukrainians killed, wounded, and driven from their country or their homes, would demand it.

Indeed, Ukrainians from President Zelensky on down were already pleading for justice because, sadly, the evidence of Russian war crimes was overwhelming. There was widespread battlefield evidence in places like Bucha, Kramatorsk, and Izium of summary executions, intentional attacks on civilians, torture, sexual violence, and countless other serious crimes. The International Criminal Court found sufficient evidence of the war crime of unlawful deportation of children from the occupied areas of Ukraine to the Russian Federation to issue arrest warrants in March 2023 for Putin and the Russian commissioner for children's rights, Maria Lvova-Belova. The Russian military's attack on and continuing occupation of the Zaporizhzhia Nuclear Power Station, near Enerhodar, was not only a likely war crime, but also extremely dangerous and a grave risk to the health of Europeans across the continent. The list of Russian atrocities was long and growing.

For two related reasons, however, I concentrated less on the crimes committed during the war and more on responsibility for its start. First, my vantage point was in Moscow, not in Ukraine near the battlefield scenes of the war crimes. I had been engaged with senior Russian government officials right up to the day the war started, on February 24, and I had gained insights into their plans, thinking, and rhetoric. As a result, I focused on the initiation of the conflict and the legal concept of aggressive war, also known as the crime of aggression or "crime against peace." European Commission president Ursula von der Leyen had a similar approach, stating on November 30, 2022, that she was planning "to set up a specialized court, backed by the United Nations, to investigate and prosecute Russia's crime of aggression."

Second, my vantage point in Moscow also gave me a historical perspective on the only successful prosecutions ever for the crime of aggression, which occurred after the Second World War. In fact, a legal architect of that crime in international law was Soviet jurist Aron Trainin, from 1945 to 1946. The most famous convictions were of the leading Nazi German defendants at the proceedings of the International Military Tribunal at Nuremberg in 1946. Any future assessment of the origins of the Russian war against Ukraine in 2022 would have to take account of the convictions of those German defendants for waging an aggressive war against Poland in 1939.

That historical focus resonated with me because my life in Moscow, like Russia itself, was steeped in the history of World War II. I had spent most of my tenure as ambassador in a mansion that had suffered bomb damage during the war. Every time I was driven to or from Moscow's Sheremetyevo Airport, I passed the memorial (giant anti-tank obstacles) marking the closest advance by the Germans to the center of Moscow and the Kremlin, in early December 1941. War memorials and remembrances were everywhere. Victory Day, May 9, was among the biggest holidays and celebrations of the year. And Putin never stopped talking about the Great Patriotic War. Almost everything was viewed through that prism.

Growing up in Boston in the 1960s in a small family for which "the War" was the pivotal and defining event in each adult family member's life, I was accustomed to that atmosphere and in some ways reveled in it while I lived in Moscow. In October 2021, I attended the annual Russian historical reenactment commemorating the Battle of Borodino Field, which was fought on October 16, 1941, as part of the larger Battle of Moscow, at the village of Borodino, seventy miles west of the city. Borodino was also the site of a larger and more famous battle between Napoleon's Grande Armée and the Imperial Russian Army on September 7, 1812, which the Russians separately reenact annually, the month before the World War II reenactment. Tchaikovsky's renowned *1812 Overture* commemorated that epic battle, waged against another invader from the West. Russians distinguish the Napoleonic Battle of Borodino by calling the World War II battle the Battle of Borodino Field.

I spent an entire Saturday at the reenactment of the Battle of Borodino Field, and it was fascinating. I had seen reenactments of Revolutionary War and Civil War battles in the United States, but I had never seen a World War II reenactment. There were a large number of reenactors in accurately styled Red Army and German uniforms who re-created the sequence of the battle with period vehicles, weapons, and aircraft. The organizers had set up a Red Army camp with vintage gear and a field hospital that spectators could walk through. I was allowed to fire (with blanks) different small arms that the Red Army had used in the battle.

In the middle of the day, I had lunch with a group of elderly, retired Russian generals who were watching the event. All of them had served in the Red Army, although none of them was old enough to have fought in the Great Patriotic War. Their identity as Russians and as soldiers was thoroughly grounded in the Soviet victory. Over many glasses of vodka, they told me about their views on the war and the importance of the historical memory of the war to the Russian people. Considering that, I was curious to know how they convinced reenactors to participate as German soldiers. It could not be a popular role, especially since one of the units participating in the battle on the German side was the infamous Waffen-SS Das Reich Division. One of the retired Russian generals smiled and pointed to a bottle of vodka on the table, suggesting a form of liquid inducement.

There was a large crowd of spectators, including many families with children, watching the spectacle. The Red Army lost the battle in October 1941 (later recapturing Borodino in January 1942), but that trivia was of no consequence to the Russians enjoying the event on the day I was there. The keen interest and sense of pride among them in the Red Army's final victory over Germany was palpable. There was no doubt in my mind why Putin found this such a powerful tool and used it repeatedly over the years to bolster his political standing, and twisted it to justify his geopolitical ambitions and actions, including the invasion of Ukraine.

The Great Patriotic War was Putin's talisman, and he wielded it relentlessly against Ukraine. The war also posed an overlooked historical challenge to Putin, however, because the victorious Allies in 1945 showed the path to postwar justice by applying the concept of aggressive war, the crime against peace, to those who had started the war in 1939. The legal doctrine of criminal aggression was novel and controversial at the end of World War II, and it remained a complex and rarely applied area of international law eight decades later, with difficult, unresolved questions concerning the scope of the crime and jurisdiction to enforce it.

After I left Moscow and retired, I spent a considerable amount of time thinking, writing, and speaking about Putin's "special military operation," its origins, and the responsibility for starting it. I was not looking to resolve the important pending legal issues surrounding the crime of aggression or how it could be charged and prosecuted against any individual defendant in the case of the war in Ukraine. Rather, I concentrated on the precedent that was set in October 1946, when the International Military Tribunal issued a decision imposing liability for the crime of aggression on the most senior Nazi German leaders in the custody of the Allies. I focused on the facts supporting the Nuremberg tribunal's judgment, the facts that demonstrated how German leaders had planned and justified their aggressive war against Poland.

Comparing the factual record at Nuremberg, which proved the crime of aggression, with what I had experienced as ambassador in Moscow from 2021 to 2022 was, I believed, a revealing exercise. I found the parallels between the German justifications for the war on Poland and the Russian justifications for the war on Ukraine to be compelling. In my public remarks in retirement, I offered those parallels for consideration, not as a historian, which I am not, nor as part of a formal legal analysis of the crime of aggression, which would require more research and scholarship. Instead, as a witness to what transpired in Moscow before and after the launch of the "special military operation," I offered those parallels as a way to put the origins of that brutal conflict in the context of how an earlier generation of Americans and Europeans (including Russians and Ukrainians) had viewed and dealt with the last major war fought on the continent of Europe.

———————

The Soviet Union, the United States, the United Kingdom, and France convened the Nuremberg tribunal in November 1945 to prosecute the twenty-two most senior former leaders of Nazi Germany who were still alive. All the defendants were present, except Martin Bormann (later concluded to be dead), who was tried in absentia. The four charges against them were crimes against peace (aggressive war), war crimes (e.g., the execution of prisoners of war), crimes against humanity (the Holocaust), and conspiracy to commit the first three crimes. Four judges, one from each of the Allies, presided. The prosecution function was divided among the four Allies, with a chief prosecutor from each country. Every defendant had legal counsel.

All twenty-two defendants were charged with crimes against peace, or conspiracy to commit crimes against peace. Not all defendants were charged with war crimes or crimes against humanity. Twelve defendants were convicted on October 1, 1946, of crimes against peace, including Foreign Minister Joachim von Ribbentrop, Field Marshal Wilhelm Keitel, and Colonel General (Generaloberst) Alfred Jodl. In addition, those same defendants (except Rudolf Hess) also were convicted of war crimes and/ or crimes against humanity, as were most of the other defendants not convicted of crimes against peace.

The parts of the Nuremberg proceedings, decisions, and judgment most relevant to the Ukraine war are the convictions under the inchoate concept of crimes against peace. The broad category of war crimes has a lengthy and established pedigree on which to judge Russian conduct in Ukraine. Moreover, Putin's "special military operation" could never approach in scale and horror the crimes against humanity committed by the Nazis against the Jews of Europe. The chief American prosecutor at Nuremberg, Associate Justice Robert H. Jackson, of the Supreme Court of the United States, concluded that the "most savage and numerous crimes planned and committed by the Nazis were those against the Jews." Putin is not Hitler, and his crimes, while severe, cannot be compared to Hitler's.

No, the primary focus on the Nuremberg trial should be on the German plans and justifications for waging an aggressive war against Poland. On that narrow ground, the comparison of the Nuremberg record with the "special military operation" is far more apt. That comparison should inform how the world responds to what the Russian government and its leaders have done in Ukraine.

As the prosecution acknowledged at Nuremberg, nothing justified the war that the Nazi defendants launched on September 1, 1939, although Germany had many grievances in the 1920s and 1930s, including serious, legitimate grievances. Looking at Germany on January 30, 1933, when he became chancellor, Hitler saw a former great country, an empire, that he believed had been duplicitously humbled, devastated, after the Great War by its enemies in the Treaty of Versailles. That is what he would have considered the "greatest geopolitical catastrophe of the century," to borrow Putin's phrase.

To begin with, Hitler believed that the Imperial German Army had not lost the war in 1918. From his perspective as Corporal Hitler, a decorated veteran of the Great War, it was traitorous civilians in Berlin—Jews, socialists, Bolsheviks, republicans—who had stabbed Imperial Germany and its military in the back. Out of that alleged betrayal grew the intolerable burdens of Versailles: solitary war guilt, massive reparations, loss of historical territories (almost 10 percent of Germany's prewar European land mass) and all its colonies, and disarmament leaving a denuded (no tanks or air force) and shrunken military (capped at a one-hundred-thousand-man army), in which Hitler had proudly served. Those were real grievances. Most Germans of the interwar period considered their country to be in a state of abject humiliation. Justice Jackson described the Germans as "a frustrated and baffled people as a result of defeat and the disintegration of their traditional government."

Hitler and the Nazis set out to redress Germany's grievances and restore German greatness in three overlapping stages. First, by crushing domestic opponents with violence and in concentration camps, eliminating democratic government, and consolidating totalitarian leadership under the führer, who eventually combined the offices of chancellor and president and ruled by decree. Second, Hitler and the Nazis rebuilt and modernized the German military, in violation of the postwar restrictions on troop strength, tanks, ships, and aircraft. Germany reintroduced conscription in 1935.

Third, after making substantial progress on its first two objectives, Germany began restoring its lost territories, where the *Deutsche Volk* were separated from the fatherland. In his opening statement at the Nuremberg trial, Justice Jackson said that Nazi Germany's answer to its significant interwar problems was "to plot the regaining of territories lost in the First World War and the acquisition of other fertile lands of Central Europe by dispossessing or exterminating those who inhabited them.... The precise limits of their ambition we need not define for it was and is as illegal to wage aggressive war for small stakes as for large ones."

The well-known historical record of Germany's territorial aggression began cautiously on March 7, 1936, when German troops entered the Rhineland, which was required under the Treaty of Versailles to be a demilitarized buffer between France and Germany. Two years later, in the *Anschluss* on March 12, 1938, German troops marched unopposed into Austria, which was annexed by Germany on the following day with the full support of most Austrians. There was faint opposition internationally, even though the annexation contravened a specific prohibition in the Versailles Treaty.

Gathering momentum, Hitler's campaign to restore German territory immediately created another crisis in the summer of 1938 over ethnic Germans in the Sudetenland, a region of Czechoslovakia (a nation created as the Great War was ending) bordering Germany and Austria. Hitler warned there would be war if Germany was not allowed to annex the Sudetenland. At the infamous Munich conference at the end of September 1938, the leaders of Britain (Neville Chamberlain) and France (Édouard Daladier), joined by Benito Mussolini of Italy, signed an agreement with Hitler providing for German annexation of the Sudetenland in return for a promise of peace. The annexation was popular with Sudeten Germans, but definitely not with the Czechoslovak government in Prague.

The *Anschluss* and the Sudeten crisis were aggressive acts by Germany, but not aggressive war. A combination of the sense that Germany had been terribly wronged at Versailles, the popularity of the territorial moves among Germans and German-speakers in Austria and the Sudetenland, and the overwhelming fear of another war led British, French, and other leaders to acquiesce in the German aggression without a military response. That would change in March 1939, when Germany, again threatening war, occupied what remained of Czechoslovakia.

Britain and France accelerated their preparations for a dreaded war they had both sought to avoid—and as they did, they soon had to deal with yet another crisis created by Germany. The new emergency concerned Poland, which had been restored as an independent nation, known as the Second Polish Republic, after the Great War. The postwar Polish state absorbed some German territory, including West Prussia and Posen, to create the so-called Polish Corridor that gave Poland access to the Baltic Sea and important trade routes. The Polish Corridor, however, separated German East Prussia from the fatherland. Moreover, the German-speaking port city of Danzig, on the Baltic, was declared a Free City under the authority of the League of Nations and was partially administered by Poland.

In early 1939, Hitler demanded the return of Danzig to Germany, and access across the Polish Corridor to East Prussia. The Poles refused and were backed by Britain and France, which issued defense guarantees to Poland in March 1939. In April, Hitler ordered the German military to prepare for war with Poland; like his hero Frederick the Great, the führer would regather the ancient Prussian lands in the east that had been lost. Subsequent intense diplomacy between and among Germany, Britain, France, and the Soviet Union could not resolve the crisis. On August 23, 1939, the Nazis and the Soviets signed a nonaggression pact in Moscow, along with a secret protocol that divided Poland and Eastern Europe into German and Soviet spheres of influence (facilitating the subsequent German and later Soviet invasions of Poland).

After the shock of the Nazi-Soviet pact, Britain and Poland signed a mutual assistance agreement on August 25. In a final shudder of diplomacy at the end of August, Hitler briefly tried to dissuade Britain from supporting Poland. He gave the British ambassador to Germany conditions for a settlement that included ceding Danzig and the Polish Corridor to Germany. Hitler also demanded that Poland engage in direct negotiations over his demands in twenty-four hours. Justice Jackson summarized the result for the judges at Nuremberg: German "demands were made for cession of territory. When Poland refused, the German forces invaded on September 1st, 1939. Warsaw was destroyed; Poland fell."

In announcing that a state of war existed between Britain and Germany, British prime minister Chamberlain stated on Sunday, September 3, that until the very end, "a peaceful and honorable settlement between Germany and Poland" had been possible. "But Hitler would not have it. He had evidently made up his mind to attack Poland whatever happened, and although he now says he put forward reasonable proposals which were rejected by the Poles, that is not a true statement." Chamberlain noted that the German proposals were "never shown to the Poles, nor to us, and, though they were announced in a German broadcast on Thursday night, Hitler did not wait to hear comments on them, but ordered his troops to cross the Polish frontier."

After the war, the Nuremberg tribunal agreed with Chamberlain's assessment that Germany did not engage in good-faith diplomacy in late August 1939. The tribunal found that German foreign minister von Ribbentrop "read to the British ambassador at top speed a document containing the first precise formulation of the German demands against Poland. He refused, however, to give the ambassador a copy of this, and stated that in any case it was too late now, since no Polish plenipotentiary had arrived." The tribunal concluded that "the manner in which these negotiations were conducted by Hitler and von Ribbentrop showed that they were not entered into in good faith or with any desire to maintain peace."

Feigned diplomacy was part of a German propaganda campaign seeking to justify what was otherwise naked German aggression in launching a war against Poland. According to Justice Jackson, more than a week before the invasion, on August 22, 1939, Hitler addressed the German High Command, "telling them when the start of military operations would be ordered. He disclosed that for propaganda purposes, he would provoke a good reason. 'It will make no difference . . . whether this reason will sound convincing or not. After all, the victor will not be asked whether he talked the truth or not.'"

Hitler's propaganda plan to justify war was to invert the truth and make Germany the victim, contending that Germans were being abused by barbarous Poles in the former German territories and that Germany itself was under attack from Poland. In an interview after the war, from his cell at the Nuremberg prison, Hermann Göring explained the need and the rationale for the German war propaganda:

> Of course, the people don't want war. Why would some poor slob on a farm want to risk his life in a war when the best that he can get out of it is to come back to his farm in one piece? Naturally, the common people don't want war; neither in Russia nor in England nor in America, nor for that matter in Germany. . . . [But] it is the leaders of the country who determine the policy and it is always a simple matter to drag the people along, whether it is a democracy or a fascist dictatorship or a parliament or a communist dictatorship.
>
> [T]he people can always be brought to the bidding of the leaders. That is easy. All you have to do is tell them they are being attacked and denounce the pacifists for lack of patriotism and exposing the country to danger. It works the same way in any country.

That is precisely how Hitler explained the start of Germany's war against Poland to the German people and the world. In his address announcing the invasion early on the morning of September 1, Hitler claimed that ethnic Germans in Poland were the targets of "bloody terror, driven from home and farm," and that Poland had engaged in "unacceptable violations of Germany's borders." He later said he was compelled to use force against Poland because German women and children were being abused by "bestial and sadistic" Poles. The Nazi Propaganda Ministry broadcast and printed fabricated stories of Polish atrocities against ethnic Germans.

It was a bitter irony, considering what the future would reveal about the Nazi's crimes against humanity in Poland, that German propaganda blamed the "barbarism of Poles against Germans"—Poland's "bestial and sadistic" treatment of Hitler's *Volk*—for the start of the war. Hitler also had the SS manufacture false-flag attacks on the German border to embellish the image of Germany as a victim. To further solidify Germany's status of "victimhood," the Nazi Propaganda Ministry would not allow the German press to call the invasion of Poland a war. Instead, the German government said the invasion of Poland was a "military intervention." It was only after Great Britain and France declared war on Germany, on September 3, 1939, that the term *war* could be used. The Nazis thereafter referred to the invasion of Poland as a "defensive war" (*Verteidigungskrieg*).

None of the German propaganda could justify an aggressive war against Poland, and calling it a "military intervention" did not change its character. More significantly, none of the legitimate German grievances growing out of the Great War and the Treaty of Versailles justified the invasion of Poland. "No one excuse[d] Germany for launching a war of aggression because she had grievances," Justice Jackson asserted at Nuremberg, and the tribunal did not decide whether Germany "had grievances. If she had real grievances, an attack on the peace of the world was not her remedy."

The Nazi defendants at Nuremberg were guilty, according to the Soviet chief prosecutor, Lieutenant General Roman A. Rudenko, because they "prepared these crimes a long time in advance and then committed them by attacking other countries, seizing foreign territories." As Justice Jackson quipped, the invasion of Poland "was not an unprepared and spontaneous springing to arms by a population excited by some current indignation." It was a long-planned and repeatedly threatened war of aggression.

---

The deep echoes in Putin's "special military operation" of what Justice Jackson called the "mad and melancholy record" of the crimes against peace proved at Nuremberg are damning. They range from the false accusations against the target of the aggression (claims of a Ukrainian "genocide," like the allegations of Polish "barbarism") to the prohibition on the use of the word "war" to describe a premeditated and massive military invasion. Yet while egregious, the uncanny similarities between the

Russian war against Ukraine and the German war against Poland are also instructive.

In each, a bit player (a corporal and a lieutenant colonel) on the losing side of a global conflict (the Great War and the Cold War), which he maintained his country did not really lose (only because of a "stab in the back" in Berlin and Moscow), rose to power by crushing a fledgling democracy in his quest to restore an empire whose territory had been sundered by evil foreign interests. Motivated by history (Frederick the Great and Peter the Great, respectively) and a profound sense of grievance, each leader sought to undo the great "geopolitical catastrophe" that his country had suffered in the twentieth century.

For both Putin and Hitler, the "geopolitical catastrophes" caused sham international borders to be imposed on their countries, severing their peoples from their ancestral homelands. For Hitler, it was a spurious border in the east with Poland, created out of the Great War, that separated the *Deutsche Volk*. For Putin, it was an artificial border in the west (what had been an internal border of the Soviet Union) that after the Cold War, became an international boundary dividing the *Russkiy mir*. Putin and Hitler both resorted to war to erase what they considered illegitimate international borders and reunite their historic peoples.

Of course, Hitler went much further than Putin in his insane quest to restore his country to greatness. It is undeniable that Nazi Germany had war aims far beyond Poland and the restoration of historic German territory. In addition to fighting a war against the United Kingdom and France (and later the United States), Hitler and the Nazis pursued a crusade for *Lebensraum* for Germany and vastly extended their aggressive war in the east with the invasion of the Soviet Union on June 22, 1941. Their crusade included the "most savage and numerous" crimes against humanity in the Holocaust that were proved at Nuremberg, and which bear no comparison to the Russian war in Ukraine.

Nevertheless, the broader German war aims and territorial aggression do not undermine the basic assessment of the original German invasion of Poland or diminish its applicability as a precedent to Putin's invasion of Ukraine. As Justice Jackson said at Nuremberg, "It was and is as illegal to wage aggressive war for small stakes [Poland or Ukraine] as for large ones [all of Eastern Europe or the territories of the former Soviet Union]." Moreover, it is impossible to say, while the "special military operation" is ongoing—as it is at the time of this writing—what Putin's ultimate objectives are, beyond his stated goals of "denazification" and "demilitarization" of Ukraine. Russia's prior aggression against Georgia in 2008, and even earlier in Moldova, suggest that Putin's territorial ambitions are almost certainly far wider and include, at a minimum, some of the other former republics of the Soviet Union.

Like the scope of Hitler's war aims described by Justice Jackson at the Nuremberg trial, however, the "precise limits" of Putin's "ambition . . . need not [be] define[d]." The incontrovertible evidence shows that Russia committed the crime of aggression, as it was defined at Nuremberg: the "invasion of its armed forces, with or without a declaration of war, of the territory of another state." There was no legal justification for its invasion of Ukraine. The Russian propaganda claim of a Ukrainian "genocide" against Russians to justify the invasion was absurd and was rejected overwhelmingly by the International Court of Justice. The ICJ ordered Russia to stop the "special military operation" immediately and withdraw from Ukrainian territory.

The other Russian justification for the invasion was self-defense, to prevent or preempt an attack by Ukraine, NATO, and/or the United States. This rationale is just as specious as Putin's debunked claim of a Ukrainian genocide by neo-Nazis in Kyiv. To be sure, waging a defensive war does not constitute the crime of aggression, as Justice Jackson explained at Nuremberg: "Exercise of the right of legitimate self-defense, that is to say, resistance to an act of aggression, . . . shall not constitute a war of aggression." For self-defense to be legitimate, however, there must be a "good-faith fear of attack." Russia had no such good-faith fear in 2022, just as Germany had no such fear in 1939.

None of the Nazi defendants at Nuremberg credibly argued that Poland had attacked Germany, but some maintained that Germany's actions were not aggressive because they "were defensive against a 'Bolshevik menace.'" Those defendants, according to Justice Jackson, claimed they "only intended to protect Germany against some eventual danger from the 'menace of Communism,' which was something of an obsession with many Nazis." The Soviet chief prosecutor, General Rudenko, scoffed contemptuously and unsurprisingly at this argument: "Could this be a defensive war? But nobody intended attacking Germany; nobody had such an idea and—in my opinion—such an idea could not have even existed."

Justice Jackson rejected the defensive war argument at Nuremberg, based on "the enormous and rapid German preparations for war," and "the repeatedly avowed intentions of the German leaders to attack." Finally, and most significantly, there was the incontrovertible "fact that a series of wars occurred in which German forces struck the first blows, without warning, across the borders of other nations." Those same arguments vitiate any Russian claim to be fighting a defensive war.

Russia brutally attacked Ukraine first, without notice and without a declaration of war. If Russia had genuinely feared an attack by Ukraine or the United States or NATO, why did Putin not raise Russia's fears with Biden at the summit in Geneva in June 2021? That was the best opportunity to do so, after Russia had raised tensions in the spring with increased troop deployments on its border with Ukraine. Instead, Russia waited several months and then created a contrived crisis—like the Sudeten crisis in 1938—over Ukraine. What Russia truly feared was not an attack by NATO eastward, but the sovereign, democratic decision of Russia's neighbors to look westward—to NATO and the EU—for their future.

In any event, considering Russia's frequent veiled threats to initiate a nuclear war, and references to its huge stockpile of nuclear weapons, what country was actually going to attack or invade Russia? No country. None. Arguing to the contrary is farcical, like arguing that Poland was going to attack Germany in September 1939. As General Rudenko declared at Nuremberg, "Such an idea could not have even existed."

In addition to creating a false crisis, the Russians mirrored Nazi Germany in the lead-up to their invasion of Ukraine by engaging in sham diplomacy for propaganda purposes. As I saw firsthand, they offered sloppily drafted treaties in December 2021 that sought unilateral and impossible concessions from the United States and NATO, and then insisted preposterously on negotiations within forty-eight hours over texts that had not even been translated. Continuing the ruse in January 2022, Russian diplomats read from scripts and refused to engage in any meaningful dialogue. As the Nuremberg tribunal concluded about Hitler and von Ribbentrop, the Russians in 2021 and 2022 did not engage in diplomacy "in good faith or with any desire to maintain peace."

This is not to say that Putin and Russia did not have grievances. They were seething with what that they considered unaddressed grievances: rampant Russophobia in the West that was hostile to, and even sought to destroy, traditional Russian culture; a relentless eastward expansion of NATO despite a (broken) promise by the United States not to do so; troop and missile deployments by the United States and NATO that threateningly surrounded Russia; an anti-Russia coup d'état in Ukraine fomented by the West—the list went on ad nauseam. I heard them all as ambassador, because one common feature of these diverse grievances was that the United States was responsible for every one of them. I spent three years debating Russian grievances with officials at every level of government in Moscow.

Russia also has a long history of being attacked and invaded, as the Russian people were frequently reminded (twice a year, for example, in the separate reenactments of the battles fought 130 years apart at Borodino). That history has given rise to what George Kennan called the "traditional and instinctive Russian sense of insecurity." And for that reason, like Chamberlain and Britain with Germany in August 1939, Biden and the United States were willing to negotiate with Russia and try to address its legitimate grievances and concerns, right up to February 24, 2022. But, as Chamberlain said of Hitler, Putin "would not have it. He had evidently made up his mind to attack [Ukraine] whatever happened." Putin's sham diplomacy was part of a larger propaganda effort to falsely portray Russia as a victim interested only in peace and security.

None of the Russian grievances, individually or combined, amounted to an attack on Russia or the "good-faith fear" of an attack that would justify a "defensive war" against Ukraine. Germany in the late 1930s had as many serious grievances as Russia in 2022, if not more (and no nuclear weapons with which to defend itself), but none of the German grievances justified an aggressive war against Poland. Justice Jackson once again had the answer in highlighting the crucial difference between the valid conclusion that Germany had committed the crime of aggression and the erroneous "position that Germany had no grievances. We are not inquiring into the conditions which contributed to causing this war. They are for history to unravel. It is no part of our task to vindicate the European status quo as of 1933, or as of any other date."

Whatever the merits of Russia's complaints about the European status quo as of 2022, nothing justified the aggressive war it launched against Ukraine. Nothing justified killing, wounding, or driving from their homes millions of Ukrainians. The persuasive force of the following statement by Justice Jackson at Nuremberg in 1946, on behalf of the four victorious Allies, including the Soviet Union, is fully applicable to Russia of the 2020s:

> Our position is that whatever grievances a nation may have, however objectionable it finds the status quo, aggressive warfare is an illegal means for settling those grievances or for altering those conditions. It may be that the Germany of the 1920s and 1930s faced desperate problems, problems that would have warranted the boldest measures short of war. All other methods—persuasion, propaganda, economic competition, diplomacy—were open to an aggrieved country, but aggressive warfare was outlawed.

In that light, despite its kaleidoscopic litany of grievances, complaints, criticisms, objections, and concerns, Russia is as guilty of the crime of waging aggressive war against Ukraine as Germany was of waging aggressive war against Poland. The fact that it did so by claiming that Ukraine was under the yoke of neo-Nazis is an added, horrible irony— one that is sure to occupy historians well into the future.

---

The convictions of the leading Nazi defendants for crimes against peace point to the legal and moral conclusions that should be drawn regarding Russia's "special military operation." The Nuremberg record does not answer, however, what should be done politically with Russia in the face of those conclusions. At Nuremberg, the victorious Allies tried individual former leaders of a Nazi government in Berlin that no longer existed. The Third Reich had been crushed into shameful oblivion—divided into four occupied zones—by the force of the Allied militaries at the cost of millions of lives lost. There was thus no issue at the Nuremberg tribunal about what to do with the state of Nazi Germany, which had been consigned to history. That is not the situation with the nation that perpetrated the "special military operation" against Ukraine.

What should be done with the Russian Federation? It is a country, and permanent member of the UN Security Council, that as of this writing continues to wage an illegal and immoral war in Ukraine, and that as Putin reminds the world regularly, also possesses an enormous stockpile of nuclear (and other unconventional) weapons and the means to deliver them against any adversary. The Nuremberg tribunal did not suggest an easy solution to such an intractable problem as the one that Russia now poses to the world. Yet this is where we find ourselves today.

Indeed, the question of how to manage our relations with Russia is one that tested the Biden administration from the start of the war, when the president issued two fundamental directives to his national security team: first, do everything possible to help Ukraine defend itself against Russia; and second, avoid getting the United States involved in a war with Russia. Putin faces a similar conundrum. As much as Russia wants to conquer Ukraine, which is vitally dependent on Europe and the United States for its survival, Russia does not want to fight a wider war against its European neighbors and the United States.

That two-sided strategic paradox is a challenge as difficult for US diplomats and policymakers as any faced by Kennan and his generation in dealing with the Soviet Union, which he had described as "undoubtedly [the] greatest task our diplomacy has ever faced and probably [the] greatest it will ever have to face." Meeting that challenge will require the same intellectual rigor, courage, and commitment to principles that prior generations of Americans have brought to bear in similar circumstances.

It will also require perseverance. The Russian people will endure, or will be forced by Putin to endure, much more suffering in carrying out the "special military operation." It remains to be seen whether the United States will be able to lead the West and rest of the world in opposition to Putin's aggressive war.

# EPILOGUE

# WHAT IS TO BE DONE?

W HEN I CONCLUDED MY SERVICE as ambassador, I planned to write a valedictory cable for officials in Washington, collecting my thoughts on
Russia, the Russian government, Putin, and his aggressive war against
Ukraine. It was common practice for an ambassador to submit a final
report—the State Department still uses the old-fashioned word "cable"
for written communications from embassies and consulates—on lessons
learned and the future. Jon Huntsman wrote a good one when he concluded his service in Moscow in 2019, on how the US embassy had been
severely impacted by diplomatic expulsions and the visa impasse with the
Russian MFA, and the consequences for US relations with Russia.

In my time in Moscow after the war started in February 2022, I
thought about what I would say in a last dispatch, whenever I concluded
my tenure, and how the document would be styled. There is an art
to writing a persuasive cable that is actually read (rather than filed) in
Washington. Kennan was, of course, the archetype. My uncle Ambassador Bill Sullivan also had a reputation for writing masterful cables.
His reports from Laos, where he was ambassador from 1964 to 1969,
during the Vietnam War, were sent directly to President Johnson at
the White House. He later wrote a significant and influential cable on
November 9, 1978, when he was ambassador to Iran, on the future of
what became the Iranian Revolution. The title of his cable was "Thinking the Unthinkable," and President Carter was not pleased with what
my uncle Bill reported from Tehran about the increasingly uncertain
prospects for the Shah and the Pahlavi dynasty.

As I learned from my uncle, a pithy title that captures the reader's attention is often useful. I had in mind using for my final cable the title of Lenin's famous revolutionary tract, *What Is to Be Done?*, which was published in 1902. I thought it might catch the eye of those familiar with the history of the Russian Revolution and evoke the calamitous upheaval in global affairs caused by Putin's aggressive war against Ukraine, akin to the impact of the October Revolution. For those with a less historical bent, the title might also attract officials interested in practical insights on the future of diplomacy with Russia (rather than idle theorizing).

Alas, my plans for a valedictory cable were overtaken by events: the tumult of my final weeks as ambassador left me little time for reflection and writing. I used the first few months after my retirement in October 2022 to rebuild my professional life. At the end of the year, I accepted an appointment as a distinguished fellow at the School of Foreign Service of Georgetown University and rejoined my former law firm, Mayer Brown. All the while, however, I never let go of the idea of putting in writing my thoughts and experiences from the extraordinary times in which I served in Russia. Eventually, my original concept of a final dispatch as ambassador from Moscow turned into this book. But the question that I planned to ask in my final, unsent cable could not be answered simply by telling the story of my time in Moscow.

That question—*What is to be done?*—has proven to be both vexing and timeless, whether it was asked about the Russian Empire (as Lenin did), the Soviet Union (as Kennan did), or the Russian Federation under Putin (as I and so many others are now doing). And as recent events have made clear, as Russia continues to wage an aggressive war against Ukraine, it will take great vision and creativity to address it when so many attempts have failed.

As I was finishing this book's final chapter, at the end of 2023, Russia had stabilized—at a huge cost in lives and treasure—the military conflict that it had started almost two years before, when it had attacked Ukraine with an arrogant confidence of a quick victory in two weeks. The war was in stalemate after high hopes for a Ukrainian offensive that ultimately made only very modest gains in 2023, compared to the Ukrainian military's successes in 2022. The Russian military did not collapse—as it had in Kharkiv Oblast in the prior fall—and it continued to launch missiles and drones against targets across Ukraine, killing scores of innocent men, women, and children. Russia was still hemorrhaging capital and literal blood—but with a much larger population and economy, Russia was better positioned than Ukraine for a war of attrition. The Ukrainian government continued to depend heavily on massive support from the West to defend itself.

The Russian losses, however, went far beyond men and money: serious flaws in the Russian military and its leadership were revealed, and its stockpiles of expensive weapons systems and equipment were being critically depleted. Even more troubling for Putin, the cohesion of the regime was briefly threatened by the unsuccessful mutiny of the Prigozhin-led Wagner Group in June 2023. Putin survived the Wagner scare and reaffirmed and consolidated his control by dealing with Prigozhin as only a good Chekist would (killing him with a bomb on a plane, which was the cause suspected by most Russia-watchers for the crash). Putin would never surrender power and, also, would never relent in his invasion of Ukraine.

The strategic picture for Putin and Russia beyond the front lines in southeastern Ukraine, however, was decidedly less favorable than before the war. NATO was unified and strengthened by the addition of Finland and Sweden as members, two countries that for decades had declined to seek NATO membership but were driven to do so by Russia's aggressive war. Indeed, by seeking to stop NATO enlargement by attacking Ukraine, Putin had blundered into creating an enlarged NATO more unified than before. Ukrainians, too, remained unified in opposition to the "special military operation" and against conceding territory to Russia. Putin's war aim of uniting Russians and Ukrainians—Russian-speaking Slavic sisters and brothers, in his view—in a unified *Russkiy mir* was shattered by the horrors that he inflicted on Ukraine and its people. The result was an even stronger Ukrainian state and national identity separate from Russia.

———————

Ironically, among the most significant developments in 2023 regarding the defense of Ukraine occurred not on the battlefield but thousands of miles away, in Washington. Some members of Congress and political commentators, inspired by statements from former president Trump, began to question whether the United States could or should continue to support Ukraine with the provision of weapons, matériel, and money. As the war settled into a perceived deadlock and the cost of supporting Ukraine remained extremely high, I understood the inclination to ask the question, but the answer had to be a resounding yes.

Continued stout support for the defense of Ukraine was vital to the national security and foreign policy interests of the United States. That had been the solid political consensus in the United States in 2022, when Kyiv was under attack, and later when Ukraine was pushing the Russians out of Kharkiv and Kherson. But it started to fray when the Ukrainian military could not overcome heavily entrenched and defended Russian positions in southern and eastern Ukraine in the second half of 2023. When the cost and difficulty of standing up to Russia's violent aggression increased, some Americans began to wobble.

In retirement, I was involved in the public debate in the United States over continued support for the defense of Ukraine, which the Biden administration sought from Congress (for my efforts, I was recently sanctioned by the Russian government). One troubling sentiment that motivated a handful of those opposed to further aid was their unwillingness to support anything for which President Biden had asked. That was not a legitimate basis on which to oppose support for Ukraine, if that support was otherwise in the vital interests of the United States, as I believed it was. Partisan politics should play no role in the discussion, and the fact that it did (even if only in part) was a troubling sign of the increasing politicization in recent years of what had been traditionally apolitical issues, like the national security of the United States.

On the other hand, I also believed that the Biden administration was open to fair and nonpartisan criticism over its cumulative decisions on support for the defense of Ukraine. My view was that the administration had not done enough, as evidenced by the slow and erratic pace in 2022 and 2023 of its approval of the provision of weapons systems to the Ukrainians that they needed urgently, like missiles, tanks, and aircraft. The administration had built a track record of first denying a weapons system to Ukraine, then reconsidering after a substantial delay, and later

WHAT IS TO BE DONE?

approving the transfer. That was no way to support a fellow democracy under attack by a much larger, aggressive, authoritarian foe.

The president's hesitancy was caused, in large measure, by his fear of provoking Putin to widen the war and attack NATO or use a tactical nuclear weapon. It was an issue that I had only observed from the sidelines in Moscow and Washington—I was not privy, for example, to discussions between the Biden administration and the government in Kyiv—and which I have not treated at any length in this book. Historians (and Monday morning policy quarterbacks) will, in time, pass judgment on the administration's record of delayed provision of weapons systems to Ukraine and assess what effect, if any, that had on the fruitless Ukrainian offensive in 2023.

Taking a broader perspective, however, I believe that the United States has generally been on the right track in facing the fundamental challenge presented by Putin's aggressive war against Ukraine. The position of the United States has been, and should continue to be, to support Ukraine's defense with everything it can provide without itself engaging in a direct conflict with Russia.

I also agreed with former Speaker of the House Kevin McCarthy that the United States should not simply write a "blank check" to Ukraine. Every weapons transfer should be vetted to insure that it is consistent with US law and policy and will not put the defense of the United States and its allies in jeopardy (for example, by dangerously depleting the stocks of an advanced weapons system). Every dollar for Ukraine should be accounted for and spent only in the manner intended by Congress and the president. That is simply a matter of good government and common sense of which Ronald Reagan would have heartily approved.

There are two important and obvious caveats to the full support of the United States for Ukraine that bear emphasis. The first qualification is that the United States should avoid a war with Russia, as President Biden has instructed. A direct military conflict between the world's two nuclear superpowers over Ukraine is just too fraught for humanity, a fact that Putin appears to delight in repeatedly reminding everyone. For that reason, it was clearly the correct decision for the United States and NATO to reject declaring a no-fly zone over Ukraine at the start of the "special military operation." Such a declaration has meaning only if it is enforced, which would have required shooting down Russian aircraft entering Ukrainian airspace. Ukraine can shoot down Russian aircraft, including with US weapons systems, but the United States should not do so (except in a case where American lives are in immediate danger).

The distinction between what Ukraine can do and what the United States should not do may sound artificial and risky, but it has solid historical and legal foundations. As Justice Jackson noted at a conference in 1945 before the Nuremberg trial started, President Roosevelt had provided weapons and material to the United Kingdom and the Soviet Union (in massive and decisive amounts that Putin was loath to acknowledge) before the United States was at war with Nazi Germany:

> The thing that led us to take sides in this war was that we regarded Germany's resort to war...as an illegitimate attack on the international peace and order. And throughout the efforts to extend aid to the peoples that were under attack, the justification was made...that this war was illegal from the outset and hence we were not doing an illegal thing in extending aid to peoples who were unjustly and unlawfully attacked.

After World War II, indirect conflict between the United States and the Soviet Union was a staple of the Cold War. The Soviets heavily armed North Vietnam and the Viet Cong with weapons to kill American troops and shoot down American aircraft during the Vietnam War. In fact, the Soviet Union went further in Vietnam than the United States has gone in Ukraine, because thousands of Soviet "experts" were on the ground advising the North Vietnamese, and some reportedly flew combat air sorties against the US Air Force (something that had also happened in the Korean conflict). And then there is the precedent of Operation Cyclone, the US program to support the Afghan mujahideen with weapons and money in their conflict with the Soviet Union in the 1980s. In short, these sorts of indirect interventions are well within bounds, both in terms of precedent and in terms of ethics.

The second caveat is that while the United States should be the leader among nations in sustaining the defense of Ukraine, it cannot and should not be the only supplier of weapons, money, and other backing to Kyiv. There must be equitable burden-sharing among every nation supporting Ukraine, including all NATO allies and European countries, which (with some exceptions, e.g., Turkey and Hungary) has generally been the case to date. Ukraine needs more resources than the United States can reasonably provide, and more Europeans are directly affected, personally and substantially, by the conflict than Americans—although, to be sure, the entire globe is adversely affected by the "special military operation," as the disruption of Ukrainian grain exports in 2022 and 2023 demonstrated.

This leads to the conclusion that the United States and its allies and partners also must increase the effectiveness of their diplomacy to convince more nations, particularly those with large economies (e.g., Brazil, India, and South Africa), to support Ukraine and oppose Russia's aggressive war. Unfortunately, the world's other great superpower, the People's Republic of China, is an unlikely candidate to come to the defense of Ukraine, because of President Xi's relationship with his "dear friend" Putin. Nevertheless, diplomacy to win more international support for the defense of Ukraine continues to be essential, even if it is focused on a question slightly different from Lenin's "*What* is to be done?"

*Why*, rather, must it be done?

Why must the United States and the world, not just the West, support the defense of Ukraine? The answer is straightforward: Russia launched an illegal aggressive war and is committing egregious war crimes in conducting that "special military operation." Putin's war is shockingly, eerily similar to Germany's aggressive war against Poland in 1939, which was condemned at Nuremberg. It also parallels Iraq's aggressive war by Saddam Hussein against Kuwait in 1990, when the dictator claimed that Kuwait was Iraq's nineteenth province. Saddam's invasion of Kuwait was condemned by the UN Security Council and was opposed with overwhelming military force by a large international coalition authorized by the Security Council and led by the United States and President George H. W. Bush.

Some world leaders, regrettably, like some members of the US

Congress, require a more detailed and persuasive rationale to support the defense of Ukraine and oppose Russia's aggressive war. In addressing their concerns, I begin where Kennan did when he laid out in the Long Telegram the basis of what became the containment strategy of the United States for the Soviet Union: the "first step must be to apprehend, and recognize for what it is, the nature of the [country] with which we are dealing.... We must see that our public is educated to [the] realities of [the] Russian situation. I cannot overemphasize [the] importance of this."

In almost six years as deputy secretary of state and US ambassador in Moscow, I observed four important features of "the Russian situation" that are most relevant to understanding and crafting a strategy to address Putin's aggressive war against Ukraine.

First, Russia is not merely an *adversary* of the United States. Putin's government in the Kremlin is a self-declared *enemy* of the United States. That was the most important reason I found that nothing was ever easy in dealing with the Russians: in engaging with the Kremlin, the United States and its allies and partners are confronting an implacable enemy, with all the security, legal, political, and social consequences that such a confrontation entails. Among those consequences will be the continued arrest and wrongful detention of innocent Americans in Russia, which was demonstrated by the arrest and detention of *Wall Street Journal* reporter Evan Gershkovich on March 29, 2023, in Yekaterinburg for espionage.

Recognizing that the Russian government considers itself an enemy of the United States leads ineluctably to the conclusion that Putin genuinely and resolutely believes he is at war with the United States and NATO in Ukraine. No goodwill gesture or search for a negotiated solution by the West will change that fact.

Second, the Russian government cannot be trusted in any context. Putin and the Kremlin are completely untethered from the truth and facts—yet another reason that nothing is ever easy in dealing with them. As Justice Jackson said of the defendants at Nuremberg, the Russian government's "attitude [is] that truth is any story which succeeds." Russian leaders—from Putin through Lavrov and on down—lied repeatedly in promising that Russia would not invade Ukraine. Indeed, Russia's leadership stated definitively that it had no plans to invade Ukraine—none—right up to the moment the "special military operation" began.

After this naked betrayal, how can anyone negotiate in good faith with Putin's government again, over Ukraine or any other issue of importance? Trust is impossible. Reagan's famous maxim of "trust but verify," *doveryai, no proveryai,* in his engagement with the Soviet Union and Gorbachev, is simply inapplicable and seems quaint now when dealing with Moscow. There is no trust, only verification. I would say about Russian diplomats, as a whole, the same thing that Justice Jackson said about German diplomats before and during the Second World War: their "readiness to pledge the German word without hesitation and to break it without shame has fastened upon German diplomacy a reputation for duplicity that will handicap it for years."

Russian "diplomacy" has been reduced to bald lies and increasingly bizarre name-calling. Putin has said that the United States and the West are now plagued with "outright satanism." I amused my colleagues and students at Georgetown when I said that I might need to call on the Jesuits at the university for an exorcism for myself and some of my former State Department colleagues.

Third, no matter what he or any other Russian leader might say, Putin's Russia will never surrender the goal of the "special military operation" to subjugate Ukraine. Never. When Putin or one of his surrogates talks of negotiations and peace, we should acknowledge and treat it as pure disinformation.

I have often been asked whether there is an "off ramp" for Putin in Ukraine. My reply has not wavered: There is none, short of victory on his terms. In a conversation in 2022 with Secretary Blinken, who also was frequently asked the same question, I said that Putin does not want an off ramp, although (continuing the highway metaphor) he might avail himself of the Vladimir Vladimirovich Putin Service Area, like the named rest stops (Clara Barton, Vince Lombardi, Walt Whitman, et al.) on the New Jersey Turnpike that I have come to know so well over many decades of travel in the Garden State. But Putin would use such a pause or cease-fire only to refit and regroup for victory—to complete his journey, so to speak, rather than to exit altogether and negotiate a durable peace.

Fourth, although my assessments of Putin and his plans for Ukraine are grim, his removal is not necessarily the answer. And it is certainly not within the remit of the United States to decide what type of government or leader Russia should have—or to try to influence regime change in Moscow. Winston Churchill once said, during the Russian Civil War in 1919 that "if Russia is to be saved, as I pray she may be saved, she must be saved by Russians." We should be saying the same prayer now. Because ultimately, the government of the Russian Federation is the responsibility of the Russian people, not the American people or their government.

When we understand and accept these four features of "the Russian situation," the answer to the question of *what is to be done* begins to take shape.

The only suitable strategy for the United States and the West must be a form of twenty-first-century containment of Russian aggression. It is, as I have argued, legally and morally imperative to defend Ukraine against a rapacious invader. But there is an even more compelling and self-interested reason for the United States to do so: Russia cannot be allowed to succeed with the "special military operation," because Putin's aggression will not stop at Ukraine if the West relents and allows Russia to topple the democratically elected government in Kyiv and subjugate the Ukrainian people—against their will—to the Kremlin.

Isolationists may argue that worrying about further Russian aggression in Europe or elsewhere is rank speculation and fearmongering, and that the fate of Ukraine does not affect the real interests of the United States. That argument is flatly wrong on both counts. First, Putin has already encroached by force on the territories of Georgia and Moldova, in addition to that of Ukraine. Many of the other former Soviet republics and Warsaw Pact countries—including the Baltic states (Estonia, Latvia, and Lithuania) that are members of NATO—have been subjected to Russian cyberattacks and military threats. Russian aggression against them is real, not speculative. Their future security will be very much imperiled if Ukraine falls.

Moreover, allowing Russia to invade and conquer Ukraine would have a disastrous effect on the security of the United States, even if Russia did not invade another country thereafter. Putin regards his invasion of Ukraine as a war against Russia's true enemy, the United States, and is not shy about sharing that view with the world. If, after publicly and decisively supporting the defense of Ukraine at the outset of Putin's aggressive war, the United States were to withdraw its support because of the perceived burden or a lack of interest either in Eastern Europe or in opposing an aggressive war by a permanent member of the UN Security Council, the effect in world capitals would be seismic.

Consider that scenario, which some in Congress have been attempting to steer us toward: Russia's aggression would be validated. Whether or not he could eventually succeed in conquering Ukraine, Putin would be able to convincingly declare victory over the United States. NATO allies, particularly in Eastern Europe, would have to seriously question whether the United States has the strength and commitment to assist in their defense, which would be more necessary than ever because of the increased threat of further aggression from Moscow. Officials in Tokyo and Seoul would be gravely concerned, at best, about the United States as an ally and world leader, while hostile governments in Beijing, Tehran, and Pyongyang would be bolstered in pursuing their own territorial aggression. The stigma of the tragic and humiliating US withdrawal from Afghanistan would be both reinforced and completely eclipsed by a greater debacle in Ukraine. It would be just as the secretary of the Russian Security Council, Nikolai Patrushev, predicted for the Ukrainians in August 2021: the Americans cannot be trusted and Ukraine will suffer the same fate as Afghanistan.

The United States, at that point, would have two fundamental choices. Either double down on the defense of its allies to reassure them, or abandon the system of alliances that has been the cornerstone of American security since the end of the Second World War. In either case—defending itself and its allies against emboldened aggressors in Moscow, Beijing, Tehran, and Pyongyang, or providing for its own self-defense without the support of effective alliances—the increased cost to the United States would far exceed what it has contributed, and would contribute in the future, to the defense of Ukraine against Russian aggression. There is no conceivable outcome in which the withdrawal of support for the defense of Ukraine materially reduces the defense budget of the United States.

Indeed, contributing now to the defense of Ukraine is less expensive in the long run. The United States is going to have to pay for its security against increased Russian aggression, and it is more effective and cheaper to do so with numerous allies vigorously supporting Ukraine's resistance, rather than defending ourselves and our allies further to the west in Europe or on this side of the Atlantic (or the Pacific and Arctic Oceans, because Russia is such a huge land mass). And we cannot break America's pledge to its allies.

Maintaining the United States commitment to NATO, and to our other alliances, is the only conceivable path forward, because abandoning them is unthinkable for American security. Trying to defend the United States without allies would be far less effective and significantly more costly than our current defense strategy and budget. As former defense secretary Jim Mattis has said, the defense of the United States "is inextricably linked to the strength of our unique and comprehensive system of alliances and partnerships. While the US remains the indispensable nation in the free world, we cannot protect our interests or serve that role effectively without maintaining strong alliances and showing respect to those allies."

Finally, no matter what the United States does, the Ukrainians will continue to resist Russia's aggression, regardless of whether Congress provides any further support, or whether the government in Kyiv falls, or whether the Ukrainian military is overrun by the sheer mass of the Russian military and mercenaries. I have in my mind the image of the Ukrainian woman in Henichesk confronting heavily armed Russian soldiers with sunflower seeds. That passionate resistance is not going to ebb because Washington goes wobbly.

At best, after the withdrawal of US support, Ukraine will remain a festering, bloody problem on the European continent until Russian aggression is contained, and that will affect not only American and global security but also the global economy and supply chains. The United States cannot, as some isolationists believe, wall itself off from major security challenges elsewhere in the world and expect to thrive as Americans have become accustomed in the post–World War II era. We tried that before in a less interconnected world, and we failed. As Justice Jackson said at Nuremberg, "Twice we have held back in the early stages of European conflict in the belief that it might be confined to a purely European affair." It was wrong in the twentieth century and it is a pure chimera in the twenty-first.

Withdrawing support for Ukraine and failing to oppose Putin's aggression would be a historic—an epoch-defining—mistake. The lesson of the dangerousness of a despot that launches an aggressive war was learned at an unthinkable cost eighty-five years ago. That lesson must be applied today without hesitation, without negotiations while Putin's war is ongoing, and without any "off ramps." History has judged Neville Chamberlain harshly for his appeasement at Munich in 1938. Imagine what the judgment of history would have been for any leader that had proposed negotiating with Germany in September 1939, after the invasion of Poland had begun? Or had asked what Germany's "off ramp" was in Poland? Or had said, "All wars end in negotiations, so let's start talking with the Germans now to avoid unnecessary further cost and bloodshed"? Such thinking might have changed history, but definitely not for the better.

———————

Of course, this application of the lessons from the start of World War II to Russian aggression in the twenty-first century has a practical limit imposed by the advent of the nuclear age in 1945 with the atomic bombs dropped by the United States on Japan to end the war. The nuclear arsenal of the Russian Federation, with its capacity to destroy civilization, puts a compelling constraint on what the United States and NATO can sanely do to oppose Putin's aggression in Ukraine. The answer to this problem, however, is also found in history: specifically, in the containment strategy applied to the Soviet Union, a nuclear-armed superpower, by the United States.

Updated for the twenty-first century, the Cold War strategy of containment would look something like this: Russian aggression, which is at least as dangerous as Soviet aggression but without the animating Communist ideology, must be opposed by the United States and its allies and partners. Resistance in other countries subject to Russian aggression must be supported, and that starts in Ukraine with weapons and assistance to the government in Kyiv to stop the advance of the Russian invasion and protect the Ukrainian people. Going further and rolling back the existing Russian gains in Ukrainian territory will no doubt be costly and take an indeterminate amount of time, as demonstrated by the unproductive Ukrainian military offensive in 2023. It might take months (as it did to expel Iraq from Kuwait), or decades (as it did for the reunification of Germany), or it may never happen (as on the Korean Peninsula).

Yet so long as the Ukrainian people are committed to the task of defending their country, so too the United States and its allies and partners should be committed to providing them the wherewithal to do so. The strategy, means, and timetable for reclaiming Ukrainian territory should be discussed with Ukrainian government officials, but decided by them. It is their country. Unlike the maliciously false accusations in the Kremlin's propaganda, the United States cannot (and should not try to) make the Ukrainian people defend themselves. But rousing the Ukrainian spirit of independence is not, and has never been, an issue.

Putin would have the world believe that a docile, Russia-loving Ukraine has been forced or duped by the United States to fight a war with Russia. In fact, a courageous and determined Ukrainian people—millions of whom have been killed, wounded, or driven from their homes by Putin—is pleading with the United States for help to defend themselves and defeat Russian aggression. To any American, Democrat or Republican, who struggles with what the response of the United States should be, I ask: what would Jack Kennedy or Ronald Reagan (or Harry Truman or Dwight Eisenhower) say? I believe the answer is abundantly clear: they would tell us to support, in concert with our allies, the defense of Ukraine.

Ultimately, if we follow a strategy of containing Russian aggression with strength and perseverance, it will pay substantial dividends, just as

Kennan correctly predicted of containment in the Cold War: "The United States has it in its power to increase enormously the strains under which Soviet policy must operate," he observed, "to force upon the Kremlin a far greater degree of moderation and circumspection than it has had to observe in recent years." In dealing with the United States and a unified West, Kennan saw, no "Messianic movement—and particularly not that of the Kremlin—can face frustration indefinitely without eventually adjusting itself in one way or another to the logic of that state of affairs." The crucial elements in this equation are strength and perseverance over time.

"Containing" Russia does not mean that we should seek regime change in Moscow—only that we should seek to moderate and restrain Russia's aggressive actions against other countries. Putin currently has a lock on the "managed democracy" in Russia and will certainly win a comfortable victory in his reelection campaign for a fifth term in mid-March 2024. He has eliminated his competition by any means available. The death of Alexei Navalny on February 16, 2024, in a Russian prison is only the most recent and notorious example.

This state of affairs, however, is not permanent; nothing is. Over time, the Russian people will decide how they want their country to participate in global affairs. My hope is that they will eventually choose a better path, as Churchill said about the Soviet people in a speech at MIT in 1949:

> The machinery of propaganda may pack their minds with falsehood and deny them truth for many generations of time. But the soul of man thus held in trance or frozen in a long night can be awakened by a spark coming from God knows where and in a moment the whole structure of lies and oppression is on trial for its life.

It took over forty years after Churchill's speech, but eventually the Soviet people proved him right by throwing off the shackles of Soviet Communism. Change is always possible, but it takes time and must develop organically from within.

Putin used a range of elaborate justifications for his aggressive war in Ukraine, many of them ludicrous. But he has one criticism of the United States that resonates with me, and it involves NATO expansion.

I am not saying that I agree that NATO expansion violated a (nonexistent) promise by Secretary of State James Baker not to expand the alliance eastward; nor do I believe that the admission of the former Warsaw Pact countries to NATO starting in 1999 (Czechia, Hungary, and Poland) and the former Soviet republics in 2004 (Estonia, Latvia, and Lithuania) was a mistake in US foreign policy. The problem, though, was the extremely negative perception in Russia of NATO expansion. It was about the effect of such expansion on the Russian psyche, because there was otherwise no rational concern that NATO, a defensive alliance, would actually attack Russia.

The most persuasive articulation of this criticism was offered by none other than my Russia muse George Kennan in an opinion piece in the *New York Times* in 1997, written at ninety-three years old, more than fifty years after his Long Telegram. Kennan warned that

> expanding NATO would be the most fateful error of American policy in the entire post-cold-war era.
>
> Such a decision may be expected to inflame the nationalistic, anti-Western and militaristic tendencies in Russian opinion; to have an adverse effect on the development of Russian democracy; to restore the atmosphere of the cold war to East-West relations, and to impel Russian foreign policy in directions decidedly not to our liking.

As always, Kennan was prescient in writing about Russia. Indeed, he was absolutely uncanny in predicting what would happen over the next twenty-five years. But I question whether it was the admission of the Eastern European countries to NATO—as opposed to other action or inaction by the United States—that was the fateful policy mistake in the late 1990s and early 2000s.

The Kennan view, which has been endorsed and elaborated on by some "realists" in the foreign policy commentariat, focuses only on Russian security perceptions and gives no weight to the aspirations and security concerns of the more than 100 million people in Eastern Europe who suffered for decades under Soviet oppression from Moscow. They remembered Brezhnev's Operation Danube, which crushed the Prague Spring in 1968. As a result, their countries sought membership in NATO; they were not coerced into joining. It was not an eastward expansion of NATO so much as a westward striving by the people of Eastern Europe, because their future peace and security was still uncertain and very much hung in the balance.

I believe that it was not a mistake to admit those countries and was entirely consistent with NATO's charter. Bringing the ancient capitals of Eastern Europe under NATO's defensive umbrella brought freedom and security to a region that had known violence and oppression for generations. I do not believe that shunning them, declining their requests for admission to NATO, would have had the same result, but it is impossible to say with any certainty twenty years later—just as it is impossible to say with certainty that declining their requests would have quelled Russian nationalism or prevented the rise of Putin.

On the question of the effect of NATO expansion on Russia, however, I agree with Kennan that the United States should have done more, following the dissolution of the Soviet Union, to reconcile with and reassure the adversary that it had defeated in the Cold War. Rather than celebrating "the end of history," that Francis Fukuyama notably proclaimed, the United States surely could have worked harder to ensure that history did not repeat itself in the rise of aggressive and destructive Russian nationalism. If there was a fateful mistake in American foreign policy during the early post–Cold War era, it was in not embracing the Russians more while also including the Eastern Europeans in NATO. At the time, the West considered extending its embrace of Russia to include admitting it to NATO. Instead, we created the NATO-Russia Council, which was a lesser consultative body.

At the end of the day, the most telling criticism of the United States that I heard from Russians across the ideological spectrum while I was in

Moscow was that Americans grossly underestimated the impact on the Russian people—emotionally and intellectually—of the end of the Cold War and the demise of the Soviet Union. They told me that the United States was distracted (with the Clinton scandals, the war on terror, and other priorities) when it should have been doing more to engage with and support Russia. I debated with my Russian interlocutors over what that additional engagement and support might have entailed and whether the Russian government, under either Yeltsin or Putin, would have been open to it. These were interesting conversations, but the answers to those questions, considered years later, were imponderable.

The entire discussion is part of an academic debate—could the United States have reconciled with Russia while also respecting the security concerns and NATO aspirations of the peoples of Eastern Europe?—that is now entirely beside the point in responding to Russia's "special military operation." Even if Kennan were absolutely correct in 1997, and even if one were to credit (contrary to fact) some of Putin's Ukraine-related grievances, none of that justifies Russia's aggressive war, which has brought death and destruction to Ukraine on a scale not seen since World War II.

Up to February 24, 2022, the United States was prepared to continue discussions with the Russians in good faith on all of their security concerns in Ukraine and in Europe. I was a participant in the discussions until that date; and there was not, at any time, the threat of an attack by any country on Russia. Nevertheless, Putin was not interested in talks with the United States; if he had been, he would have raised his issues and grievances with Biden in Geneva. Instead, like the Germans in August 1939, the Russians feigned negotiations starting in mid-December 2021 by making demands and reading from their talking points. They created a crisis and then set unreasonable time deadlines to resolve it. They stoked fear among Russians with false accusations of Nazis in Kyiv plotting to attack Russia as Nazi Germany had in June 1941. Their behavior was pure bad faith.

In the final analysis, I witnessed the leader of a great country—a permanent member of the UN Security Council that should be committed to peace—calculatingly decide to start a major war without justification to address his security concerns and grievances. Putin was not forced to do so by any country or by any circumstances; there was no legal claim to self-defense. He decided that Russia would invade Ukraine and that no one—not the United States, not NATO, and certainly not the United Nations—could stop him. That choice changed everything.

———————

It is now up to the United States, as flawed and imperfect as our union may be, to continue to lead the West and try to gather the rest of the world in opposition to Russian aggression against Ukraine. We must do so while simultaneously addressing other serious (perhaps even more danger-ous) challenges to our security and the security of our allies around the world. The burden on the United States is extremely heavy and cannot be avoided without creating even more dire consequences. Yet, as daunting as that may sound, as tempting as it may be to listen to those who believe that we can wish (or talk) our security challenges away, Americans should be reassured by the fact that our current burden is not unprecedented.

Prior generations of Americans during the Second World War and the Cold War successfully bore similar if not greater burdens. Their service, their sacrifice, and their commitment to our Constitution, and the princi-ples and values to which we have aspired as a nation since our founding, point the way forward. The unanswered question is how the American people will respond to the challenging and dangerous times in which they find themselves in the third decade of the twenty-first century.

Will they "[pull] themselves together and [accept] the responsibilities of moral and political leadership that history plainly intended them to bear," as Kennan urged Americans at the start of the Cold War? Or will they say the burden is too great? Putin is counting on the latter response. The only way that he can achieve the objectives of the "special military operation" is if Americans ignore Russia's brutal military aggression, which is clearly directed not only at Ukraine but also at the United States and our allies. In fact, it is an even greater challenge than that.

The containment of Russian aggression is not predominantly a mili-tary strategy or problem. Putin views the current hostilities between the United States and Russia as a clash of "civilizations," which conjures the Cold War confrontation between Communism and liberal democracy. Kennan viewed that prior conflict not as a military affair but rather as "a test of the overall worth of the United States as a nation among nations." It was a test in which the United States needed to "measure up to its own best traditions and prove itself worthy" to resist Soviet Communism and preserve its system of government with private property, individual freedom, and the rule of law (rather than the rule of Communist Party leaders through the KGB).

The Russian aggression led by Putin in this century seeks to overturn not liberal democracy directly, but the post–World War II international order, which is the system that for example, made it illegal for any nation to engage in aggressive war. Putin uses many tools, including disinformation and propaganda (mixing truth with lies), to attack this system, to which he objects because it limits his power over the hundreds of millions of people on Russia's borders. He desires a world in which Russian power (which means his personal power, like that of the tsars of the Russian Empire) is unconstrained by international norms, rules, and obligations. His argument is that the United States does not follow these rules, so why should Russia. That is the heart of Russian whataboutism.

Putin's attack is directly on the United States and our merits as a nation and as the principal creator of the postwar international order. He wants to undermine the confidence of the American people in the United States and its role in the world. But the response of the United States to this challenge should be neither despair nor self-righteousness. The United States is not and has never been faultless in either its foreign or domestic policies—what country is? Our system of government, our democracy, was and is imperfect, but what is the alternative? As Churchill famously said in the House of Commons in 1947: "Many forms of Government have been tried, and will be tried in this world of sin and woe. No one pretends that democracy is perfect or all-wise. Indeed it has been said that democracy is the worst form of Government except for all those other forms that have been tried from time to time." Our task is to improve our democracy, not abandon it.

I would make the same argument about the international system that was built out of the wreckage of the Second World War. Does it need to be modernized and improved for the twenty-first century? Of course. If it is overturned completely, as Putin urges, what is the alternative? A world of aggressive wars and might makes right? If so, then we have turned the clock back to 1939.

Americans have traditionally been an optimistic people with hope for the future, which is not surprising for a nation of immigrants, like my family and Grace's family, seeking a new life in this country. This optimism is what made Reagan popular in the 1980s, got Bill Clinton elected in 1992 as the man from Hope, Arkansas, and gave us the Obama "Hope" poster in 2008. Putin, and those like him who attack the United States, want to crush that hope. He wants Americans to believe that our country is every bit as lawless and brutal as the Russia he seeks to create.

The increasing polarization and politicization of American society since the end of the Cold War, a historical trend that has been intensifying rapidly in recent years, is an Achilles' heel that Putin seeks to exploit with the Kremlin's global propaganda. Without that, Putin has no persuasive case to make for the decline of America. Thus, the ultimate answer to the aggression of Putin's Russia is to strengthen the United States from within, just as it was during the Cold War. As Kennan said about the confrontation with Soviet Communism, "Every courageous and incisive measure to solve internal problems of our own society, to improve self-confidence, discipline, morale and community spirit of our own people, is a diplomatic victory over Moscow."

Success or failure in stopping Russian aggression depends more on the health and vigor of American society than on any arcane foreign policy decisions or complex military actions. It comes down to Americans respecting our Constitution, our political system, and each other. If we do, we will restore hope in America and its future. But if, as Kennan warned, "we cannot abandon fatalism and indifference in face of deficiencies of our own society, Moscow will profit."

This, ultimately, is the answer to the question *What is to be done?* We Americans must acknowledge our faults and seek to overcome them— just as we have throughout our history. Not with complete success every time, but with sufficient progress to maintain our hope and optimism for the future. Bolstered by this history, I can still say today what I said before I departed for Moscow in January 2020: I believe in America.

# ACKNOWLEDGMENTS

I owe debts of gratitude to many people and institutions that made it possible for me to write this book. They are far too numerous for me to list. I can highlight only the most significant, and I begin with my parents, Jack and Julia Sullivan. Their quiet example of authentic American patriotism—as active members of the generation that fought and won the Second World War—started me on a path of service to a nation that as they taught me, deserved everything I could give and more. They and their siblings set a high standard for public service. My mother's brother Edward Clark was a US Army World War II combat veteran. My father's brother Bill, the real Ambassador Sullivan in the family, was another important role model.

I am profoundly grateful to and proud of my extraordinary children Jack, Katie, and Teddy Sullivan, and Katie's partner, Amanda. We have supported each other since their mother passed away in 2022, and without their encouragement I would not have been able to write a book. I am further indebted to my amazing mother-in-law, also named Grace Rodriguez (the apple did not fall far from the tree), and sister-in-law, Susan Rodriguez. My whole family, led by my wife, Grace, made it possible for me to have the extraordinary experiences in government service that form the basis for this book. I will never be able to thank them enough.

For almost six years, I was honored to serve with the women and men of the US Department of State. They were an inspiration for me during my tenure as deputy secretary and ambassador, and I thank each and every one of them. Two individuals stand out for their leadership of the office of the deputy secretary, Greg LoGerfo and Kate Nanavatty. They, along with Orlando Davis and our many gifted colleagues in the deputy's office, worked long hours to keep pace with events and prepare me to do my job. Taryn Fridenes, Amanda Jessen, and Jennifer Ehlinger were stalwarts in their work on my nomination to be Ambassador to Russian. In addition, all the men and women, and their families, who served with me at the US mission to Russia are owed a heartfelt debt of gratitude for their commitment to and sacrifices for our country. They were led by a courageous and selfless American, Bart Gorman, our deputy chief of mission and my friend. I am also grateful to Maddison Buser, Daniel Sanborn, and Anne Barbaro in the State Department office that reviewed and cleared my manuscript for publication promptly and professionally.

My literary agent, Mel Berger, and his team at William Morris Endeavor, including Cashen Conroy and Ty Anania, got my book project started. Mel convinced me that I had a book to write and introduced me to the world of publishing. He has been an invaluable advocate and guide from beginning to end.

The hard work of writing a book was made much easier for me by my superb editor, Alex Littlefield, at Little, Brown and Company, who has been a wise and patient tutor for a neophyte author. He is not only a keen editor with a flair for English prose, but also a polymath who advised me on a wide variety of subjects covered in the book. It has been a real pleasure to collaborate with him and the other remarkable professionals at Little, Brown, including Linda Arends, Albert LaFarge, Taylor Navis, and Morgan Wu.

Several friends and colleagues were exceedingly generous with their time and read a draft (or portions thereof) of my manuscript: Bart Gorman, Marik String, Angela Stent, Kate Nanavatty, and Jill Dougherty. Their insightful comments and edits improved the book, and I am thankful for their friendship and willingness to share their immense talents and experiences with me.

Mayer Brown LLP has been my professional home in the private sector since December 1992, when I received an offer to join the law firm after President George H. W. Bush lost his reelection campaign. Over more than three decades, I left the firm twice to reenter public service and each time my partners welcomed me back after my service was concluded. It was Mayer Brown partners Ken Geller, Andy Frey, Steve Shapiro, Dick Favretto, Bob Helman, Richard Ben-Veniste, Erika Jones and many others who trained me as a young lawyer and were role models over my legal career. Most recently, the firm provided unparalleled assistance after I returned from Moscow and began writing this book. I am indebted to our chairman Jon Van Gorp and my partners and dear friends Mike Lackey, Raj De, and Liz Stern in the Washington, DC, office; as well as my assistant Jan Buzard and my colleagues Kate Angel and Elizabeth Powell.

Grace and I were supported while I was deputy secretary of state and ambassador by many friends and colleagues, including Lisa Vahdat, Gina Maya, Doug Cox, Julie O'Sullivan, Bob Fiske, Tom Hemingway, Fr. Samuel Giese, Lily Claffee, Catherine Stevens, Toby Moffett, and Fr. Robert Casey, and I am thankful for all they did for Grace and me over the years. Because Grace was a partner for over two decades in King & Spalding, I sometimes felt like a virtual member of the firm. Her partners and colleagues—too many to acknowledge individually—provided vital assistance and consolation to me and my family after Grace died, and we will always remember their generosity.

The Center for Eurasian, Russian and East European Studies at the Walsh School of Foreign Service at Georgetown University has been an academic home for me since I retired from government service. I am grateful to Dean Joel Hellman and professors Michael David-Fox and Kelly Smith for welcoming me to the university as a Distinguished Scholar. In writing this book, I have benefited immensely from the Georgetown students who have participated in a discussion group with me and reviewed my manuscript: Scott Buchholtz, Jaine Archambeau, Grace Fay, Kamen Kirov, Nigel Li, Mikael Pir-Budagyan, and Ilya Yudkovsky.

My alma mater Columbia University, where I have been appointed a distinguished fellow by the School of Law and by the School of International and Public Affairs, also deserves my thanks. I am indebted, in particular, to Deans Gillian Lester and Keren Yarhi-Milo, and to my old friend and fellow law clerk for Justice David Souter, Professor Matt Waxman. At Columbia, I have worked with talented research assistants, Talia Abrahamson, Irene Jang, and Jemima Baar, who have helped me in finishing this book.

## ACKNOWLEDGMENTS

I owe an incalculable debt to my two best friends for over fifty years, Jack McCormick and Scott Smith, who encouraged me while I wrote this book and sustained me as I tried to adjust to life without Grace. We met as freshman at Xaverian Brothers High School in Westwood, MA, and have remained brothers for life. I also want to express my gratitude to the administration, faculty, students, and alumni of Xaverian, on whose board of trustees I am proud and honored to serve. And a special thanks to two great men of faith and scholarship, Brother Joe Gerard Teehan, CFX, and Brother Paul Feeney, CFX.

I conclude as I began this book with a dedication to my wife, Grace. She was the love of my life, and for that reason I was the luckiest man in the world. In recognition of that fact, I have even started rooting for the Amazin' Mets.

# INDEX

# INDEX

# INDEX

# ABOUT THE AUTHOR

**John J. Sullivan** is an American attorney and government official whose career spans four decades in the public and private sectors. He has served five presidents in prominent diplomatic and legal positions, including as US ambassador to the Russian Federation under Presidents Joe Biden (January 2021 to October 2022) and Donald Trump (December 2019 to January 2021). Before his post in Moscow, he served for almost three years as the US deputy secretary of state. He is currently a distinguished fellow at Georgetown and Columbia Universities, a foreign affairs contributor to CBS News, a partner in Mayer Brown LLP, and a member of the congressionally chartered, bipartisan Commission on Reform and Modernization of the Department of State. He splits his time between the Washington, DC, area and Connecticut.